Gesine Müller
Crossroads of Colonial Cultures

Gesine Müller
Crossroads of Colonial Cultures

Caribbean Literatures in the Age of Revolution

Revised and considerably expanded version,
translated by Marie Deer

DE GRUYTER

Original title: *Die koloniale Karibik. Transferprozesse in frankophonen und hispanophonen Literaturen* (De Gruyter 2012)

ISBN 978-3-11-049500-3
e-ISBN (PDF) 978-3-11-049541-6
e-ISBN (EPUB) 978-3-11-049233-0

Dieses Werk ist lizenziert unter der Creative Commons Attribution-NonCommercial-NoDerivatives 4.0 Lizenz. Weitere Informationen finden Sie unter http://creativecommons.org/licenses/by-nc-nd/4.0/.

Library of Congress Control Number: 2018936209.

Bibliographic information published by the Deutsche Nationalbibliothek
The Deutsche Nationalbibliothek lists this publication in the Deutsche Nationalbibliografie; detailed bibliographic data are available on the Internet at http://dnb.dnb.de.

© 2018 Gesine Müller, published by Walter de Gruyter GmbH, Berlin/Boston
Cover image: ThePaul/photocase.de. Gestaltung: Tobias Kraft
Printing and binding: CPI books GmbH, Leck

www.degruyter.com

For my parents

Contents

I	Introduction —— 1
I.1	The Colonial Kaleidoscope of the Caribbean —— 1
I.2	Premises —— 5
I.3	Colonial Dynamics in the Caribbean (1789–1886) —— 24
I.4	Debates over Abolition in France and Spain —— 38
I.5	Issues of Conviviality —— 51

II	Literature and the Colonial Question —— 56
II.1	Notions of Citizenship (*Citoyenneté/Ciudadanía*) on the Eve of Independence —— 56
II.2	Between Francophilia and Attempts at Autonomy: The Formation of Postcolonial Theory and the Nineteenth Century —— 67
II.3	Spatial Dynamics and Colonial Positioning —— 80

III	Literary Snapshots of the In-Between —— 93
III.1	The Creole Upper Class —— 95
III.2	The Conceptual Inadequacy of the Terms *patrie*/Nation/Exile —— 100
III.3	Haiti As an In-Between Culture —— 110
III.4	Transfers of Ideas between the Center and the Colony —— 117
III.5	The In-Between and the Figure of the Mulatto —— 123
III.6	The Island Function, or between Nature and Culture —— 125
III.7	Between Trans-Tropical Dimensions: Xavier Eyma and the Philippines —— 129
III.8	Between Literature and the Natural Sciences —— 132
III.9	Digression: Sugar and Skin Color between Metropolis and Colonial Projection —— 135

IV	Processes of Ethnological Circulation —— 145
IV.1	"Labeling People": Discourses of "Race" in France and Spain —— 147
IV.2	The *Revue des Colonies* as a Transfer Medium Within a French-Speaking Colonial Diaspora —— 154
IV.3	Haiti and the *Revue encyclopédique* —— 189
IV.4	Literary Transfer Processes in the *Revue des deux mondes* —— 196
IV.5	Conclusion —— 229

V	The Imperial Dimension of French Romanticism: Asymmetrical Relationalities —— 231
V.1	Towards Madrid or Paris? —— 231
V.2	The Dominant Reception of French Romanticism —— 233
V.3	Variations of Reception —— 235
V.4	Hugo as a Model —— 237
V.5	Chateaubriand as a Model —— 240
V.6	The Reception of French Romanticism and Its Cultural-Hegemonic Consequences —— 248
V.7	Conviviality and Relationalism in the French Colonial Empire: A Transoceanic Comparison —— 250
VI	Transcaribbean Dimensions: New Orleans as the Center of French-speaking Circulation Processes —— 263
VI.1	France and Spain as Colonial Powers in Louisiana —— 263
VI.2	Caribbean Louisiana —— 265
VI.3	*Les Cenelles:* Writing in the In-Between —— 276
VII	Excursus: Paradigm Change within Historical Caribbean Research and Its Narrative Representation —— 282
VII.1	Reading Gómez de Avellaneda with Maryse Condé —— 282
VII.2	Raphaël Confiant —— 287
VII.3	Khal Torabully —— 299
VII.4	J.-M.G. Le Clézio, Édouard Glissant, and Epeli Hau'Ofa: Avant-Gardes in Oceania —— 305
VIII	Knowledge about Conviviality, or on the Relevance of Research into the Nineteenth-Century Caribbean —— 316
VIII.1	Norms of Knowledge about Conviviality: Utopias of Caribbeanness —— 316
VIII.2	Forms of Knowledge about Conviviality. An Ethnographic Quest, or the Question of Distance and Separation from the Other —— 322
VIII.3	The Rejection of Essentialist Models of Identity —— 326
IX	Conclusion —— 329
X	Works Cited —— 338
X.1	Primary Sources —— 338
X.2	Ethnological Journals —— 342
X.3	Secondary Literature —— 342

Afterword —— 359

I Introduction

I.1 The Colonial Kaleidoscope of the Caribbean

A look at the kaleidoscope-like world of the nineteenth-century Caribbean can give us completely new insights into the early processes of cultural globalization; phenomena of which we are only now becoming aware were anticipated there. Racist discourses, established models of "white" abolitionists, the politics of memory, and the role of the Haitian revolution (which for a long time was barely recognized) form an amalgam that puts our conventional understanding of a genuinely Western modernity into question.

Migration, circulation, and interconnections among the most diverse geographical areas, along with rootlessness and a lack of direction, are considered to be characteristics of our societies of today. But these phenomena of deterritorialization can already be observed in the Caribbean islands in the nineteenth century, where, for example, pirates and slave traders sailed back and forth between empires and continents; writers fled from one exile to the next; and illiterate peddlers served as messengers between worlds. This is what makes the nineteenth-century Caribbean a fascinating starting point for the examination of the (cultural) fracture points of colonial systems that finally end in cultural (and political) emancipation.

The nineteenth-century world of the Caribbean islands can be read as a kaleidoscope of colonial structures and dynamics,[1] in which colonial experiences come together in a dense network within the sphere of influence of a great variety of hegemonic and peripheral systems and give rise to dependence and separation, to exchange and confrontation. This study focuses on the processes of cultural transfer that play out in, are directed towards, or originate from the Caribbean in a particularly fascinating phase of the colonial transition period, to which little attention has been paid: the years 1789 to 1886, from the French Revolution, with its proclamation of human rights and the immediate effects on the revolutionary events in Haiti, to the abolition of slavery in Cuba (1880 to 1886). Within this time period we can see an intense distillation of the experiences that take place between dependence and independence.

Some voices, taken from documents of that time, will convey an impression of this Caribbean kaleidoscope, already strongly shaped by global interconnect-

---

[1] These island worlds always operate according to their own rules of logic. See Ette's theories about islands in *Writing-between-worlds* 135. See also Ette, *Alexander von Humboldt* 32, and Müller, "El Caribe."

edness. Writing in the Parisian periodical *Revue des deux mondes* (Journal of the Two Worlds) in 1850, a Frenchman makes an observation that could just as well have come out of our own current phase of globalization: "What is new and particular about our time consists in the multidimensionality of its relationships, in the speed of its electric communication media, which leads to the fact that we are constantly finding out what is happening at this moment in other latitudes" (Mazade 1018).[2]

Or to move to another scene: fathers and sons in Guadeloupe. A paternal lecture in Levilloux's 1835 *Les créoles ou la Vie aux Antilles:*

> My son ... I believe I can see in your letters a marked tendency to become passionate about these dogmas that you call regenerative, but that can only be that after they have killed us. ... Beware of making yourself equal through bonds of friendship with compatriots of color. ... Do not look only at external signs; they can be misleading. (23)[3]

The son in this case had left Guadeloupe to study in Paris, which is where he had been contaminated by these "ideas": philanthropic, revolutionary ideas that put slavery into question. Reason enough for the father to want to show the son the error of his ways. (After his return, the son did indeed finally convince himself that slavery was in fact the most humane invention—for blacks.)

Or, to change the scene again: in Gómez de Avellaneda's abolitionist novel *Sab*, a slave (the title character) speaks for himself: "I have no homeland to defend, because slaves have no homeland" (Servera edition 36).[4] Statelessness at the height of nationalism!

Or, again: turmoil for Maynard de Queilhe, also in 1835. The poet was traveling back home from the French mainland, home to Martinique. As they said their good-byes, Victor Hugo was envying his fellow poet, at least some of the time: "Altogether, there are times when I envy you, you a poet exiled in a sunny land, an exile which Ovid would have loved, in that beautiful Martinique

---

[2] "Ce qui est plus nouveau et plus particulièrement propre à notre siècle, c'est que la multiplicité des rapports, la rapidité électrique des communications nous font assister pour ainsi dire à tout ce qui se fait ou se tente sous toutes les latitudes." Unless otherwise indicated, translations in this book are by Gesine Müller and Marie Deer.
[3] "Mon fils, ... j'ai cru deviner, par tes lettres, une tendance marquée à t'exalter pour ces dogmes que tu nommes régénérateurs, mais qui ne peuvent l'être qu'après nous avoir tués. ... Garde-toi de t'égaler par des liens d'amitié à des compatriotes de couleur. Ne t'arrête pas aux signes extérieurs, ils sont souvent trompeurs."
[4] "No tengo tampoco una patria que defender, porque los esclavos no tienen patria."

which you have described so admirably" (*Letters* 56).⁵ In Maynard de Queilhe's novel *Outre-mer* (Overseas), however, we hear a very different tune. The protagonist complains: "But as for me, why must I leave my fatherland [England]? Why is there this cursed island named Martinique?" (I:43).⁶

Another change of scenery. Now we're in Louisiana, in mid-nineteenth-century New Orleans. The free people of color here are refugees from the Haitian revolution, most of them having come via Cuba. Their descendants have never seen their native Haitian soil, but they want to go "back," and their literature strengthens their resolve. In an 1867 story by the Louisianan author Joanni Questy, for example, "Monsieur Paul" says: "My friend, you should send Georges to Haiti. After all, he is smart, young, talented, and not superstitious. He will find his way in that country. Georges has an awe-inspiring feeling for freedom. Don't forget that, my friend."⁷ And in fact, on July 25, 1860, two hundred and fifty emigrants really did return to Port-au-Prince, on board the ship *Lara*. *Le Progrès* (Progress), Haiti's most important daily newspaper of the time, cheered: "We welcome the arrival of our new brothers. ... We will experience freedom and equality under the Haitian palms, in Port-au-Prince, ... the capital of the black race in the civilized world" (September 8, 1860, quoted in Duplantier 163).⁸

Transatlantic solidarity was even announced on street signs, for example in the Calle O'Reilly in Old Havana: "Two island peoples in the same sea of struggle and hope, Cuba and Ireland" (Adams). Irish emigrants were mostly drawn to the British colonies of Barbados and Jamaica, but many also landed in Cuba.

The anti-slavery Parisian journal *Revue des Colonies* (Journal of the Colonies), which was read throughout the French colonies, started dreaming of a future mixing of the races in the early eighteen-forties (even before slavery was abolished). These ideas can be found again just a few years later among the progressive intellectuals of Cuba:

> These whites, blacks, and reds will become a new mixed race of Europeans, Africans, and Americans. In a few generations and after various intermixings, they will create new colors:

---

5 "Il y a des heures où je vous envie, vous poète exilé sous le soleil, exil qu'Ovid eût aimé, dans cette Martinique que vous avez si admirablement peinte" (*Bug-Jargal* 69).
6 "Mais, moi, abandonner ma patrie [Angleterre]. ... Pourquoi existe-t-il une île appelée Martinique?"
7 "Mon ami, vous enverrez Georges en Haïti. Brave, jeune, intelligent, doué d'excellentes qualités, pas superstitieux, il fera son chemin dans ce pays-là. Georges a un amour de la liberté à faire trembler, n'oubliez pas cela, mon ami."
8 "Nous nous félicitons de la prochaine arrivée de ces nouveaux frères. ... Que tous viennent se joindre à nous pour jouir de la liberté, de l'égalité sous le palmier d'Haïti, ... la métropole de la race noire dans le monde civilisé."

from earth-colored, fawn-brown, and nougat to shades of orange and a pale copper yellow. (*Revue des Colonies* July 1836, 20 ff.)[9]

In 1870, Eugenio María de Hostos, from Puerto Rico, gave voice to the crucial issue that haunts the entire nineteenth century. In a speech, he asked the question:

> What are the Antilles?" in the same way that elsewhere the question was being asked, what is Germany, what is France ... ? Was he talking about a pan-Antillean nationalism, à la Bolivar? His answer disabuses us of any such idea. Once again, we feel transported into the twenty-first century: he went on to say that the Antilles are "the bond, the connection between the fusion of European standards and ideas in North America and ... Latin America. They are the natural geographic median between both parts of the continent as well as the producers of a transcendental fusion of races ... the definitive crucible of races. (Diary, March 28, 1870)[10]

Against this background, Édouard Glissant's answer in his *Caribbean Discourse*, written more than a hundred years later, sounds less sensational: "What is the Caribbean in fact? A multiple series of relationships."

The purpose of this study is to point out the cultural mechanisms of a variety of colonial regimes. It compares transfer processes along the axis between the center and the periphery—whether intraperipheral, going through the center, or trans-area—in which all sides engage in dynamic interactions. Literary representations will be situated in the broader context of the circulation of culture and knowledge. The comparison between the French-speaking and Spanish-speaking Caribbean will show the variety in the reception, appropriation, and transculturation of discourses from the mother country as well as their bounceback effects on the images of the "other" in the metropolis.

Three main theses guide this study:

1. France's strong influence and binding force can be traced back to its ability to integrate the colonial Other or, alternatively, to transform itself in the presence of the Other. The reorganization and institutionalization of knowledge in

---

[9] "De ces blancs, de ces noirs, de ces rouges, il se fondera une race mélangée d'Européens, d'Africains et d'Américains, qui en quelques générations et au travers des croisements divers, arrivera, par le brun, le carmélite, le prune – monsieur, l'orangé, à un jaune pâle, légèrement cuivré."

[10] "El lazo, el medio de unión entre ... ideas europeas de Norte América y ... la América Latina: medio geográfico natural entre una y otra parte del Continente, elaborador también de una fusión trascendental de razas, ... el crisol definitivo de las razas" (*Diario*, March 28, 1870, 284 ff., quoted in Gaztambide Géigel 48).

the early nineteenth century (especially in the context of the emergence of ethnology as a scientific discipline) are symptomatic of this.

2. In the case of the Spanish colonies, the loss of a culturally binding center is a productive force for colonial literature, insofar as it promotes the search for new points of connection and interlinking and thus gives rise to a kind of multirelationalism (which increasingly marks Caribbean literature). This "writing-between-worlds" produces literary forms that, while they can aptly be described as "foundational fictions" (Doris Sommer), are difficult to integrate into the category of national literatures.

3. The study of the Caribbean in the nineteenth century, far from being confined to that time frame, can provide a perspective for current discussions about questions of identity in the fourth phase of rapid globalization. Instead of the concept of identity, what turns out be vastly more fruitful is the question of knowledge about *conviviality*, which not only gives us a new way of looking at nineteenth-century texts but is also well-suited to providing an familiar context within which to look at contemporary literary productions and cultural debates.

This study is intended as a rehabilitation of Caribbean literatures. The idea that the French- and Spanish-speaking Caribbean of the nineteenth century can only be understood as an outpost of the European metropolises of Madrid and Paris will prove, in the following, to be problematic in multiple respects.[11]

I.2 Premises

I.2.1 The Subject of the Study

This study addresses the literary and extraliterary forms of representation, along with the constantly increasing intersections between them, that developed during a time of colonial upheaval. In order to pursue the question of how various versions of colonialism are reflected and shaped in various textual media, I will look at parallel and concurrent transfer processes between mother countries and colonial spheres of influence, also taking into account intercolonial exchanges, even though they are overlaid with the asymmetrical relationship of the center to the periphery. The spatial and temporal dimensions are as follows:

---

[11] See Tim Watson's introduction to his *Caribbean Culture:* "My book works against the idea that the Caribbean was a nineteenth-century 'outpost' easily relegated to the mode of historical romance while the real story took place at the imagined centre, with the history of England" (4).

I treat the islands of the Caribbean as a cohesive and at the same time heterogeneous and disparate space, in which the Spanish and French spheres of authority are in the foreground, along with the former island of Hispaniola, encompassing Haiti, which was already independent in 1804, and the later Dominican Republic, with its turbulent history of varying dependencies. This covers the extremes of a field within which multiple and diverse processes of circulation take place; a field that extends from the earliest separation, in the case of Haiti, to the continuing connection to the (French) mother country in the cases of Guadeloupe and Martinique; and from the social revolution and emancipation of the black underclasses (Haiti) to the late abolition of slavery in Cuba (legislated in 1880 and implemented in 1886). This is not, however, a hermetically closed field, but rather a dynamic one, open to the world. This work also takes as its starting point an understanding of the Caribbean that always also includes the regions surrounding the Caribbean. The larger Caribbean, the *Gran Caribe*, I take to include the tropical and subtropical Atlantic coastal fronts from Charleston to Rio, in other words the coasts and estuaries of Brazil (as far as Bahia and Rio), Venezuela, New Granada / Colombia, Florida, and Louisiana (and, for the purposes of research on slavery, the coastlines of the Carolinas and Virginia), along with the Greater Antilles (Cuba, Saint-Domingue / Haiti / Santo Domingo, and Puerto Rico), the diverse Bahamas, the Lesser Antilles, and other archipelagos in the Caribbean; for certain purposes, the Caribbean coasts of Central America and Mexico are also included as well as the Pacific coasts of Colombia and Ecuador (the transitional zone of Darién and Chocó). Michael Zeuske makes it clear that research on the history of the "greater" Caribbean is growing exponentially, both internationally and transdisciplinarily,[12] now that all of the countries of the region, after centuries of an inward-oriented "nationalism," have discovered the resources of their Caribbean periphery and the connective power of the concept. The regions of the "greater" Caribbean all have things in common in addition to their distinct characteristics. In all of them, the Indian populations collapsed under the pressure of the *conquista*, unaccustomed forced labor (slavery or *encomienda*), and the diseases brought by the Europeans, leading to the demographic catastrophe of the fifteenth and sixteenth centuries. The resulting large "uninhabited" spaces made it possible for the colonial elites and the Creole upper classes[13] to establish colonial slavery as an important export economy and the slave trade of Africans and their descendants as a way to accumulate

---

[12] For important dimensions of the transatlantic perspective, see Abel, *Transatlantisches KörperDenken*.
[13] I deal with the complex concept of the "Creole upper classes" in detail in chapter IV.

wealth. In the "greater" Caribbean, the competition among the great Western colonial empires (Spain, France, England / Great Britain, the Netherlands, Denmark, and later also the United States) played an overwhelming role, with important consequences for the building of fortifications, shipbuilding, the development of the military, and urbanization, as well as piracy and smuggling, which some historians consider to be a "Caribbean" economy. This competition continued later on in the context of the unequal development of abolition in the different empires.[14]

When we talk about the period from 1789 to 1886, we are talking about a colonial threshold situation between dependence and independence. I have chosen these parameters for the sake of the history of ideas, political history, and social history: from the French Revolution, with its proclamation of human rights and the immediate effects of that proclamation on events in Haiti, to the abolition of slavery on the last (and also the largest and most important) island in the Caribbean, namely Cuba, in 1886. This covers a large arc, from the launching of the idea of equality in Europe all the way to its final implementation in the central issue of slavery and abolition, which is finally a much more important issue in the colonies at that time than the question of independence (which generally only becomes a burning issue at a point in time when abolition has already been achieved). As a former colony, the United States can provide a possible model for both sides here, for the abolitionists as well as for the defenders of slavery, given the strong tensions between the northern and southern states. The chronological framework of this study, therefore, is driven by the fundamental shift in the conception of humankind and of society that took place over the course of the nineteenth century and was transmitted, in a transformative way, to the colonies.

In terms of literary history, the emphasis here is on Romanticism, which begins as a transregional phenomenon that characterizes revolutionary and post-revolutionary Europe and then goes on to be received and implemented in all of Latin America and the Caribbean region from around 1830 to 1870, much later than the political ideas of the revolution. At the same time, it should be noted that because of the chronological overlap and in view of the eclecticism displayed by many Caribbean writers (even while they adopt the European terminology for the periods), the Enlightenment and Romanticism cannot readily be separated from each other in the Caribbean.

---

14 See for example Downey, who describes the British-American crisis following the slave rebellion on board the *Creole*, and Chambers. Misevich and Mann provide a good overview of Atlantic slavery. Schmieder compares the abolition process in Cuba and Martinique.

And as indicated in my third thesis, above, the time frame I indicate here is actually transcended when we begin to look at the ways in which the cultural representations of the nineteenth-century Caribbean can connect to our current literary interpretations and to the interpretations of today's literary and cultural studies. Thus, I propose to look at the cultural and political "trans-area" exchanges taking place throughout the nineteenth-century Caribbean,[15] with a particular focus on three different geographical and political areas: 1. the hegemonic domain of colonizing Europe; 2. the external periphery in the form of Africa and of the two Americas; and 3. the dynamic of the internal translinguistic and transcultural exchanges among the islands.

As far as *hegemonic colonizing Europe* is concerned, the connections and influences are particularly clear: each colony was tightly connected with its mother country. In the case of the Spanish-speaking Caribbean, however, the situation becomes more complicated, because Spain's cultural weakness caused it to lose a lot of its influence as a colonial center. This created an opening for a variety of other cultural influences and models, which not only made for disorientation in the Spanish colonies but also, to an important degree, stimulated cultural production. The question of the bounceback effects of these cultural manifestations on the European mother countries is connected to this "productive multirelationality."

Included in the category of exchanges with the *external periphery* are the transfer processes, which have so far barely been studied, with the young United States. Towards the end of the century, of course, the United States increasingly plays the role of a colonizer, not only in terms of economics but also militarily and politically. But the northern neighbors are, first and foremost, colonies that have freed themselves from dependence and are therefore definitely able to serve as a model, at least in cases where the actors understand independence to be on their horizon. In addition, there is the question of slavery, so central to the United States, where it ends in the American Civil War; the two opposing

---

[15] This study relies on the toolkit of trans-area studies, in the sense that the focus is on those processes of exchange and transformation that run directly between various cultural areas without any immediate centering via Europe. See Ette, *ZusammenLebensWissen* 11 ff. It goes without saying that this method does not ignore the historical realities of the nineteenth century, a period when, because of the colonial configurations, the centrality of Europe was unquestioned. On the trans-area dimension of Caribbean writing see also the Puerto Rican cultural theorist Torres-Saillant, who, though unlike Ette he does not use the term itself, does work with it indirectly: "The world consists of culture areas and distinct regions whose interconnectedness does not preclude their discreteness. As a chronicle of Caribbean thought, this work enacts a postulation of the need to subdivide the intellectual history of humanity into manageable chunks, namely, countries, regions, culture areas, and the like" (1).

sides of that conflict are of great interest to the upper and lower social strata of the Caribbean, respectively. Does the American Revolution offer a model for the islands of the Caribbean? And if so, what is the relevance of the issue of slavery, its suppression during the revolution, and its role in the simmering conflict between the northern and southern states? Is North American literature, as a postcolonial literature, a source of inspiration for Caribbean writers in its search for new modes of expression and its own identity, as well as in its efforts to distance itself from literary England?

The transfer processes with the Latin American neighbors in Central and South America are similar to those with the United States, although in a weaker and less ambivalent form. In this case, Spanish-speaking writers needed no translation (or interlingual reception). There was even the possibility of a direct exchange with the cultural producers there, because a large number of Caribbean writers went into exile on the mainland. Might it even be the case that the shared-language cultural exchange with the subcontinent thrust itself into the void left by the mother country?

In the above-mentioned cases, in spite of a certain asymmetry,[16] we can assume that the processes of transfer took place in both directions; the exchange with Africa and Asia, however, was surely mostly one-directional, with the greatest cultural significance attaching to the black population that was enslaved in Africa and shipped to the Caribbean, later replaced by Indian laborers. And yet, in spite of the one-sidedness of this transfer, the influence of African and also Asian cultures played an important role, of course. These cultures and their bearers, for their part, undergo complicated transfer processes in their new heterogeneous environment, and it remains to be clarified what contribution those processes made to the classics of nineteenth-century literature.

In the case of the transfer processes within the Caribbean, we can assume that, in spite of the difficulties posed by the limited transportation network, they were highly symmetrical. What forms, then, did this intra-Caribbean exchange take—first of all among the various islands of the archipelago, some of them speaking the same language and some of them speaking different languages; and secondly, on the former Saint-Domingue, between the two so different parts of the island, Haiti and the Dominican Republic (occupied by Haiti for twenty-two years, from 1822 to 1844), with their very distinct colonial, political, and cultural make-ups? It is only in this intra-Caribbean exchange, tightly bound

---

[16] Lüsebrink, referring to Michael Werner, distinguishes the following kinds of asymmetry: chronological asymmetry, spatial and geographic asymmetry, and multidimensional asymmetry (*Interkulturelle Kommunikation* 131).

into the network of external colonial and collateral relationships, that the kaleidoscopic multidimensionality of the colonial dynamics can be fully realized.

I.2.2 Comparing Processes of Circulation and Transfer

In comparing the cultural production of the former French and Spanish colonies of the Caribbean, we are not looking at static constructions but, rather, at processes of transfer and circulation that took place side by side and with very different dynamics during this time of transition, processes that were also interwoven with each other in places and influenced each other.[17] Thus, there were hardly any nineteenth-century Caribbean writers who did not live outside the Caribbean for years or even travel back and forth multiple times between their birth or home islands and the mother country or other places of exile. Most of these exiled writers were in Europe (mainly in Paris), but some of them went to the American colonies that had already gained their independence, namely to the United States or to Mexico. In addition, almost all of these writers were politically engaged, so that even beyond their writings they were in the public eye (some of them even holding public office), which makes them particularly interesting as nodal points for transcontinental transfer processes across multiple categories.

Starting in the late eighteenth century, European scholars of all different sorts set off for remote transatlantic regions and then wrote down and published their impressions and experiences in various forms (Lüsebrink, *Das Europa der Auflärung* 11ff.). The reorganization of systems of knowledge that was triggered by the fundamental paradigm shift of the French Revolution was reflected in and lastingly promoted by the Napoleonic modernization of institutions; the emergence and institutionalization of ethnology, in particular, profoundly changed the viewpoint of travelers to the New World. As scientists, writers, politicians, and stakeholders of various sorts—or even several of these things at once, like the particularly prominent Alexander von Humboldt—these travelers were driven by completely other interests and desires for knowledge than were the missionaries and colonial officials with whom the islanders had had contact (on their home island territory) in earlier eras. As a result, the perception of the overseas colonies also changed in the centers themselves, where Rousseau's exotic, proto-Romantic ideas of the noble savage met flesh-and-blood embodi-

---

17 This takes the form of an *histoire croisée* (entangled history), as called for in Werner and Zimmermann. See also Lüsebrink, *Interkulturelle Kommunikation* 129.

ments, which had far-reaching effects on those ideas. Contact in the center and in the periphery between the cultural elites of both places gained a new intensity, and there were visits, encounters, and responses in both directions; at that point, literary portrayals, travelogues, ethnographies, and political opinion were sometimes indistinguishable from each other. It was only within this constellation of intensified encounters and mutual exchange that the first important foundational fictions developed, and this happened, interestingly enough, where these encounters were not confined to the simple bipolarity of colonizer and colonized, but where actors were also open to multilateral processions of transculturation. This makes the search for intra-Caribbean contacts and mediating figures particularly significant.[18]

The strong cultural connection to France that characterizes both the French-speaking and the Spanish-speaking Caribbean had opposite effects on the emancipation movements of the two groups, because for the French colonies, it involved a strong connection to the mother country and a tendency to want to preserve the status quo, while for the Spanish colonies it involved a cultural dependence on a foreign mother country and therefore a separation from their own; the multiplicity of relational connections, meanwhile, had an effect on the productivity and originality of cultural production, which in turn contributed indirectly to the political affirmation of a separate identity. As a result, the bipolar orientation of the French colonies had a mimetic and therefore stabilizing effect on the status quo.

Although the Caribbean writers mostly belonged to the elites, the quantity and accuracy of the information available about their lives and work, in addition to their texts themselves, differ vastly: for the canonized writers of the Spanish Caribbean, a great deal is known, in particular because of the broad-based literary and political debates that took place, whereas for the French-speaking writers, there is often only very scanty material. As a result, the study of these writers needs to be approached using a variety of methodologies. It is not always possible to document encounters and contacts in the lives of the writers, but in fact the key thing here is the textual representation itself, which—unlike personal

---

18 Raphaël Confiant, in his novel *Adèle et la pacotilleuse*, has memorialized one of these mediating figures in the nineteenth-century world or, more precisely, worlds, of the Caribbean islands in the form of the *pacotilleuse*, the itinerant vendor. This black peddler, goods transporter, and commuter among the Caribbean islands takes the disturbed daughter of Victor Hugo, who has landed in the Caribbean in her search for her mysterious lover, under her wing; the *pacotilleuse* takes her to St.-Pierre, the capital of Martinique, from which the two of them then finally take off together for the "mother" country and to see the famous father of the white woman. See also section VII.2 of this book.

meetings and connections, though these undoubtedly gave a great deal of impetus and inspiration to cultural activity—when published, was able to produce a broad impact. In the foreground are intertextual references, motifs, genre-specific citations: in short, relationalisms, which can be deduced from a differentiated juxtaposition of the various cultural productions. The most valuable material includes magazines that are primarily dedicated to ethnological and literary questions, although it is not yet possible to categorize them into different specialties.

With respect to the study of intra- and cross-Caribbean receptions and forms of communication among the islands, Janett Reinstädler, in her pioneering study of Caribbean theater, points out that theater groups also moved among the islands, and that therefore there was not only a direct exchange, but this exchange also took place in the context of immediate and physical contact and interaction with a broad public that included the lower classes and even slaves. These contacts, hitherto completely unexplored, can provide us with insights into mutual reception and influences.

The main focus of this book is to examine transfer processes, using a variety of methods that have gained particular attention in the wake of a so-called transnational turn. One important pillar is made up of *histoire croisée* ("entangled history"), developed by Michael Werner and Bénédicte Zimmermann.[19] This study subscribes to a basic interest in overcoming nationally bound historical perspectives. *Histoire croisée* attempts to construct the specific connections among observer positions, perspectives, and objects. This is no longer a matter of interconnectedness as a new object of research in itself but, rather, of the production of new insights out of a constellation that is itself already interconnected. *Histoire croisée* arose in France, as an attempt, among other things, to expose the prominent field of comparative studies as too static and to propose an alternative model. Given the central issue of this study, which is a comparison of French and Spanish colonialism, it is worth considering to what degree a comparative approach is compatible with *histoire croisée* methods.

The fundamental problem that accompanies comparative inquiries is that as cognitive operations, they assume synchrony, but as history they always deal with diachrony. Transfer history, in contrast, positions itself in a diachronic context from the outset. Unlike comparison, transfer history by definition takes processes as its exclusive object. It describes changes: processes of acculturation, socialization, and appropriation. It avoids the cognitive aporias of historical

---

19 Graham and Raussert's study is a convincing example of *histoire croisée* with a special focus on the Americas. I am grateful to Johanna Abel and Leonie Meyer-Krentler for valuable pointers and discussions on this topic.

comparison by trying not to assume any abstract constructions that would shape the outcome ahead of time. It pays attention to interactions and to how those interactions change historically constructed entities. And an important concern is to investigate the mechanisms of reception and reinterpretation and to examine the processes of cultural translation. This translation work can be evaluated not only from the perspective of the appropriation and adaptation of what is foreign but also as an opening and an enrichment that changes the receiving culture. Transfer history attempts to transcend rigidified national paradigms by emphasizing the ways in which culture and nation are processes, the fluidity of border demarcations, and the constant redefinition of their contents. When we talk about contacts, transfers, and relationships, we are no longer only talking about connections or about similarities between different assemblages but about a kind of interconnectedness that reshapes the assemblages themselves and rewrites their identities (Werner and Zimmermann 613 ff.).

Of what do the boundaries of transfer history consist? Even the analysis of interactions cannot completely do away with the reification of nationally marked beginning and ending points. The difficulty with nationally delineated categories of description and analysis is that they locate the transfer analysis within the respective systems and cultural, social, economic, and political models, which means that the transfer analysis always implies a comparative dimension, whether that is explicitly named or only indirectly constructed. Comparative studies and transfer history share the same comparative dimension in their national categories of analysis. This becomes problematic when the implicit comparative structure is not revealed or the transfer perspective is played off against the comparative perspective. A polarized confrontation between comparative analysis and transfer history is not sustainable:

> It follows from this that the investigation of transnational transfers often leads to a relativization, on the one hand, but also a consolidation, on the other, of the national frame of reference. Analyses of cultural exchange relationships among nations open up a richer and subtler picture, mostly of the importing, receiving culture. The ideological construct of the national culture is of course scrutinized; the foreign elements it contains are noted; the porousness of the borders is pointed out. But the picture of the national culture of reception, thus differentiated, is not itself questioned. In fact, one might even say that it is strengthened and secured. (615)[20]

---

[20] "Daraus ergibt sich, dass die Untersuchung von transnationalen Transfers vielfach zur Folge hat, dass der nationale Bezugsrahmen einerseits relativiert, andererseits aber auch konsolidiert wird. Analysen von kulturellen Austauschbeziehungen zwischen Nationen eröffnen ein reicheres, subtileres Bild vor allem auf die importierende Rezeptionskultur. Zwar wird das ideologische Konstrukt der Nationalkultur hinterfragt, zwar wird auf die Fremdanteile verwiesen, die

It is the connection of a comparative perspective with processes of transfer and circulation that is the decisive factor. In the context of the second phase of accelerated globalization, Ottmar Ette, talking about Alexander von Humboldt, points out that the phenomenon of worldwide interconnectedness cannot be addressed epistemologically through the use of comparisons between different spaces alone. "Alexander von Humboldt understood that static comparisons had to be raised to the level of mobile relationalisms." It was a matter of "putting things into relationship (and into movement) through comparison" (*Alexander von Humboldt* 116).[21] The current study would like to take this ambition of Humboldt's as the guiding principle of its approach.

In her study of transamerican literary relations, Anna Brickhouse has identified the formation process of a transcultural current she calls the transamerican renaissance. This transamerican renaissance spans the period from the anonymous publication, in 1826, of the historical novel *Xicoténcatl*, ascribed to Félix Varela, to the 1856 appearance of Faubert's Haitian drama, *Ogé ou Le préjugé de couleur*.[22] Ottmar Ette has long argued for a paradigm shift from a spatial history to a history that concerns itself with movement, and Anna Brickhouse subscribes to this movement-oriented history as well, which is slowly establishing itself; it aims to challenge the historiographic model in which the center and the periphery are fixed points on an analytical map and the United States is set up as the regional linchpin, in contrast to a homogenized and predictably marginal Latin America and an even more marginal Caribbean (Ette, *ZusammenLebensWissen* 16; Brickhouse 27–28). Brickhouse emphasizes the fact that the dominant public domains of the United States and of its rivals—both

---

es enthält, wird die Durchlässigkeit der Grenzen betont. Doch das in dieser Weise differenzierte Bild der nationalen Rezeptionskultur wird als solches nicht in Frage gestellt. Eher, so möchte man meinen, wird es gestärkt und gesichert."

21 "Alexander von Humboldt begriff, daß statische Vergleiche auf die Ebene mobiler Relationalitäten gehoben werden mussten"; "durch Vergleich in Beziehung (und in Bewegung) zu setzen." Ette also stresses that comparison provokes mental development, so long as it does not aim to use comparisons to make things equal (*Alexander von Humboldt* 152). For a similar connection between comparing and understanding, between comparative studies and intercultural communication (Lüsebrink's key expositions), see Lüsebrink, *Interkulturelle Kommunikation* 33. Haesendonck and D'Haen offer a good example of the comparative approach to Caribbean literature.
22 Félix Varela y Morales (born 1788 in Cuba; died 1853 in the United States), a priest, teacher, writer, philosopher, and politician, was an important figure in the intellectual life of Cuba in the first half of the nineteenth century. He is considered to be a pioneer for the Cuban nation and taught some of the outstanding thinkers of that era, including José Antonio Saco, Domingo del Monte, and José de la Luz y Caballero. Pierre Faubert (born 1806 in Haiti; died 1868 in France), a Haitian poet and playwright, was a diplomat for Haiti in Europe. I am grateful to Stephan Eberhard for some essential pointers in engaging with Brickhouse's work.

French- and Spanish-speaking, abolitionist and anti-colonial—often intersect. At the same time, she addresses the connection between the phenomena of literary transnationalism and of imperialism, which can go hand in hand (Brickhouse 29). She cites a particularly clear example from the *North American Review:* an article that appeared in 1849 on the poetry of "Spanish America" charged its United States readers with the "patriotic duty" of learning about Latin American literary traditions, given the "indefinite boundaries of our country" and all the "mysterious tropical nations, with whom it is [our] 'manifest destiny' ... to be more and more closely connected" (Hurlbert 135, 131, quoted in Brickhouse 29).

Brickhouse is interested in a new approach to the literary history of the nineteenth-century United States, using perspectives from the greater Americas. Knowledge that was developed outside the territorial boundaries of the United States is key here. This kind of knowledge shares important characteristics with what Walter Mignolo calls "border gnosis," in other words knowledge production from both the interior borders of the modern/colonial world system (imperial conflicts, hegemonic languages, directionality of translations, etc.) and its exterior borders (imperial conflicts with cultures being colonized, as well as the subsequent stages of independence or decolonization) (*Local Histories* 11, quoted in Brickhouse 30).

The modern/colonial world system that Mignolo theorizes emphasizes "internal and external borders," which "are not discrete entities but rather moments of a continuum in colonial expansion and in changes of national imperial hegemonies" (*Local Histories* 33; cf. Brickhouse 30).

The Americas of the nineteenth century play a pivotal role in the development of border gnosis. Spain, France, England, and, increasingly the United States were fighting over territories and islands in the Western hemisphere and demanding linguistic and cultural purity. None of them, however, was able to control the pace of decolonization nor the mobility of the intellectual work and translation that were taking place within the public spaces of the disputed areas. Brickhouse has determined the extent of the "transamerican renaissance": from del Monte's circle in Matanzas, Cuba, to the subversive Spanish-language publishing centers in Philadelphia and New York; from the intersecting cultural exchange of the famous Mexican Society for Geography and Statistics (*Sociedad Mexicana de Geografía y Estadística*) to the contested Texas Territory, where United States soldiers read Prescott as preparation for war; and from the exiled intellectuals of Haiti and Martinique, who established the Society for Men of Color (*Société des Hommes de Couleur*), to Louisiana's French-speaking Creole culture (Brickhouse 30).

I.2.3 Text Corpus

The time period I have selected for this investigation, 1789 to 1886, makes it possible for me to allow literary actors from the French and Spanish colonial Caribbean spheres—some of them from still-intact colonies and some from states (Haiti and the Dominican Republic) that were already independent—to have their say. I have chosen the most prominent authors for the text corpus, writers who represent a variety of stages of Romanticism and who apparently enjoyed a relatively broad reception. These literary texts come from the pens of a Euro-Creole elite. With a very few exceptions, then, this is a white literature. For the writers of the French-speaking Caribbean, in particular, we can say that their literature is an attempt to tell the story of the French colonies from the point of view of the plantation-owner class. It will also become clear that one of the biographical characteristics shared by the writers discussed here is that they all traveled between worlds; for a Caribbean writer, in other words, it was impossible to gain an audience if one never left one's own island. Politically, the result is that Creole fiction always represents a "vacillation between loyalty and opposition" (Watson 18). Generally speaking, the writing of the Caribbean's Creole upper class is a colonial discourse in opposition to the metropolises, but it is not an opposition that expresses itself in a questioning of the colonial status quo.

I use "the Caribbean" to refer not only to the Caribbean island world but also to the regions surrounding the Caribbean, and I will be highlighting Louisiana, in particular. It is not possible to think about Caribbean transfer processes, especially in the French-speaking sphere, without including the hub that is New Orleans. I take it for granted in this book that it is problematic to adopt standards of national literatures. This does not mean, however, that the criterion of the "island of origin" is not decisive. Given these parameters, I have chosen the following literary texts:

Spain's (post)colonial sphere[23]
Condesa de Merlín, Maria de las Mercedes Santa Cruz y Montalvo (Cuba, 1789–1852): *La Havane* [1844].
Galván, Manuel de Jesús (Santo Domingo, 1834–1910): *Enriquillo* [1879].
Gómez de Avellaneda, Gertrudis (Cuba, 1814–1873): *Sab* [1841].

---

[23] Where no biographical information is available, I have had to leave out birth and/or death dates.

Heredia, José María (Cuba, 1803–1895): "Himno del desterrado" [1825]; "A Bolívar" [1825].
Hostos, Eugenio María de (Puerto Rico, 1839–1903): *La peregrinación de Bayoán* [1863].
Manzano, Francisco (Cuba, 1797–1853): *Autobiografía* [1835].[24]
Tapia y Rivera, Alejandro (Puerto Rico, 1826–1882): *La palma del cacique* [1852].

France's (post)colonial sphere
Bergeaud, Émeric (Haiti, 1818–1858): *Stella* [1859].
Coicou, Massillon (Haiti, 1867–1908): *Poésies nationales* [1892].
Coussin, J.H.J. (Guadeloupe, 1773–1836): *Eugène de Cerceil ou le dernier Caraïbe* [1824].
Eyma, Louis-Xavier (Martinique, 1816–1876): *La Vie aux États-Unis* [1876].
Lanusse, Armand (New Orleans, 1810–1868) (ed.): *Les Cenelles* [1845].
Levilloux, J. (Martinique): *Les Créoles ou la Vie aux Antilles* [1835].
Lespinasse, Beauvais (Haiti, 1811–1863): *Le Chevalier de Mauduit* [1836].
Maynard de Queilhe, Louis de (Martinique, 1811–1836): *Outre-mer* [1835].
Nau, Ignace (Haiti, 1808–1845): *Isalina ou une scène créole* [1836].
Prévost de Sansac, Auguste Jean: *Les amours de Zémedare et Carina et description de l'île de Martinique* [1806].
Questy, Joanni (New Orleans, 1817–1869): "Monsieur Paul" [1867].
Séjour, Victor (New Orleans, 1817–1874): "Le mulâtre" [1837].

In addition to these, I look at classics of French Romanticism and Exotism such as Chateaubriand, Pierre Loti, and Victor Hugo. Alongside the literary evidence, I also examine contemporary magazines that deal with ethnological, literary, and literary-historical questions: the *Revue des Colonies*, the *Revue encyclopédique*, and the *Revue des deux mondes*. And finally, as a comparison with these nineteenth-century writings, I bring in some current works: *Traversée de la Mangrove*, by Maryse Condé (1989), *Adèle et la pacotilleuse*, by Raphaël Confiant (2005), *Cale d'étoiles, Coolitude*, by Khal Torabully (1992), *Raga*, by Jean-Marie Gustave le Clézio (2007), and *We are the Ocean*, by Epeli Hau'Ofa (2008).

---

24 There are disagreements about Manzano's birth and death dates and about the publication date of his *Autobiografía*. I rely here on William Louis's scholarly foreword to the 2007 Vervuert edition.

I.2.4 About the Structure of this Book

This study is based on three central arguments that connect with individual subsections of the book in various ways. The first is a comparison, using literary and cultural forms of expression, of France and Spain as colonial powers; the second builds on the first, addressing the greater inclusivity of French colonialism; while the third digresses a little, opening up the nineteenth century as a period of investigation by looking into paradigms of Caribbean research and presenting a critical review of constructions of identity. After the object of study has been geographically and temporally defined and the text corpus introduced, I present the state of the research, which is guided by the methodology of transfer history and the history of interconnectedness, albeit without explicitly rejecting comparative issues (see proposition 1 in section I.1).

The preliminary work in this study includes a diagramming of the complex political relationships between the Spanish and French Caribbean, whose history has been relatively little studied until now. The process of outlining these historical situations always includes a presentation of the state of literary affairs. In terms of content, the positions taken by the texts on slavery as well as on the colonial status quo are always a central issue. One chapter section gives an overview of the debates on abolition in France and Spain. Finally, in connection with my third argument above, I introduce the concept of conviviality and its positioning within current cultural theory debates and then reflect on the possibility of applying the concept to the nineteenth century. In order to do that, it turns out to be crucial to clarify its anthropological foundations.

In chapter II, "Literature and the Colonial Question," I lay out the literary positions taken by the various writers towards the colonial status quo. I have chosen a few key aspects that demonstrate a political dimension of the novels: citizenship (*citoyenneté*); positions for and against independence; and issues of spatial dynamics. To illustrate these themes, I have chosen one literary representative each from the French- and Spanish-language colonial spheres to juxtapose and compare. This approach, which might appear static at first, is intended to illuminate the much-discussed political opinions on the basis of literary texts. This chapter, therefore, is more concerned with whether these aspects are present and less with how they are treated. The necessity of this approach has to do with the paucity of research so far on the literatures of the French-speaking Caribbean.

While the aim of chapter II is to establish the value of literature within comparative research on colonialism, chapter III, "Literary Snapshots of the In-Between," changes course. In terms of its strategy, chapter III might appear to contradict the expositions that precede it. While the previous chapter works to uncover the writers' positions on colonial questions, in chapter III it becomes clear, on further examination, that it is impossible to establish a clear colonial position for each writer, because the literate Creole upper class was in a permanent in-between state. This chapter attempts to capture various dimensions of this in-between-ness, which eludes any clear definition: established categories such as fatherland (*patrie*), nation, and exile prove to be inadequate; Haiti can only be grasped as a transitional culture; transfers of ideas from the center are difficult to apply to the colonies; etcetera. The chapter closes with a digression on sugar and skin color—the two cornerstones of the (anti-)slavery debates—between the metropolis and colonial projections, and identifies a discourse around "foreign things" as forms of cultural representation of the in-between, based on eighteenth-century travelogues.

Chapter IV, "Processes of Ethnological Circulation," introduces yet another change of perspective, which has to do with the second thesis of this book. At the beginning of the nineteenth century, more than thirty ethnological journals were started in France. They are a symptom of the much-cited epistemic turn and the reorganization of knowledge in the wake of the French Revolution and of Napoleonic expansions into areas outside Europe. New institutions for teaching and research divided scholarship into different branches, and polymaths were replaced by specialists, including ethnologists.

Among these journals were the *Revue des Colonies*, the *Revue des deux mondes*, and the *Revue encyclopédique*, and an analysis and overview of these provides some useful information about the ways in which the Caribbean region was covered in the journals. I look at their sources and methods and the images that they transmit, using these components to get a picture of the researchers, their travels, and their contacts with actors in the Caribbean itself. Any positions or actions taken directly or indirectly by the scholars on the debates of the time over colonial politics are of particular interest, especially with regard to the debate on abolition, along with the arguments it involved, which called for scientific authority.

Writers from the mother country were disproportionately represented in these political debates. Some of them (for example Chateaubriand) traveled to the colonial areas themselves und wrote about their travel experiences. French literature seems to have been particularly adept at making use of specialized scholarly discourse and thus played an important role, at the very least, in the dissemination of scientific findings about the colonial Other. Chapter V, therefore, investigates the colonial dimension of French Romanticism, asking to what degree the discourses of French Romanticism prevailed in their reception in the Caribbean and thereby played a role in stabilizing the power structures there. And finally, a look at questions of conviviality and relationality in Victor

Hugo's Atlantic-oriented and Pierre Loti's Pacific-oriented texts affords us a transoceanic perspective.

In order not to fall into the trap of approaching the thesis of the multirelationality of the Spanish-speaking Caribbean too categorically, chapter VI looks at trans-Caribbean dimensions that go beyond the island world and include the Caribbean periphery. New Orleans played a pivotal role for the colonial centers in the French-speaking colonial empire, although the city changed colonial masters in the eighteenth century. It remains to be seen to what extent the ties of colonial culture remain structurally defining after a political emancipation, as in the case of Haiti.

In chapter VII, finally, I illustrate my third argument and allow myself a digression, leaving the time period under discussion and focusing on two contemporary writers of the French-speaking Caribbean. First, I ask how Maryse Condé can help us to read Gómez de Avellaneda in a new way. And then, using Raphaël Confiant's novel *Adèle et la pacotilleuse*, I look at the reenactments that the Caribbean island world of the nineteenth century can undergo in literatures of the present day. In the process, we will see paradigm shifts in research on the Caribbean translated into literature, which in turn corroborates the assumption that the region is a privileged space for theory production. Khal Torabully's concept of coolitude is relevant here, involving as it does the experiences of Indian contract workers in the Caribbean without giving in to essentialist imputations. And finally, the contemporary writers J.-M.G. Le Clézio, Édouard Glissant, and Epeli Hau'Ofa provide a transoceanic perspective and open up the question of a transoceanic avant-garde.

My final observations (chapter VIII) build on these arguments, rejecting essentialist concepts of identity and replacing outdated approaches with a new focus on the promising question of conviviality.

I.2.5 The Context for the Research

In the search for focal points in phases of accelerated globalization (Ette, *Weltbewußtsein* 26),[25] the Caribbean, a trading center subject to the most varied in-

---

[25] Ette distinguishes four phases of accelerated globalization: the first begins with the so-called discovery of America by Christopher Columbus in 1492; the second, involving discovery expeditions by various European seafarers, provides important insights into European colonialisms; the third made itself felt in the last third of the nineteenth century in Europe but most of all on the two American continents; and the fourth phase, finally, based on the dramatic development and dissemination of electronic media and storage systems, made it possible for a world-

fluences, can be understood as a laboratory for modernity, increasingly not only providing material for European (postcolonial) theory development but also rising to become itself a place for the production of theory (see Martínez-San Miguel, Sifuentes-Jáuregui, and Belausteguigoitia), a Euro-centrifugal development that would appear to be a manifestation of a worldwide phenomenon—one has only to look at the backgrounds of the leading proponents of postcolonial theories (see Ette, *Literature on the Move* and *Writing-between-worlds*). Ottmar Ette, who has set the tone in important ways in international literary and cultural research on the Caribbean in recent years, traces this development back to (among other things) the constant movement and rootlessness of Caribbean intellectuals and their interconnections in the manifold geographical spaces there, a phenomenon of deterritorialization that is not simply about the immigrant background of its actors and is therefore not reducible to the category of migration literature.

Of course, the kind of ubiquitous, even if not simultaneous, interconnectedness that is characteristic of the dislocated intellectual world of the twentieth-century Caribbean[26] cannot be directly projected onto the nineteenth century, because in the nineteenth century colonial ties still provided more or less clear guidelines for the lines of interconnectedness, even if those boundaries were constantly being overrun. But this is exactly what makes the nineteenth-century Caribbean into a fascinating starting point for the investigation of the (cultural) fracture points of colonial systems that lead, in the longer term, to cultural (and political) emancipation. And beyond that, the contemporaneity of very different parallel developments in the various colonial frames of reference (not in the sense of the kind of "phase shift" that a monistic theory of progress would claim) makes it possible to add something new to the debate on postcolonialism using the concept of interconnectedness, involving comparative inquiries into processes of transfer and circulation, without blindly committing to that approach.

This is a new kind of asymmetric strategy, pulling together extremely dissimilar spaces that have been researched to very different degrees, usually as studies of a regional, national, colonial, or postcolonial literature or focused on a center in the form of a particular colonial or imperial domain. The relevant geographical spaces are the French-speaking and Spanish-speaking Caribbean, France, Spain as a colonial power, the neighboring Caribbean islands, and the American mainland. The research on French-speaking Caribbean literature and early

---

wide system of networking and global communication to arise over the course of the last third of the twentieth century.

26 For the world war era see for example McIntosh.

French ethnology is the thinnest, except for that on early Spanish ethnology, which is even sparser. Nineteenth-century French Caribbean literature has so far been barely addressed, and even the primary texts are very hard to find. For nineteenth-century Spanish Caribbean literature, on the other hand, even though there has been quite a bit of research, questions of relationality have hardly been touched.

It is not possible for me to give a comprehensive overview of the secondary literature here; instead, I refer my readers to the notes in the text and will concentrate here on a few more recent works that are especially valuable for this project. Two studies that look at nineteenth-century Spanish- and French-language Caribbean literature together were important for the present study: Janett Reinstädler's "Theatralisierung der Karibik" and Gudrun Wogatzke's *Identitätsentwürfe*.[27]

Reinstädler's postdoctoral thesis examines theater in the nineteenth-century Caribbean and touches on questions of transfer and exchange in the process, especially in the context of the reception of the hegemonic cultures. Using documents such as season programs and theater reviews, she shows what was being produced where and addresses how they were received by the audience and the general public. She finds that the works on offer were mostly works from the respective mother countries. In the theater, where the underclasses were included in the audience, language barriers were a much bigger issue than they were in the interlingual reception of prose and poetry by intellectuals that we find in the texts under discussion here. This makes it clear that multirelationality begins as an elite phenomenon, which can only be brought to "the masses" once it has been processed and converted through domestic literature. The Spanish colonies produced a significant amount of homegrown theater, while the French Antilles had only a negligible amount. For Reinstädler, who takes a consistently symmetrical approach, this can be traced back primarily to the smaller population in the French-speaking Caribbean (as well as to Haiti's special position and economic misery), but from my perspective the deeper reason lies in the uneven strength of the respective mother countries' cultural influence, especially since the population density on islands like Martinique was much greater than that on Cuba.

Wogatzke's study investigates an extremely comprehensive textual corpus (including both poetry and prose) of the nineteenth-century Spanish and French Caribbean, providing very important groundwork. Her imagological perspective

---

27 See also Reinstädler, "*La répetition interrompue.*"

leads to interesting choices of emphasis, some of which I pursue further in this book, even though her approach is somewhat static.

There are, in addition, a very few individual monographs on the little-studied literature of the French-speaking Caribbean that also address the nineteenth century (usually only in subsections, unfortunately).[28] The Spanish-speaking nineteenth-century Caribbean, on the other hand, has been much better researched: Doris Sommer, for instance, has declared no fewer than three novels of the Spanish Caribbean (Gómez de Avellaneda's *Sab*, Villaverde's *Cecilia Valdés*, and Galván's *Enriquillo*) to be foundational fictions. Nevertheless, even for the Spanish-speaking Caribbean, there are relatively few studies of the nineteenth-century literary realm overall.[29]

There have been many investigations of images of the foreign in nineteenth-century French literature. For this project, studies of the nineteenth-century travelogue (Wolfzettel; Korte; Hölz) play a crucial role, because this genre, whose popularity was then at its apex, stood at the threshold between (proto-)scientific scholarly interest and the broader public's taste for the exotic. The public's interest was an essential precondition for the legitimation of colonial and imperial domination (for the case of England, see Korte 120); at the same time, traveling scholars provided a bridge to early ethnology (which has so far been greatly neglected by research on that period) and may even have served as ethnological informants, whether directly or through their travelogues. The studies of exoticism, therefore, are also worth paying careful attention to, even if they are mostly concerned with orientalism. Using the primary French texts, especially the French Romantics, which have been extensively studied (Matzat; Küpper; Warning), I look into the influence of specific literary models from the mother country and of the imperial cartography that makes its appearance there. The only study that deals explicitly with the representation of the Antilles in nineteenth-century French literature, however, is Romuald Fonkoua's doctoral thesis, which provides an enormous amount of material but is, overall, mostly descriptive.

Hans-Jürgen Lüsebrink's *Das Europa der Aufklärung* is an important resource on the dissemination of European constructs beyond Europe (especially in the eighteenth century). Since Foucault, many Romance scholars have engaged with the reorganization of systems of knowledge and the transformation of cul-

---

[28] Particularly noteworthy texts on Guadeloupe and Martinique are Maignan-Claverie; Corzani; Toumson; and Antoine. For the special case of Haiti, see the following notable works: Hoffmann, *Littérature d'Haïti*; Middelanis; and especially Fischer.

[29] Gewecke's works are important exceptions: see for example her *Der Wille zur Nation* and *Die Karibik*. Also important are Fleischmann and Bremer.

tural conceptions of order at the turn from the eighteenth to the nineteenth century. And finally, an important resource that should not be neglected is the research on literary anthropology.[30]

I.3 Colonial Dynamics in the Caribbean (1789–1886)

In the Caribbean, as in many Latin American countries, the traditional patterns of political and cultural orientation began to lose their binding force by the end of the eighteenth century, creating an increased need for a new collective positioning and identity (cf. Müller, "Processes of cultural transfer"; Müller, "Las letras").[31] In the second half of the eighteenth century and up through the Congress of Vienna (November 1814 to June 1815), many of the islands had been subjected to a quickly changing series of colonial masters; in addition to this, Europe was reorganizing politically, and the great revolutions in North America and France were exerting their influence. In this atmosphere of ongoing threat and constant fluctuation and change, the process of grounding went hand in hand with a search for points of reference, not just political but also cultural, outside the islands. The relationship to the mother country had been called into question and had to be redefined in one way or another. This situation had the potential to deterritorialize concepts of identity, a development that manifested itself first in Spanish-language Caribbean literature, which was visibly marked by it in the nineteenth century; over the course of the twentieth century, the phenomenon spread to the entirety of the cultural production of the Caribbean islands, and at times it has been projected to be the model for literature the world over, given the accelerated globalization of the means of communication, digitized to the speed of light.

For the nineteenth century, however, directly shaped as it was by the power structures of colonial politics, it would be a mistake to deny the analytically privileged position of the relationship between the center and the periphery. On the other hand, we must also not lose sight of the multirelationalism (both potential and, often, actual) that surrounded that relationship, with the Bolivian movement for independence and unification, and its accompanying cultural and literary awakening, having a political effect on the Caribbean that was comparable to that of the Haitian revolution. Haiti, however, was seen less as a role model than

---

30 For an overview from the point of view of German literary studies, but with reference to tendencies in Romance literatures as well, see Riedel. See also Thoma; Garber and Thoma.
31 I am grateful to Malte Griesse for crucial suggestions and discussions concerning this chapter and much more.

as a cautionary tale, not only because the conflict there was so brutal and the economic decline so unparalleled (making the jewel of the French colonial empire into a long-term poorhouse), but also because of the cultural stagnation that followed the decades-long expulsion and extermination of the white elite: the first Haitian novel to be published after the revolution was *Stella*, by Émeric Bergeaud (1818–1858), published in 1859. It is indicative of the hierarchy of relationalisms here that it apparently took the literary interventions of Hugo (in his debut work *Bug-Jargal*, 1818/1826) and Lamartine (in his play *Toussaint Louverture*, first performed in 1850, so not until after the 1848 revolution and the abolition of slavery) to make the Haitian revolution even worthy of discussion in the Caribbean. Even then, Spanish writers proved to be much more receptive to the social-revolutionary Romanticism that went along with the revolution than were French writers; even in Haiti itself, it was only after there were models from the French mainland that its own revolution against the political domination of such models was able to become the subject of prose representations.

I.3.1 The Spanish-Speaking Caribbean

While the writers and intellectuals of the French-speaking periphery seem to have largely contented themselves with redefining their relationship to the center and adjusting to the changing conditions, one has the sense that for Spanish-speaking intellectuals, their own cultural center had lost any influence it might have had. Some of the more radical expressions of that can be found in the words of Félix Tanco,[32] a sharp-tongued polemicist and abolitionist in del Monte's circle in Cuba.[33] Tanco was not shy with his vituperative tirades about how derivative (how "epigone-like") contemporary Spanish literature was: in 1837, for example, he mocked the Neoclassicists, while a few years later it was the Romanticists in the group around Zorrilla, Espronceda, and Bréton de los

---

32 Félix Tanco y Bosmeniel, who was born in Colombia in 1796, fled with his parents to Cuba in 1812. In the repression that followed the so-called *Conspiración de la Escalera* (Ladder Conspiracy) anti-slavery uprising, Tanco, known for his anti-slavery views, had to flee, first to the United States and then on to Spain. He was able to return to Cuba in 1850, but he spent the last two years of his life in New York, where he died in 1871.

33 Domingo del Monte, born in Venezuela in 1804, lived in Cuba from the time he was five years old and became well-known there as a literary critic. He became the center of a circle of intellectuals and writers, some of whom met regularly for the famous *tertulias* (literary gatherings), and some of whom were in regular contact with del Monte from exile. Del Monte himself, suspected of having been part of the *Conspiración de la Escalera*, had to leave Cuba; he died in Madrid in November 1853.

Herreros that he targeted, saying that, "like all of Spanish literature," they were not producing anything original anymore (Wogatzke 100). Although this judgment may be harsh, it reflects the effects on the colonial empire of Spain's cultural (self-)marginalization. Insofar as Spain was becoming a kind of European periphery, one could think of the colonies as a periphery of the periphery, or in Tanco's polemical words: the epigones of the epigones. However, that is in no way an accurate description of the Spanish-language literature of the Caribbean, which was much more inclined to give up its (former) center as a primary cultural point of reference. That meant that this literature was floating freely among the force fields of the various centers of gravity of the time, to which it was fundamentally receptive. It is no secret that French literature played a prominent role in this process. In Europe, French literature was already ubiquitous, because anyone with any claims to education spoke and read French; in addition, after Rousseau, French Romanticism concerned itself explicitly with the New World and its people. Even though most of the Spanish-speaking Caribbean writers may well have read French, translations also played an important role, which makes it clear that the act of translation from French into Spanish was an important intermediary for this primary reception.[34]

But for the hypothesis of the multirelationalism of a literature that has moved beyond the one-way street of colonialism to hold up, there has to be evidence of influences from and exchanges with other cultures as well. In a few articles, José Maria Heredia (*Prosas*) gives reading recommendations not only from the French literature of his time but also from British and United States literature.[35] He even visited the United States (where Cirilo Villaverde lived in exile[36]) and wrote letters, travelogues, and articles expressing his admiration for Washington and the American people, who so bravely fought for their independence, thereby at least implicitly proposing a model for Cubans (and potentially for other inhabitants of the Caribbean as well) (192 ff.). Writers like Lord Byron are particularly popular with Heredia. Might it be the Romanticist travel motif, and in the case of the English satirist Byron in particular, the fact that he permanently left his home country (for Italy)—an uprooting that in Byron's

---

34 On the phenomenon of translation as a part of cultural transfer, see Lüsebrink, *Interkulturelle Kommunikation* 143 ff.

35 Heredia (Cuba 1803–Mexico 1839) was a pre-Romantic poet and writer whose short life took place between Cuba, Santo Domingo, Venezuela, Mexico, and the United States.

36 Villaverde (Cuba 1812–New York 1894), a Cuban poet, journalist, and freedom fighter and author of the novel *Cecilia Valdés*, was forced to flee to the United States in 1849 because of his involvement working for Cuban independence; in the United States he was the publisher of several exile newspapers.

case has a very different context, but that could be seen as creating a parallel between his fate and the biographical experience of the writing-between-worlds of so many Spanish-language writers of the Caribbean—that is especially appealing to these writers?[37]

Villaverde's novel *Cecilia Valdés*, one of the best-known Cuban novels, also suggests readings in which colonial control is being infiltrated by the Creole writer. Villaverde intentionally appropriated nineteenth-century European literary models, but then, after thoroughly advertising that, finally failed to follow them (Mateos).[38]

As for the Spanish-language literatures of the Latin American mainland, they did not even need to be translated, and Heredia, in particular, spent a long time in exile in Mexico. Which authors were read, and what kind of interaction was there, with the South American continent and South American authors such as Bello, Fernandez de Lizardi, Sarmiento, Altamirano, or Echeverría? Might the cultural exchange with the likewise Spanish-speaking subcontinent have possibly even filled the vacuum left by the mother country when it was pushed to the sidelines?

I.3.2 The French-Speaking Caribbean

Although it might sound paradoxical, the main problem for the cultural production of the French Caribbean, unlike for that of the Spanish colonies, was that it suffered from the extraordinarily strong cultural influence of the mother country, which led to what we call a brain drain today. France, especially the French capital, offered excellent opportunities for education and development, which meant that the most forward-looking thinkers stayed there rather than returning to their home islands. A contemporary witness commented in 1842 that "almost all of the youth of our colonies is educated in France: the young men in Paris's

---

37 It is significant that Heredia refers particularly to Byron's famous epic poem *Childe Harold's Pilgrimage*, which is essentially Byron's poetic travel journal. It includes a Romanticist rendition of the Spaniards' freedom struggle against Napoleon and a dramatic lament of the foreign rule of Greece by Turkey. The experiences and descriptions of nature have elements that echo Rousseau's *Nouvelle Héloise* as well as his *Rêveries du promeneur solitaire*, which play a prominent role in contemporary Latin American and Caribbean reception. All over Europe, romantic young people identified with Byron's heavily autobiographical protagonist, with the pathos of his search for freedom and shedding of old ties.
38 Mateos emphasizes how Villaverde's "strategy of apparent incompetence" can be unmasked as a way of playing with colonial expectations, thus expressing its Caribbean autonomy. Compare Abel, "Tagungsbericht" 474.

academies and the young women at Saint-Denis and Sacré-Coeur" (Granier de Cassagnac 102 ff.; Wogatzke 56).³⁹ People like the Creoles Estève and Edmond in Levilloux's novel *Les créoles ou la Vie aux Antilles*, who went home to Guadeloupe after enjoying an education in the metropolis, felt melancholy about leaving the mother country:

> With their eyes turned towards that land that was sinking on the horizon, they counted all the blessings they had received from it: science, the lifting of their souls, a new moral existence. ... And completely occupied with France and its glory, their pure souls breathed a hymn of love and gratitude. (Levilloux 32)⁴⁰

For many writers, their country of origin hardly even seemed to matter anymore.⁴¹

Another reason for the elite's strong orientation towards Paris had to do with the terrified fear on the part of the white upper classes (the *Békés*) of rebellions and slave uprisings, a sense of menace that was surely not entirely unjustified and was of course also heavily fueled by what they had seen happen in Haiti. As a result, there were few efforts to ease the tensions by making concessions to the lower classes and the slaves, much less by abolishing slavery. This sense of menace becomes clearer if we look at the demographics: in 1820, Cuba's slaves made up 36% of the total population, which was high for the Spanish Caribbean (in Puerto Rico, for instance, it was only 9%);⁴² in French-speaking Guadeloupe and Martinique, however, where the population was also very much denser, the slaves made up 78% and 79% of the total population, respectively.⁴³ In Saint-Domingue (Haiti), the proportion of slaves in colonial times (1760) had been only a little greater than it was on the two smaller French Caribbean islands, which meant that their demographic structure seemed to harbor a similar potential for danger. And in fact, following the revolution, there had

---

39 "presque toute la jeunesse de nos colonies est élevée en France, les jeunes gens dans les Collèges de Paris; les jeunes personnes à Saint-Denis et au Sacré-Cœur."
40 "Les yeux tournés vers cette terre qui s'abaissait à l'horizon, ils comptaient tous les bienfaits qu'ils en avaient reçus; science, élévation de l'âme, nouvelle existence morale. ... Et tout occupés de la France, de sa gloire, leurs âmes pures soupiraient d'un hymne d'amour et de reconnaissance." See also Levilloux 28 and Wogatzke 301.
41 Reinstädler ("Theatralisierung") lists a whole string of playwrights from Martinique and Guadeloupe who barely even mention any Caribbean themes or motifs in their plays.
42 Experts have interpreted the historical demographic data in different ways. See Zeuske, *Sklavenhändler* 209–317.
43 Concerning the history of slavery and African forced labour in the French Caribbean see Flory.

been serious clashes between royalists and republicans, accompanied by unrest among the slaves and the free mulattos,[44] not just in Saint-Domingue but also in Martinique. In a letter to his father from the Martinique writer Maynard de Queilhe, published with his novel *Outre-mer*, it can be clearly seen that the Antilles are in such a tense political situation that the literary view of them as a source of exotic projections is long out of date:

> All that is left for me, my father, is to hope that this book engages you. If it is full of blood, you will not complain about that, you who have twenty times seen your lands overrun by flames and rebellion piling up corpses at Grosse-Roche, this Clamart of the Paris of the Antilles. The colonists of all the colonies know well that it is no longer possible today to write about their societies in beautiful volumes scented in rosewater or orange flowers. May cheerful things be born! This is what I call for, with all my heart. My God! you who have prodigally given to these climates your magnificences, your rarest splendors, now give them a gift even more beautiful and more precious, my God! give them peace. (Preface)[45]

After the free mulattos had been granted legal equality (1792), things went no further and slavery was not abolished, because the royalists and the vast majority of white plantation owners, who were prepared to defend their privileges at any cost, supported the British invading army, which ultimately restored the previous status quo.

After the islands were finally back under the French flag, which did not happen until 1815, writers like Prévost de Sansac[46] defended himself and his peers against the implied rebuke of betrayal and "Anglomania." All he had to do to justify the alliance with the British was to paraphrase what Napoleon had said at a meeting of the state council in 1803, when he declared that if he had been in Martinique in 1794, he would have been for the British, because one's

---

44 The term "mulatto" refers to people with both African and European ancestors; there were both free and enslaved mulattos. I use the term "mulatto" based on its historical usage in both literary and cultural forms of representation and not as a description of skin color from today's perspective.

45 "Il ne me reste plus, mon père, qu'à souhaiter que ce livre vous attache. S'il est tout sanglant, vous ne vous en plaindrez pas, vous qui avez vu vingt fois la flamme courir sur vos terres et la révolte amonceler des cadavres à la Grosse-Roche, ce Clamart du Paris des Antilles. Les colons de toutes les colonies savent bien qu'il n'est plus possible aujourd'hui de composer sur les faits de leur société de jolis volumes qui soient à l'eau de rose ou à la fleur d'oranger. Naissent des choses riantes! c'est ce que j'appelle de tous mes vœux. Mon Dieu ! vous qui avez prodigué à ces climats toutes vos magnifices, vos magnificences les plus rares, faites-leur un don plus beau et plus précieux, mon Dieu ! donnez-leur la paix."

46 There is very little in the way of biographical information that has survived on Auguste Jean Prévost de Sansac, the Count of Traversay. His family apparently settled in Martinique in the eighteenth century. In 1806 he published *Les amours de Zémédare et Carina*.

first concern is to save one's life. Prévost de Sansac also stressed the natural loyalty of the Martinicans to France and the variety of the ties "so strong and so sweet" (in other words cultural) to the mother country:

> In this colony … we will never forget that it is to the generous protection [of the English] that we owe the preservation of men and of properties … but to conclude from that that the inhabitants of Martinique, *all of them true Frenchmen, naturally loyal, good, and loving*, could wish to become English and break the *multiple links, so strong and so sweet, which attach them to France*, is the most odious slander. (250–252, emphasis mine)[47]

I.3.3 For Slavery

The white French Caribbean *Béké* writers of the first half of the nineteenth century seem to have been most eager to draw a peaceful, almost beatific picture of small plantations where the master looked after his slaves like a father. Subversive ideas (like the 1794 confrontation with the British) were dismissed as European imports that only arose because people in France did not understand the actual situation in the colonies. Here we can see an astounding overlap between literary representations and actual political statements. In Maynard de Queilhe's *Outre-mer*, his protagonist, Marius, convinced of the inhumanity of slavery and imbued with European social-revolutionary (abolitionist) ideas, returns to the Caribbean, where he is finally convinced of the basic error of his ideas about the life of the slaves on the plantations:

> He had been told that they were exposed to the elements in all seasons and weathers, defenseless and without clothes; what he learned was that these men received two jackets and two pairs of pants every year, the women two jackets and two skirts, and that if one sometimes saw them half-naked, it was because they found that more pleasant. … Their work brought with it no suffering nor pains. (I:105 ff.)[48]

---

[47] "Dans cette colonie … l'on n'oubliera jamais que c'est à la généreuse protection [des Anglais] que l'on doit la conservation des hommes et celle des propriétés … mais en conclure que les habitants de la Martinique, *tous vrais Français, naturellement fidèles, bons et aimants*, puissent désirer devenir anglais et briser les *liens multiples, si forts et si doux, qui les attachent à la France*, c'est la plus odieuse calomnie."

[48] "On lui avait dit qu'on les exposait aux intempéries des saisons, sans défense, sans vêtements; et il apprenait que ces hommes recevaient par an deux casaques et deux caleçons, les femmes deux casaques et deux jupes: que si parfois on les voyait à moitié nus c'est que cela leur était plus agréable. … A ces travaux ne se joignaient ni douleurs ni peines." For a very similar picture, see Eyma, "Les Borgias Noirs" 118: "In order to correct … his judgments and to initiate him into the splendors of this vegetation, which has no parallel anywhere in the world, and the sight of all the activity of a plantation, of the expanse of the properties, of all that is curious

The assessment presented by the delegates of the colonies to the center in 1838 sounds almost like an echo of these literary representations:

> If we consider [the colonies] on their own terms, in their own internal condition ... there is nothing that would make the abolition of slavery urgent or necessary. The regimen of the plantations is gentle and progressive, and no native passion or opinion asks for any radical transformation; in the presence of the public opinion of Europe, however, and under the influence of the measures that that opinion has already ordered, the serious discussions that it provokes and multiplies, and even of the effects that these causes produce on the moral and economic condition of the colonies, it is no longer possible to maintain slavery in a comprehensive and sustainable way. (*Avis des Conseils coloniaux* [*Opinion of the Colonial Councils*], quoted in Gisler 129)[49]

What still requires examination is how the undiminished enthusiasm and admiration for France as a haven of culture, and the very strong grounding in (and even imitation of) French culture overall and French literature in particular, can be made to square with this unilateral positioning of harmful ideas as coming from the mother country.

How was the image of France constituted, and what are the literary models that were used, in terms of content as well as form? Which philosophical ideas were picked up and reshaped, and how? In addition, we have to ask to what extent and in what way a myth about slavery was disseminated, across categories and media and in literary and extraliterary forms of representation. Or, to put it another way: how did the picture drawn by the *Béké* writers shape the French notions of the social conditions and the relations between the races overseas, possibly even influencing French historiography? The reports by Maynard de Queilhe and the delegates are clearly contradicted by the reality of multiple slave revolts in the French Antilles (in 1822, 1830, 1833, and 1848), which were accompanied by the abolitionist movement (though it was a weak one) of the in-

---

and unique in the relationship between master and slave, I resolved to take him ... to one of the island's largest sugar plantations." ("Afin de rectifier ... ses jugements et de l'initier ... aux splendeurs de cette végétation qui n'a pas sa pareille dans le monde, au spectacle de l'activité d'une habitation, de l'étendue des propriétés, du côté curieux et original des rapports entre le maître et l'esclave, je résolus de le conduire, ... sur une des sucreries les plus considérables de l'île.")

49 "Si on les considère [les colonies] en elles-mêmes, dans leur état intérieur ... il n'y a rien qui rende urgente ni nécessaire l'abolition de l'esclavage. Le régime des habitations est doux et progressif, et aucune passion, aucune opinion indigène n'en demande la transformation radicale; mais en présence de l'opinion publique d'Europe, sous l'influence des mesures qu'elle a déjà commandées, des discussions graves qu'elle provoque et multiplie, des effets mêmes que ces causes produisent sur l'état moral et économique des colonies, le maintien intégral et durable de l'esclavage n'est plus possible."

tellectuals in Cyrille Bissette's circle.⁵⁰ In other words, the slaves were not just egged on by unqualified, foreign European ideas, as Maynard de Queilhe and others suggest, but there were educated local mentors—or philosophers, as the proponents of slavery dismissively characterized them—who committed themselves to the slaves' cause and were very well acquainted with the actual situation.

This myth also incorporates the Martinican abolition of 1848, which in the official reports is always traced back unilaterally to the confirmation by the revolutionary government in Paris in 1848 of Victor Schœlcher's emancipation decree; in other words, it is represented as a gift from the mother country whereas in fact, before the news of the change in the law had arrived, the slaves had already rebelled and thereby forced an announcement of their liberation. Édouard Glissant, referring to this myth, deplores the "discursive negation of Afro-Caribbean contributions" to Martinique's development: "The absence of any historical memory facilitated the projection of these elitist pseudo-histories onto the popular consciousness" (*Le discours antillais* 646).⁵¹ He sees the stubborn persistence of "Schoelcherism" as arising from the repressive political strategy of suppressing the development of a locally rooted historical consciousness in Martinique; this absence of a historical memory, in turn, creates the necessary conditions for an interpretation of the past that is targeted to the metropolis. Here, again, we must ask how literature and culture have contributed to the discursive construction of these deeply problematic politics of memory or, rather, formations of knowledge.

I.3.4 Against Slavery

Not all writers, however, talk about the plantations in such glowing terms as do the white *Békés* Prévost de Sansac, Eyma,⁵² Maynard de Queilhe, and Rosemond

---

50 Cyrille Bissette (Martinique 1795–Paris 1858) was one of the most committed Caribbean abolitionists and came close to having to pay for his engagement with a lifelong sentence to galley slavery. History, however, has unjustly left him in Victor Schœlcher's shadow, where he has been almost forgotten.
51 "L'absence de mémoire historique favorise la projection de ces pseudo-histoires d'ordre élitaire sur la conscience populaire." See also Glissant, *Mémoires*; Reinstädler, "Theatralisierung" 19.
52 Louis-Xavier Eyma (1816–1876), a Martinican writer, spent his life between the Antilles, Louisiana, and France. He used the impressions he gathered on his travels in his literary descriptions of Caribbean and American slaveholding societies.

de Beauvallon.⁵³ Levilloux, Chapus, Bonneville, and Agricole⁵⁴ are all considered sympathetic to the slaves, even though their novels could certainly not be called abolitionist (or at least not militantly so). The image of the island societies that they convey is problematic and fissured: confrontations between the members of the different races play a central role, but the attributes and the complexity of the characters are not tied to their skin color. In the works of these writers, historical events occupy an important position and are explicitly thematized (in contrast to the work of the "hard-liners" among the white *Béké* writers, with their Romanticist idealization of nature). In Levilloux's work, these events are made up primarily of the revolutionary developments in Martinique and Guadeloupe, and in his writing, among other things in his interpretation of the Haitian revolution and the separatism of the black rebels, we can hear a modest counter-narrative to the official representation. In Levilloux's novel *Les créoles ou la Vie aux Antilles*, for example, General Dugommier says that the white oligarchs in Martinique, as well as in Saint-Domingue, are only exploiting the revolutionary turmoil in France and the war in Europe in order to strengthen their own position and make themselves independent from the mother country (249).⁵⁵ The charge of disloyalty to the mother country, to which Prévost de Sansac was reacting when he defended the behavior of the white plantation owners at the time of the British invasion, is made explicit here. The separatist opportunism of the white landowners is contrasted with the patriotism of Estève, the novel's mulatto protagonist, who has internalized the ideals of the French Enlightenment and who, along with Dugommier, dies for France's revolutionary cause at the end, in the battle against the Spaniards in Catalonia's *Selva negra*.

There is a clear conflict of the literary discourses around the historical representation of the events that emerges here. What were the interactions between literature and historiography? How were views of history formed at the intersections between literary and extraliterary representations? Were there open discussions among the few French-speaking writers who were active in the French Antilles and who wrote about historical events? What was the role of censorship in

---

53 Jean-Baptiste Rosemond de Beauvallon (1819–1903), a journalist from Guadeloupe, used his descriptions of Caribbean societies to try to convince mainland France of the advantages of slavery.
54 Levilloux and Chapus were apparently both mulattos; see Wogatzke 451, although she gives no evidence for the claim. Maignan-Claverie, on the other hand, appears to imply that Levilloux can be counted as part of *Béké* literature (320). Bonneville was married to a mulatto woman; Eugène Agricole (1834–1901), a politician born in Guadeloupe, is considered to be the first black writer in Martinique, although he does not appear until 1870.
55 "se constituer indépendants de la France en profitant des embarras de la lutte européenne."

the relative restraint these writers showed in expressing (or rather insinuating) any critique of slavery? How were the novels received, and by whom? And what connections did the writers have to the explicitly abolitionist movement in the Antilles, about which we still know so little but which contemporaries linked, significantly, with the Freemasons (Hoffmann, *Le Nègre* 136; Maignan-Claverie 259)?

Levilloux's and Chapus's novels, in which the social-revolutionary dimension of European Romanticism is particularly in evidence (even though at times it turns inwards, towards the philosophical and contemplative [Maignan-Claverie 259]), are very comparable to texts from the Spanish Caribbean. However, there is not the least sign to be found in the work of these two authors of any move whatsoever towards independence; quite the contrary. The question of abolition, on the other hand, occupies an important position in both the French and the Spanish narratives, though it never crystallizes into an explicit call for the abolition of slavery, which would not have passed the censors in either case.

More than the question of the freeing of the black slaves, then, it is the figure of the mulatto that is given a central position: the primary focus is on the emancipation of mulattos and their chances for social advancement; and their inner conflicts of identity and belonging, fueled by the racially discriminatory environment, are examined in great detail, with a measure of introspection. In both French- and Spanish-language Caribbean literature, it is very hard to separate the figure of the mulatto from the essentialist characterizations that, finally, define the mulatto's legal position, and in spite of the demand for equal rights in principle, the mulatto is always pulled back into the equation of black ancestry with a closeness to nature and lack of culture that can only be overcome—and it is overcome—with a great deal of hard work at self-improvement. While writers like Maynard de Queilhe and Eyma see in the free mulatto (*affranchi*) the epitome of a seditious threat—because mulattos, with their advancement and their access to education and culture, could acquire revolutionary ideas and then in turn stir up the "contented slaves"—others, such as Villaverde, the Cuban-Spanish writer Gómez de Avellaneda, and Levilloux place all their hopes in the figure of the mulatto as a mediator, the only one who is in any position to soften the antagonistic stances taken up in their strictly segregated societies. Thus, for example, racial and gender-related essentialist characterizations are blurred in the person of the slave Sab in Gómez de Avellaneda's eponymous novel *Sab*, and for that very reason Sab is able to serve as a figure of integration and cohesion. Similarly, the racial identity of Levilloux's protagonist, Estève, can barely be determined from his appearance. When we look at these fictional characters, and the images that they convey of society and its conflicts, alongside literary and political discussions about slavery, for example those that took place in the illustrious circle centered on del Monte, it becomes clear what kind of utopias were connected to the figure of the mulatto. These utopias seem hair-raising to our modern-day sensibilities, with our paradigms of multi-, inter- and transculturalism, and yet we cannot simply dismiss them as absurd if we want to understand the conceptual world and the categories within which the Caribbean actors thought, communicated, acted, and wrote, and which certainly had repercussions for Europe as well. Even in progressive literary circles, integration was thought of in terms of homogenization, to prevent the danger of Africanization: *limpiar* (cleaning), *blanquear* (whitening), and *controlar* (controlling) were the watchwords (Zeuske, *Kleine Geschichte* 119 ff.). Thus, del Monte is concerned with "cleansing Cuba of the African race (*limpiar Cuba de la raza Africana*, Reinstädler, "Theatralisierung" 42). José Antonio Saco, the famous Cuban philosopher and politician, explains in a letter to his compatriot José de la Luz y Caballero written in the eighteen-forties what this "cleansing" was supposed to look like (from our perspective today, of course, we cannot help but be reminded, when we hear the word, of the twentieth century's brutal "ethnic cleansings"—but note that *limpiar* does not imply "killing" here at all). Saco recommends a conscious policy of encouraging educated white Europeans to immigrate and promoting ethnically mixed marriages, in order to "breed out" or domesticate the African element (cf. Llorens 90 ff.); in other words, a proto-eugenic project to create equality and culture in a humane way.

Were there similar discourses in the French colonies of the Caribbean? And what was the effect of the much higher proportion of slaves there on literary and extraliterary reflections on racial mixing and its dangers and potentials? What discussions were ethnologists in Paris having at that time on these questions, and what was the relationship between those discussions and the Caribbean debates both in France's own and in Spain's colonies? Could the prominence of the question of independence in the Spanish texts be merely the result of the political immobility of the mother country, which was unwilling to allow any serious discussion of the question of abolition, whereas the fictional mulattos from the French Caribbean rightly saw belonging to the French mother country, with all the vehemence of its egalitarian principles, as the only realistic prospect for their own emancipation? Given that ethnic differences and the problem of overcoming them (in whatever way) were given such priority, may there actually have been a direct exchange between intellectuals of the Spanish and French Caribbean? What kind of effects did the abolition of slavery in the French Caribbean in 1848 have on literature and debates, given that slavery had been replaced by wage labor but the wages were starvation wages and abolition was accompanied by repressive political measures, and those who bore the brunt of them were not only blacks but also the Asians who were immigrating in ever increasing waves

I.3.5 Haiti: On the Dialectics of Imitation

Finally, we must also ask what intra-Caribbean transfer processes looked like in contexts where Spanish and French speakers were able, at least in theory, to meet directly, without having to overcome a dividing sea but with an even deeper rift between them: on the island of Hispaniola, divided into Haiti and Santo Domingo and forcibly united, for a period of twenty years (1822–1844), by the Haitian occupation. This was also the only part of either the French Caribbean (Haiti) or Spanish Caribbean (Santo Domingo) that could call itself independent in the time period under examination (though for Santo Domingo it was only temporary, from the eighteen-forties to the eighteen-sixties).[56]

Paradoxically, the social Romanticism of the Dominican Galván,[57] whose hero Enrique invokes "the great Hugo" and emphatically calls for humane treatment for the Spanish prisoners of war, stands in contrast to the high degree of dependence on French culture in Haiti, as paradigmatically expressed in Bergeaud's novel *Stella*. Haitian poetry has a certain amount to offer in this regard as well:

> Oh France, we love you, like many, no doubt
> Of your own children will never love you;

---

56 Cf. Gewecke, "Saint-Domingue/Haití—Santo Domingo." Gewecke deals with the Haitian occupations of Santo Domingo in the period from 1795 to 1865, which led to repeated temporary reunifications of the island. She shows how the opportunity to found a transcultural state out of the revolutionary West and the Spanish/Dominican East according to Toussaint's ideal of a "single and indivisible island" (*île une et indivisible*) was lost in the conflicts of hegemonic interest between the colonial powers of France, Spain, and England. Due to marked anti-Haitian sentiment on the Dominican side, which alternated over the course of the nineteenth century between European protectionism and U.S.-American annexationism, transfers between the French-speaking and Spanish-speaking parts of the island went down in history as highly aggressive and conflict-filled, she writes, while the dynamic potential of other possibilities was often repressed in the historical record, though that was in fact several times the historical reality of the entire island.
57 The Dominican diplomat and journalist Manuel de Jesús Galván (Santo Domingo 1834–Puerto Rico 1910) was a Spanish loyalist who become known for his historical novel *Enriquillo* (1879/1882). On Galván, see also Torres-Saillant 206.

And everywhere that your finger points the way
That is where we will search for harmony and peace. (Coicou 113 ff.)[58]

In this hymn of praise by Massillon Coicou (1867–1908), the Haitian writer calls himself a better patriot even than the French. There was a kind of Francophilia, consistently glorifying the mother country, that could be encountered very frequently in Haiti. The country's various attempts to define its own self-image as Latin America's first independent black state soon gave way to a renewed understanding of France, the onetime mother country, as a guiding influence. French culture held a special position as the only cultural model: those who had it were guaranteed a special status in their own country and the ability to advance; it was also a way to prove the injustice of racial discrimination by the French (and all whites). Most cultural aspirations in Haiti involved gaining acceptance for Haiti from the countries that had Western culture, and as a result, all of the African cultural manifestations that still held any meaning were denounced as backward, while parallels with France were glorified. The aim was to demonstrate the equality of blacks and whites.

Hans-Jürgen Lüsebrink, writing about "cultural transfers and the postcolonial legitimation of power" during the reign of Haiti's King Henry Christophe (1807–1811), shows how present these ambitions were in the press and in literature during that time. Using examples from texts from 1800 to 1820 by Abbé Henri Grégoire, Antoine Métral, and the Baron de Vastey, he convincingly shows how central a role the print media played in the legitimation of Haiti's independence. Haitian writers, in imitating the "courtly" writing style of the French ancien régime, made a decisive contribution to the international recognition of the new state's intellectual capabilities, "degree of civilization," and self-government. This creative appropriation of Western forms of representation was a key factor in the postcolonial state's ability to maintain its position of power.[59]

---

[58] "Oui, France, nous t'aimons, comme plusieurs, sans doute, / De tes propres enfants ne t'aimeront jamais / Et partout où ton doigt nous indique la route / C'est là que nous cherchons l'harmonie et la paix." See Hoffmann, Littérature 92.

[59] "Haitian literature was intended, by its very existence, to represent a sort of essential 'piece of evidence' ... (to use Grégoire's legal metaphor) in order to 'prove,' in the eyes of Western public opinion but also of its own people, the young Haitian nation's capacity for intellectual development, in other words its ability to succeed even in the poetic genres that were understood by the poetic world of that time to be the most sublime genres and, by making 'progress' that external observers such as Grégoire, Sismondi, and Métral found astonishing, to rapidly reach advanced stages of 'civilization.'" ("La littérature haïtienne se voulait représenter, de par son existence même, une sorte de 'pièce à conviction' ... [pour reprendre la métaphorique judiciaire utilisée par Grégoire] essentielle visant à 'prouver,' aux yeux de l'opinion publique occidentale,

The fact that the idea and the language of the revolution were white was crucial for the further course of Haitian history. The black slaves did not create the revolution on their own independent initiative but as mimicry of the rhetoric of their white masters. Michael Zeuske points to one of the first narratives featuring revolution in the Spanish empire, translated from French into Spanish by Juan López Cancelada. This story places a demiurge, a mysterious mentor to the blacks, on Saint-Domingue at the beginning of the slave revolution, a leader who had been the house slave and barber of a French lawyer and had adopted his master's way of talking and thinking (Zeuske, *Schwarze Karibik* 169). This view is also very clearly on display in Émeric Bergeaud's 1859 novel *Stella*, in which the Haitian revolutionary leaders love the white protagonist, Stella. She is an allegory for revolutionary France who suggests the idea of freedom to them and gives them the courage to fight for it and to rise up against colonialist France. What meaning does Francophilia have in this exclusively black context, unique in the Caribbean? In spite of the mimicry, could we say that the racist and essentialist categories that were the norm on the other islands were "culturalized" in this case? Did French culture take the place of (white) skin color?

I.4 Debates over Abolition in France and Spain

I.4.1 Debates over Abolition in France (1789–1848)

In the case of France, it does not really make sense to talk about *the* abolitionist movement, because there was such a variety of motivations behind the abolitionist demands of the various social groups and individuals. Because of these divisions, the abolitionists in France were never able to organize effectively until slavery was in fact abolished. The movement in France towards lasting abolition was not linear and should be understood as a complex array of different forces.[60]

The first group to agitate for abolition in France was the *Société des amis des Noirs*, the Society of the Friends of the Blacks, founded in 1788. Martin Klein compares the situation in France to that in Great Britain and the United States,

---

mais aussi de son propre peuple, la capacité d'évolution intellectuelle de la jeune nation haïtienne; c'est-à-dire sa faculté de réussir même dans les genres poétiques considérés comme les genres sublimes par l'art poétique de l'époque et d'atteindre rapidement, à travers des 'progrès' jugés étonnants par des observateurs externes comme Grégoire, Sismondi et Métral, des stades avancés de la 'civilisation.'") (Lüsebrink, "Transfers" 321; cf. Abel, "Tagungsbericht").
60 I am grateful to Hafid Derbal for some important suggestions that informed this chapter. See also Müller, "Koloniale Achsen".

describing how this first French group was founded relatively late, compared to those in the Anglo-Saxon world, and was also much more elitist. It had very few members, though they were very influential. The group did not have its roots in the church, nor did it have an explicit goal of reaching the public (Klein 28). It was, instead, a lobbying force, submitting complaints and grievances to the 1789 National Assembly. There can be no doubt that the Enlightenment had led to an atmosphere that was conducive to a positive attitude towards the rights of blacks and the abolition of slavery, but the fact that the question of abolition played a role throughout the revolution can be largely traced to the work of this first Society. According to Klein, the Society also worked to incite dissatisfaction and revolt in the colonies. Many of its members, including the Marquis de Condorcet, were republican Girondins who were executed during the revolution (273 ff.).

In 1791 the National Assembly granted citizenship to Caribbeans of color (*gens de couleur*), which heightened tensions in Saint-Domingue. In 1794, the Assembly abolished slavery in all of France's colonies and also made it illegal for slave owners to bring their slaves with them to France. Henri Grégoire (called Abbé Grégoire, 1750 – 1831), among the most prominent members of the Society of the Friends of the Blacks and the leading figure among the proponents of abolition at that time, published a pamphlet in 1791 entitled "A Letter to the Citizens of Color and Free Negroes of Saint-Domingue," in which he argued for mulattos' right to vote. He also kept up a correspondence with the Haitian leader Toussaint Louverture and became a mouthpiece for Haitians in France (Klein 160 ff.). Neither these activities of Grégoire's nor the work of so many others was able to bring about abolition at that early date, when France and its colonies were not yet ready for a lasting implementation of abolition, but Grégoire's commitment was nevertheless tremendously important, because it caused the issue to continue being discussed and kept it visible as an item on the political and economic agenda. Grégoire was also one of the best-known critics of the 1802 reintroduction of slavery under Napoleon Bonaparte. But when the revolutionary powers attempted to reorganize the church, Grégoire was one of the few clerics who accepted the reforms, and that made him into a controversial figure, which ultimately hurt the abolition movement: his involvement with the cause made the church less willing to support it.

Seymour Drescher describes the role of the Catholic Church, which now found itself facing a dilemma ("Two Variants"). The Church was hostile to the Enlightenment and the revolution, and considered abolition, and forces such as the Society of the Friends of the Blacks, to be part of those developments (Klein 84). The Enlightenment and the revolution had severely shaken the Church's dominance, and its main concern was for its own survival in post-revolutionary France. Therefore, the Church's efforts went towards preserving peaceful relations with the new ruling powers, who had reintroduced slavery. In addition, as a result of the pro-government role that it had agreed to, the Church had committed itself not to interfere with the colonial status quo (Drescher, "Two Variants" 42).

Jean-Marcel Champion notes that the 1802 law making slavery legal again was really only making official what had never actually changed anyway (230). There was hardly anywhere where slavery had actually been abolished. Bonaparte's attitude towards slavery was based on three main objectives: first, he aspired to reestablish France's rule and authority in all the colonies; second, he wanted to lead them back to economic wealth; and third, he intended to use the Antilles, especially Saint-Domingue, as a platform from which to pursue active politics in the Americas. Champion notes that Bonaparte's pragmatic politics sometimes hardened, depending on the situation; his primary goal was to maintain the colonial status quo. But Bonaparte also made it clear that he would not meddle with abolition in regions where it was already established (Guadeloupe, where abolition had been briefly enforced, was an exception: Antoine Richepanse reintroduced slavery there in 1802) (Champion 232 ff.).

Paul Michael Kielstra concludes that up until 1814, the French abolitionist movement was fragmented and disorganized (21). It included Protestant intellectuals like Madame de Staël and Victor, Duke of Broglie, whose position was both religiously and politically grounded and who were opposed to the Bourbon Restoration, as well as conservative aristocrats who spoke out against the slave trade for a variety of reasons. Although these proponents of abolition were able to keep the debates on the issue alive, they made very little difference, because the ruling powers needed the slave trade and the colonial status quo in order to regain the wealth that had been destroyed by a quarter century of war. Those in power during the Restoration, including the liberals, were clearly pro-slavery. Francis Arzalier points out that they had certainly taken note of the increasing British pressure and of the slave uprisings. As a result, they understood that in the long term, slavery would come to an end, but that did not by any means make them abolitionists. The ties to the old colonial system were still too strong for that (Arzalier 261).

The pragmatic politics of the Restoration, aimed at stabilizing postrevolutionary France and its colonial empire, were shaped by the generation that had experienced pre-1789 France and, in part, wished for its return. Gaspard Théodore Mollien, for example, had helped to negotiate Haiti's independence and the issue of its debts. From 1827 to 1831, he wrote hundreds of manuscript pages about the loss of the colonies and their condition, pages that betray a definite nostalgia for prerevolutionary times. Although Mollien accepted that there was no future for slavery, he found that unfortunate (Arzalier 262).

The numbers that are mentioned in various parliamentary debates during the Restoration make it clear how much the French economy suffered under the Revolution. The volume of trade in France's colonial empire was a hundred thousand metric tons of freight before the Revolution; by 1813, that number had fallen to barely seven thousand. The new governments that took power starting in 1814 concluded that France could not recover, and that it was impossible to regain the prerevolutionary levels of colonial prosperity. Saint-Domingue played a prominent role in these debates: on the eve of the Revolution, of the 165 million francs yielded by colonial products, approximately 120 million came from Saint-Domingue alone. In the early years of the Restoration a number of shipowners and brokers, including Admiral Dufort de la Rochelle and Lezurier de la Martel, played key roles; they had a political and strategic interest in returning to the old colonial order, and they were supported by members of the military who found an audience in the parliament (Démier 237–239).

The economic interests involved in the slavery question are a central issue in the economic thought of the industrialization period, as Francis Démier makes clear. The interests of the sugar industry, in particular, had a growing influence on the debates over abolition.[61] In the eighteen-twenties, economic crises badly shook global market prices for sugar, and the price of sugarcane fell by half, with devastating consequences for the French colonies and severe losses. Around the same time, in 1816, the price of slaves rose dramatically. These circumstances led many people in Paris as well as in the colonies to start thinking about alternative farming methods but also, especially, workforce alternatives. Most of the plantation owners, however, resisted any change, and they organized and financed a lobby for their interests in Paris. (They also sent a fifty-two-member delegation, with deep financial resources, to Bordeaux, a crucial city for Atlantic concerns, for several months, to represent the interests of the large landowners in the Antilles.) Their political leaders and direct speakers in the parliament were the Duke of Fitz-James, the Marquis de Lally Tollendal, the Comte de Sesmaisons, Révillière, and various deputies and soldiers, such as General Lieutenant Ambert, who were in direct contact with colonial circles. This movement was connected with the extreme right, and its interests were closely intertwined with those of the navy and the military. Colonial holdings always involved a need for a strong marine fleet (Démier 241–242). Philippe Vigier (251) also mentions the Council of Colonial Delegates (*Conseil des délégués des colonies*) in this context, and the influence of that body on both chambers of the parliament.

---

61 For a historical analysis of *Slavery in the Circuit of Sugar* in Martinique, see Tomich.

At the same time, a slow but steady increase and strengthening could be seen in various attitudes that favored the abolition of slavery. This was especially the case with individuals who saw themselves as the heirs of the Enlightenment and of the Revolution. These attitudes were also an indication that there was a new generation of writers and politicians emerging that had not personally experienced the prerevolutionary period and that therefore perceived the Haitian revolution, for example, differently. According to Arzalier, these were most often faithful monarchists, whose rejection of slavery was founded on a humanitarianism tinged with religion: moderates such as Victor, Duke of Broglie, and his friend Benjamin Constant; François Guizot; Antoine d'Argout; and Auguste de Staël (Arzalier 262).

During the Restoration, liberal calls for the abolition of slavery on economic grounds, which also made the colonial question into a key economic issue, grew increasingly vocal as well. They took the position that focusing only on the colonies and clinging to the old colonial system meant preventing trade with the young, independent states of Latin America. Liberals of this stripe joined up with other abolitionists in the Society for Christian Morals (*Société de la morale chrétienne*), which in 1822 established a Committee for the Abolition of the Black Slave Trade (*Comité pour l'abolition de la traite des Noirs*). They enjoyed the support of, among others, Benjamin Constant and Jacques Antoine Manuel, and they found outlets for their positions in various press media, including *Commerce*, *Producteur*, and *Le Constitutionnel* (Démier 243–244).[62] And although the pro-abolitionist attitude of these liberals can be traced much more to concrete economic interests than to any sympathy for blacks, it should not be forgotten that they were instrumental in moving these questions, which included the question of slavery, to the center of the political debates of the time. Most of the position statements of that time argued for a transition, seeing reforms as necessary measures towards the step-by-step abolition, or at least modification, of slavery. Radical voices calling for immediate abolition were still the exception then, but they did exist: in an 1830 pamphlet, for instance, P.A. Dufau, a well-known philanthropist, tried to convince the plantation owners that it was in their interest to introduce reforms to slavery, arguing that such reforms were essential to the modernization of their plantations (Démier 244). I should also point out that anyone calling for abolition at that time was also subject to the accusation of working for England, since the climate of the times included a general anti-England attitude (Vigier 252).

---

62 The issue of abolition shows up again and again in Constant's speeches as he argues that France is increasingly isolating itself within a progressive Europe.

The fact that the period following the French Revolution of 1830 took on an increasingly abolitionist character had to do not only with the generational change that was taking place but also, very clearly, with the new international geopolitical context and the changing economic conditions, mentioned above. This change could be felt as early as the beginning of the eighteen-twenties, as can be seen in an 1822 comment by Count Molé, Minister of the Navy and of the Colonies: nothing, he said, could save the slavery-based colonial system from its own collapse (Arzalier 262). As a result, it was only a matter of time before the French government, following the general trend and also bowing to the heavy pressure from England, outlawed the slave trade in 1827. The law passed by a delegate vote of 220 to 64. And though France did very little at first to fight the still existing, though now illegal, slave trade, the endorsement of this law shows how clearly the prevailing attitudes towards slavery had changed among France's political and social elite. Arzalier (262) points out that this reversal can be seen in the literary production of the time as well, where it reflects the change in opinion not only of the authors but also of the readers.[63]

There is a parallel between this development and France's attitude towards the declining Ottoman Empire: the Society for Christian Morals launched a campaign to free the Greeks from their Turkish "slavery." Some of the members of that campaign, including d'Argout, Guizot, and the banker Jacques Laffitte, obtained high-level political offices after the Revolution of 1830. And even though the complete abolition of slavery in the French colonies had to wait until 1848, the demand to abolish slavery in the Ottoman Empire offered a potential for propaganda that France took advantage of, using abolitionist arguments to try to legitimize its conquest of northern Algeria in 1830. At the time of the French conquest there were virtually no more slaves in Algeria, but France justified its expedition and conquest with the desire to end the piracy and enslavement of Christians there (Arzalier 264).

This attitude is reflected in a variety of texts: most of the Romantics, including Alexandre Dumas, combined their opposition to slavery with a denunciation of Islam, which was seen as supporting slavery (Arzalier 267). Victor Schoelcher made the same connection between the two, and his 1845 trip to Egypt gave him the opportunity to brand Mohammed Ali personally, as well as Islam, as advocates for slavery. In 1848 he started a petition calling for the liberation of the

---

[63] Arzalier's article is particularly noteworthy in that he analyzes well-known and lesser-known literary works as well as political and historical discourses of the time in order to portray the changing attitude.

slaves in Algeria.[64] Thus, abolition was increasingly used as a way to justify the colonization of new regions, and it became an established part of the discourse of France's new political and social forces. But the growing strength of these new forces did not mean that the old powers had disappeared, by any means. As late as the early eighteen-thirties, there was a variety of works published that explicitly called for the maintenance of the old structures and drew a positive picture of slavery (Arzalier 264 ff.).

The events of 1830, taken together, paved the way for a reorganization of the efforts towards abolition in France; as Philippe Vigier makes clear (248), calls for abolition were by no means a marginal phenomenon involving only individual figures and their representatives in Parliament. Thus, in 1833, the French Society for the Abolition of Slavery (*Société française pour l'abolition de l'esclavage*) was established, counting Victor Schœlcher, without a doubt the best-known figure in this movement, as one of its founding members. This group aimed to influence public opinion and exert pressure on both of the chambers of parliament and on the various French governmental regimes that followed.

The abolition movement, however, cannot be subsumed within clearly defined circles or groups: it brought together figures from very different political camps and denominations. Important leftists such as Alexandre Ledru-Rollin and Pierre-Jean de Béranger were connected here with centrists such as Alphonse de Lamartine and Alexis de Tocqueville,[65] moderate Orléanists such as Odilon Barrot, Lafayette, Molé, and Achille de Broglie, and liberals like the religiously motivated reformer and journalist F.R. de Lamennais and like Charles de Montalembert, who starting in 1831 clearly denounced slavery, noting that Christianity had freed the Roman Empire of it (Arzalier 265). Arzalier explains the merging of these very different forces by the fact that abolition was much more of a moral than a political demand (120). And yet, as Démier makes clear (242), economic interests must be taken into account as well.

Klein notes that about seventy percent of France's overseas trade involved Caribbean imports and exports (without however specifying the time period) (82). The issue of sugar, which had strongly marked a large part of the eighteen-twenties and was closely linked to the issue of slavery, had seemed to become less important by the beginning of the eighteen-thirties. In the eighteen-

---

[64] The political call to actively fight slavery in Algeria must, of course, be subjected to a discourse analysis. Drescher shows that for reasons of pragmatic politics, that fight was never actually undertaken ("British Way" 167).

[65] Tocqueville was one of those who called for a compromise on the question of slavery. He supported abolition, but he also believed it should be paired with compensatory payments (Vigier 249).

forties, however, the sugar beet and sugarcane producers came into conflict with each other. Sugarcane had become the most important product of the colonial economy, but it was coming under pressure from sugar beets, which were cheaper, more "ethical," and more modern. This also had consequences for the slavery question (Démier 246). On July 18, 1845, a law was passed guaranteeing a small sum of money to freed slaves and allowing them to own property. This was seen as a definitive step in the direction of abolition once and for all (Vigier 252; Drescher, "British Way" 166).

Last but not least, the Republican press played an important role in these debates. In this context, it is worth mentioning Philippe Buchez's *L'Atelier*, as well as Ledru-Rollins's *La Réforme* and *Le Siècle*, along with the work of centrists such as Lamartine. Vigier names other newspapers as well in which the debate over abolition took place. The *Journal des débats*, which Vigier considers to have been the semi-official organ of the Orléanists, condemned the colonists for their efforts to preserve the system of slavery, though the newspaper was clearly rightist. Victor Considérant's *Démocratie pacifique* was also abolitionist, but it was much more radical and politically leftist. Vigier also mentions Cyrille Bissette, the publisher of the *Revue des Colonies* (250), a mulatto who had emigrated from the Antilles and become a dedicated crusader for the cause of the blacks in opposition to the Creoles.[66] In 1824, the royal tribunal in Martinique found Bissette, along with Louis Fabien and Jean-Baptiste Volny, guilty of wanting to overthrow the civil and political order of the French colonies, because Bissette had written a pamphlet in which he criticized the unfair treatment of free mulattos on the island and demanded equal rights for them. In response, leading lawyers and liberals in France started a campaign in 1827 and were able to overturn the sentence. But Bissette was banished, and went to Paris. His arrival there revived the interest in colonial questions and generated public sympathy for people of color (Mesnard 255, 257). Drescher describes Bissette as one of the hardest-working petitioners in eighteen-forties Paris ("British Way" 169).

In conclusion, we can say that the debates over abolition in France were shaped by moral, political, economic, and social factors, all of which can be placed within a changing national and international context. The successive regimes in France (1789–1802, 1802–1815, 1815–1830, and 1830–1848) of course provide a helpful way of understanding the development of the debates, but we must not make the mistake of seeing this development as linear and organized. The various influences should instead be understood as multidirectional.

---

[66] Vigier relies here on the work of Stella Pâme, whose doctoral thesis describes the life and work of Cyrille Bissette.

When new factors and powers emerged, it did not by any means imply that the old ones had disappeared. And while some of these became weaker at times, that kind of change could always quickly shift again because of developments on the national or international scene. And yet, while there was no *one* abolitionist movement, and there was no linear development in France towards abolition, the central question remains: what connection can we find between abolitionist engagement and positions on the colonial status quo? It might surprise the reader to learn that in this atmosphere of intense debate, and with so much potential for social critique, questions about the colonial status quo in the Caribbean (with the exception of Haiti) just did not play the kind of role in French discourse that they did in neighboring Spain.

I.4.2 Debates over Abolition in Spain (1810–1886)

Questions about slavery and abolition in nineteenth-century Spain always have to be understood in a transatlantic dimension, encompassing not only the Cuban "sugar barons," alert to implications for their own hold on power, and the abolitionist efforts of the Puerto Rican reformers, but also interests within Spain, especially those of moderately liberal circles.[67] These circles had an interest in economic protectionism and the maintenance of the slave trade, as the source of great and multiple riches.

Enriqueta and Luisa Vila Vilar point out that the development of the debates over abolition in Spain took a paradoxical course: "it is in Spain that we find pioneering abolitionist protests ... and at the same time it is in Spain—if we exclude Brazil—that the burden of slavery persists the longest" (Vila Vilar and Vila Vilar 12).[68] These authors also speak of an uncomfortable silence around this subject in both science and literature:

> With a few notable exceptions, it is rare to find writers who take a stance or who refer openly to the issue of slavery, outside of the propagandistic sphere of the Abolitionist Society. ... On the other hand, it is important to keep in mind that freedom of expression was curtailed for most of the century. (ibid.)[69]

---

[67] I am grateful to Ana Mateos for important suggestions with respect to this section.

[68] "es en España donde se dan manifestaciones abolicionistas absolutamente pioneras ... y al mismo tiempo es en España —si exceptuamos Brasil— donde la rémora de la esclavitud permanece por más tiempo."

[69] "Salvo algunas notables excepciones es raro encontrar escritores que tomen postura o que se refieran abiertamente al tema esclavista fuera del ámbito propagandístico de *La Sociedad Abo-*

Jordi Maluquer de Motes makes it clear that given this

> politics of silence [about slavery and slave ownership], along with the growing disrepute [of the institution of slavery] in international public opinion, even among the Antillean slavers themselves, ... this desire to shut down the debate that was opened up by Turnbull's proposals is well reflected in the words of an anonymous Spanish slaveowner: "we beg the government, for the sake of reclaiming its honor and that of the nation, someday to declare ... that slavery no longer be discussed." In other words, the law of silence. (311)[70]

The Vila Vilars, along with Mario Hernández Sánchez-Barba, define three distinct periods in which slavery was a subject of debate: the periods from 1810 to 1814, from 1835 to 1845, and again from 1869 to 1886.

The liberal thinker Francisco de Arango y Parreño initiated a precursor to the debates over slavery and abolition with his 1792 publication of *Discurso sobre la agricultura de La Habana y medios para fomentarla* (Discourse on the agriculture of Havana and ways of promoting it), dedicated to King Carlos IV, in which he defended the slave trade. Just a few years later, however, he turned away from this position after recognizing the political consequences of such a stance. Isidoro de Antillón (1778–1814), who fought against the French occupation and was active in the Cádiz Cortes (national legislative sessions during the occupation), should also be mentioned as an important early defender of abolitionist positions in Spain; in 1811, he published a *Disertación sobre el origen de la esclavitud de los negros, motivos que la han perpetuado ventajas que se le atribuye y medios que podrían adoptarse para hacer prosperar sin ellos a nuestras colonias* (Dissertation on the origin of the enslavement of the Negroes, motives for its perpetuation, advantages that can be attributed to it, and measures that could be taken to allow our colonies to prosper without them [the slaves]). In this document, he reprinted a speech he had given in 1802 (Vila Vilar and Vila Vilar 33).

Spain was occupied by Napoleonic troops from 1808 to 1814. In San Fernando and later in Cádiz, tribunals (*cortes*) were established to indicate that their members rejected the installation of Napoleon's brother, José I, as king. Representatives of the American territories, including Cuba, were invited to participate in these tribunals, and the plan was to extend equal rights to all of them. This

---

licionista. ... Por otra parte hay que tener en cuenta que los derechos de expresión estuvieron cercenados durante casi toda la centuria."
70 "el silencio como política y el creciente desprestigio entre la opinión pública internacional incluidos los propios esclavistas antillanos ... esta aspiración a cerrar el debate abierto por las propuestas de Turnbull queda bien reflejada en las formulaciones de un anónimo esclavista español: 'suplicamos al gobierno que, volviendo por su honor y por el de la nación decrete un día ... De la esclavitud no se hable más.' Es decir, la ley del silencio."

undertaking failed, however, and what followed it were liberation movements in the various kingdoms.[71] In the context of the discussions of the "equality of rights and representative equality," people also thought about abolition (Hernández Sánchez-Barba 25). (It is interesting to note that in this context, Spain was talked about as having a "slave situation," by contrast with France.) One important question was how the right to vote in the Spanish tribunals should be organized, that is to say which people should receive census-based suffrage. In 1811, the representative from Galicia suggested that slavery should be abolished and advocated giving blacks the right to vote. Antillón and the Mexican representative, María Guridi, agreed. The representatives of Venezuela (Esteban Morales) and Columbia (Mejía Lequerica) were vehemently opposed, and a representative from Peru pointed out that blacks had no right to representation, since they were originally from Africa, not America (Hernández Sánchez-Barba 26 ff.). Agustín Arguelles, the representative from Asturias, drafted the ban on the slave trade and suggested postponing the question of abolition for the time being. The large estate owners from Cuba immediately sent a letter, written and signed by Arango y Parreño, as a "Representation of the city of Havana to the tribunal, opposing abolition as proposed by Jose María Guridi and Agustín Arguelles" (*Representación de la ciudad de la Habana en las Cortes, en la que se oponían a la abolición con motivo de las proposiciones hechas por Jose María Guridi y Agustín Arguelles*) (Pons 67). None of the abolitionist suggestions were finally successful, and Cádiz's 1812 constitution failed to recognize the black population, in the sense that they were ignored in the calculations to determine the number of representatives.

Another strong proponent of abolition in those years was José María Blanco White (or Blanco y Crespo) (1775–1841), a Catholic cleric, from an Irish background, who had converted to Protestantism. Blanco White, who represented liberal Anglo-Saxon positions, fought the Napoleonic troops, participated in the Cádiz tribunal, and, finally, emigrated to Great Britain when absolutism arrived in Spain in the person of Ferdinand VII. Blanco White used the British abolition of slavery as the context for his abolitionist positions, and in 1814 published his "Draft on the slave trade" (*Bosquexo sobre el comercio de esclavos*) based on a petition translated from William Wilberforce's famous 1811 letter on abolition.

In spite of the tribunals set up in Cádiz, Ferdinand VII returned to Spain, nullified the 1812 constitution, and established a conservative, absolutist regime that was in accord with the Russo-Austro-Prussian Holy Alliance. In 1817, he signed an agreement with England pledging to renounce the slave trade in ex-

---

[71] For a summary of the various possible reasons for the failure of these dialogues, see Breña.

change for four hundred thousand pesos. This agreement, however, was not implemented.[72] It was not ratified until 1835, by Queen Maria Cristina.

Spain's second abolitionist phase began, then, with the reign of Maria Cristina, widow of Ferdinand VII and mother of the future Queen Isabella. She felt compelled to ratify the agreement banning the slave trade so that British liberals would support her daughter's accession to the throne against the conservative Carlists, who wanted to seat Ferdinand's brother Carlos on the throne. The 1837 constitution thus outlawed slavery on the Iberian Peninsula and its neighboring islands, although not in Spain's overseas provinces (Hernández Sánchez-Barba 28, 29; Vila Vilar and Vila Vilar 18). The Vila Vilars provide the text of the ambiguous March 5, 1837 law outlawing slavery, which acknowledges both abolition and, at the same time, the law's lack of effectiveness in the overseas territories:

> Guided by these principles and desires, the commission wishes for slavery to be abolished from this day on and forever, not only on the Spanish continent but also in its overseas possessions, such that the condition of servitude should have no value or existence next to free Spaniards. But the commission believes that while this reform, demanded by reason, humanity, and religion itself, can be easily and quickly carried out on the peninsula and in the neighboring islands, that is not the case in the overseas provinces. (18)[73]

This law also raised a series of economic questions. The growing Cuban sugar industry was too tempting and attractive to be scorned simply for philanthropic reasons (19). The Vila Vilars show that for this reason, the abolition of slavery experienced a setback compared to the debates that had taken place in the Cádiz tribunals in the previous era.

Antillean representatives, including José Antonio Saco, were invited to participate in the preparation of the constitution. No sooner had they arrived, however, than the Iberian representatives voted to exclude them, arguing from the fact that the islands were an exceptional situation, where the system of slavery constituted an essential characteristic. The proposal to give the Antilles some "special laws," falling outside of the framework of the constitution, met with approval. These laws, however, were never implemented, which confirmed the ab-

---

[72] On British pressure against slavery and the slave trade, see Roldán.
[73] "Guiada la comisión por estos principios y deseos quisiera que de hoy mismo para siempre quedara abolida la esclavitud, no sólo en el continente español sino también en sus posesiones ultramarinas que la condición de siervo no tuviese valor ni existencia al lado de españoles libres. Pero la comisión cree que esta reforma, exigida por la razón, la humanidad y por la religión misma, si es de fácil y expedita ejecución en la Península e islas adyacentes, no así en las provincias de Ultramar."

solute authority of the Captain General there. José Antonio Saco argued against the exclusion of the representatives from the Antilles, pointing out that the liberal European constitutions were themselves far from establishing the equality of their inhabitants (Fradera 153–166). Piqueras provides an overview of the economic benefits that Queen Maria Cristina and one of her most trusted followers, Leopoldo O'Donnell (Captain General of Cuba and the founder of Spain's *Unión liberal*), had gained from the slave trade (277, 284).

The founding of the Abolitionist Society (*Sociedad Abolicionista*) in 1864, by Julio Vizcarrondo (from Puerto Rico) and Rafael María Labra (who was born in Cuba but grew up in Spain), marked an important moment in the third period of Spanish abolition.[74] Labra was a proponent not only of abolition but also of Cuban independence and the end of colonization. The Abolitionist Society published newspapers such as *El Abolicionista* and sponsored competitions for abolitionist texts.[75] Schmidt-Nowara describes contacts between this group and the Free Society for Political Economy (*Sociedad Libre de Economía Política*), whose members included Segismundo Moret and Laureano Figuerola, a member of the Prim government. Schmidt-Nowara mentions that the abolitionism of this period was driven by three main currents: the economically liberal positions of the Free Society for Political Economy, the doctrine of Krausism, and the Democratic Republican Party (*Partido Democrático Republicano*) (Schmidt-Nowara 74).

This third period of debates over abolition reached its apex in the 1868 revolution. Some people in Spain had already accumulated great riches by this time through trade, including the slave trade, with the Antilles and in particular with Cuba. Historians such as Piqueras and Fontana have even argued that the revolution consolidated the power of the Cuban lobby in Spain with the arrival of the Bourbon Restoration in 1874. There were many different parties sharing the political landscape at the time; some of the most notable were the Progressive Party (*Partido Progresista*, Prim); the Liberal Union (*Unión Liberal*, Serrano); and the Republican Democratic Party (*Partido Demócrata Republicano*, Castelar, Pi Margall). After the elections, several abolitionists managed to acquire seats in the house of representatives. Emilio Castelar gave a speech in 1870, entitled "The abolition of slavery" (*La abolición de la esclavitud*), which became famous. 1870 was also the year in which the Moret Law was passed, declaring the children of enslaved mothers to be free. In Puerto Rico, slavery was abolished in

---

[74] Maluquer de Motes mentions the possible existence of an Abolitionist Society in 1835 ("Abolicionismo y resistencia").

[75] Vila Vilar and Vila Vilar (14) also mention the following Madrid newspapers that were open proponents of the abolition of slavery: *La Discusión*, *La Propaganda*, and later *El liberal* and *La Tribuna*.

1873. The Republican Party introduced a draft constitution in 1873, which was never approved, but that declared slavery to be abolished in Cuba. The popular rebellions backed by the Republican Party, the endless war in Cuba, and the institutional chaos all facilitated the turn to the Restoration under Cánovas del Castillo and the consolidation of the colonial lobby in Spain (Piqueras Arenas). In 1880, the system of *patronato* (a system of "apprenticeship" for freed slaves) was approved, and in 1886 abolition was introduced for good. On the subject of the difficulties of the transition from the *patronato* to abolition, Durnerín describes the violent debates in the tribunals and the stormy campaigns of the Abolitionist Society, on the one hand, but also notes the absence of any notice of these in Spanish newspapers (with the exception of *El liberal* and *El imparcial*) or in public opinion. There is no question but that the Abolitionist Society played a leading role in changing the minds of Spanish politicians.

I.5 Issues of Conviviality

Let us now go beyond the level of the specific subject of this research and consider the higher-level issue of the contemporary cultural and theoretical debates; these debates have a universal character, but if we do not refer back to the nineteenth-century Caribbean, we will lose sight of one of the most significant, not to say existential, aspects of what they show us. In what follows, I will be looking at current programmatic cultural-theoretical attempts to understand *conviviality in peace and difference*, attempts that are particularly important in the early twenty-first century,[76] developed as the response to unsuccessfully labeled multiculturalism[77] or as the rejection of an essentialist concept of identity. It is clear, for a variety of reasons, that intellectuals from the Caribbean and its diaspora are also carrying on intensive debates on this topic. Over the last few decades, this very richly literary region[78] has become one of the most privileged sites of theory pro-

---

[76] On the singularly great challenges that arise with respect to the foundations and conditions of global conviviality in the fourth phase of accelerated globalization, see Ette, *ZusammenLebensWissen* 169 ff. and 183; see also Ette, *Konvivenz* and Ette and Mackenbach.
[77] On the concept of multiculturalism, see Lüsebrink's fundamental proposition: "Multiculturalism is usually used to mean the parallel existence of various cultures (in the anthropological sense of word) within a social system (usually a nation)." ("Unter Multikulturalität wird im Allgemeinen das Nebeneinander verschiedener Kulturen [im anthropologischen Sinn] innerhalb eines sozialen Systems [meistens einer Nation] verstanden.") (*Interkulturelle Kommunikation* 16 ff.).
[78] The Caribbean has made a particular name for itself as a privileged region for "literatures without a fixed abode." See Ette, *Writing-between-worlds* 135–166.

duction: négritude, *Créolité*, and relationalism have, in turn, tried to concretely consider *conviviality* in the Caribbean and its diaspora or used it as a starting point from which to develop universal categories, as Édouard Glissant (in *Poetics*) and Antonio Benítez Rojo, most prominently, have done. In this process, the question that remains unanswered to this day is how to understand ethnic difference without falling back on essentialisms. Along lines that are similar to the critique of multiculturalism that has come from leading intellectuals in the Anglo-Saxon tradition (such as Arjun Appadurai and Paul Gilroy [in *After Empire*]), Walter Mignolo, talking about the discourse of *Créolité*, notes quite critically that:

> Creoles, Caribbeanness, and Creoleness are still categories that overlap but which belong to different levels. Being or defining oneself as Creole means identifying a group of people, differentiating them from others. Thus, to say that "neither Europeans, nor Africans, nor Asians, we proclaim ourselves Creoles" [Bernabé, Chamoiseau, and Confiant 75] is an identification in relation to a territory, and to the historical processes that created that territory. (*Local Histories* 241 ff.)

But what responses are there to this critique? Glissant calls his alternative model "creolization":

> an encounter between cultural elements coming from completely different horizons and which in actuality creolize themselves ... in order to produce something completely unpredictable. ... The creolization that takes place in the New America, and the creolization that is taking over the other Americas, is the same one that operates in the entire world. The thesis that I will defend ... is that *the world is becoming creolized*, that is to say that the cultures of the world, connected with each other today in an electrifying and totally conscious way, change themselves by exchanging themselves through irremediable clashes and pitiless wars but also advances of conscience and hope. (*Introduction à une poétique* 15)[79]

Because the current, specifically postcolonial, situation of Caribbean societies is impossible to understand without confronting its colonial dimensions (in *The Repeating Island*, Benítez Rojo already talked about a mutual interdependence between today's discourses of creolization and the historical plantation econo-

---

79 "une rencontre d'éléments culturels venus d'horizons absolument divers et qui réellement se créolisent ... pour donner quelque chose d'absoument imprévisible. ... [L]a créolisation qui se fait dans la Néo-Amérique, et la créolisatiom qui gagne les autres Amériques, est la même qui opère dans le monde entier. La thèse que je défendrai ... est que *le monde se créolise*, c'est-à-dire que les cultures du monde mises en contact de manière foudroyante et absolument consciente aujourd'hui les unes avec les autres se changent en s'échangeant à travers des heurts irrémissibles, des guerres sans pitié mais aussi des avancées de conscience et d'éspoir."

my⁸⁰), let us now turn back to the nineteenth century. What is the specific literary potential of the knowledge of conviviality in nineteenth-century Caribbean literatures (see Ette, *ZusammenLebensWissen* 80)? I divide this question into two levels:
1. *Norms* of knowledge about conviviality. By this I mean the explicit dissemination of a program for good or ideal conviviality.
2. *Forms* of knowledge about conviviality. By this I mean the dissemination of a literary content of conviviality,[81] a level that can be explicitly or implicitly legible (cf. Ette, "Literaturwissenschaft" 27).

It makes sense that in the nineteenth century, when discourses of racism were established, the issue of conviviality would have been particularly closely intertwined with them, because the concept of "race" was decisive for the development of the political anatomy of the nineteenth century. Insofar as this became a scientific concept, it remained an important aspect of European geopolitics as they progressed towards global supremacy, supported and legitimized by Darwin's insights (Gilroy, *After Empire* 6). In light of the ubiquitous manifestation of ethnic difference that dominated that epoch, conviviality thus needs to be captured through an ethnographic lens.[82] Current efforts, such as those of Mignolo

---

80 This essay has become a classic. In it, Benítez Rojo shows that every understanding of creolization processes requires a confrontation with the system of plantation society: "Well then, what relationships do I see between the plantations and creolization? Naturally, first, a relationship of cause and effect; without one we would not have the other. But I also see other relationships." ("Bien, entonces, ¿qué relaciones veo entre plantación y criollización? Naturalmente, en primer término, una relación de causa y efecto; sin una no tendríamos la otra. Pero también veo otras relaciones") (*La isla* 396; not present in English translation). For a recent discussion of creolization, see Müller and Ueckmann, *Kreolisierung revisited*. On the question of the applicability of postcolonial theories to the nineteenth-century Caribbean, see Müller, "Entre la francofilia y las aspiraciones."
81 In other words, a knowledge "that is constantly in contact with the extraliterary living environment, [which] can be understood ... through the specific autonomy and the self-will of literature" ("das stets im Kontakt mit der außerliterarischen Lebenswelt steht, [das] aus der spezifischen Eigengesetzlichkeit und dem Eigen-Sinn der Literatur heraus verstanden ... werden kann") (Ette, *ZusammenLebensWissen* 114).
82 Benítez Rojo pointed out that from the moment one stepped onto the plantation, skin color became the operative line of demarcation: "Thus, in the Caribbean, skin color denotes neither a minority nor a majority; it represents much more: the color imposed by the violence of conquest and colonization, and especially by the plantation system. Whatever the skin color might be, it is a color that has not been institutionalized or legitimized according to lineage; it is a color in conflict with itself and with others, irritated in its very instability and resented for its uprootedness; it is a color neither of the Self nor of the Other, but rather a kind of no-man's land where

or Glissant, attempt to expose earlier concepts of identity as essentialist, but for the nineteenth century in particular the most challenging question is to what extent it is possible to critically examine constructions of essentialism in an age that has gone down in history as the very heyday of racism. Could a sharper look at representations of conviviality lead to a relativization of the canonical frames of reference, such as race and nation, that we have for the nineteenth century? Because the question of conviviality requires more nuanced answers than, for example, simply stressing the ethical dimension of the abolitionist novel and its contribution to the end of slavery. Nor can it entirely be a matter of pointing out such things as how a foundational novel such as *Cecilia Valdés* could conjure up a transcultural Cuba. In other words, the issue goes beyond the question of politically committed literature.

I.5.1 Who Is Human?

Let us now turn to the height of the Caribbean plantation economy, on the eve of the French Revolution. The decisive issue in the problem of human conviviality was not so much the how of it as the question of who was even allowed to call themselves human (see Meyer-Krentler, "Los perros ingleses y los perros esclavos"). Hans Blumenberg has vividly shown, in connection with the French Revolution, how ungraspable the concept of life is. Georges Clemenceau, in response to a question from his secretary, Jean Martet, about the French Revolution and its bloodiness, is supposed to have said: "What do you expect? The Revolution … the principles are excellent, but the people, the people!" (Blumenberg 14). If the very definition of a person is already such a challenge, then the concept of life, which lies at the foundation of being, becomes even more complicated, leading directly to the question of conviviality. Here Michel-Rolph Trouillot has pointed out a crucial event, getting to the heart of the anthropological dimension of the constellations of colonial politics in Paris at that point in time.[83] He de-

---

the permanent battle for the Caribbean Self's fragmented identity is fought" (*The Repeating Island* 169). ("Así, en el Caribe el color de la piel no representa ni una 'minoría' ni una 'mayoría'; representa mucho más: el color impuesto por la violencia de la conquista y la colonización, y en particular por el régimen de la Plantación. Sea cual fuere el color de la piel, se trata de un color no institucionalizado, no legitimado por la estirpe; un color en conflicto consigo mismo y con los demás, irritado por su propia inestabilidad y resentido por su desarraigo; un color que no es el del Yo ni tampoco el del Otro, sino una suerte de tierra de nadie donde se lleva a cabo la batalla permanente por la fragmentada identidad del Ser caribeño" [*La isla* 241]).

83 On this particular point, I rely directly on Michel-Rolph Trouillot's exposition.

scribes how, in July 1789, just a few days before the storming of the Bastille, plantation owners from Saint-Domingue came together in Paris to ask the new French National Assembly to include twenty deputies from the Caribbean among their ranks (90). The growers had arrived at this number by using the exact same methods used in France as well to calculate the distribution of representatives, but the growers had deliberately included the black slaves and the *gens de couleur* in their calculation of the island population, while never for a moment considering giving the vote to the nonwhites. Honoré Gabriel Riquetti, the Count of Mirabeau, took the floor in the session of July 3, 1789, to expose the absurdity of the growers' calculations:

> Do the colonies count their Negroes and their *gens de couleur* as belonging to the category of human beings or to that of the beasts of burden? If the colonies would like to see the Negroes and the *gens de couleur* counted as human beings, they should first give them the right to vote, so that all could vote and all could be counted. If not, however, we would like to point out to them that in distributing the number of deputies across the population of France, we have taken neither the numbers of our horses nor those of our mules into consideration. (Archives Parlementaires 1789, 8:186, cited in Trouillot 90)

Mirabeau wanted to convince the French National Assembly to reconcile the philosophical position of the declaration of human rights with the assembly's political position towards the colonies. However, the declaration spoke of the "rights of the human being and of the citizen," a title that was contradictory in itself.

Trouillot shows how, in the case at hand, the citizen triumphed over the human being, or at least over the nonwhite human being. The National Assembly allowed the Caribbean sugar colonies only six representatives. This was more than they would have been allotted on the basis of their white inhabitants alone, but significantly less than their numbers would have come to if the Assembly had recognized the full political rights of blacks and *gens de couleur*. Their pragmatic political calculations meant that the half a million slaves on Saint-Domingue/Haiti und several hundred thousand in the other colonies yielded exactly three deputies, who were of course white (Trouillot 91).

Against the background of this high degree of uncertainty over the question of who even counts as a human being, it is not surprising that the authors of the following textual examples struggle so intensely with ethnic categories.

II Literature and the Colonial Question

II.1 Notions of Citizenship (*Citoyenneté/Ciudadanía*) on the Eve of Independence

¡Bolívar inmortal! ¿Que voz humana
Enumerar y celebrar podría
Tus victorias sin fin, tu eterno aliento?
Colombia independiente y soberana
Es de tu gloria noble monumento.
Del vil polvo a tu voz, robusta, fiera,
De majestad ornada,
Ella se alzó, como Minerva armada
Del cerebro de Júpiter saliera.
...
Jamás impunemente
Al pueblo soberano
Pudo imponer un héroe ciudadano
El sello del baldón sobre la frente.
El pueblo se alza, y su voraz encono
Sacrifica al tirano,
Que halla infamia y sepulcro en vez de trono
Así desvanecerse vio la tierra
De Napoleón y de Austria la gloria,
Y prematura tumba los encierra
Y la baña con llanto de la Victoria.[1]

These verses are from the Cuban writer José María Heredia's 1825 poem "To Bolívar" (*Niagara* 84). This hymn to the "citizen hero" Bolívar plainly shows the connection between the ideas of the French Revolution and the Latin American wars of independence.

---

[1] "Immortal Bolívar! What human voice / Could number and celebrate / Your endless victories, your eternal breath? / Independent and sovereign Colombia / Is a noble monument to your glory. / From vile dust she rose at your voice, / Robust and fierce, decked in majesty, / Like armed Minerva rising / From Jupiter's brain. / ... / Never with impunity / Could a citizen hero / Impose the seal of this affront / On the forehead of the sovereign people. / The people rises, and its ravenous resentment / Sacrifices the tyrant, / Who finds infamy and a sepulchre instead of a throne / Thus the earth saw the glory / Of Napoleon and of Austria vanish, / And an early grave enfold them / And bathe the earth with Victoria's tears."

II.1.1 Rousseau's Reflections on the *citoyen* and Their Consequences for the French Revolution

While the 1807 occupation of Spain by French troops is generally considered by historians to have been the immediate cause for the political transformation of the colonies into sovereign republics, the cultural ramifications of the French Revolution had a decisive impact, even if indirectly, on the inspiration to fight for independence. In particular the declaration of human rights on August 26, 1789; the proclamation of the constitution on September 3, 1791; and the issuance of the *Code civil* (the Napoleonic Code) in 1804 released a great deal of revolutionary potential. These ideas were adopted in the European States, a little later in Latin America, and finally everywhere as the model for political, economic, and legal modernization.

In these legal texts, which usher in an epochal upheaval, the word "citizen," *citoyen*, is used very frequently, with a new matter-of-factness. What lies behind this guiding concept of the French Revolution? As we know, the cultural backdrop of the French Revolution should not be underestimated, as the ideas of the Enlightenment philosophers prepared the ground for the later events. For this new understanding of the citizen it was most of all the ideas of Jean-Jacques Rousseau, from Geneva, that were key; in his *Social Contract*, he explains what he means by "citizen": "The real meaning of this word has been almost entirely lost in the modern world when a town and a city are thought to be identical, and a citizen the same as a burgess. People forget that houses may make a town, while only citizens can make a city" (Rousseau, *Contract* 61).[2] The original meaning of the word, which for Rousseau is closely connected to the *cité*, the self-governing settlement, and also has to do with community, has been lost. Rousseau makes this particularly clear in a quotation from *Emile:* "Public instruction no longer exists and can no longer exist, because where there is no longer fatherland, there can no longer be citizens. These two words, *fatherland* and *citizen*, should be effaced from modern languages" (40).[3] After first pointing out the opposition between the human being and the citizen, Rousseau arrives at the following hierarchy: "We conceive of our general society in terms of our particular societies, the establishment of small Republics leads us to think of the large one,

---

[2] "Le vrai sens de ce mot s'est presque entièrement effacé chez les modernes; la plupart prennent une ville pour une Cité & un bourgeois pour un Citoyen. Ils ne savent pas que les maisons font la ville mais que les Citoyens font la Cité" (Rousseau, *Du contrat social* 361).
[3] "L'institution publique n'existe plus, et ne peut plus exister, parce qu'où il n'y a plus de patrie, il ne peut plus y avoir de citoyens. Ces deux mots patrie et citoyen doivent être effacés des langues modernes" (Rousseau, *Émile* 250).

and we do not properly begin to become men until after having been Citizens" (*On the Social Contract, with Geneva Manuscript and Political Economy* 15).[4] This new meaning of citizenship, of *citoyenneté*, is necessarily dependent on the frame of reference of the fatherland, the *patrie:*

> If I spoke to you of the duties of a citizen, you would perhaps ask me, "Which is my country?" And you would think you had put me to confusion. Yet you would be mistaken, dear Emile, for he who has no country has, at least, the land in which he lives. There is always a government and certain so-called laws under which he has lived in peace. (Rousseau, *Emile* 357)[5]

Rousseau's observations provided an important basis for the understanding of citizenship in the French Revolution. Irene Castells shows how the revolutionary concept of citizenship touches on three different levels: first, the legal level, which makes all citizens equal before the law; then, the political level, which has to do with active participation in public affairs; and finally, the national level, on which affiliation with the nation replaces the old class structures (Castells 2; Rétat). According to Castells, the emancipation of the citizen was implemented by ordinary people taking part in public life, within the framework of revolutionary institutions, leading to far-reaching change and a lasting democratization of the political space, which from that point on was no longer just the sphere of governments and interest groups but became a matter of everyday life (5).

The French Revolution's concept of citizenship, then, is grounded in an identification of the Revolution with the *patrie* and the Nation, and naturally, this new (self-)understanding had consequences for the construction of national identity. The nation defined itself through the integration of all citizens, who gave up their personal interests in order to enter into the *cité*, and not because of any law but on the basis of a collective enthusiasm (8).

---

4 "Nous concevons la société générale d'après nos sociétés particulières, l'établissement des petites républiques nous fait songer à la grande, et nous ne commençons proprement à devenir hommes qu'après avoir été citoyens" (*Du contrat social ou Essai sur la forme de la République. Manuscrit de Genève*).

5 "Si je te parlais des devoirs du citoyen, tu me demanderais peut-être où est la patrie, et tu croirais m'avoir confondu. Tu te tromperais pourtant, cher Émile; car qui n'a pas une patrie a du moins un pays. Il y a toujours un gouvernement et des simulacres de lois sous lesquels il a vécu tranquille" (Rousseau, *Émile* 858).

II.1.2 Between the "Noble Savage" and the Citizen: Rousseau's Case Study of the Caribs

In his *Discourse on the Origin and Basis of Inequality among Men* (*Discours sur l'origine et les fondements de l'inégalité parmi les hommes*, 1755), Rousseau develops his speculative theory of evolution, from which his political magnum opus, *The Social Contract* (*Du Contrat Social ou Principes du droit politique*, 1762) follows (Fink-Eitel 17). Although the phrase "back to nature" has often been (falsely) attributed to him, what Rousseau wanted was not a natural paradise but a social contract. His main example is the society of the Caribs, who had supportive, reciprocal, egalitarian social relations and bitterly resisted colonial violence. The situation of the Caribs at the time of their first encounter with the colonial powers is described in very positive terms. This point in time was supposed to have been humanity's happiest and most lasting time, because it struck the true happy medium between the laziness of their original condition and the misguided efficiency of self-love. Rousseau therefore judged this condition as being the one that was the least subject to revolutions and the best suited to humanity. In savages, who were usually in fact encountered in this very condition, he found the confirmation that the human race was destined to remain in that state (Fink-Eitel 173).

Rousseau goes one step further, however: these people are neither wild nor noble. Their situation is in fact exemplary, but it is not free of conflict, neither among themselves nor within the colonial system. They are in need of a social contract in order to live humanely and to interact with each other as citizens. The concept of the *ciudadano*, which is a crucial one for the Latin American independence movement, is an import from the French Revolution, which in turn was primarily developed by Rousseau on the basis of his reflections on Caribbean society. We are dealing here with a complex transfer process from center to periphery to center, which will become a complex process of circulation through further mechanisms of reception.

II.1.3 *Citoyenneté* und Its Reception in the Caribbean

How were the ideas of the French Revolution received in Latin America and the Caribbean? Rousseau, at any rate, was widely read at the beginning of the nineteenth century: in 1811, four hundred copies of his *Social Contract* arrived in Chile (Gazmuri Riveros 98). In 1815, Fray Melchor Martínez, the royal chronicler of Chile's wars of independence, described the rapid spread of Enlightenment ideas in the wake of the French Revolution. He wrote that the philosophy of Enlightenment, incorrectly considered modern since it had been lying dormant, out of sight, for several centuries, had by means of the Revolution acquired an incalculable level of influence over people's reason and could now be considered to be the only valid science. From France, this philosophy had spread across the entire earth, and Latin America had shown itself to be particularly receptive to these revolutionary (and from the point of view of the chronicler, pernicious) ideas, because they corresponded to Latin America's desires for a cutting of the apron strings and for autonomy (cf. Martínez, cited in Gazmuri Riveros 81).

Accordingly, the precepts of the French Revolution are also reflected in the formation of the Latin American nations. For the first Mexican constitution, for example, the new understanding of the citizen, the *ciudadano*, was very much a guiding principle, as Borrego Plá explains (22): the citizenry, the *ciudadanía*, included everyone born in Mexico, regardless of the color of their skin, but also foreigners living there, as long as they were on the side of patriotism and adhered to Roman Catholicism. The status of citizen, which even nonresident Mexicans of the Catholic faith possessed, could also be forfeited if a person became guilty of heresy, apostasy, or an insult to the nation. All citizens enjoyed the same rights as those that were proclaimed in France in 1789 and went down in history as "human rights." Borrego Plá explains that the authors of the constitution, who met in Apatzingán, followed the French example in making the principles of freedom, equality, security, and property their top priorities, but that these were taken not as abstract concepts but as the concrete social implementation by means of which feudal structures were to be democratized. She particularly stresses Rousseau's role in pioneering the concepts behind the conviction that all human beings are born equal and that no citizen could place him- or herself above the others by means of inherited rights and privileges (23).

Unlike on the Latin American mainland, the intellectuals of the Caribbean had "more time" to grapple with the aforementioned theoretical achievements of the French Revolution *within* colonial structures. In what follows, using texts by José María Heredia and J. Levilloux, we will take a look at the respective and varying ways in which the concept of citizenship was received in the French and Spanish colonial Caribbean.

II.1.3.1 José María Heredia: A Reader of Rousseau

José María Heredia was born in Santiago de Cuba in 1803 and died in Mexico, in 1839. He led a very peripatetic life: he lived a total of only six years in Cuba, five and a half in Venezuela, four in the United States, and nineteen in Mexico, where he was an active participant in literary and political life and where he was generally taken for a Mexican. And yet he himself confidently self-identified as

Cuban and was a close friend of José Antonio Saco, Félix Varela y Morales, and Domingo del Monte (Padura Fuentes 9; Poumier 266). He was mostly known as a poet, though he also translated French drama, English novels, and Italian poetry. He studied law and first worked as a lawyer in Matanzas; later he held a variety of law positions in Mexico. The fights for independence on the continent (especially in Venezuela and Mexico) had a strong influence on him. Because of his activities (from within Mexico) conspiring towards Cuba's independence, as a member of the secret society Suns and Rays of Bolívar (*Soles y Rayos de Bolívar*), he was sentenced to death in Cuba in 1831. He was actively involved in a variety of political debates and understood himself as a *ciudadano*, fighting for the rights of other *ciudadanos*, an attitude that also comes through very clearly in his poems, for instance in "To the Greeks in 1821" ("A los griegos en 1821") and "Ode to the Inhabitants of Anáhuac" ("Oda a los habitantes de Anáhuac," 1821–1822) (Padura Fuentes 31). The best-known example of the poetic processing of the fight for independence is his "Hymn of the Exile" ("Himno del desterrado"):

> ¡Cuba! Al fin te verás libre y pura
> como el aire de luz que respiras,
> cual las ondas hirvientes que miras
> de tus playas la arena besar.
> Aunque viles traidores te sirvan,
> Del tirano es inútil la saña,
> que no es vano entre Cuba y España
> tiende inmenso sus olas el mar. (Heredia, *Niagara* 68)[6]

Heredia's "civic poetry" encompasses the Enlightenment ideal of freedom, peace, and justice. His self-understanding as a politically engaged writer can also be seen in the lines in which he writes very positively about Ferdinand VII, who had (temporarily) abolished slavery:

> Aquí una voz: "¡Oh negros desdichados
> Ya vuestros males término han tenido

---

6 "Cuba! I will finally see you free and pure / like the light-filled air that you breathe, / like the seething waves that you watch / kiss the sand of your beaches. / Although you are served by vile traitors, / The viciousness of the tyrant is futile, / Not in vain between Cuba and Spain / The sea extends its enormous billows." W. H. Hurlbut translated the first four lines of this as "Cuba! thou still shalt rise, as pure, as bright, / As thy free air, – as full of living light; / Free as the waves that foam around thy strands, / Kissing thy shores, and curling o'er thy sands!"

> Ya no seréis del África arrancados
> Fernando libertarlos ha querido!" (Heredia, *Obra poética* 157)[7]

Heredia's sympathy for Ferdinand VII was of course not destined to last long. In his translation of Joseph-Marie Chénier's 1819 novel *Tibère*, he saw Ferdinand VII as a spiritual heir of the Roman tyrant (Poumier 264). He also translated Victor-Joseph-Étienne de Jouy's 1821 play *Sylla*, which caused a heated dispute between him and del Monte. Del Monte considered that the dictator was depicted in a very positive light, where Heredia saw the dictator's abdication. Del Monte commented as follows:

> And what about *el Sila* [the play *Sylla*]? How was it represented in Mexico's theater? And did the voices of Prieto and Garay [Spaniards who were Mexico's best actors] make the lines "Je me fis dictateur: je sauvais la patrie" [I made myself dictator; I saved the fatherland] resonate in their coffered republican ceilings? O imprudent friend of liberty, why are you inviting imitations of the Roman dictator's example in Tenochtitlan? Iturbide could say the same, and so could all the usurpers. These are not the pictures that should be presented to a newly created people. (del Monte 23, cited in Poumier 267)[8]

While del Monte, in Cuba, was "only" interested in the attainment of independence, Heredia, in already-independent Mexico, was problematizing the ruling elite, and specifically the consolidation of political power in one person (del Monte 23, cited in Poumier 267). On the cultural level, however, del Monte went further: he criticized Heredia for importing foreign elite cultures. But Heredia was attempting to create a symbiosis: he wanted to transplant the heroes of European literature into American mythology.

Heredia was a great connoisseur of French literature. Not only did he translate Florian, Millevoye, and Lamartine into Spanish, but he also directed theatrical adaptations in Mexico of Voltaire, Chénier, and d'Alfieri, all of them writers deeply involved in the cultural French Revolution (Poumier 263). Meanwhile, he also published articles in the Mexican press on Rousseau and on Victor Hugo. Menéndez Pelayo pointed out Rousseau's influence on Heredia early on:

---

[7] "Here is a voice: 'O unfortunate Negroes / Your troubles have now found an end / And you will not be ripped out of Africa / Ferdinand has wanted them liberated!'"

[8] "¿Y el Sila? Con qué se representó en el teatro de México; y las voces de Prieto y de Garay hicieron resonar en sus republicanos artesones el Je me fis dictateur: je sauvais la patrie ? ¿A qué invitas, oh amigo imprudente de la libertad, a imitar en Tenoxtitlán el ejemplo del dictador romano ? Iturbide también pudo decirlo y todos los usurpadores lo mismo. No son esos los cuadros que deben presentarse a un recién nacido pueblo."

> We should not believe that Heredia ... ought to be taken for a Romantic poet. He is part of a different school, which was like a vague prelude, like a dim dawn of Romanticism. ... His true affiliation is obviously with that sentimental, descriptive, philanthropic, and nonphilosophical school that derived mainly from the prose of Jean-Jacques Rousseau and which had distinguished members in all of the European literatures in the late eighteenth century. (Pedraza Jiménez and Alonso Martín 104)[9]

Alongside his political and literary activities, Heredia was also interested in the history of the New World. Columbus occupied a prominent position in his historical research; for Heredia, Columbus had given the Europeans back their innocence and opened the way to revolutions and greater democracy for them. These ideas have their roots in Rousseau and in his reflections on the state of nature: by making it possible for Europeans to discover the "noble savage," Columbus initiated the purification of political mores. Heredia was clearly convinced by the path that Rousseau indicated for attaining the ideal state of society, in which freedom and equality reign, in other words the state in which actions are motivated only by the general will and an insight into the common good. Rousseau's path provided protection against legal inequality and against the pernicious, civilization-produced, and historically embedded privileges of individuals and of individual social groups, but not against the demagoguery and tyranny of such individuals and groups when they believe themselves to represent the common will. These assumptions are clearly expressed in Heredia's problematization of tyranny in *Sylla* and in his dispute with del Monte, because in Rousseau's conception, only those who are morally good and possessed of virtue belong to the people. Thus, the political opponent is automatically morally corrupt, because that is the only explanation for that opposition, that is to say, the opposition to what is best for everyone. And if in fact the majority is itself corrupt, as in the case of Cuba's Spanish Creole elite, then the virtuous minority is justified in using all power to help virtue to victory. The force that it uses in such a case is only the means to helping the unfree egoist to his own true will, to wake the citizen in him (Schulin 1989). This conviction of Heredia's is reflected in his yearslong struggle as one of the circle of conspirators in the society of Suns and Rays of Bolívar.

---

9 "no se ha de creer que Heredia ... deba ser tenido por poeta romántico. Su puesto está en otra escuela que fue como vago preludio, como aurora tenue del romanticismo. ... Su verdadera filiación está evidentemente en aquella escuela sentimental, descriptiva, filantrópica y afilosofada que, derivada principalmente de la prosa de J. Jacobo Rousseau, tenía a fines del siglo XVIII insignes afiliados en todas las literaturas europeas."

II.1.3.2 J. Levilloux: *Les créoles ou la vie aux Antilles* (The Creoles or Life in the Antilles) (1835)

There is no biographical information for J. Levilloux, aside from the fact that he is a man, referred to as "J. Levilloux of Martinique" (his first name is sometimes given as Jules, sometimes as Joseph). His *Les créoles ou la vie aux Antilles* is a historical novel, a reinterpretation of the revolutionary events of 1789 in the French Antilles. Estève, a mulatto, becomes friends with Edmond Briolan, because they are both from Guadeloupe and both attend a prestigious French school, the Collège de Navarre. After a certain period of time, Estève discloses his secret, that he is not a "pureblooded white man," to Edmond. This leads to a dilemma: should the ethnic caste system in the colonies be accepted as it is or broken apart?

The fact that both of the protagonists are being educated in the same establishment in the metropolis is a crucial element of the novel. In his preface, Levilloux talks about new kinds of access to education, along with their impact on the colonial societies:

> The constant activity of the press and of the forums of the metropolises has legally won in the Lesser Antilles what the revolution undertook to do with violence. For seventeen years, multiple generations of Creoles who have visited the schools and universities of Europe have, through rubbing up [against the others], lost the savage roughnesses that characterized them. Their contact with the brothers of the mother country has rendered them more receptive to ideas of progress, more flexible in the hands of the legislator. The work of the political emancipation of the colored race is done; and that race, having achieved the goal of its ambition, has laid down the passionate bitterness that explains every state of conflict, and it too has enjoyed the circulation of the vivifying lights of education. (preface)[10]

Levilloux is committed to drawing as detailed a picture of his time as he possibly can. He addresses himself very explicitly to the European reader, to whom he wants to convey a description of the conditions on the island after the effects of the French Revolution, like a storm, have passed through: "The principles of the Revolution passed like a hurricane over these lands of privileges and slav-

---

10 "L'action constante de la presse et de la tribune des métropoles a conquis légalement dans les Petites Antilles ce que la révolution avait entrepris avec violence. Depuis dix-sept ans, de nombreuses générations de créoles visitant les collèges et les universités d'Europe ont perdu par le frottement les aspérités sauvages qui distinguaient leur caractère. Elles sont devenues, au contact des frères de la mère-patrie, plus pénétrables aux idées de progrès, plus flexibles aux mains du législateur. L'œuvre émancipation politique de la race de couleur est accomplie; celle-ci ayant atteint le but de son ambition dépose cette aigreur passionnée qu'explique tout état de lutte, et chez elle aussi ont circulé les vivifiantes lumières de l'instruction."

ery, sowing some fertile ideas for the future and leaving a great ruin as a monument to their invasion" (Levilloux 6, cited in Toumson 190).[11]

Levilloux insists on freeing himself of prejudices about race, etcetera, which live on stubbornly in spite of the changed political climate: "habitual attitudes, laborious creations of time, ... still resist in social practices and in social relations, even when the political principles that should transform them already prevail in the spirit" (preface).[12] But there are nevertheless some racist prejudices in the novel, a fact that comes through in the conversation between Estève, the mestizo, and his rival, the young white Creole Thélesfore: "Ah! If only I could love you like a brother, mingle my fates with yours, march forever along with you in search of the happiness that we would share like children of the same blood" (64).[13]

Levilloux's description of the various island population groups is also marked by essentialist attributions and value-laden racial stereotypes. This can be seen, for instance, in his characterization of the colonists: "intellectual lightweights, generally uncultured, but very alive and penetrating, enthusiasts for whatever is marvelous, disdainful of Europe's philosophical knowledge. ... They take advantage of the nobility of whiteness" (preface).[14] The free mulattos, meanwhile, are described as ambitious beneficiaries of the new circumstances:

> Born of the commerce between white men and negresses: freedmen ambitious for political rights and social equality; men of strong passions, of a hardy nature, participating in both the intellectual qualities of the whites and the physical vitality of the blacks, they aspire to build, on their own behalf, on the ruins of the Creole's privileges. (preface)[15]

---

11 "Les principes de la Révolution passèrent comme un ouragan sur ces terres de privilèges et d'esclavage, semant quelques idées fécondes pour l'avenir, et laissant une grande ruine, monument de leur invasion."
12 "Les mœurs, créations laborieuses du temps, ... résistent encore dans les usages et dans les rapports sociaux, quand les principes politiques qui doivent les transformer règnent déjà dans les esprits."
13 "Ah! que ne puis-je vous aimer comme un frère, confondre mes destinées avec les vôtres, marcher toujours avec vous en quête du bonheur que nous partagerions comme des enfants du même sang."
14 "intelligences légères, en général incultes, mais vives, pénétrantes, enthousiastes du merveilleux, dédaigneux des connaissances philosophiques de l'Europe. ... Ils se prévalent de la noblesse de la couleur blanche."
15 "Nés du commerce des blancs et des négresses: affranchis ambitieux des droits politiques et de l'égalité sociale; hommes aux passions fortes, d'une nature hardie, participant, à la fois des qualités intellectuelles des Blancs et de la vigueur corporelle des Noirs, ils aspirent à fonder pour leur compte, sur les ruines des privilèges du Créole."

About the black slaves, on the other hand, he writes:

> They make up the majority, but they are ignorant, superstitious, cunning by necessity, prone to sublime devotions and atrocious cruelties, gifted with a poetic imagination and often joining slavery with several virtues that one is surprised to find in this state of degradation. (preface)[16]

While the storyline would tend to imply an author who is quite critical of the system, if we look more closely, we can see that Levilloux actually explicitly justifies the existing conditions of slavery:

> whatever his prejudices, which are vices that can be traced to his education and to the social state in which his childhood is formed, the colonist is a man of the elite who can invite hatred, but never scorn. ... The dominance [of the colonists] over the African race is shaped, is explicable, is even justifiable to this day. (preface)[17]

Levilloux's main concern is with rehabilitating the class of mulattos, but not that of blacks. There is not, in Levilloux, any conceptual confrontation with the idea of the citizen, along the lines of what we find in Heredia. In fact, tellingly, the word can barely be found on the lips of Estève, the Creole protagonist. He regrets not having supported the French mother country better, as a perfect *citoyen:*

> There is in me an urgent need to sacrifice myself to a holy cause, to devote all of the resources of my youth and of my knowledge to the service to some cherished beings and to the realization of some pure and generous sentiment. Such is the moral life of the young man of our time. Happy are those who can reproduce it outside themselves! Therefore, not having been able to make myself a useful citizen in the revolution of our beloved France, I feel that there is, at least, even in this country, a great deal of room for devotion to the cause of humanity. (48)[18]

---

[16] "Ils sont les plus nombreux; mais ignorants, superstitieux, rusés par nécessité, susceptibles de dévouements sublimes et d'atroces cruautés, doués d'une imagination poétique et affectant souvent l'esclavage à côté de plusieurs vertus qu'on est surpris de rencontrer dans cet état de dégradation."

[17] "quels que soient les préjugés, vices de son éducation et de l'état social où se moule son enfance, le colon est un homme d'élite, qui peut attirer la haine, mais jamais le mépris. ... La domination [des colons] sur la race africaine se conçoit, s'explique, se justifie même jusqu'à nos jours."

[18] "Il y a en moi un besoin impérieux de me sacrifier à une sainte cause, de consacrer toutes les ressources de ma jeunesse et de mon savoir au service de quelques êtres chéris et à la réalisation de quelque sentiment pur et généreux. Telle est la vie morale du jeune homme de notre époque. Heureux ceux qui peuvent la reproduire au dehors! Ainsi, n'ayant pu me rendre citoyen utile

In another context, he asks, "Will you accept us as fellow citizens, as brothers?" (183)[19] but there is no programmatic enactment of this in what follows.

If we compare how present the ideas of the French Revolution are, and how concrete the concept of the citizen is, in the work of José María Heredia and J. Levilloux, it turns out that they occupy a great deal of space in Heredia's work, while in Levilloux's they do not appear at all. This result is definitely symptomatic. The choice of these two authors may appear arbitrary, but their political positions are representative of the respective colonial spheres of Spain and France. And the simple fact of dealing with the French Revolution, which is always a natural move for every writer in the French colonial sphere, does not mean that its political philosophy is taken as an opportunity to reflect critically on questions of colonial law.

II.2 Between Francophilia and Attempts at Autonomy: The Formation of Postcolonial Theory and the Nineteenth Century

Let us now juxtapose two more literary representatives of the Spanish and French colonial spheres, looking at their respective positions with respect to the colonial status quo. Gertrudis Gómez de Avellaneda and Louis de Maynard de Queilhe are the two writers I would like to compare here. What connects these two writers? What will a comparison of their most important novels, *Sab* (1841) and *Outre-mer* (Overseas) (1835), bring to light? The two novels appeared almost at the same time in the Caribbean. Maynard de Queilhe is from Martinique, Gómez de Avellaneda from Cuba, and they are representative examples of the literary Creole upper class of their respective islands of origin, both of which (unlike the Latin American mainland) were still under colonial rule at the time. Both writers did their writing in the mother country: Gómez de Avellaneda, the Cuban, wrote from Madrid, while Maynard de Queilhe, the Martinican, wrote from Paris. And while Cuba became independent in 1898, Martinique was given the status of a French overseas department (*Département d'outre-mer*), which it still retains, in 1946. Even in the twenty-first century, the French Antilles are still involved in the complications of a (post-)colonial situation, as became clear in 2005 when a law drafted by the National Assembly mandating that

---

dans la révolution de notre chère France; je sens du moins que même dans ce pays, il y a large place pour le dévouement à la cause de l'humanité."
19 "Nous acceptez-vous pour concitoyens, pour frères?"

the positive influence of colonialism should be taught in French schools led to heated debates (see Glissant and Chamoiseau).

But to what extent does working with the concepts of postcolonial theory provide a fruitful way of engaging with the Latin American literatures of the nineteenth century? While the actual formation of nation-states on the Latin American mainland had been completed by the end of the eighteen-twenties, the processes of independence in the Caribbean (with the exception of Haiti, which won its independence in 1804) continued on for much longer. If we think of postcolonialism in purely chronological terms, it would in fact be problematic to use the concept with respect to a theoretical literary and cultural analysis of the nineteenth-century Caribbean. But it can nevertheless be helpful to use the tools of postcolonial theory as a guide. I take my cue from the work of Bill Ashcroft and Walter Mignolo. Ashcroft, Griffiths, and Tiffin argue that postcolonialism should not be understood as a (historical) moment *after* but as a *process* of confrontation with structures that are replaced by new ones, and he therefore includes Latin America (and also the Caribbean) in his postcolonial analyses (cf. Reinstädler, "Theatralisierung").

First of all, I want to introduce the two novels; it will quicky become clear that for both of them, the central question has to do with the relationship between colonizer and colonized. In the Caribbean, this relationship is shifted onto the level of a social and ethnic master-slave issue, since the original indigenous population was mostly wiped out around 1492. In comparing *Sab* and *Outre-mer*, then, I focus on the following central questions:

1. Walter Mignolo suggests that in using the terminology of "postcolonialism," we separate out and differentiate between the concepts of historical postcolonialism and epistemological postcolonialism. Epistemological postcolonialism is connected to postcolonial reasoning (*razón postcolonial*), a mental attitude that makes it possible to look critically at colonialism and the colonial heritage (Reinstädler, "Theatralisierung"; Mignolo, "La razón postcolonial"). Using this logic, novels written before political independence can already include postcolonial discourses, for instance if they undermine dichotomous hierarchies and propose a plurality of values. Can Mignolo's insight be fruitful in comparing novels that may in fact take very different positions towards the colonial situation?
2. What European discourses have the authors appropriated? In doing so, are they claiming the cultural identity of their own islands of origin? In what way do they reflect on the potential contradiction between emancipation and a commitment to a Europe-oriented history of ideas? Are there certain texts that have been particularly successful? And in what way does an inten-

sive textual reception contribute to the breaking down or, alternately, the consolidation of constellations of cultural hegemony?
3. Is the representation of colonial structures based on a system of binary opposites? And if so, does that intensify and stabilize the division between colonized and colonizers (Castro Varela and Dhawan 85)?
4. Does the literature of the Antilles help to illustrate Edward Said's thesis that colonialism is always a result of imperialism (and not the other way around) (Castro Varela and Dhawan 13 ff.)? And to what extent does literature anticipate political developments?
5. To what extent are stereotypes, such as the idea of the "noble savage," then transplanted back into the region from which they originally came?
6. Do these two texts have the characteristics that would allow them to be considered and read as foundational fictions, according to Doris Sommer's categorization?
7. Both writers were born in the Antilles, but, as we have seen, did their writing in the capitals of their respective mother countries (Gómez de Avellaneda in Madrid and Maynard de Queilhe in Paris). Does this mean that they perpetuate the writing of colonial discourses? To what extent does this writing influence that perspective?

II.2.1 Gertrudis Gómez de Avellaneda: *Sab* (1841)

In the choice of her subject, Gómez de Avellaneda[20] follows Victor Hugo's early work *Bug-Jargal* (1826): Sab, a slave, falls in love with Carlota, his mistress, but rather than becoming the romantic hero of a slave rebellion that would tear down the social and ethnic barriers that separate him from his beloved, he chooses the path of self-abnegation and passion for the sake of his love, a love that is not really reciprocated because of the stable social order within which Carlota lives and, what is more, a love that (as Gómez de Avellaneda, in differentiating herself from Hugo, seems to suggest) can never really be imagined, much less acted upon, in that society. While Hugo was writing about Saint-Domingue's wars of liberation after the fact, Cuba, at the time of *Sab*'s publication, still had more than half a century of colonial rule ahead of it, and in fact the book, even with its apparently "soft" criticism of the stark social reality, immediately fell victim to colonial censorship. If we look at Sab's actions against the

---

20 Regarding Gómez de Avellaneda, see also Müller, "Transkoloniale Dimensionen"; Müller, "Variantes de miradas."

background of the wars of liberation in the context of already-independent Latin America, we can also see his self-sacrifice as a sacrifice on the altar of the longed-for national independence, because he renounces an escalation of the social and ethnic conflicts for the sake of inner (national) unity, although that escalation is certainly contemplated as an option, giving us a glimmer of the basic existence of such potential issuing from the mutually supportive relationships among the slaves.

> I also thought of taking up arms against our oppressors, arms shackled with their victims; of throwing out among them the terrible cry of freedom and vengeance; washing myself in the blood of the whites; trampling with my feet the cadavers and their laws and then myself perishing among their ruins. (Gómez de Avellaneda, *Sab*, ed. Servera 157)[21]

Gómez de Avellaneda, however, also takes the love story extremely seriously (note that she herself, around the same time—though with the sexes reversed—experienced an unrequited love), and in so doing, along with the ethnic dimension, she also points to a gendered dimension of social oppression. The asymmetries in the power relationships are not purely external; they are deeply inscribed into the consciousness of human beings, and in particular also into the consciousness of the oppressed themselves. But what is often overlooked in research focused on gender is that not only does Carlota not return Sab's unspoken love, but for her it is in fact quite simply unthinkable to love a slave. When, on her wedding day, she learns of Sab's death from her deeply shaken relative Teresa, she dismisses her bridegroom's conjecture that Teresa had loved Sab with the words: "Love him!—Carlota repeated—Him! A slave! ... I know that his heart is noble, good, capable of the greatest sentiments; but love, Enrique, love is for tender and passionate hearts ... like yours, like mine" (251).[22]

Unlike Hugo's Bug-Jargal and his comrades-in-arms, who care precious little about the feelings and wills of the white women that they desire and for whom these women are finally objects, just as they are for the white men, Sab attains a moral and reflective depth that is incomparably more meaningful. The traditional romantic pictures of the impulsive "noble savage" and the "good Negro" (*bon nègre*) are revolutionized when Sab, in renouncing her, takes Carlota seriously as

---

[21] "He pensado también en armar contra nuestros opresores, los brazos encadenados de sus víctimas; arrojar en medio de ellos el terrible grito de libertad y venganza; bañarme en sangre de blancos; hollar con mis pies cadáveres y sus leyes y perecer yo mismo entre sus ruinas."
[22] "¡Amarle! –repitió Carlota– ¡A el! ¡A un esclavo! ... sé que su corazón es noble, bueno, capaz de los más grandes sentimientos; pero el amor, Enrique, el amor es para los corazones tiernos, apasionados ... como el tuyo, como el mío."

a subject, without however losing sight of how much his beloved, in her perceptions, is governed by socially dominant thought patterns, by means of which she subjectively internalizes her own position as an object. Thus, Sab compares his role as a slave with the lot of woman: "Oh, women! Poor, blind victims! Just like slaves, they patiently drag along their chains and bow their heads to the yoke of human laws. With no other guide but their *ignorant and credulous hearts*, they choose a master for their whole life" (270; emphasis mine).[23] Note the use of the active voice: the women choose, they let themselves be led by their own unknowing and gullible hearts; or, to put it in the language of the Enlightenment: their lack of responsibility is entirely their own fault!

> The slave, at least, can change masters and can hope that by gathering gold, he will some day be able to buy his freedom, but the woman, when she lifts her gaunt hands and her ravished forehead to beg for freedom, hears the monster with the sepulchral voice shouting at her: "In your grave!" (271).[24]

Sab's dilemma is grounded in the situation itself: the sensitivity of his perceptions, the depth of his reflection (and self-reflection) on the social power structures, which he does not at all see as a purely external force, along with the incredibly high moral expectations he places on himself, drive him to his own self-sacrifice. He clearly sees the weakness of character in Carlota's fiancé, Otway, who, under the influence of his avaricious father, wants to cancel the already scheduled wedding when he finds out that Carlota's family is in a worse financial position than he expected. After an exhausting internal battle and in spite of his expectation that she will have an unhappy marriage, Sab hands over his lottery winnings to Carlota to allow her to make a free choice.

It is only after a number of sobering years of marriage, at the moment when her relative Teresa dies in the convent, that Carlota finally sees Sab's farewell letter, not only disclosing the slave's story to her but also, for the first time, giving her her own history. This belated insight into the moral superiority of the slave, who showed himself to be capable of much more than just a passionate love, finally allows the unhappily married woman to see the absurdity of her ethnic and social prejudices. More than simply calling for a fight against external oppres-

---

23 "¡Oh! ¡las mujeres! ¡Pobres y ciegas víctimas! Como los esclavos, ellas arrastran pacientemente su cadena y bajan la cabeza bajo el yugo de las leyes humanas. Sin otra guía que su *corazón ignorante y crédulo*, eligen un dueño para toda la vida."
24 "El esclavo, al menos, puede cambiar de amo, puede esperar que, juntando oro, comprará algún día su libertad, pero la mujer, cuando levanta sus manos enflaquecidas y su frente ultrajada para pedir libertad, oye al monstruo de voz sepulcral que le grita: 'En la tumba!'"

sion, the novel targets the internal systems of power from which social, ethnic, and sexual structural inequalities draw their stability in the first place. Sab does not divide society up according to class warfare but is instead made into a figure of integration for a new, united Cuban identity. It is significant that he eludes clearcut, essentialist attributions: although he is mulatto, people have a hard time determining what his skin color is; and although he is a man, he is drawn with characteristics that are very feminine, particularly the fact that he freely chooses the path of suffering, which he sees to be the lot of woman in a patriarchal society that needs to be overcome. The choice of this path of suffering seems to me to refer back strongly to the biblical Passion story: in the same way that Jesus of Nazareth becomes a focal point for a new religious beginning by rejecting the zealots' armed resistance to the foreign rule of the Romans, so too does Sab became an integrating figure for a new national beginning. The identity-defining project offered by *Sab* thus outlines the perspective of a new, future-oriented, national consensus, which cannot take any exclusive ethnic or gender criterias as its basis and in which it is only the Otways, as the male representatives of a colonial gambler morality, who are (voluntarily, in the end) left behind: for them, Cuba is only a waystation in their worldwide hunt for ever more new riches, and they have no interest in truly and lastingly integrating themselves there.

II.2.2 Louis de Maynard de Queilhe: *Outre-mer* (1835)

Maynard de Queilhe's *Outre-mer* (Overseas) was written in 1835. The context was that the ideas of the 1830 July Revolution in France were slowly spreading out into the furthest-flung corners of France's colonial empire. And along with the Revolution's ideas, questions about the abolition of slavery also profoundly affected the tenor of the philosophical and political debates taking place in Paris. The model for this was England, where abolition had already been achieved in 1835; in France, preparations were being made for the 1840 Broglie Commission, which finally led to abolition in 1848.

Maynard de Queilhe was a *Béké*, a member of Martinique's white Creole upper class, which in 1835 was primarily concerned with preserving the old order of things. Their wealth was mostly based on the successful functioning of the plantation economy, which relied on slavery. The revolutionary ideas coming from Europe were seen as a great danger by the *Békés*. It seemed to them as though the nightmare of 1789 were just being repeated all over again. In his preface, Maynard de Queilhe gives the reasons for his literary testimony: "[This present book] has two faces, one that is literary and the other political, or rather social. ... I have tried to be impartial. ... I have told stories. ... I don't pretend to deny that there is a lesson, or rather an opinion, hidden in the fable and in its resolution" (I:II).²⁵

The action of the novel takes place in 1830; at the heart of it is the passion of Marius, a mulatto, for a white Creole woman, Julie de Longuefort. Such a connection must be contrary to nature, according to Maynard de Queilhe, and can only be explained by a corrupt upbringing: Julie grew up in the French capital and was exposed there to the pernicious influence of romantic appeals. Her character, therefore, lacks the clarity and consistency of the young Creoles of the "good old times." Marius, for his part, has only recently returned to Martinique. His corrupt upbringing was due to his adoptive father, Sir William Blackchester, a philanthropist and an Englishman to boot. (Because slavery had already been abolished in England in 1833, Englishmen were even more unpopular with the white Martinicans than were the liberal French.)

Early on, Marius is aflame with political enthusiasm, strongly under the influence of European Enlightenment, and calls for revolt. The slaves, he believes, are too passively acquiescent: "I don't understand it at all. They are insulted, and they lower their heads; they are beaten, and they kneel down; they are killed, and they say thank you. What is this, good God? I come from a country where the very beasts could teach you your human duty" (I:41).²⁶ His words almost anticipate some of the later positions of négritude, to the point that he buys and frees a black woman in order to marry. But he soon returns to reality, and it becomes to clear to him that they are worlds apart. Marius realizes that he can only love a "real woman": that is to say, a white woman.

His new realization puts Marius in a position that is diametrically opposed to his political convictions. Torn between his hatred of whites and his love for Julie, Marius joins a group of insurgent *marrons* (runaway slaves) and takes part in a few revolts. His experiences after he returns to Martinique, however, lead him to revise his opinion about slavery. Monsieur de Longuefort, who is white, explains to the mulattos that the prejudices against the blacks are completely justified (I:86; cf. Corzani II:338). And in fact, Marius is delighted by his visit to an *habitation*, one of Martinique's vast sugar cane plantations, a model of the old aristocracy. Here he discovers how well the slaves are actually treated: so well, in

---

25 "[Mon livre présent a] deux faces, l'une qui est littéraire, l'autre qui est politique ou plutôt sociale. ... Je me suis efforcé d'être impartial. ... J'ai raconté. ... Je ne prétends pas nier qu'une leçon ou plutôt qu'un avis ne soit caché dans la fable et dans son dénouement."
26 "Je n'y comprends rien. On les insulte, ils baissent la tête; on les bat, ils s'agenouillent; on les tue, ils remercient. Qu'est-ce que cela, bon Dieu? Mais je viens d'un pays où les bêtes pourraient vous enseigner votre devoir d'hommes."

fact, that they have almost become lords and masters themselves. They even receive a piece of land from the colonist overlord. After his visit to the *habitation*, Marius rejects his revolutionary ideas from Europe.

> Sure, the whip did ring out at intervals, but in the air and not on the back of the slave, and it was just to stimulate the energies of those who had fallen asleep, or to reach the ears of those who were furthest away. The earth was not watered with their sweat, but possibly with the syrup that they can have at any time, and that they tend to drink diluted with water. ... He had been told that there would be many cries and moans, but he only heard them laugh and chatter. (I:105 ff.)[27]

The plantation, far from being the opposite of paradise, is instead an extension of it, and the harvest time is a time of positive activity and happy singing. The French plantation owner is generally depicted as a generous patriarch, who is seen by his slaves as a father and who, for his part, lovingly cares for them. He builds handsome housing for them in the countryside; they plant their own gardens and receive medical care from the plantation's hospital (Wogatzke, *Identitätsentwürfe* 164).

So that is how blacks are portrayed in *Outre-mer*. Even more important, however, is the novel's characterization of mulattos, represented in the person of the main protagonist, Marius himself. The author endows Marius with a certain level of intelligence, putting him almost on the level of the whites; at every possible opportunity, however, his black background is emphasized, for example in the form of his passionate propensity for violence, his latent barbarity, etcetera. Thus, as the novel goes on, Marius eliminates all of Julie's suitors, and after he has killed the son of the Marquis de Longuefort, he exploits the blind father's generosity and becomes his trusted steward. There is nothing exceptional in the fact that Marius is in love with a white woman. But the fact that a white woman expresses her feelings for a mulatto, on the other hand, is a scandal. Julie admits to him, as he is beating her to death: "My Marius, I loved you!" (II:376).[28] And at the moment at which Monsieur de Longuefort is trying to ensure that justice prevails by decapitating his daughter's murderer—in the very moment in which Marius is baring his neck—an old black woman notices a scar and recognizes him as the son that she once had with the Marquis himself. The virtues of the white race

---

27 "Par intervalles certes le fouet retentissait, mais en l'air et non sur le dos de l'esclave et c'était uniquement pour exciter l'ardeur des endormis ou pour se faire entendre des plus éloignés. La terre n'était point arrosée de leurs sueurs mais peut-être du sirop qu'on ne leur refuse en aucun temps, et qu'ils ont l'habitude de boire délayé dans l'eau. ... On lui avait annoncé beaucoup de cris et de gémissements, et il ne les entendait que rire et jaser."
28 "Mon Marius, je t'aimais!"

are thus confirmed on yet another level: what Julie saw as a passionate love turns out to be the affection of a sister for her half brother. Marius, the mulatto, on the other hand, is stigmatized in multiple ways at the end of the novel: he is the murderer of his brother, the poisoner of his brothers-in-law, and the lover and murderer of his sister. He is the extreme offender, who has dared to return to his home island without respecting its rules. There is nothing left for him but the melodramatic production of his suicide.

Marius's fate can be summed up in the following sentence, from his own mouth: "in a country of privileges, a brilliant education is the most disastrous gift to a man of an inferior caste" (II:163)[29]—the mulattos who have risen in society and have returned from their studies in Paris infected with revolutionary ideas are seen as the true enemies of the aristocratic order (Corzani II:341). The novel's conservative audience finds the confirmation of its own attitudes in the description of Julie's mental state, shocked as she is at the mediocrity of Saint-Pierre's mulattos.

> This discovery was, in effect, the withering of all that past in which she had loved Marius against the law and the customs of her country: which she, poor child, had had the weakness to blame on the faith of others! Now she saw with her own eyes the mistake she had made. Who would ever believe that Marius was an exception! And moreover, who would dare to abolish the rule just for one exception! (II:163)[30]

The novel shows the Creole upper class neglected by the metropolis and betrayed by France's liberal constitutional July Monarchy. According to a decree from the Colonial Council (*Conseil des colonies*), abolishing slavery was in fact not really necessary from the point of view of the colonies, and the problem was just the "philanthropic pressure" coming from Europe; the *habitations*, according to this, were managed very progressively, with a gentle hand, and the locals had no wish, and were not interested in demanding any radical changes. But because of public opinion in Europe, given the measures already taken and the serious discussions about slavery that were constantly rekindled, with their negative consequences for the colonies, both moral and economic, it was

---

[29] "dans un pays de privilèges, une brillante éducation est pour l'homme de la caste inférieure le présent le plus funeste."
[30] "Cette découverte, en effet, c'était la flétrissure de tout ce passé où elle avait aimé Marius contre la règle et les usages de son pays: qu'elle, pauvre enfant! avait eu la faiblesse de blâmer sur la foi des autres! Maintenant elle voyait de ses propres yeux quelle erreur elle avait commise. Qui voudrait jamais croire que Marius fût une exception! Et d'ailleurs, pour une exception, qui oserait abolir la règle!"

no longer possible to countenance the comprehensive and lasting continuation of slavery (cf. Gisler 129).

The ambition of *Outre-mer* is highly political: to convince the philanthropists to give up all their calls for abolition and at the same time to clear the colonists of any slander. The novel's characterization of them as fatherly masters is intended to counteract their reputation as oppressive slave lords (Wogatzke, *Identitätsentwürfe* 214): "They would be the first to approve of any laudable effort that might be made for the sake of the slaves and the freedmen, as long as their goodwill is not exploited by sacking their properties and delivering up their lives to the Negroes' cutlasses" (Maynard de Queilhe II:168 ff.).[31]

II.2.3 Literary Stagings of Spanish and French Colonialism

The writers Maynard de Queilhe and Gómez de Avellaneda can be seen as exemplars of the literary worlds of their respective islands of origin. This juxtaposition of the two illustrates the different positions taken by intellectuals of the French and the Spanish Caribbean with respect to colonial issues. The ideas of Gómez de Avellaneda were near to those of del Monte's circle, and *Sab*, one of the earliest antislavery novels of the Americas (O'Brien n.p.), can be seen as belonging to the cluster of abolitionist novels coming out of Cuba, which also includes the works of Anselmo Suárez y Romero (1818–1878), Cirilo Villaverde (1812–1894), and Francisco Manzano (1797–1853).

It is telling that there was no comparable intellectual circle in Martinique. The few other writers from the French colonial Caribbean (not including Haiti, independent since 1804) take a position similar to that of Maynard de Queilhe, arguing for the preservation of the status quo. In the time period we are looking at one could also mention J. Levilloux, whom I have already discussed, as well as Poirié Saint-Aurèle[32] and J.H.J. Coussin.[33]

---

[31] "Ils seraient les premiers à seconder toute tentative louable qu'on ferait en faveur des esclaves et des affranchis, pourvu toutefois qu'on ne profitât point de leur bonne volonté pour saccager leurs propriétés et livrer leur vie au coutelas des Nègres."

[32] Jean Pierre Aurèle Poirié, known as Poirié Saint-Aurèle, was a plantation owner and poet from Guadeloupe. He was born in British Antigua in 1795, during his family's short period of exile there, and died in Guadeloupe in 1855.

[33] Aside from his birth and death dates, the only biographical information that is known about the writer J.H.J. Coussin (Guadeloupe 1773–1836) is that he was a writer in Guadeloupe's royal law court.

While *Outre-mer* affirms the existing colonialist discourses, what we find in *Sab* is a clearly anticolonial position, which can also be described using the concept of epistemological postcolonialism, mentioned above. And yet, in spite of these clear differences between the social politics of Gómez de Avellaneda's and Maynard de Queilhe's novels, they are very close together in their literary orientation, both of them drawing on French Romanticism. Marius, as a romantic hero, is caught in an existential dualism that can be traced back to the influence of Victor Hugo, who was a friend of Maynard de Queilhe's. In his famous preface to *Cromwell*, Victor Hugo touches on the genuine ambivalence of human nature:

> "Thou art twofold, thou art made up of two beings, one perishable, the other immortal, one carnal, the other ethereal, one enslaved by appetites, cravings and passions, the other borne aloft on the wings of enthusiasm and reverie—in a word, the one always stooping toward the earth, its mother, the other always darting up toward heaven, its fatherland." ("Preface to Cromwell")[34]

In *Outre-mer*, Longuefort assigns this double nature to Marius, the mulatto, in a racist way: "Remember that the mulatto was not a man like other men. He was like those powerful places in nature full of precipices, poisonous plants, and treacherous animals, but which are nevertheless where you have to go to find the universe's most valuable marvels" (II:16).[35]

In a certain sense, Marius can be said to partake of what Homi Bhabha describes as mimicry, because he can only ever be a partial representation of the colonial master. There is no noble savage to be found in Maynard de Queilhe. Anything that is noble is confined to the beauty of white women, who are of course not "savage." And while the representations of nature are very positive, the author explains in the preface that because of the tense political situation, Antillean literature could no longer offer exotic images of nature as a place of refuge. Sab, on the other hand, does have some of the traits of the noble savage. As the archetype of the romantic hero, he also corresponds to the social-romantic dimensions of readings of Victor Hugo.

---

34 "'Tu es double, tu es composé de deux êtres, l'un périssable, l'autre immortel, l'un charnel, l'autre éthéré, l'un enchaîné par les appétits, les besoins et les passions, l'autre emporté sur les ailes de l'enthousiasme et de la rêverie, celui-ci enfin toujours courbé vers la terre, sa mère, celui-là sans cesse élancé vers le ciel, sa patrie'" (Hugo, "Préface de Cromwell," cited in Maignan-Claverie 250).
35 "Le mulâtre, il ne faut pas l'oublier, ce n'était pas un homme comme un autre. C'était une image de ces fortes natures où les précipices, les plantes vénéneuses et les animaux malfaisants abondent, mais où néanmoins on doit aller chercher les merveilles les plus estimées de cet univers."

In the case of Gómez de Avellaneda, the reliance on French precedents means a turning away from the literary production of Spain, her mother country, and therefore also a kind of emancipation, which of course also has to do with the omnipresence of French Romanticism at the time. Marius and Sab both embody basic features of Romantic mythology. While Sab represents the positively marked superhero, however, Marius is the "rebellious Satan" (Maynard de Queilhe II:16), the "product of the love between heaven and earth" (I:350; Maignan-Claverie 251). In these two novels, therefore, the reception of the same literary model, namely French Romanticism, is developed with completely different effects: in *Outre-mer* constellations of cultural hegemony are reinforced, while in *Sab* they are cracked open.

In *Outre-mer*, the depiction of colonial structures is based on a system of binary oppositions: the novel works with descriptions of essentialist identities, dividing the world into good whites and bad blacks, and the mulattos represent the dangerous and problematic intermediate position between these two poles. This representation deepens segregation and solidifies colonial structures. In *Sab*, meanwhile, we also find binary structures, especially with respect to ethnic backgrounds. But while its attributions of identity are likewise essentialist, the very positively marked figure of the slave Sab is such a strongly unifying force that, as with Cirilo Villaverde's *Cecilia Valdés*, the process of transculturation can allow something to develop that is truly new.[36] This function of Sab's is also connected to the fact that the novel can be read as a foundational fiction (in the sense developed by Doris Sommer). It is not for nothing that it belongs to the constitutive canon of Cuba's national literature. And even putting aside the issue that Martinique never did become an independent nation, the novels of the nineteenth-century French Antilles could not take on any such function. Both *Outre-mer* and *Sab* anticipate political developments. With its emotional appeal and the shock that its self-sacrifice produces in the reader, *Sab* had a very sizable historical effect. After being banned for thirty years, the novel was finally published in a revolutionary Cuban newspaper and then immediately became a part of the struggle for independence and the abolition of slavery.

---

36 On *Cecilia Valdés*, see Ette, "Cirilo Villaverde"; Ortiz. On transculturalism, which I have already mentioned several times, see in particular Lüsebrink's explanations, which also explicitly cite Fernando Ortiz. Lüsebrink's focus on the interconnective approach is very instructive here: "The term 'transculturalism' ... serves to denote plural cultural identities, which arise from the high degree of interconnectedness and intertwining of many contemporary cultures." ("Der Begriff Transkulturalität ... dient zur Bezeichnung pluraler kultureller Identitäten, die durch die hochgradige Vernetzung und Verflechtung vieler Kulturen der Gegenwart entstanden sind.") (Lüsebrink, *Interkulturelle Kommunikation* 17).

As I mentioned earlier, one of the main things that these two authors have in common is that while they were both born in the Antilles, they both also left and did their writing from the capital of their respective mother countries, placing them in an intermediate space. In the case of *Outre-mer*, it becomes clear within the text itself that as particular ideas and theories of the metropolises are translated to the colonies, they are subjected to processes of hybridization in the course of their rearticulation within the imperial domain (Castro Varela and Dhawan 89): the revolutionary ideas of the book's protagonist, Marius, arise in Paris, the center of France's colonial power, and cannot be realized or carried out in the colony itself.

In the case of Gómez de Avellaneda, these issues show up not within the text, on the level of the plot, but rather when we look at how the text uses its literary models. For this Cuban writer, the in-between-ness of her situation is much more complex: it is from the outside and from a distance that she inscribes herself and her literature into the fight for political emancipation and, to a certain degree, cultural emancipation as well. What we see in her work is that when the categories, models, and discourses of identity that are available all come from the very center from which one is trying to differentiate oneself,[37] the attempt to establish a non-European identity often creates a kind of tension that cannot simply be eliminated through a dialectical synthesis.

With respect to both Maynard de Queilhe and Gómez de Avellaneda, we can say that whatever the motivation for their exile to the mother country, and no matter how strongly they might identify with the colonial power or former colonial power, every postcolonial position taken and act of self-determination has to involve a conceptual balancing act because of the mother country's discursive dominance over the colonies. And while relationships to the respective colonial powers of France and Spain are addressed and dealt with very differently in the work of these two authors, there are some extremely revealing similarities in the colonial relationships: while models and ideas from the mother country are reproduced and repeated in the colony, they can never be identical to the supposed original. The process of translation—the duplication but within a different context—necessarily carves out a gap in the apparent original, such that colonialism itself fragments the identity and authority of the colonizers. The colonizer requires the colonized to take on the external forms of the ruling power and to internalize its values and norms. Bhabha's concept of mimicry is therefore also an

---

[37] In the text corpus presented in this book, this holds true not only for Gómez de Avellaneda but also for Eugenio María de Hostos, discussed in section II.3.3.

expression of the European civilizing mission,[38] which took as its objective the transformation of the colonized culture according to the colonizers' ideals, though it must also be said that in the first half of the nineteenth century, France's model was more successful than Spain's.

Finally, as a conclusion to these concrete findings, it is also worth taking a quick look at the theoretical metalevel: the toolkit of postcolonial theorization provides crucial insights for the identification of the political stances that are taken towards the colonial status quo through literature, but it will also become clear that the vocabulary of postcolonialism also runs the risk of producing overly schematic results. The defining characteristic of the Caribbean literatures, with which chapter III concerns itself, cannot be grasped using a binary of center versus periphery, nor does a focus on a so-called third space allow for an understanding of the complex in-between-ness that cannot simply be dissolved in a further, third dimension.

II.3 Spatial Dynamics and Colonial Positioning

> Know ye the land of the cedar and vine,
> Where the flowers ever blossom, the beams ever shine;
> Where the light wings of Zephyr, oppress'd with perfume,
> Wax faint o'er the gardens of Gúl in her bloom;
> Where the citron and olive are fairest of fruit,
> And the voice of the nightingale never is mute;
> Where the tints of the earth, and the hues of the sky,
> In colour though varied, in beauty may vie?
>
> (Lord Byron, *The Bride of Abydos*, Canto the First, cited in Bergeaud trans. Hossman 7)

This romantic praise of nature, a quotation from Lord Byron, can be found at the beginning of *Stella*, a novel published in 1859 by the Haitian writer Émeric Bergeaud (Byron, whom we have already mentioned, was already heavily canonized in his own time). Lord Byron's poem in turn, at least in its first line, quotes directly from Goethe's "Mignon." Why is it that Caribbean writers take descriptions

---

38 Jürgen Osterhammel (826) has pointed out that the concept of civilization can only make sense in inextricable tension with its opposite: civilization reigns where barbarity or savagery has been conquered; civilization needs its opposite in order to remain recognizable. If barbarity were to disappear from the world, then we would have no standard of measurement with which to satisfy the civilized world's aggressively self-satisfied or defensively anxious need for validation. The less-civilized are necessary as an audience for the great spectacle of civilization.

of Italian nature by German or English poets and transfer them to Haiti in order to extol what is supposedly their "own"?[39]

The spatial tension that is thereby generated in this novel, the first novel of Haiti, still a very young state and therefore in an explicitly postcolonial situation, directly evokes the central question I will be addressing in the following: namely, what are the spatial dynamics that underlie the nineteenth-century texts that emerged from a specifically colonial or postcolonial situation? Or, more concretely: to what extent can a look at the staging of spatial dynamics in literary texts from a variety of colonial spheres contribute to the comparative research on colonialism? Using this approach, the first thing that becomes apparent is a paradigm shift from a spatial history to a history of movement (cf. Ette, *ZusammenLebensWissen* 16).

In order to make sure that our investigation is as representative as possible, we will hear from three literary exemplars from a variety of Caribbean colonial areas. I will be foregrounding the novel I cited above, *Stella* (1859), by the Haitian writer Émeric Bergeaud. In addition, we will also look briefly at *Outre-mer*, by Louis de Maynard de Queilhe and published in 1835, which has already been introduced, and *La peregrinación de Bayoán* (The pilgrimage of Bayoán), from 1863, by the Puerto Rican writer Eugenio María de Hostos. This gives us three voices from three very different colonial spheres: Bergeaud, from Haiti, which has gained its independence from France, contrasts with Maynard de Queilhe, a writer from the French colony of Martinique, which never became independent. Hostos, finally, as a representative of the Spanish colonial sphere, is the only one of the three who, even just from the point of view of the language, is situated in a context in which the pursuit of independence had a completely different meaning than what it had in the French colonial empire; the Caribbean islands, after all, were the last dependent American enclaves of Spain, the mother country (*Madre Patria España*). Simply looking at it from a historical viewpoint, therefore, *Stella* is the only one of these novels that can be considered part of a postcolonial situation. We will also need to examine here whether and to what extent the two other novels, which were both written before independence was achieved, can be read in the light of Ashcroft, Griffiths, and Tiffin's procedural understanding of the postcolonial.

The following analyses of the three novels will, on the one hand, concentrate on the novels' respective conceptions of space and their dynamics, taking into consideration the fact that spaces are culturally constituted or outright produced (in the sense of a pragmatic cultural concept of space); and, on the other, exam-

---

[39] For the following remarks cf. Müller, "'Une misérable petite île!'"

ine how they position themselves with respect to the colonial status quo. I will also look at possible interactions between these two phenomena. And in addition to these central questions, I will also be looking at an overarching issue that arises here: although it is not new to talk about a "spatial turn," my remarks in the following use this turn in the historical sciences, first noticed in the nineteen-sixties, as well as the "topographical turn" in the cultural sciences, as an occasion to explore the staging of spatial dynamics in nineteenth-century texts.[40]

I will also use this sharper focus on the staging of spatial dynamics to reexamine the assumption that the nineteenth century was a century defined by time. There is a long-established presumption that the supremacy of the spatial perspective was increasingly superseded by a temporal perspective, starting with the developmental and progress-oriented paradigm of the eighteenth-century Enlightenment; this is only strengthened by the colonialist conceptions of development, in conjunction with the nineteenth century's progress-related historical notions (Bachmann-Medick 212). The "topographical turn" is based on the experience of a break in the established equation of cultural identity with national territory or, to follow Benedict Anderson, the imagination of territorial spaces as homogenous spaces. This experience of a break is concentrated in the figure of displacement, which has taken the place of conventional concepts about migration such as exile and diaspora (Weigel 156).

Although the project of "cultural identity" already existed as a conceptual construct in the nineteenth century, it still seems to make sense, with texts from that time, to expect a literary arrangement that conveys precisely this equation of cultural identity with national territory. Thus, defenders of the "spatial turn" acknowledge that an age of imperialism necessarily involves a confrontation with the idea of space. And yet, from their point of view, this does not take into account an understanding of space in the sense of the "spatial turn," because it primarily concerns static structures and space as a purely physical mass.

The privileging of time in the nineteenth century seems particularly active in literary texts from Latin America and the Caribbean, where Chateaubriand was extremely popular. His omnipresent historical-chronological grounding is epitomized in his famous sentence from his *Memoirs from beyond the Tomb:* "I have found myself between two centuries as at the junction between two rivers; I have plunged into their troubled waters, regretfully leaving behind the ancient strand

---

[40] This is therefore not a systematic implementation of new categories, in the sense of a Kuhnian paradigm shift. For an overview of the state of the study of nineteenth-century American literature, with special regard to the series of field redefinitions that have taken place over the past two decades and have been consistently described as "turns," whether transnational, hemispheric, postnational, spatial, temporal, postsecular, aesthetic, or affective, see Blum.

where I was born and swimming hopefully towards the unknown shores where the new generations will land" (5).[41] It is an intense experience of time that is expressed here and, specifically, the prevailing feeling that the good ancien régime is in decline. Before I turn to the novels themselves, let me just say that I am primarily concerned here with interpretations of three texts that are representative of their respective colonial spheres, and that in these interpretations I focus on spatial dynamics, the positioning of the novels vis-à-vis the colonial status quo, and the interaction between these two phenomena. In a broader concluding discussion, then, I will also look briefly at the question of the overarching scholarly paradigm and address its applicability here.

II.3.1 Émeric Bergeaud: *Stella* (1859)

In writing *Stella*, Émeric Bergeaud (1818–1858) produced independent Haiti's first novel. The story takes place between 1789 and 1804, a time of political upheaval including the French Revolution and the abolition of slavery that radically changed the former island of Hispaniola and led the country into a long struggle for freedom as an independent nation.[42] Bergeaud employs the form of a fictionalized historiography, infused with elements of a tradition of poetic allegory, to describe the time of the wars of independence, using the example of the brothers Romulus and Remus as well as the figure of Stella, a personification of freedom, ending in a glorifying final scene in which he sings the praises of Haiti as a unified nation (Thiem 57). Marie l'Africaine, the mother, from the shelter of her little hut, tells her two sons, who have different skin colors, about their original roots: Romulus is the son of an African tribal chief, who was killed in a war in Africa; because he could no longer protect his village from the slave traders, the remaining members of the tribe were sold into slavery overseas. Romulus, therefore, conceived in Africa but born in the colony of Saint-Domingue, symbolizes the African origins of the Haitian population. Remus, on the other hand, is the result of Marie's rape by the plantation owner. His skin, therefore, is lighter than his brother's, and he stands as a symbol for the mulattos (61).

The treatment of space in the novel is immediately noticeable as a structuring framework. Because of how certain aspects of the content are attached to certain realms, a variety of different spaces arise that are characterized by their re-

---

41 "Je me suis rencontré entre deux siècles comme au confluent de deux fleuves; j'ai plongé dans leurs eaux troublées, m'éloignant avec regret du vieux rivage où je suis né nageant avec espérance vers une rive inconnue" (Chateaubriand, *Mémoires* 1047).
42 In my comments about *Stella* I am guided by Annegret Thiem's analysis (61 ff.).

spective semantic unity and therefore also delimitation. These spaces are, primarily, places, in the sense of geographical areas, which can be both concrete places with an extraliterary referent, such as for example Haiti, Paris, and Africa, and accessible places that have no direct extraliterary referent. Mountains, cities, and forests, for instance, are certainly places that are accessible to our field of experience, but in the text they represent a mixture of possible and fictional places, which means that they do not refer to anything outside of the text and that their spatial extension in our imagination is a purely intra-literary manifestation. Annegret Thiem sees the text as a whole as divisible, with the help of graphic fields, into five spheres or spaces that make it possible to understand the action of the story within a spatial structure; these five spheres are:

1. Saint-Domingue/Haiti: the homeland (*patrie*);
2. Europe/France/Paris: the mother country (*mère-patrie*);
3. battlegrounds: cities, forts, and fortifications (*villes, fort, fortification*);
4. natural spaces: mountains, woods, caves, rivers (*montagne, bois, grotte, rivière*); and
5. Africa.

The relationships among the various spaces are highly variable: there is a fundamental spatial opposition between the two spheres of Saint-Domingue/Haiti and Europe, which influence each other, refer to extra-literary places, and make it possible for figures to cross borders. On the other hand, in the spaces of Saint-Domingue/Haiti and of *montagne, bois, grotte, rivière*, the extraliterary and the intra-literary intermix, in a relationship of mutual influence (72). But the two spaces cannot possibly come into direct contact with each other.[43] The African sphere, though it has far-reaching consequences for the other spaces, shows no movement beyond Marie l'Africaine's original border crossing; this sphere is otherwise characterized by its static nature. The first sphere, that of Saint-Domingue/Haiti, has a double dimension: in most of the book, it functions as the space of colonial Saint-Domingue, but in the last two chapters it comes to fruition as the independent nation of Haiti. In the last chapter, the borders between the individual spheres become porous, thus allowing the spaces to interconnect with each other. They are synthesized here into one new, common space, the Haitian nation. Thus, the novel's spatial structure serves as a textual support

---

[43] In talking about the battleground, Thiem speaks of a "third space" (64). But in the light of how the term has been shaped by Homi Bhabha, I would just call this an "intermediate space," without however meaning the postcolonial "in-between" in this case.

for the nation's founding myth as well as anticipating that nation's hybrid and syncretistic character (64).

The territorial beauty of what is later to become the national space is decisive for the cultural positioning here. This is why Bergeaud, in describing the colony of Saint-Domingue, quotes Byron's and Goethe's paradisiac images, in order to emphasize the claim to the founding space that is yet to be established (68). The hymn of praise to nature is introduced with elements of romantic fairy tale structure: "In a fortunate land, at the heart of a captivating and lavishing environment ..." (Bergeaud trans. Hossman 7).[44] The audience is called upon directly to visit this island and allow itself to take in the influence of its natural beauty (Thiem 68). But the crucial element here is the omnipresence of knowledge about Western culture, according to which this beautiful nature must still be tamed and civilized. This, too, finally comes to pass in the final chapter, in which the foundations of civilization constitute the bedrock on which the nation can be formed (69).

> They know that one can only be truly happy via the soul and achieve strength with intelligence, and that these sublime faculties can only be developed after contact with civilization. Civilization does not exclude; it attracts rather than repels. It is through it that human bonds must be constructed. Thanks to its all-powerful influence, soon there will be no blacks, no whites, no yellows, no Africans, no Europeans, no Asians, no Americans, but only brothers. Civilization dispels, with all its light, barbarity when it wishes to hide. Wherever barbarity, in its dying voice, counsels war, civilization advocates for peace. When the word hate is uttered, civilization answers love. (Bergeaud trans. Hossman 201)[45]

This rigorous orientation towards European values means that the African sphere remains a place of memory alone (cf. Thiem 76)[46]: Thiem emphasizes, rightly, that here the actual civilizational values for establishing a cultural identity are directly connected to the European value system, and that the African space is therefore reduced from the status of a dynamic field of action to the

---

44 "Sur une terre fortunée, au sein d'une nature séduisante et prodigue de ses dons les plus précieux ..." (Bergeaud, *Stella* 1).
45 "Ils savent qu'on n'est réellement heureux que par l'âme, fort que par l'intelligence, et que ces facultés sublimes ne se développent qu'au contact de la civilisation. La civilisation n'est pas exclusive; elle attire au lieu de repousser. C'est par elle que doit s'opérer l'alliance du genre humain. Grâce à sa toute-puissante influence, il n'y aura bientôt sur la terre ni noirs, ni blancs, ni jaunes, ni Africains, ni Européens, ni Asiatiques, ni Américains: il y aura des frères. Elle poursuit de ses lumières la barbarie qui se cache. Partout où celle-ci, de sa voix mourante, conseille la guerre, la civilisation prêche la paix; et quand retentit le mot haine, elle répond amour" (Bergeaud, *Stella* 324).
46 This is not, however, a place of memory in Pierre Nora's sense.

purely imaginary status of a memory that has become static. This memory is one-dimensional and does not convey any movement. The author uses this national myth to attempt to lead Haiti out of the position of the Other and into the ranks of Western nations. In *Stella*, nation building takes place as an allegorical spatialization of historical time and events (Thiem 76). Its allegorical character expresses itself above all in the abstract figures, thus reinforcing the static and reduced image of the spatial configurations.

II.3.2 Maynard de Queilhe: *Outre-mer* (Overseas) (1835). Or: Creole Lianas

This brings us now to the representative from the French colonial sphere, Maynard de Queilhe, from Martinique. As is the case for most writers from the French Antilles, we have almost no exact biographical information about Maynard de Queilhe. What we do know is that he lived in Paris for a while, where he wrote his novel *Outre-mer*,[47] and that he was friends with Victor Hugo. There are some indications as well that his family sought political exile in Martinique after the French Revolution.

The long preface to *Outre-mer*, which contains a kind of ethnographic introduction, is revealing. It becomes clear that the Creole upper class is perfectly capable of identifying its spatial affiliation. Maynard de Queilhe expresses it this way: "The colonists only think of themselves as travelers in a land of exile; they always have their wings half-spread, ready to return to their former homeland" (Maynard de Queilhe I:13).[48] At the most, we might be able to detect a spatial indecisiveness with regard to the audience of the book: "There are, therefore, many things in this book which will seem strange, whether to the people of the country where I am or to the people of the country where you are" (I:12).[49] Alienation on both sides of the Atlantic? Not really, because in each case he is talking about the French or, respectively, Creole upper class.

Within the fiction of *Outre-mer*, it is the spatial positioning of the class of free mulattos that is thematized. Marius, the protagonist, is presented as being homeless; or, more precisely, he considers England, the country of his philanthropic adoptive father, to be his own spiritual fatherland:

---

[47] For a short summary of the contents of the novel, please see section II.2.2.
[48] "Les colons ne se considèrent que comme des passagers sur une terre d'exil; ils ont toujours les ailes entrouvertes, pour regagner leur ancienne patrie."
[49] "Il est ensuite beaucoup de choses de ce livre qui paraîtront étranges, tantôt aux personnes du pays où je suis, tantôt aux personnes du pays où vous êtes."

But for me to abandon my fatherland [England], not the one where I first saw the light of day [Martinique], a terrible day, which I curse and would be happy to return; no, the fatherland of my soul, where I grew up, where I was happy and free, where my intelligence was enriched and developed; to my eternal damnation, as I recognize now. Why is there an island called Martinique? Why am I here instead of somewhere else? (I:43)⁵⁰

While no scenes in the novel are actually set in England, the tension of the England-France-Martinique triangle pervades the entire novel, with Marius undergoing a purification process along the exact lines of the hero of a classical bildungsroman: from the youthful hero in postrevolutionary Paris, inspired by philosophy and revolution, to the more jaded, disillusioned advocate of the aristocratic, prerevolutionary system of slavery and the plantation economy.

The novel takes place in three geographical settings: Martinique, the colony; France, the mother country (*mère-patrie*); and the ship, which is clearly bound for the French mother country. The ship's focus on its destination and the straightness of its route, however, only emphasize the bipolarity between mother country and colony. This spatial bipolarity is also reflected in the textual space: first, on the level of the constellations of protagonists, namely good Creoles, bad blacks, and the supposedly noble mulatto who is unmasked in the end as a rebellious Satan; and second, on the level of the book's literary role models, because the author's reliance on Bernardin de Saint-Pierre, Victor Hugo, and George Sand is everywhere in evidence, in the sense of René Girard's mimetic theory or, to use the vocabulary of postcolonical theory, as mimicry.[51] It is not for nothing that Maynard de Queilhe's mimetic proceedings have been compared to the behavior of the tropical climbing liana (Bongie, *Islands and Exiles* 319). Lianas shoot into the air without branching; the colonial offshoots cluster around the mother plant.

The bipolar spatial structure that is found in *Outre-mer* is also underscored by Martinique's function as an island.[52] This takes place in the context of a con-

---

50 "Mais, moi, abandonner ma patrie, non celle où j'ai reçu le jour, jour affreux, que je maudis et que je suis prêt à rendre; mais celle de mon âme, où j'ai grandi, où j'ai été heureux et libre, où mon intelligence s'est enrichi et développée; pour ma damnation éternelle, je le reconnais à cette heure. Pourquoi existe-t-il une île appelée Martinique? pourquoi suis-je ici plutôt qu'autrepart?"
51 The fact that the literature of the nineteenth-century French Antilles—which Patrick Chamoiseau and Raphaël Confiant call "doudouist literature"—lacks originality has already become almost a cliché of Franco-Caribbean literary studies. But this observation does not in any way detract from the wealth of cultural history that is transmitted through a careful analysis of the process of copying.
52 On the island function, see also III.6.

temporary trend in island motifs: as with the Île de Bourbon (actually Réunion Island) in George Sand's *Indiana* and the Île de France (in other words, Mauritius) in Bernardin de Saint-Pierre's *Paul et Virginie*, Martinique is characterized here by an island semantics of isolation and exile (Ette, "Von Inseln" 143).

II.3.3 Eugenio María de Hostos: *La peregrinación de Bayoán* (The Pilgrimage of Bayoán) (1863). Or: A Pilgrim in the Mangroves

> Going to Cuba, to Darién, from Darién to Peru, from Peru to Mexico, from Mexico to Havana ... and staying in Nuevitas to go to Cat Island (San Salvador de Colón, the Indian Guanahani) and then, when I return, visiting my friends, ... and with all this effort preparing myself for my pilgrimage to Europe. (Hostos, *Peregrinación* I:108)[53]

This quotation, out of the mouth of the homeless protagonist in *La peregrinación de Bayoán*, is a pronouncement of a programmatic nature. Significantly, the novel was confiscated by the Spanish authorities shortly after its appearance. This may have been because of the text's anti-Spanish goals and because of the rebellion of the Antilles against the oppression of the Spanish nation, both of which Hostos makes explicit in his novel. The political dimension of the novel is the utopia of a search for a universal Caribbean identity (Thiem 184).

> To leave! In order to find a way to make my unhappy Boriquen happy, to set an example, and to prepare for the emergence of a country that I do not yet have? ... To leave ... ! But where to? To travel through continental America, to think about its future and to provoke it? To Europe, in order to convince it that America is the predestined site for a future civilization? ... I will leave. (Hostos, *Peregrinación* I:149)[54]

In an obvious allusion to Christopher Columbus's travel journals, the novel, written in the form of a diary, begins with notations for October 12th, the day of Columbus's discovery of America.[55] The young Puerto Rican Bayoán, whose name

---

53 "ir a Cuba, al Darién, del Darién al Perú; del Perú al Méjico; de Méjico a La Habana ... y en Nuevitas quedarme para ir a Cat Island (San Salvador de Colón, indiana Guanahaní) y al volver, visitar a los amigos, ... que en tanto empeño tiene en que me prepare, para mi peregrinación a Europa."
54 "¡Partir! ¿Para encontrar los medios de hacer feliz a mi infeliz Boriquen, para dar el ejemplo, y preparar el advenimiento de una patria que hoy no tengo? ... ¡Partir ... ! ¿adónde? ¿A viajar por la América continental, a pensar en su porvenir y a provocarlo? ¿A Europa, a convencerla de que América es el lugar predestinado de una civilización futura? ... Partiré."
55 It is not an accident that Bayoán's travels do not start with some beginning point but instead take Columbus's discovery document as their basis. The figure of Columbus, as presented by

is borrowed "from the first native of Boriquen who doubted the Spaniards' immortality" (according to Hostos, in the novel's guide to names), leaves his home island by ship with the goal, at first only vaguely formulated, of visiting the Caribbean islands and the Latin American mainland (Thiem 186). Bayoán records some notes while on board. In this novel, the ship, unlike in *Outre-mer*, represents a kind of threshold space. It can be seen as a vehicle that crosses the boundaries of timeframes, transporting the protagonist from one level to another, thus allowing an oscillation between timeframes and spaces: "The wind pushed the frigate, and the frigate walked the way that I walk, pushed by a wind about which I still do not know whether it leads to port" (Hostos, *Peregrinación* I:192).[56]

Bayoán is torn back and forth between the Antilles and Spain (and wants to prove his strength to Spain); his inner struggle has to do with the future direction of his life (Thiem 199). This ever-present conflict and process of initiation leads him to develop his consciousness, so that at the end, he, who was homeless, clearly realizes where his voyage is going to lead: "America is my homeland" (*América es mi patria*; Hostos, *Peregrinación* I:355; cf. Thiem 199). Bayoán's pilgrimage structures the literary space: "I am a man wandering in a desert, and you [addressing his homeland] are my only oasis. I am a pilgrim. ... Must I make this pilgrimage? Well then, onward!" (Hostos, *Peregrinación* I:18).[57] His voyage appears as a multidimensional search, an expression of openness but also of foreignness; the pilgrimage motif includes being oriented towards a goal but also the idea of the journey as the goal. This results in a circular structure that is often broken.

In taking on the pilgrimage as a literary element that structures space, the open status of the pilgrimage is constitutive: the construction, institutionalization, and functionalization of the system of the pilgrimage are subject to evolutionary dynamics that are linked, to varying degrees of looseness or strictness, to the developments of the overarching functional religious system (Hassauer 19). In the transmission of the medieval pilgrimage motif, the idea of sacrifice is cer-

---

Hostos, is in a constant state of flux: on the one hand, Hostos emphasizes Columbus's importance (particularly with respect to his concern with fulfilling a civilizing mission, opening America up to Europeans, and saving the continent from darkness and savagery); on the other, Hostos definitely also problematizes the negative side of the arrival of the Europeans. Richard Rosa makes it clear that Bayoán cannot take sides either for or against the figure of Columbus.

56 "El viento empujaba a la fragata, y la fragata andaba como ando yo, empujado por un viento que aún no sé si lleva a puerto."

57 "Yo soy un hombre errante en un desierto, y mi único oasis eres tú [se está dirigiendo a su patria]. Yo soy un peregrino... ¿Necesito peregrinar? Pues, ¡adelante!"

tainly uppermost, and that is what we see reflected in Bayoán, on a political level. Although I cannot claim that Hostos had read the works of Hegel or Nietzsche, the novel was produced in the context of the modern critique of sacrifice, in an environment that was critical towards religion and in which Anselm of Canterbury's satisfaction theory of atonement, which formed the basis of the Christian doctrine of sacrifice, had gained a political dimension. This is also how Bayoán's pilgrimage should be interpreted, because he has to make a sacrifice for the freedom of the Spanish colonies by undertaking the arduous journey through the Caribbean archipelago, Latin America, and Europe. And it is not for nothing that the structure of the circle is what the pilgrimage motif makes into the central structure here, given that Hostos's allusion to Columbus's logbook is so crucial. It was after all the return to his starting point in Europe (and the honor he was given there by the Catholic monarchs) that gave meaning and legitimacy to Columbus's voyage of discovery, with its first stop in the Antilles.

Pilgrimage is a very fundamental literary motif in the nineteenth century. The single greatest bestseller of that time was Lord Byron's *Childe Harold's Pilgrimage. A Romaunt*; as I have already mentioned in the context of Bergeaud and Heredia, Byron was extremely popular, and with the publication of *Childe Harold* in 1812, 1816, and 1818, Byron became famous overnight. The protagonists of such canonical novels as Jorge Isaacs's *María* and José Mármol's *Amalia* can be found reading the book. How can we explain this fashion trend? Is it the romantic symbol per se of an unbridled yearning for freedom? The sublime image of the ocean: unlimited, timeless, not subject to humankind? (Post)colonial reception theory offers us the following possible interpretation: Byron explains Ireland's "oriental status" first through its subjugation to England and secondly by ascribing the attributes of "wildness, tenderness and originality" to Ireland (Ogden 117). This combination may have been what fostered the large number of references to Byron among Latin American and Caribbean authors; Hostos himself expressed a deep admiration for Byron. He was finally less interested in freedom, which only concerned Puerto Rico, than in sketching out a complete Spanish-American project that included the beginnings of an Antillean confederation. Although the clearly political dimension, transmitted in particular through the option of sacrifice, belongs to an earlier century, the pilgrimage motif can definitely be read as an early form of nomadism, à la Vilém Flusser, or of the rhizomatic migrant, à la Deleuze/Guattari. The most convincing reading is Hostos's anticipation of the ideas of Édouard Glissant, specifically Glissant's concept of *Antillanité*, which is not based on any one-dimensional nationalistic perspective but, rather, on the structure of the mangrove.

II.3.4 Conclusions

All three of these texts suggest a reading based on the equation of cultural identity with national territory. Thus, in this respect, it cannot be said that the nineteenth-century novels described here manifest a clear paradigm shift towards the topographical. And yet the examination of spatial dynamics in the three works has provided important new recognitions within the context of comparative postcolonial research.

It is undisputed that the literature of the nineteenth century is characterized by physically perceptible conceptions of space. In my analysis here, however, I have not been able to confirm the generally accepted thesis that the nineteenth century is a century defined by time, but this is not by any means because the category of time was deliberately ignored. On the contrary, insofar as time functions as a constitutive factor of dynamics and movement, it was the juxtaposition of the two ship metaphors that was able to make the various spatial dynamics productive. It cannot be equally claimed for all three of the novels that the figure of displacement, in Sigrid Weigel's words, has replaced the conventional migration concepts of exile and diaspora. And yet the toolkit of spatial theory provides important keys to the basic understanding of postcolonial positioning. Guadeloupe and Martinique, subject to France's division into departments, have not lost their colonial status to this day. The political and cultural gravitational pull of French colonialism was far more formative and effective than the Spanish model. Thus, in *Outre-mer*, the concept of exile works strikingly well. The binary opposition between the metropolis and the colony is unbroken there. The novel can be read as a perfect example of the "mapping of empire," as Edward Said uses the term (Bachmann-Medick 235).

In *Stella*, the much more complicated spatial structure suggests that the multirelationalism of young Haitian society has far-reaching spatial implications. *Stella* represents colonial independence in that the novel shows the extent to which the young country of Haiti consolidates the connections between external and internal relationalisms. The individual spaces in *Stella*, however, appear to be very static. This has to do with the irresolvable contradiction in Haitian self-understanding, proclaiming political independence while simultaneously affirming cultural dependence.[58] While Haiti is a special case in every respect, not only in the Caribbean but in the entire Western hemisphere, the two other novels con-

---

[58] Masillon Coicou's famous 1892 pronouncement is a symptom of this: "Yes, France, we love you very much, in a way that several of your own children will never love you." ("Oui, France, nous t'aimons beaucoup, comme plusieurs de tes propres enfants ne t'aimerons jamais.") (113).

vey spatial perspectives that differ from this, as clearly reflected in the titles: *Outre-mer* (Overseas) by Maynard de Queilhe, as an affirmation of the colonial status quo, represents the one-dimensional colonial view, while *La peregrinación de Bayoán* (Bayoán's Pilgrimage) is based on the moment of movement. *La peregrinación de Bayoán*'s understanding of the Caribbean archipelago projects an island-based logic and emphasizes the internal relationalism of that logic (Ette, *Writing-between-worlds* 153). In this novel, the Caribbean symbolizes the concept of a third space (in Bhabha's usage of that term), which offered itself beyond the "hypnoses Europe and Africa" (Bernabé, Chamoiseau, and Confiant 22, cited in Ette, *Literature on the Move* 256). Where *Outre-mer* presents a colonial discourse, oriented towards Europe, and *Stella* puts forward an anticolonial discourse, oriented towards Africa, what we find in *La peregrinación de Bayoán* is a different, postcolonial discourse, one which makes a new kind of spatial conception possible. *Bayoán* is an American discourse, with independentist traditions, making reference to the connections across all of the Americas. Although nineteenth-century texts do not manifest the same kind of radical structure of movement that we see in twentieth- and twenty-first-century texts, *La peregrinación de Bayoán* and, to a certain extent, *Stella* as well, do anticipate Glissant's assertion of a relational conception of space. The spatial turn asserts that it refers not to physical space nor to natural space but to socially produced space as a dynamic process. Physics and nature are undeniably important categories for the nineteenth century, and postcolonial interpretation would not be possible without them. And yet the new theories of interconnectedness, relationalism, and movement sensitize us to dimensions that were more present, even before the postmodern turn, than has been assumed. These three novels convey the overlaps that result from the simultaneity of unequal spaces and territories, the ways in which spaces are charged through imperial inscriptions, hidden hierarchies, displaced experiences, and breaks in continuity.

III Literary Snapshots of the In-Between

"Who knows how many slaves will someday owe their freedom to the poets!" writes the Cuban Félix Tanco enthusiastically, in a letter to Domingo del Monte. The following observations support the thesis, of which Tanco's statement is the best illustration, that literature, as Edward Said says, anticipates political developments and that cultural dimensions are what make up the depths of imperialism, or may even precede political imperialism. In the light of these assumptions, this chapter responds to two main questions:

1. In my opinion, colonialism research (which continues to flourish) tends to divide its field of study into linguistic and cultural units, whereas its theorization aims to find generalizations. The colonial history of cultural and literary entanglement, in the sense of a colonial *histoire croisée* (the history of colonial interconnections), on the other hand, tends to be somewhat neglected. And this is exactly where the Caribbean offers an enormous potential for examining not just the hegemonic axes but also intercolonial transfers, thanks to the immediate juxtaposition of different colonial cultures. It is well-known that French nineteenth-century colonialism was far more successful than the Spanish version. Long before the loss of its last colonies in 1898, Spain was already in a steady decline, whereas it was not until the nineteenth century that the French idea of a civilizing mission really blossomed (aside from the painful loss of Haiti, whose violent emancipation was taken as an alarm signal far beyond the French colonial sphere). On the political level, France's cultural gravitational force proved to be long-lasting: the French Antilles remained a part of the mother country and became overseas departments in 1946. I would like to take these rough findings as a starting point for asking in what ways the literary texts of the Spanish and French Caribbean anticipate political developments. What can they contribute to an examination of a colonial *histoire croisée?* And very specifically: does the literary production of the French and Spanish Caribbean offer us indications of the perpetuation of the French model and the decline of the Spanish one? I will focus here on how the literature positions itself with respect to colonialism, primarily in terms of the two main themes of the nineteenth-century Caribbean, namely independence and abolition.
2. I will be looking primarily at literary transfer processes within, into, and out of the Caribbean, which have been relatively neglected until now. This involves both extraliterary and intra-literary dimensions. Which transfers are staged how? Or: which versions of reception, appropriation, and transformation have taken which paths?

I do not by any means propose to consider the two constellations of questions in isolation from each other; the interconnections between, on the one hand, the scope, character, and range of the transfer and, on the other, the political and cultural positioning are precisely what interest me.

Transfer processes are multidimensional, whether in the framework of investigations of the festival as a basic anthropological constant and site of transculturation, or in the context of a history of harbors, seen as inherent meeting places. There are also, of course, important transfers that take place within the circulation of ideas, for our purposes in particular very often in reference to the various ways in which the Haitian Revolution is transmitted. Further examples could include traveling theater groups (Reinstädler, *Theatralisierung*), immigration policies that emphasize whiteness out of fear of Africanization (cf. Naranjo Orovio; Chinea),[1] and carriers of subversive knowledge, such as pirates, as the protagonists of an early version of globalization from the bottom up (cf. Arnold). What all of these investigations (which I believe are very valuable) have in common is that they look away from static comparative models towards forms of exchange and new forms of movement that have so far been underestimated.

In the following expositions, we will be dealing with literary snapshots of an in-between; I consciously refrain from typologizing them and instead use them to try to capture a multiplicity of aspects. The time period under consideration, 1789 to 1886, is one that, for the Caribbean in particular, consolidates the results of the second phase of accelerated globalization;[2] on the literary level, all of the

---

1 Naranjo Orovio shows the kinds of fearful reactions that were unleashed on the neighboring island of Cuba by the Haitian Revolution and its upheavals. Naranjo Orovio addresses the "ghost of barbarism," a fear legend that the Spanish colonial authorities and the local elites nourished and used to fortify Spain's colonial preeminence in Cuba and Puerto Rico through the end of the nineteenth century. The well-established concepts of civilization and barbarism, and their inversion in Haiti's case, played an important role here. Cf. also Abel, "Tagungsbericht" 476. Chinea shows how the fear and anxiety of the slave owners, provoked by the immigration and the presence of Free People of Color coming from the Caribbean to Puerto Rico, led to racist laws.

2 The dynamics of globalization in the nineteenth century are particularly intense around the connection between globalization and the civilizing mission. In the early modern period there did not yet exist the conviction that European civilization was the only civilization worthy of the name; this globalization of civilizational norms was new in the long nineteenth century and presumed that older balances, whether military, economic, or cultural, between Europe and the other continents, had been disrupted. The successes of the nineteenth century's civilizing missions were based on two further preconditions as well: first, the conviction (not just on the part of the representatives of the European power elites but also on the part of private agents of globalization of many different kinds) that the world would be a better place if as many non-Europeans as possible were to adopt the accomplishments of the superior civilization; and sec-

authors presented here are committed to the ideal of romantic writing. Insofar as we think of time and space together, in the history of movement that derives from their combination, and focus primarily on the transfer and translation of knowledge, we will be looking at "thinking about globality as the archeology of its mobility" (to use Ottmar Ette's words about Alexander von Humboldt) (Ette, *Alexander von Humboldt* 92).[3]

In both of the colonial empires, this is a time of overlaps in which, as far as colonial dependence is concerned, the colonial status quo is maintained, with the sole exception of the island of Hispaniola. The year 1848 marks an important dividing line, when slavery is abolished in the French colonial empire. Because of that, the texts are grouped around an event that radically changed the societies or, in the case of the Spanish colonies, made the question of abolition even more pressing because of what was happening in their immediate surroundings. Almost all of the textual examples are the literary testimonies of the writing Creole upper class, which, although it does not come anywhere near to reflecting the "holistic condition" of a society, is nevertheless alone responsible, in a decisive way, for the establishment of the prevailing discourses and is therefore writing an *écriture blanche* (cf. Bremer 336). However, this does not mean that this is the gaze of "imperial eyes" (cf. Pratt).

III.1 The Creole Upper Class

Creole writing was the expression of a permanent in-between-ness, an inner rift, that could on the one hand have very destructive effects, keeping the writer rigidly stuck in conservative thought patterns, but could also, on the other hand, be highly productive.[4] The very term "Creole" is already very difficult to define. The following examples come from the pens of Euro-Creoles, that is to say representatives of the white upper class who were born in the Antilles and stayed in constant contact with the metropolises of their respective mother countrys. The difficulty of establishing any clear position often manifests itself in a particularly fraught struggle by this colonial class for the confidence that they are compatible

---

ond, the appearance of social forces at the numerous peripheries that shared this view as well. Cf. Osterhammel 911 ff.

[3] "Denken der Globalität als Archäologie ihrer Mobilität."
[4] It has never been possible—even before the nineteenth century or in parts of the world other than the Caribbean—to write a history of the Creoles from one central perspective, and definitely not according to the European pattern of a "total, panoramically illuminating, central perspective." Cf. Ette, *ZusammenLebensWissen* 17.

with the elite of the center. Thus the thriving theater life in Saint-Pierre, then the capital of Martinique, is described as follows in Prévost de Sansac de Traversay's *Les amours de Zémédare et Carina* (The Loves of Zémédare and Carina) (1806)[5]:

> Saint-Pierre was the only city in Martinique that had a theater. Troupes would come from Paris every year to put on shows there. And these shows were usually good, because the public was knowledgeable and sometimes quite demanding, especially in matters of singing or music. (8)[6]

Prévost de Sansac's description of the inhabitants of what he calls the richest French colony of the time is similar:

> Martinique, one of the windward islands in the American archipelago, is today the most flourishing and most precious of France's colonies. The richness of its soil, the beauty of its climate, and its cleanliness make it worthy to be inhabited by the most generous, the most affable, and the best of men. The Martinicans, who are naturally spiritual, loyal, loving, and in general well-made, are all valiant. There are few countries where one sees a larger number, proportionally speaking, of pretty women. (21)[7]

Mr. Saimprale, one of the main characters in *Les amours de Zémédare et Carina*, has never been to Europe. But the narrator immediately attempts to defuse this "deficit" by referring to his excellent education: "Mr. Saimprale had never been to Europe; nevertheless, the care that his father had taken with his education put him on a level with men who were considered to be of the best society. His morals were tender, his face pleasant" (25).[8] Behind such descriptions there lurks the idea that the Creole upper class should be described in a thoroughly positive

---

[5] Corzani (II:301) describes *Les amours de Zémédare et Carina* as the first novel about Martinique by a Martinican writer.
[6] "Saint-Pierre était la seule ville de la Martinique à posséder un théâtre. Des troupes venaient, chaque année, de Paris, y donner des spectacles. Et ces spectacles étaient généralement de qualité, car le public était connaisseur, et il se montrait parfois exigeant, surtout quand il s'agissait de chant ou de musique."
[7] "La Martinique, une des îles du vent de l'archipel américain, est aujourd'hui la colonie la plus florissante et la plus précieuse de celles que la France possède. La richesse de son sol, la beauté de son climat et sa salubrité, la rendent bien digne d'être habitée par les plus généreux, les plus affables et les meilleurs des hommes. Les Martiniquais, naturellement spirituels, fidèles, aimants, en général bien faits, sont tous braves. Il est peu de pays où l'on voie, proportion gardée, un plus grand nombre de jolies femmes."
[8] "M. Saimprale n'avait jamais été en Europe; cependant le soin que son père avait pris de son éducation le mettait de pair avec les hommes réputés pour être de la meilleure société. Ses mœurs étaient douces, sa figure agréable."

way. *Les amours de Zémédare et Carina* is a colonial pro-slavery novel. It develops the picture of a Creole slave owner who is primarily a protector:

> The fair master is always well served by his slaves, esteemed by his compatriots, and protected by the government. The cruel master ... there isn't any among the white men on Martinique; looked on with horror by all, he would soon be forced to leave the island. Without trying to justify slavery here, I simply observe that the world's earliest records speak of its existence: we have seen it persist across all the centuries, and even in Sparta, the most republican of all governments. It has never been possible to successfully entrust the cultivation of the soil in the tropics to white men; they cannot endure this arduous work. The Negroes, all across the vast expanse of the coast of Africa, only use their freedom to satisfy their stupid ferocity, to make war on each other, to destroy and devour each other. In our colonies, in contrast, see their gaiety, their pleasures, and the moderation of their work; they are without worries for the future; they know love and can freely enjoy the happiness of being fathers. ... Laborers of Europe, ... and you especially, you serfs attached to the land in Poland and in Russia; you whom we so often see anxious about your existence and that of your family: tell us whether the Negroes in the colonies are the unhappiest beings on earth. (61)[9]

It is characteristic of the Creole upper class's orientation towards France that they always keep one foot in the mother country: "We shall not transport our fortune there, because it may well be that one day some of our children, or even we ourselves, will be very glad to find it again in France" (183).[10]

In J. Levilloux's novel *Les créoles ou la Vie aux Antilles* (The Creoles or Life in the Antilles),[11] France is consistently glorified as a colonial power and a site of education. The reason for Estève being sent to France is clearly articulated: "his

---

[9] "Le maître juste est toujours bien servi par ses esclaves, estimé de ses compatriotes et protégé par le gouvernement. Le maître inhumain ... il n'en existe point parmi les hommes blancs, à la Martinique, vu avec horreur par tous, on le forcerait bientôt à sortir de l'île. Sans vouloir chercher à justifier ici l'esclavage, j'observai seulement que les premiers annales du monde parlent de son existence: on l'a vue se maintenir dans tous les siècles, et même à Sparte, le plus républicain de tous les gouvernements. La culture des terres, entre les tropiques, n'a jamais pu être confiée, avec succès, à des hommes blancs; ils n'y peuvent résister à ce travail pénible. Les nègres, dans toutes la vaste étendue de la côte d'Afrique, n'usent de leur liberté que pour assouvir leur stupide férocité, se faire la guerre, se détruire et se dévorer entr'eux. Dans nos colonies, au contraire, voyez leur gaîté, leurs plaisirs et la modération de leur travail; ils sont sans souci sur l'avenir; ils connaissent l'amour, et jouissent librement du bonheur d'être pères. ... Journaliers d'Europe, ... et vous surtout, serfs attachés à la glèbe en Pologne et en Russie; vous que l'on voit si souvent inquiets sur votre existence et sur celle de votre famille, dites-nous si les nègres, dans les colonies, sont les êtres les plus malheureux sur la terre."
[10] "Nous n'y transporterons point notre fortune, parce qu'il est possible que quelques-uns de nos enfants et peut-être nous-mêmes, nous soyons très aises un jour de la retrouver en France."
[11] For a short summary of the novel please see section II.1.3.2.

father, a planter in Guadeloupe, had sent his son to France when he was very young to draw from the beautiful knowledge that at that time was rarely to be found in the colonies" (20).[12] Just before the two protagonists return to Guadeloupe from Paris, Edmond (a white Creole) reassures Estève (who is mulatto), telling him that it is still too early for them to worry about the survival of their friendship: "We are still in France, let us take advantage of the equality that we are fortunate enough to enjoy here. On the other side of the ocean our friendship, even in its embarrassment, will draw the means to sustain itself without exciting the scandal of color-based prejudice" (32).[13] Meanwhile, Edmond's sister Lea is particularly excited about her brother's return because he will be bringing her news from the metropolis:

> She impatiently awaited the return of her brother Edmond, who was bringing her seductive accounts of the marvels of Paris and whose science, enlarged by her naïve imagination, would reveal to her a multitude of secrets that only a young man raised in Europe could know. (38)[14]

Les amours de Zémédare et Carina refers to two academies on Martinique, not exactly offering an equivalent option to the fixation on Paris's educational institutions but at least presenting an alternative solution on the island:

> If this boarding school and Saint Victor's Academy, which have already rendered the greatest services to this colony, were to cease to exist, it would be an incalculable loss for all the inhabitants of Martinique and of the neighboring islands who are not wealthy enough to send their children to France to be raised there, or who do not want to send them there until they are of a certain age, and to perfect their earlier education. It is, if I dare say so, in the interest and the duty of the government to devote all its care to preserving these two important establishments. (Prévost de Sansac 142)[15]

---

12 "son père, planteur à la Guadeloupe, avait envoyé son fils, jeune, en France, y puiser ces belles connaissances qui, à cette époque, se rencontraient rarement aux colonies."
13 "Nous sommes encore en France, profitons de l'égalité dont on a le bonheur d'y jouir. Au-delà de l'Océan notre amitié puisera dans sa gêne même les moyens de s'entretenir sans exciter le scandale des préjugés de couleur."
14 "Elle attendait avec impatience le retour de son frère Edmond qui lui apportait de séduisans récits sur les merveilles de Paris, et dont la science agrandie dans sa naïve imagination lui révélait une foule de secrets que pouvait seul connaître un jeune homme élevé en Europe."
15 "Si cette pension et le collège de Saint-Victor, qui ont déjà rendu les plus grands services à cette colonie, cessaient d'y exister, ce serait une perte inappréciable pour tous les habitants de la Martinique et ceux des îles voisines, qui n'ont pas assez de fortune pour envoyer leurs enfants en France pour y être élevés, ou qui ne veulent les y envoyer qu'à un certain âge et pour y perfectionner leur première éducation. Il est j'ose le dire, de l'intérêt et du devoir du gouvernement d'apporter tous ses soins à la conservation de ces deux établissements importants."

In spite of all of the glorification of the metropolis, however, the colonies themselves also serve as models for the future, even appearing as sites for utopias: "People felt the old world crumbling beneath their feet and were already throwing themselves towards that future, so near, where a new society was to be rebuilt" (Levilloux 21).[16] The political environment of the July Monarchy seemed favorable for an imminent abolition of slavery, which brought up urgent fears of loss among the plantation-owning oligarchy. In the eighteen-thirties, people were reminded of the runup to 1789. The loss of the ancien régime still haunted the writers of the Creole upper class.

Reading Maynard de Queilhe's 1835 novel *Outre-mer*, one gets the sense of a society that is stuck, a Creole caste driven by fear of losing its old privileges. Two of the protagonists have the author's particular sympathy: Mme de Château, who brings the news of the *trois glorieuses* (the three glorious days of July 26 through 28, 1830) and who wears a black dress that she never takes off anymore; and the Marquis de Longuefort, who says "The people of France are a horrible people" (Maynard de Queilhe II:178, 183).[17] The utterances of Marius, the mulatto, seem to be written into a discourse of dissension. After his studies in France he curses Martinique, the island of his origins:

> A miserable little island! Less than an island, a kind of islet; fevers, snakes, and beings that give themselves lashes of the whip because they are not equally yellow, or because some of them are too much so and others not enough; or maybe because there are some of them who are not yellow at all. Misery! Miseries! (I:42)[18]

The narrators of the two novels *Outre-mer* and *Les créoles* evaluate the fixation on France and the rejection of the colonial homeland by their respective mulatto heroes in entirely different ways, however. Marius reproduces the slogans of equality that he has picked up in the mother country and gets worked up about the racial mania of his country of origin, only to gradually realize, after his return, how unrealistic the egalitarian ideas of the French Revolution are and how thoroughly they miss the point of the colonial reality and the actual inequality and unequal value of people of differing skin colors and origins. In a

---

16 "Les hommes sentaient le vieux monde s'abîmer sous leur pieds et se jetaient déjà vers cet avenir si prochain où devait se reconstruire une nouvelle société."
17 "C'est un affreux peuple que ce peuple de France."
18 "Une misérable petite île! moins qu'une île, une espèce d'îlet; des fièvres, des serpents et des êtres qui se donnent des coups de fouet, parce qu'ils ne sont pas tous également jaunes, ou parce que les uns le sont trop et les autre pas assez; ou parce qu'il y en a qui ne le sont pas du tout. Misère! misères!"

process of refinement, along the lines of a classical bildungsroman, he laboriously discovers that the philanthropic ideas that come out of certain circles in Paris and London unfairly discredit the well-established plantation system.

The fate of Levilloux's mulatto protagonist, Estève, on the other hand, is tragic, not just because the societal barriers mean that he cannot live out his love for his white friend's sister but because, in his fruitless attempts to gain recognition in white Creole society, he also enrolls in the fight against the rebellious black slaves. In order to be whiter than the whites, he allows himself to be yoked into the active exclusion of those who are racially even lower than he is, instead of seeking solidarity with them; he participates in the suppression of one of the numerous rebellions of the black slaves. While Estève's hymn of love to the mother country is enduring, and is able to withstand the repugnant and anti-egalitarian reality of the colony, for Marius the "achievements" of the mother country prove to be nothing more than hot air. It is not that the colony is hobbling after the mother country in vain, but that the ideas of the mother country have not caught up with reality and with the specific experiences of the *conviviality* of various races in the colonies. The revolution's castles in the air, which ultimately turn out to be foolish, seriously threaten the status quo, represented as a paradise.

The Creole upper class is a population group that is in a genuinely in-between space, even if this brokenness and turmoil manifests itself in very different ways.

III.2 The Conceptual Inadequacy of the Terms *patrie*/Nation/Exile

What the literary texts of the French and Spanish Caribbean have in common is that the attributions of nation, *patrie*, and exile are not always able to work unambiguously. The writing Creole upper class was in a permanent state of in-between-ness. In the valuable paratext of his foreword to *Outre-mer*, Maynard de Queilhe describes the self-understanding of the Creoles as exiled French people, ready at any moment to return home to the "old father country" (I:13): in other words, the colonies are just a way station. The novel itself is clearly marked: it is signed by a "Frenchman from America." Maynard de Queilhe himself is living an exile experience in the Antilles, characterized by longing for the mother country.

On an intra-literary level, it is telling for our line of questioning that with his hero, the mulatto Marius, Maynard de Queilhe transfers a particular kind of exile experience, one that is symptomatic for the new competitors of the *Békés:* that of the class of free people of color, a class that first began its social rise in 1830 and has almost the same rights as whites do. This new class is homeless, which means that precisely because of its homelessness, it can freely choose its new spiritual home. And what it has chosen as its *patrie* is not France, but England. No wonder, especially since slavery has long since been abolished in the British colonial empire and the mulattos, too, already had other rights (I:43).

In Levilloux's work, France always represents a clear point of reference, for instance when the principal introduces Edmond Briolan as a new student. The colony is "*le pays*," "the country": "'My children,' says the principal, 'I present a new classmate to you. His country is far away, and being alone in France now, he will need your friendship'" (Levilloux 20).[19] A return to the island of Guadeloupe, however, means a return to the *patrie:* "We are returning to our fatherland [*patrie*], but at least we know the obstacles that our affection will have to overcome" (21).[20] On the other hand, from the moment that Briolan and Estève leave the French mainland, they are "exiles." More than that, they are like travelers heading off into the desert:

> Thus our young exiles took away with them in their hearts an entire France of emotions, of memories, and of consoling thoughts for the hours of bitterness. In this they were like travelers leaving for the desert who put their hopes of salvation in the abundance of their supplies. But the fires of the sun will dry up their wineskins, the impure insects will taint their fruits and meats; and the unhappy travelers, instead of being able to draw life from them, will find there only disgust and more regrets. (32)[21]

While on the one hand their absence from Paris is described as an exile, the Caribbean also appears, on the other hand, as a place of longing, and the thought of an exile is always present when Edmond's and Estève's native region is discussed:

---

[19] "Mes enfants, dit le recteur, je vous présente un nouveau camarade. Son pays est éloigné, et bientôt seul en France, il aura besoin de votre amitié."
[20] "Nous retournons dans notre patrie, mais nous connaissons du moins les obstacles que notre affection aura à surmonter."
[21] "Ainsi nos jeunes exilés emportaient dans leur cœur toute une France d'émotions, de souvenirs et de consolantes pensées pour les heures d'amertume. En cela, semblables aux voyageurs partant pour le désert, et qui mettent leurs espérances de salut dans l'abondance de provisions. Mais les feux du soleil dessècheront leurs outres, les insectes impurs corrompront leurs fruits et leurs viandes; et les malheureux, au lieu d'y puiser la vie trouveront que dégoût et surcroît de regres."

> Martinique sketches its fertile shores in front of my eyes ... but in the middle of my emotions a bitter thought cuts across my soul, and I avert my gaze to turn it towards this land of exile. (201)[22]
>
> Weary of the land of exile, not knowing where to lay his head, which no longer slept. ... I cannot die in exile. (208)[23]

The concept of the "nation" is also used in an interesting way here. In *Les créoles ou la Vie aux Antilles*, for instance, the black population groups are referred to as nations: "He had barely pronounced the first words when some Bambaras, a nation that was an enemy to his ..." (116).[24] The term is also used similarly in *Les amours de Zémédare et Carina*: the variety in physiognomy of the black population is traced back to their differing African ethnicities, which the narrator refers to as nations:

> The European can barely distinguish one Negro from another, they all look equally black to him; all he sees are flat noses, thick lips, and kinky hair. But the Creole, used to living with them, can not only distinguish the individuals among them, he will also be able to tell you at first glance to which nation he belongs. The Mocos have teeth separated into festoons. ... The Calvaire Negro is distinguished from all others by the perfect blackness of his skin as well as by the beauty of his contours; it is from among those of this nation that the sculptor and the painter should choose their models. On Sundays and holidays, the most genuine gaiety reigned throughout the establishment; the Negroes and Negresses of the neighboring dwellings came to add to the pleasures with their presence. They separated out by nations, thus forming that many different groups, and each one had its own particular dance. (Prévost de Sansac 62)[25]

---

22 "La Martinique dessine ses fertiles rivages devant mes yeux ... mais au milieu de mes émotions une amère pensée traverse mon âme, et je détourne les regards pour les porter sur cette terre de l'exil."
23 "Fatigué de la terre de l'exil, ne sachant où reposer sa tête qui ne dormait plus. ... Je ne peux mourir dans l'exil."
24 "A peine avait-il prononcé les premiers mots que des Bambaras, nation ennemie de la sienne ..."
25 "L'Européen sait à peine distinguer un nègre d'un autre, tous lui paraissent également noirs; il ne voit que des nez plats, de grosses lèvres et des cheveux crépus. Mais le créole, habitué à vivre avec eux, distingue non seulement les individus entr'eux, il vous dira même, à la première vue, à quelle nation il appartient. Les Mocos ont les dents séparées en feston. ... Le nègre Calvaire se distingue parmi tous les autres par la noirceur parfaite de sa peau, ainsi que par la beauté de ses formes; c'est parmi ceux de cette nation, que le sculpteur et le peintre doivent choisir leurs modèles. Les dimanches, et les jours de fête, la gaîté la plus vraie régnait dans tout l'atelier: les nègres et les négresses des habitations voisines venaient, par leur présence, ajouter aux plaisirs. Ils se divisaient par nations, et formaient autant de groupes différents, et chacun avait sa danse particulière."

III.2 The Conceptual Inadequacy of the Terms *patrie*/Nation/Exile

A look at a representative example from the Spanish Caribbean, on the other hand, shows that questions of exile are negotiated differently there. Thus, they do not play any explicit role in the novel *Sab*. They are, however, translated to the slaves themselves in a further sense:

> Nor do I have a homeland to defend, because slaves have no homeland; I have no duties to carry out, because the duties of the slave are the duties of the beast of burden that walks as long as it can and lies down when it can no longer walk. If at least the white men, who cast out of their societies anyone who is born with a differently colored complexion, would leave him in peace in their forests, then he would have a homeland and loves there. (Gómez de Avellaneda, *Sab* ed. Servera 36)[26]

What is also revealing in Gómez de Avellaneda, for the question of possibilities of expression from exile, is that she rescinds her authorship to a certain extent when she integrates her writing process into the novel itself and ascribes it to her male protagonist. Towards the end of the novel, it becomes clear that the entire narrative is a farewell letter from Sab, a slave and the eponymous hero. This has two results: first, it gives an *author*itative (*author*ial) voice to the hero of the novel, who is ethnically and socially more or less excluded, and that voice lifts and transforms him from a colonial object into not only the subject of his own story, but also the subject of his own discourse; second, it moves the narrative word from far away (Madrid) into the scene of the novel, thus somewhat moderating the perceived illegitimacy of a statement coming from the outside (and from the land of the colonizers).

Let us stay with this author and turn our attention to a dimension outside the narrative: in 1859, after a twenty-three-year stay in Spain, she came "back" to Cuba for the first time in all that time, and her reception by Cuban intellectuals was ambivalent. In literary circles, the question of her national affiliation sparked a lively debate, called "The Avellaneda Question." Thus, in a newspaper article from the *Aurora del Yumurí*, dated August 27, 1867, we read:

> The "Areopagus" literary club, meeting in Havana to choose which compositions are worthy of being included in the book "The Cuban Lyre," has determined to exclude the poetess Mrs. Gertrudis Gómez de Avellaneda, considering her to be not Cuban but from Madrid. On

---

26 "No tengo tampoco una patria que defender, porque los esclavos no tienen patria; no tengo deberes que cumplir, porque los deberes del esclavo son los deberes de la bestia de carga que anda mientras puede y se echa cuando ya no puede más. Si al menos los hombres blancos, que desechan de sus sociedades al que nació teñida la tez de un color diferente, le dejasen tranquilo en sus bosques, allá tendrán patria y amores."

the other hand, it seems that Mr. Saturnino Martínez and Mr. Antonio Enrique de Zafra will from now on be regarded as Cuban writers. (Gómez de Avellaneda, *Cartas* 62)[27]

A few months later (January 15, 1868), a completely different opinion appears in the same newspaper:

> Junta – The literary club of our high school met last night, at the request of one of its members, to deal with the Avellaneda question. We were not able to attend this meeting, but we are informed that it was agreed that the literary club considers Mrs. Gertrudis Gomez de Avellaneda to be one of the literary glories of which Cuba can be proud, and it was also agreed to prepare a certificate of this resolution for appropriate purposes. (62ff.)[28]

Whether the author belongs to Cuba or to Spain is decided arbitrarily and strategically, case by case.

---

[27] "El Areópago literario reunido en la Habana para escojer las composiciones dignas de figurar en el libro, 'La Lira Cubana', ha determinado escluir a la poetisa Sra. Dª Gertrudis Gómez de Avellaneda, por no considerarla cubana sino madrileña. En cambio, parece que los Sres. D. Saturnino Martínez y D. Antonio Enrique de Zafra serán mirados en lo adelante como escritores cubanos."

[28] "Junta – La Sección de Literatura de nuestro Liceo celebró anoche, a petición de uno de sus miembros, para ocuparse de la cuestión Avellaneda. No pudimos asistir a esa reunión, pero nos informan que en ella quedó acordado que la Sección literaria considera a Dª Gertrudis Gómez de Avellaneda como una de las glorias literarias de que puede Cuba enorgullecerse, y se convino igualmente estender una acta certificada de esa resolución para los fines oportunos." The Spanish literary critic Bravo Villasante, commenting on an 1859 correspondence, remarked that: "Her situation in Cuba is both gratifying and thankless at the same time, involving both praise and reproaches, and her double situation, being both Cuban and Spanish, is ambiguous. The fact that she arrived as the partner of a representative of the Central Government can be uncomfortable for the revolutionaries, who are working towards Cuban independence, although it might be premature. She is intelligent, notices everything, and debates the alternatives that are presented to her. In terms of politics, she loves the people and at the same time reveres His Majesty; she feels like a child of Cuba and of Spain at the same time and when they wanted to leave her out of an anthology of Cuban poets she was offended, even though also does not relinquish the glory of belonging to Spanish literature." ("Su situación en Cuba es grata e ingrata a la vez, al homenaje se une el reproche, y su doble aspecto de cubana y española es equívoco. Su llegada como consorte de un representante del Gobierno Central puede resultar molesto a los ojos de los revolucionarios, que intentan la independencia de Cuba, aunque sea prematura. Ella, inteligente, se da cuenta de todo, y se debate en las alternativas que se le presentan. Políticamente ama al pueblo, y al mismo tiempo reverencia a su majestad; se siente hija de Cuba y de España a la vez y cuando intentan de dejarla fuera de una antología de poetas cubanos se siente ofendida, aunque no renuncia tampoco a su gloria de pertenecer a la literatura española.") (cited in Servera 38).

For the texts of both the French and the Spanish colonial spheres, we can say that the categories of nation, exile, and *patrie* cannot be used according to clearly delineated criteria but adapt themselves, instead, to the particular situation. This shows a kind of fragility in the concept of the nation that is not what we would have expected for that time period.

III.2.1 "A Writer from Cuba is Not Always a Cuban Writer": The Countess of Merlin

"A writer from Cuba is not always a Cuban writer" (Díaz 58).[29] These introductory words of Roberto Ignacio Díaz's about the Countess of Merlin (which are just as valid for Gómez de Avellaneda, discussed above), point to the central issue with which any discussion of the countess, a writer and musician who was born in Cuba in 1789 and died in Paris in 1852, has to grapple. Even deciding which version of her name to use presents difficulties: María de las Mercedes Santa Cruz y Montalvo is better known as Condesa de Merlín, but also Comtesse Merlin (Díaz 58; Abel, "Viajes corporales"). She writes in French, and she is a woman. This may well explain her absence from the official literary canon of nineteenth-century Cuban literature.

Shortly after she was born, her family emigrated to Madrid, but she spent the first twelve years of her life in Cuba with her grandmother. In 1802, during the French occupation of Madrid, her forward-looking mother married her off to the Count Antoine Christophe Merlin (1771–1839), a general in Bonaparte's army (Méndez Rodenas, "Journey" 708). Because they were French, the Merlins were forced to leave Spain in 1812, after Bonaparte's defeat. Between 1813 and 1839, the young Creole Santa Cruz y Montalvo became one of the leading *belles dames* of Paris's cultural establishments. Her salon at no. 40, rue de Bondy attracted important musicians and writers of the time. After 38 years in France, and exactly one year after the death of her husband, she returned to Cuba in 1840 for seven weeks. In 1844 she published *La Havane*, a travelogue based on that visit (in three volumes and a thousand pages) that is committed to romantic ideals (cf. Díaz 57). But the work constantly breaks the boundaries of the genre. The text consists of 36 letters, most of which are addressed to the author's daughter, Madame Gentien de Dissay, but some of them are addressed to a series of important European personalities: René de Chateaubriand, Prince Frederick of Prussia, George Sand, and Baron Rothschild.

---

29 "Una cubana escritora no es siempre una escritora cubana."

After her Atlantic crossing on her way to Cuba, her first stops were New York and other cities on the East Coast of the United States. The Countess of Merlin's comments on the United States are characterized by the clarity of her own self-understanding as a foreigner: her lack of involvement in the world that she describes is plain to see. From the moment when she disembarks in New York, she describes herself as a "stranger to everything around me" (Condesa de Merlín, *La Havane* I:65).[30] Her apparently neutral outsider position is further reinforced by statements such as "One has to see this nation in order to form an idea of its mores" (I:118).[31]

When she arrives in Cuba, this attitude changes immediately: now she wants to present herself to the reader as a Cuban who is describing her own familiar country. In her foreword, addressed to the captain-general, she writes: "Allow me, general, to place this work, conceived by a woman's patriotic feeling, under your protective auspices; it was inspired solely by the ardent desire to see my country happy" (I:5).[32] The book is dedicated "To my compatriots" (I:7). This struggle to be recognized as Cuban is a common thread running through the text, so insistent as to be almost overpowering. Where and how can we see this? In her descriptions of the island, the author's references to the sixteenth-century Spanish "Chronicles of the Indies" are omnipresent, and overtly so. She very often mentions the chroniclers, foremost among them Columbus himself, as a direct source.[33] Right at the beginning, she paraphrases Columbus's *Diario de a bordo*; like her, he believed he had now encountered the most beautiful country in the world when he arrived in Cuba. In more than one place she uses his descriptions of it as an idyllic sanctuary. This focus also manifests itself in her stylized portrayal of the indigenous population, which in actuality no longer exists on the island but which she depicts in very effusive language (cf. Díaz 62):

> Some distance away, and closer to the coast, I come upon the village of Puerto Escondido: from those conical cottages, covered with palm branches all the way down to the ground; from the bushy banana trees whose large leaves protect the houses from the heat of the sun; from these canoes moored along the shoreline; and from the silent quietude of the

---

[30] "étrangère à [...] tout ce qui m'entoure."
[31] "Il faut voir cette nation pour se faire une idée de ses mœurs."
[32] "Permettez, general, que je place sous votre égide protectrice cette œuvre conçue par le sentiment patriotique d'une femme, le désir ardent de voir mon pays heureux, l'a seul inspirée."
[33] On the Countess of Merlin's constant reliance on outside sources (in one case, actually revealed as plagiarism), Silvia Molloy writes: "Rediscovery came to her less from what she saw on that trip than from what she read, remembered and imagined" (93). Cf. also Ianes 214.

noon hour, you would say that these beaches are still inhabited by Indians. (Condesa de Merlín, *La Havane* I:276)³⁴

In general, discovery and conquest are the Countess of Merlin's central themes. Her descriptions of nature are a particularly striking expression of an interpretation of the Caribbean as a predestined site for the symptomatic triad of "finding —inventing—experiencing" (cf. Ette, *ZusammenLebensWissen* 32).

> When I perceive these age-old palm trees, which bend their proud foliage right down to the edge of the sea, I feel as though I am seeing the shadows of those great warriors, those men of resolution and will, the companions of Columbus and Velazquez; I see them, proud of their most wonderful discoveries, bowing down in their gratitude in front of the Ocean to thank it for such a magnificent gift. (Condesa de Merlín, *La Havane* I:269)³⁵

---

34 "À quelque distance, et plus prêt de la côte, je découvre le village de Puerto Escondido; à ces chaumières de forme conique, couvertes jusqu'à terre de branches de palmiers; aux buissons touffus de bananiers qui, de leurs larges feuilles, protègent les maisons contre les ardeurs du soleil; à ces pirogues amarrées sur le rivage, et à la quiétude silencieuse de l'heure de midi, vous diriez que ces plages sont encore habitées par des Indiens."
35 "Lorsque j'aperçois ces palmiers séculaires, qui courbent leur orgueilleux feuillage jusqu'au bord de la mer, je crois voir les ombres de ces grands guerriers, de ces hommes de résolution et de volonté, compagnons de Colomb et de Vélazquez; je les vis, fiers de leurs plus belles découvertes, s'incliner dans leurs reconnaissance devant l'Océan, pour le remercier d'un si magnifique présent." Cf. Díaz 64. In referring to a new reading of *La Havane* based on this triad, however, I want to warn against the danger of reducing Ette's concept to a way of interpreting individual passages in the text. In fact, on the contrary, the reference is intended to provide a graphic example of how to appreciate a literary text on its own merits, in an unbiased way, that might otherwise most obviously provoke ironic interpretations. The conceptual orientation of the triad finding–inventing–experiencing is etched into the fundamental redefinition of the concept of literature as possessing an overarching character rather than simply being something with which to enrich the interpretation of individual textual passages: "being open to a triangular relationship of terminologies could be the key to breaking out of the simplistic opposition between 'reality' and 'fiction,' between 'facticity' and 'fictionality,' and to gain a more complex (and simultaneously more dynamic) insight into historic, cultural, or literary processes such as those that, in the sphere of the Caribbean, ... positively force us into an investigation of the relationality between the found, the invented, and the experienced." ("In der Öffnung auf eine terminologische Dreiecksbeziehung könnte der Schlüssel zur Lösung einer Problemstellung liegen, die darauf abzielt, aus der simplistischen Gegenüberstellung von 'Realität' und 'Fiktion', von 'Faktizität' und 'Fiktionalität' auszubrechen und eine komplexere (und zugleich dynamischere) Einsicht in ebenso historische wie kulturelle oder literarische Prozesse zu gewinnen, wie sie gerade auch im Bereich der Karibik [...] zu einer Untersuchung der Relationalität zwischen Gefundenem, Erfundenem und Erlebtem förmlich zwingen.") (Ette, *ZusammenLebensWissen* 32).

Just like the Spanish conquerors, the Countess of Merlin sees Cuba's greatness and beauty as a gift from nature to the newly arrived Europeans. Nature to her is a literary kingdom, a source of exotic representations. And as for Cuba's cities, she sees them as places whose lack of history is made up for by exactly that impressive natural wonder on the island:

> Our buildings have neither history nor tradition: the Havanan is entirely in the present and the future. His imagination is only struck and his soul is only moved by the sight of the nature that surrounds him; his castles are the gigantic clouds shot through by the setting sun; his triumphal arches are the vaulted sky; instead of obelisks, he has palm trees; instead of seigneurial weathervanes, the brilliant plumage of the guacamayo; and instead of a painting by Murillo or Raphael, he has the black eyes of a young girl, lit up by a moonbeam through the grating of the window. (Condesa de Merlín, *La Havane* II:210 f.)[36]

The way that the Countess of Merlin uses possessive pronouns can be problematic; it is often difficult to clearly understand their referents. Who, for example, are "our poets"? Does she mean French, Spanish, or Cuban poets? The text does not make it clear, because she uses "our" (*nos* and *notre*) to mean all of those things: "our richest Parisian hotels" (I:74); "our European world" (II:49); "our elegant salons" (II:54); but also "our *guajiros*" (II:51; cf. Díaz 63). While her stubborn self-representation as a Cuban is obvious at first glance, however, there is also a fractured experience of identity that resonates at times (cf. Méndez Rodenas, "Journey" 709). Who am I? Now and here in the tropics? Countess or Creole woman? Santa Cruz y Montalvo or the Countess of Merlin?[37] This ambivalence is closely connected to her political convictions: she sees herself not as a foreigner but rather as a colonizer, but one who understands her opinions as particularly legitimized by her rootedness in the island.

---

36 "Nos édifices n'ont pas d'histoire ni de tradition: le Havanais est tout au présent et à l'avenir. Son imagination n'est frappé, son âme n'est émue, que par la vue de la nature qui l'environne; ses châteaux sont les nuages gigantesques traversés par le soleil couchant; ses arcs de triomphe, la voûte du ciel; au lieu d'obélisques, il a ses palmiers; pour girouettes seigneuriales, le plumage éclatant du guacamayo; et en place d'un tableau de Murillo ou de Raphaël, il a les yeux noirs d'une jeune fille, éclairés par un rayon de la lune à travers la grille de sa fenêtre." Cf. Díaz 65.
37 This turmoil also finds a clear expression in her memoirs, published in 1836: "There are two 'I's within myself that constantly struggle with each other, but I always encourage the 'strong' one, not because it is 'stronger' but because it is the more wretched, the one that achieves nothing." ("Existen en mi dos 'yo' que luchan constantemente, pero estimulo siempre al 'fuerte,' no por ser el 'más fuerte' sino por que es el más desgraciado, el que nada consigue.") (*Souvenirs et mémoires de Madame la Comtesse Merlin, publiés par elle-même*, Paris, 1836, p. 246, quoted in Méndez Rodenas, "Voyage" 80).

She consistently rejects the kind of national projects that one finds in Heredia or Villaverde. And with respect to political independence, her loyalty to Spain is unambiguous: "As for us, I repeat, we are deeply, exclusively Spaniards. ... Spain's interest is our own; our prosperity would be in service to the prosperity of Spain" (Condesa de Merlín, *La Havane* II:285).[38] Her views on the contemporary debates over the abolition of slavery are equally radical. In her eyes, the enslavement of the blacks in fact represents civilizational progress for Africa, since it has led to a mitigation of the earlier barbaric customs that prevailed there with respect to the treatment of prisoners: "When a tribe took prisoners from an enemy tribe, if they were cannibals, they ate these captives; if they were not, they sacrificed them to their gods. The advent of the [slave] treaty introduced a change in this horrible custom: the captives were sold" (II:89).[39]

Given her radically conservative attitude, in a political climate that was set by such liberal debates as those that took place in the del Monte circle, it is no wonder that the Countess of Merlin met with quite a lot of contemporary criticism. This criticism was not, however, leveled only at her extremely conservative positions. Significantly, the main criticism against her had to do with her claim to be speaking as a Cuban, a claim that local writers considered to be completely without foundation. Félix Tanco wrote a number of articles in the *Diario de la Habana* in which he mocked her writing about Cuba from a European perspective: "The señora de Merlin, I will say it once and for all, saw the island of Cuba through Parisian eyes and could not understand that Havana is not Paris" (Méndez Rodenas, "Journey" 711).[40]

Taken as a whole, the Countess of Merlin's work conveys the sense of an extraterritoriality, to use George Steiner's terminology. *La Havane* is an important example of "unhousedness," which is so characteristic of Cuban literature. The text is a hybrid construction built on a series of paired opposites: Cuba vs. France; Spanish vs. French; localist *costumbrismo* vs. European exoticism; memory vs. present. She writes in an *in-between*, an intermediate space. Given her interest in cementing Spanish colonialism, her strained efforts to stage Cuban identity can only result in a fractured self-understanding as it relates to

---

38 "Quant à nous, je le répète, nous sommes profondément, exclusivement Espagnols. ... L'intérêt de l'Espagne est le nôtre; notre prospérité servirait la prospérité espagnole."
39 "Lorsqu'une tribu faisait des prisonniers sur une tribu ennemie, si elle était anthropophage, elle mangeait ces captifs; si elle ne l'était pas, elle les immolait à ses dieux. La naissance de la traite détermina un changement dans cette horrible coutume: les captifs furent vendus." Cf. also Díaz 68, and the Countess of Merlin's article on the topic: Condesa de Merlín, "Les esclaves."
40 "La señora de Merlín, por decirlo una vez, ha visto la isla de Cuba con ojos parisienses y no ha querido comprender que La Habana no es París."

identity. The experience of French colonialism and its more effective gravitational power is apparently what has led her to this colonizing behavior, but in her case it is not in the service of Paris but rather in the sense of the mother homeland Spain, *Madre Patria España*. However, she did not disappoint in service to France, as *La Havane*, which was intended for a French audience, would certainly have fulfilled that audience's exotic expectations. A model example of transcolonial knowledge transfer.

III.3 Haiti As an In-Between Culture

III.3.1 The Haitian Turn

With her 2004 book *Modernity Disavowed*, Sibylle Fischer, drawing on Michel Trouillot, introduced a new paradigm to research on the Caribbean. Fischer notes that Western philosophy fails to mention the Haitian Revolution, even though it was the only revolution whose central issue was racial equality.[41]

The colonial slave trade led to the development of a heterogeneous, transnational cultural network across an entire hemisphere. Fischer describes this cultural network as an "interstitial culture" (1): an intermediate culture, a landscape made up of heterogeneous facts, practices, and ideas that are broken up by disciplinary boundaries to this day. Haiti and the Haitian Revolution represent a central coordinate in this landscape, because there was a confluence of political imaginations and struggles for emancipation that developed precisely around the riddle of the Haitian Revolution—although it is often only graspable as the unspeakable, as a trauma, utopia, or fleeting dream (Fischer 2).[42] What is crucial in Fischer's approach is that according to her, the true battles were fought in imaginary settings: "Imaginary scenarios became the real battleground" (2).[43]

---

[41] I am grateful to Johanna Abel and Leonie Meyer-Krentler for comments on Sibylle Fischer and Chris Bongie.

[42] An instructive example of looking at Haiti as an in-between culture can be found in Bandau, who uses an impressive textual example of the testimony of a white refugee about the events of the Haitian Revolution to examine the transcultural circulation of knowledge about Haiti in the area surrounding the Caribbean and the hemispheric space between Saint-Domingue, New Orleans, France, and New York. She addresses the media's negotiation and representation of the revolutionary events of 1791 to 1804 and asks to what extent the genre of the eyewitness report ensures the translatability of the events or, rather, regulates how they are represented. Cf. Abel, "Tagungsbericht" 476. On the Haitian Revolution see also, notably, James.

[43] For interesting firsthand accounts written by white colonists trying to come to grips with a world that had suddenly disintegrated, see Popkin.

The radical anti-slavery movement left a deep imprint on the psyche of the society that was built on the slave trade and the plantations: fantasies, paranoia, desires for identification, and denial were always a part of this formation (ibid.). Fischer strives to construct a landscape that lays bare the unspoken, the hidden, and the silenced in the historical evidence.

In the Caribbean, it was Cuba and Santo Domingo that were most directly affected by the events in Haiti: over time, Cuba took the place of the former Saint-Domingue as the Caribbean's major producer of sugar. Cuba's particular territorial position naturally meant that Haiti was at the same time far enough away and dangerously close (cf. Fischer 3). Significantly, from 1791 to 1805 there was not one single mention of the Haitian Revolution in Havana's *Papel periódico* (ibid.). This politics of silence also entailed the fact that in contemporary reports such as letters or articles, the revolution never came up as a political or diplomatic matter.[44]

In order to understand this phenomenon and to conceptually define the underestimation of Haiti's role in official historiography, Fischer suggests the concept of the disavowal, or denial, of modernity, both in the conventional sense (as a refusal of recognition) and the psychoanalytic sense (the repression of a traumatic experience). The disavowal thesis, somewhat like Paul Gilroy's "counterculture," has more to do with an attitude toward, or a perspective on, the past than with the supposed character of a particular historical moment. The concept of disavowal only works when we know that there is something that is being disavowed. It is a matter of identifying that which is forsworn and asking who is suppressing or disavowing it and why (cf. 37 f.).

> Unlike the notion of trauma, which becomes politically inert when it cannot properly distinguish between, for instance, a traumatized slave and a traumatized slaveholder, disa-

---

[44] Important encyclopedia articles are missing entries on colonialism and slavery to this day. In political theory, too, the case of Haiti is problematic. In her history of revolution, Hannah Arendt (*On Revolution*, 1936) leaves Haiti out. She excludes slavery from the social question. In Arendt, slavery cannot be discussed, because it does not fit in anywhere in her framework of the social versus the political. Slavery disappears in invisibility: literally, because institutions conceal it, and conceptually, in the abyss between the social and the political. Haiti becomes unthinkable. The same is also true from the perspective of economics: Adam Smith, Karl Marx, and Max Weber categorize slavery as pre-capitalist and therefore excluded from the discussion, even though the plantation economy was the economic foundation of European industrialization and only works in a capitalist global market. The conclusion of this intellectual history is that colonialism and slavery are only "noise," disturbances on the margins of history, anomalies, more or less disturbing irregularities in the triumphal march of progress and the development of individual liberties. Cf. Fischer 8 ff.

vowal does not foreclose the political by rushing to assign victim status to all who find it difficult to deal with reality. (Fischer 38)

Chris Bongie, on the other hand, has noticed a scholarly shift since 2008 towards the Haitian Revolution, a shift that he calls the "Haitian turn" (*Friends and Enemies*). He highlights a political shift in the entire field of postcolonial studies, dating from September 11, 2001 and resulting in the inflationary interpretation of Caribbean cultural production as political and revolutionary. According to Bongie, this perspective is part of a prejudice on the part of the entire discipline, based on a confusion between the cultural and the political. Bongie's rebuttal uses Peter Hallward's designation of the culturalist approach as a nonsensical "disastrous confusion of spheres" (Hallward XIX, cf. Bongie, *Friends and Enemies* 263) that starts from the assumption that culture must always translate directly into progressive politics. The essence of Bongie's book *Friends and Enemies* is a critique of cultural politics and therefore, also, implicitly of Fischer, because she assigns a high level of political influence to culture.

The political shift in postcolonial studies involves a movement away from the enthusiasm of the nineteen-nineties for hybridity and (back) towards political engagement: Bongie designates this pole as "properly or substantively political" (328), unlike the popular culturalist studies of postcolonialism. It involves a departure from the consensus-oriented post-political ethos that marked postcolonial studies at the end of the twentieth century and a turn towards the willingness to establish boundaries that is a basic precondition for politics in the first place, just as the hostility of the Haitians towards the French was a precondition for their revolutionary victory. This brings us back to the divisive logic of the political, which Peter Hallward calls "divisive universality" and Chantal Mouffe defines as follows: "there is no consensus without exclusion, no 'we' without a 'they' and no politics is possible without the drawing of a frontier" (73, quoted in Bongie, *Friends and Enemies* 15).

According to Bongie, this more militant form of postcolonial studies offers a desperately needed counterbalance to the unchanging culturalist excesses of the same old postcolonialism, but it also opens up the horizon of (exclusionary) violence and terror that allows the "skeptical humanist" in all of us to judge the Haitian Revolution. Bongie formulates the difficulty of this turn as follows: "It is not easy to encompass the fractionalist logic of the political—the violent exclusion with which the distinctions between friends and enemies reveal themselves—in a critical environment like ours in which the imperatives of an integrationist pluralism seem like common sense" (Bongie, "Politique" 234).[45]

In a strong, five-page-long critique of his favorite enemy, Nick Nesbitt, and his most recent book, *Universal Emancipation: The Haitian Revolution and Radical Enlightenment* (2008), which jumps onto the bandwagon of mainstreaming Haiti, Bongie stresses that Nesbitt leaves the afterpains of the Haitian Revolution out of his observations because the chronology of the events would disprove the thesis that the Haitian Revolution was a globally significant event ("Politique" 242–246). Current research on Haiti, Bongie continues, ignores the existence of two rival Haitis, drawing a careful line between the "good memory" (of the successful anti-colonial struggle and the "1804 idea" of radical racial equality) and the "bad memory" (of the racially divided nation(s) of Haiti in 1804 to 1820, the years immediately following the revolution): Alexandre Pétion's southern Republic, led by mulattos, and the "black" kingdom of Henri Christophe in the north replicate, says Bongie, the binary division into "friends and enemies" that is inherent in all politics. The fact that the world-historical triumph of the Haitian Revolution became bogged down in racism and absolutism and was, therefore, ultimately a failure is consistently ignored in the Haitian turn of postcolonial studies (241).

III.3.2 Haiti Reception in the Caribbean Literatures

How, then, are literary representations articulated with respect to Haiti? The fear of Saint-Domingue is a frequent theme in Caribbean literatures, especially in the first half of the nineteenth century.[46] Maynard de Queilhe, for instance, talks about how slaves must be handled with severity and justice in order to avoid a second Saint-Domingue—this is the attitude of the slave-owning protagonists of the novel *Outre-mer*, where the concept of justice is interpreted as that which conforms to colonial jurisprudence, in other words with the right of the slave owner to act as he sees fit.[47] The free blacks and mulattos are portrayed as opportunistic egotists, who want to create Haiti-like conditions on Guadeloupe and Martinique for the sake of their own private appetites (Wogatzke

---

45 "Il n'est pas facile, en un mot, d'englober la logique fractionniste du politique—l'exclusion violente avec laquelle les distinctions entre amis et ennemis se révèlent—dans un milieu critique comme le nôtre où les impératifs d'un pluralisme intégrationniste relèvent du sens commun."
46 On this topic see for example Johnson's historical study, *The Fear of French Negroes: Transcolonial Collaboration in the Revolutionary Americas*.
47 For more detailed information see Wogatzke 505.

506). "Martinique, December 29, 1830, will become a second Saint-Domingue, a France of the Antilles! I am all for being named a deputy immediately afterwards" (Maynard de Queilhe II:182, cited in Wogatzke 506),[48] one of the ringleaders declares, while another one is stirring up the masses with an encouragement to take whatever the whites do not freely offer: "But they offer nothing, so let us take everything. Saint-Domingue should attract and keep your eyes and your spirits. Saint-Domingue is the star of everything that we are going to do" (Maynard de Queilhe II:160, cited in Wogatzke 506).[49] In the novel, it is only thanks to the stupidity of the slaves and the farsightedness of the masters that a second Saint-Domingue can successfully be prevented (cf. Wogatzke 507).[50]

In Levilloux's *Les créoles* there is barely any mention of Haiti. This is all the more surprising given that the novel is set during the time of the Haitian revolts and that slave unrests in Martinique and Guadeloupe constitute a central theme of the novel. The erasure of Haiti is particularly noticeable because the novel, which covers the peak period of the revolution, the seventeen-nineties, is looking back from the retrospective viewpoint of forty-five years later at a time when all of the discussions on the French mainland about the recognition of Haiti (which became final in 1825) had already taken place. In the following, I summarize the few places where Haiti is in fact mentioned. One particular episode is Thélesfore's first report on the Haitian events, which are characterized as directly linked to the French Revolution:

> "Great news, gentlemen," exclaims Thélesfore as he enters, "news from Saint-Domingue!"
>
> "From Saint-Domingue? What is it? What is it?" These exclamations arise from every corner of the apartment.
>
> Thélesfore, with the importance felt by anyone in possession of an interesting secret, begins by stretching out in an armchair after having tossed his hat and his gold-handled cane to his young slave.
>
> "Come on, what is it? The news!" they shout at him all at the same time, with redoubled curiosity and anxiety.
>
> "It is nothing less than the infernal trail of powder whose head is in Paris and the tail here; it it starting to catch fire."

---

[48] "La Martinique, le 29 décembre 1830, sera devenue une seconde Saint-Domingue, une France des Antilles! Je suis pour qu'on me nomme député immédiatement après."
[49] "Mais, ils ne donnent rien, prenons tout. Saint-Domingue doit attirer et fixer vos yeux et vos esprits. Saint-Domingue est l'étoile de tout ce que nous allons faire."
[50] Walsh provides interesting insights into the very different decolonization of the French Caribbean.

"What!" says Desvallon, "the principles that are being forged in the clubs have been pushed by the revolutionary hurricane as far as the great colony?" (Levilloux 70)[51]

The debates taking place in the clubs of Paris seem to have found a resonance even in the great colony, the pearl of the French colonial empire. In the novel, what is revealing is Estève's immediate reaction: he pricks up his ears as soon as he learns that Vincent Ogé, in other words a mulatto, was the mastermind of the events in Haiti. And it goes on:

"That's exactly it," Thélesfore continues, "they send word from Port-au-Prince of the conspiracy by the mulatto Vincent Ogé, recently arrived from France."

"Conspiracy!" several of the assistants repeat, in terror.

"Vincent Ogé, mulatto!" Estève says in a muffled murmur. (70)[52]

The plantation owners react very negatively to the fact that the revolt originated with a mulatto. In answer to a question about the motivation of the rebels, "'Ogé was demanding civic and political equality in the name of who knows what madness,' Thélesfore responds, affecting a disdainful air" (71).[53]

Significantly, in Levilloux, it appears that the revolutionary events in Haiti must have been transmitted by way of French literature. It is therefore no accident that Levilloux uses Adonis as an important liberator, thereby borrowing from the first story by a French writer colleague about the Haitian Revolution,

---

51 —"De grandes nouvelles, messieurs, s'écria Thélesfore en entrant, des nouvelles de Saint-Domingue!
—Saint Domingue! Quelles sont-elles? Quelles sont-elles!" Ces exclamations partent de tous les coins de l'appartement.
Thélesfore, avec l'importance de tout possesseur d'un secret intéressant, commence par s'étendre dans un fauteuil après avoir jeté son chapeau et sa canne à pomme d'or à son jeune esclave.
"Enfin, qu'y a t-il? Les nouvelles! Lui crie-t-on à la fois avec un redoublement de curiosité et d'anxiété.
—Il ne s'agit de rien moins que de l'infernal traînée de poudre dont la tête est à Paris et la queue ici; elle commence à prendre feu.
—Quoi! dit Desvallon, les principes qui se forgent dans les clubs sont été poussés par l'ouragan révolutionnaire jusque dans la grande colonie?"
52 —C'est cela, continue Thélesfore, on nous apprend du Port-au-Prince la conjuration du mulâtre Vincent Ogé, récemment arrivé de France.
—Conjuration! Répètent avec effroi plusieurs des assistants.
—Vincent Ogé, mulâtre! Murmure sourdement Estève.
53 "'Ogé réclamait l'égalité civile et politique au nom de je ne sais quelle folie,' répond Thélesfore en affectant un air dédaigneux."

which shares the name: Picquenard's *Adonis ou le bon nègre* (Adonis or the good negro).

But how is the relationship to the Haitian Revolution articulated in Haiti's own literary production? A look at Émeric Bergeaud's novel *Stella*, published in 1859, shows that while the revolution is present there, its legitimacy derives only from the legacy of France, the former mother country. *Stella* gives the impression that from a constitutional point of view, all that the Haitians did was to assert the ideas of the rightful French government of Haiti, namely revolutionary France, against the will of the evil white Creoles (cf. Wogatzke 508). In Haiti it was the blacks and the mulattos who, together, rescued the high ideals of the French Revolution, which were diametrically opposed to the base interests of the plantation owners. Revolutionary France and freedom appear in the form of Stella, who at first participates actively in the struggle for human rights for all of Haiti's population groups, but then retreats into the mountains and leaves it to the brothers Romulus and Remus to carry out the fight for freedom (cf. ibid.; Bergeaud, *Stella* 91–97; Bergeaud trans. Hossman 83–89).

It is a credit to Haiti's mulattos and blacks that, in the end, they won their own freedom. Nevertheless, Stella, or also revolutionary France, is seen as the "initiator of the revolt," as an "adviser and moral support." Because of their "inexperience" the Haitians were dependent on the help of those who were more politically and strategically adept (Wogatzke 509).

Bergeaud honors the African roots of the Haitians, but the relationship to Africa is different in the work of his fellow Haitian writer Ignace Nau. In *Isalina ou une scène creole* (Isalina or a Creole scene) (1836),[54] Nau describes the physiognomy of Galba, a friend of the protagonist's, Paul, as follows: "His broad, hairy head in no way resembles the true African type, which is considerably improved in our country" (Nau 46).[55] Also notable in *Isalina* is the representation of the plantation economy, which is reminiscent of the idyllic picture painted in Maynard de Queilhe's *Outre-mer*. The story is set among the plantation workers, using the atmosphere of daily life and its sounds: the noise of the sugar mill, the comings and goings of the workers, and their singing convey a very particular mood. "Indeed, is there anything more lively, anything more varied and more picturesque than the sugar cane harvest?" (27).[56] This critical attitude towards Africa, along with the endorsement of the plantation system, which in Haiti

---

[54] I am grateful to Leonie Meyer-Krentler for comments on *Isalina*.
[55] "Sa tête large et velue ne ressemble nullement au vrai type africain qui s'améliore considérablement dans notre pays."
[56] "En effet, est-il rien de plus animé, rien de plus varié et de plus pittoresque que la roulaison!"

right after the revolution are reconciled with Francophile tendencies, is at the same time juxtaposed with the positive presentation of the voodoo cult. Thus, Galba has a viper that he talks to so that it will not attack travelers. Paul brings him a problem, and he asks him to describe it. Paul asks him three questions: whether it was her injury that threw Isalina into a delirium; who it was that gave her the injury; and, if she has indeed been put under a spell, who it was that cast the spell over her. Galba asks what name she names in her delirium. In the following voodoo ceremony, Paul has the opportunity to see the answers to his questions on two cards as well as in a water jug, and he is given an antidote to the spell. Isalina is saved. In his gratitude, Paul offers to make Galba his adoptive son.

This ambivalence, in which relationships are explicitly affirmed that would be mutually contradictory in Western logic, corresponds to the specific dialectical situation that was discussed in the first chapter in the context of nineteenth-century Haitian literary production (see I.3.5).

III.4 Transfers of Ideas between the Center and the Colony

III.4.1 Philanthropy in the Center: Failed Transfers of Ideas

The white *Béké* writers of Guadeloupe and Martinique never tried to claim anything other than French identity (Wogatzke 56). As the contemporary witness cited in the introduction to the French-speaking Caribbean commented, there was a downright brain drain towards Paris (Granier de Cassagnac I:102 f.; Wogatzke 56). The *Békés* acted as though culture were equivalent to French culture, which was reserved to the metropolis of Paris, while Creole culture was identified with the growing of sugar (Wogatzke 56). The only place where cultivated Frenchmen from overseas could find an atmosphere that suited them was in the metropolis:

> The Creole world barely focused on intellectual and artistic work and disinterestedness. The only culture that was important to it was the cultivation of sugar cane. The few writers of Caribbean descent who stand out ... in literature will stay in the metropolis, where they will almost entirely forget the country of their birth. (Corzani II:24)[57]

---

[57] "L'univers créole ne privilégiait guère le travail et le désintéressement intellectuel et artistique. La seule culture qui lui importait était celle de la canne à sucre. Les rares écrivains d'origine antillaise à s'illustrer ... en littérature resteront en métropole où ils oublieront à peu près totalement leur pays natal."

The result of this division, into a cultural center located in France and an economic center located on the islands, was that the written culture of the French Antilles consisted mostly of historical and economic texts, which among other things pointed out the lack of their own historiographic or literary tradition and bemoaned the metropolis's lack of interest, but also criticized the apathy of a population that, in its own country, behaved as though it were only passing through.

The difficulty of transferring ideas from the metropolis to the colony is one of the central themes of the nineteenth-century French-speaking Caribbean. In Levilloux, the Creole Edmond Briolan is seized by the revolutionary atmosphere and develops philanthropical ideas there that cannot be implemented in the colonies.

> There, his vigorous memory retraced his earliest impressions for him, too vivid to be erased from a sensitive soul. He felt how incompatible his philosophical convictions were with the social realities in whose midst he was destined to live. Born Creole, a member of a privileged caste whose power could only be maintained by the prestige of its superiority, he had been nourished on the most independent doctrines and dreamed enthusiastically of their political application. (21)[58]

In a letter, Edmond's father warns his son against trying to transfer the ideas that the French Revolution might have inspired in him in Paris: equality cannot exist in the colonies (23). In a conversation between Edmond's mother and his sister, Lea, they are preparing for Edmond's arrival. Lea assumes that he will have been successfully assimilated in the capital and that he therefore belongs to the Parisian establishment. She tries to imagine the kinds of circles that her brother would have been a part of in Paris, at which point her mother corrects her.

> "Mother, he must have gone to court, because a young Creole is never out of place anywhere. We who are in the highest position here cannot in France descend from our rank."
> "Court! My daughter, are you forgetting the scorn and the anger that the court inspires in Edmond? His letters are only full of the new principles that are tormenting all the minds in France. I tremble at the thought of how his feelings and his enthusiastic character will be threatened by severe trials in this country." (38)[59]

---

58 "Là, sa vigoureuse mémoire lui retraçait ses premiers impressions trop vivaces pour s'effacer d'une âme sensible. Il sentait l'incompatibilité de ses convictions philosophiques avec les réalités sociales au sein desquelles il était destiné à vivre. Né créole, membre d'une caste privilégiée dont le prestige de supériorité pouvait seul entretenir la domination, il s'était nourri des doctrines les plus indépendantes et rêvait avec enthousiasme leur application politique."

59 "'Maman, il a dû aller à la cour, car un jeune créole n'est déplacé nulle part. Nous qui sommes les premiers ici, nous ne pouvons pas en France descendre de notre rang.'

Upon his arrival, Briolan thanks the slaves for their work, to which he owes his opportunities for further education: "And you, my good slaves, whose work has nourished my youth, has paid for my education, has woken me to the life of the mind; for you I will continue my mother's care and my father's gentleness. Come to my bosom; it is vast enough to hold all of you" (48).[60]

The non-transferability of antiracist ideas is an omnipresent problem. In Paris, unlike in the colony, skin color makes hardly any difference: "There he is, that pure-bred Creole, the living incarnation of a hateful privilege who would walk as my equal in France and here simply kicks me away within the unassailable circle of prejudices" (63).[61] In the metropolis, racism is lifted for the benefit of praise for France: we see "good people of all colors of skin uniting for the triumph of France" (251).[62]

III.4.2 Successful Transfers of Ideas

In the Spanish Caribbean, the gaze is consistently directed towards Europe, often in order to copy the fashions found there. In Gómez de Avellaneda's *Sab* we see this most clearly in the citations that preface each chapter, drawn from French and Spanish Romantic literary models, making the orientation towards Europe explicit. Other important transfers play out primarily on an economic level: such things as the gambler's morality of the English, in the person of Otway, and the function of the lottery play a prominent role.

In Manzano's *Autobiografía*,[63] the French proponents of the Enlightenment are present as Anti-Christs: Manzano's mistress sees his future as being

---

'La cour! ma fille. Tu oublies donc le mépris et les accens de colère qu'elle inspire à Edmond? Ses lettres ne sont pleines que des principes nouveaux qui, en France, tourmentent tous les esprits. Je tremble que ses sentimens et son caractère enthousiaste ne soient menacés de bien rudes épreuves dans ce pays.'"

60 "Et vous, mes bons esclaves, dont le travail a nourri ma jeunesse, a payé mon éducation, m'a fait naître à la vie de l'intelligence; pour vous je continuerai le soins de ma mère, la douceur de mon père. Venez dans mon sein, il est assez vaste pour vous contenir tous."

61 "Le voilà donc ce créole de pure race, l'incarnation vivante d'un odieux privilège qui, en France, marcherait mon égal, et ici me repousse du pied dans le cercle infranchissable des préjugés."

62 "les braves de toutes les peaux s'unir pour le triomphe de la France."

63 Juan Francisco Manzano (Cuba, 1797–1853) was a slave and a novelist. Most of his works were written when he was still a slave; he probably wrote his autobiography in 1835, encouraged by Domingo del Monte, on whose initiative a group of liberal intellectuals bought Manzano's freedom in 1837. Cf. Bremer ("Juan Francisco Manzano"), who explores the reception history

"worse than that of Rousseau and Voltaire," which she takes as a justification for her rigorous suppression of his intellectual talents. There are also connections to French opera; to the landowners of the Iberian Peninsula (Galicia); to the English drawing instructor, Mr. Godfria; but there are trans-Caribbean connections as well, to emigration from Santo Domingo. In spite of the critical portrayal of the treatment of slaves, the picture that has already been drawn, in the context of Haiti, of a dialectical relationship to the master appears as well. When Manzano was sixteen years old, for instance, he was so fascinated by the newly produced gold coin bearing the likeness of the Spanish king Ferdinand VII that he kept it and cherished it.[64]

The issue of transfer processes in the Spanish Caribbean is more complicated in Galván's[65] *Enriquillo* than in Gómez de Avellaneda or Manzano; in Galván, "colonial transfers of beauty" (Abel, "'Aunque la virgen'") are staged between Italy, Spain, and the Americas. Galván often talks about the manner of dressing according to Milanese fashion (Galván, *Enriquillo*, Notas 135): a case of reverse exoticism. Another transfer theme can be found in the communication difficulties that arise from misunderstandings and hurdles on the information paths, namely the slow-grinding mills of transatlantic bureaucracy (372). Transfers of egalitarian ideas, on the other hand, occur much more frequently in a trans-Caribbean dimension. Thus, for instance, the trans-Caribbean resistance of the Taínos constitutes a central axis in *Enriquillo*: Hatuey (from Haiti) flees to Cuba and organizes the fight against the conquest of Cuba by spying between the islands (294 f.) The multirelational orientation of the Spanish Caribbean also functions on a subversive level: pirates use the colonial masters to transport Indian slaves

---

of this, the only known autobiography of a former slave in the Spanish Caribbean, examining the transfer processes of its reception between Cuba, Spain, England, France, Ireland, and Haiti. A central question for Bremer is to what extent Cuban literature was given an initial push by British abolitionists like Richard Madden, who, working as eyewitnesses and agitators against slavery, politicized the literary discourses of the Caribbean islands. After reports by English travelers had considerably sharpened the tone of the discussions between the Spanish and English crowns about the abolition of slavery, there followed a further internationalization of the reception of Manzano's autobiography when the abolitionist Victor Schoelcher translated it into French in 1840.

64 I am grateful to Johanna Abel for comments on Manzano, *Enriquillo*, and Tapia y Rivera.
65 Manuel de Jesús Galván (1834–1910), a diplomat and political functionary, had a classical humanist academic education. His life is closely intertwined with the history of the Dominican Republic's independence: he was first a staunch annexationist (in 1861), only to become a supporter, in his thirties, of the *Partido Azul* under Luperón (starting in 1868). As a diplomat, he was active in France, among other places. It was in Paris, in the *Bibliothèque nationale*, that he conceived his single novel, *Enriquillo* (first published in 1879, and first complete edition in 1892).

among the Caribbean islands (410). On a fundamental level, the novel exhibits a deep understanding of the zeitgeist of the Spanish conquests. Galván paints a haunting portrait of Castilian court culture and of the conquistadors' sense of mission. There is a pervasive latent sympathy for the world power that is Spain, with the great minds of Columbus and Las Casas. This does not exclude the possibility, however, unlike in the literary examples from the French Caribbean, that Enriquillo could rebel in anticipation of the struggles for liberation and wars of independence with the Spanish colonial power: "The uprising of the Bahoruco is seen as a reaction; as the prelude to all the reactions that will annihilate the right of conquest in the New World within less than four centuries" (Galván, *Enriquillo*, Notas 534).[66] In a critique of the times by Galván there is a reference to Spain's political decadence:

> The Royal Council of the Indies, against the perverse hopes of King Ferdinand and *inspired by the dignity and independence which so ennobled Spanish institutions in that century*, unanimously decided in favor of the rights demanded by Don Diego, reinstating Columbus's achievement in all its pure brilliance. In spite of this glorious triumph of justice over power ... (115; emphasis mine)[67]

In Tapia y Rivera's *La palma del cacique* (The chieftain's palm tree),[68] the relationship to contemporary Castilian literature constitutes an important axis; this can be seen, for example, in an intertextual reference to Cervantes and the imaginary folly of the chivalric novel: the protagonist, Sotomayor, wants to accomplish heroic deeds in the New World before his wedding.

> These ideas, on the other hand, were very natural and proper among the distinguished youth of his time, because the chivalric structure that Henry I of Germany had established was still in place, and the greatest and most exceptional of satirists had not yet torn it down with his implacable pen. Once the Iberian Peninsula was free of Muslim dominion, with the capture of the Granadan stronghold, the adventurous and militant spirit of the Spaniards discovered a new and larger terrain in which to express itself than what Flanders and

---

66 "El alzamiento del Bahoruco aparece como reacción; como el preludio de todas las reacciones que en menos de cuatro siglos han de aniquilar en el Nuevo Mundo el derecho de conquista."
67 "El Consejo Real de Indias, contra las protervas esperanzas del Rey Fernando, *inspirándose en la dignidad e independencia que tanto enaltecieron en aquel siglo las instituciones españolas*, falló unánimemente en favor de los derechos reclamados por Don Diego, reintegrando en todo su puro brillo el mérito de Colón. Sin embargo de este glorioso triunfo del derecho sobre el poder ..."
68 Alejandro Tapia y Rivera (Puerto Rico, 1826–1882) was a prolific writer and essayist, working in many genres, who is considered the "father of Puerto Rican literature." He was also active in the causes of abolition and women's rights.

Italy could offer; thus, it was not surprising that ardent youth should swarm to the newly discovered lands *where a thousand fanciful ventures took place in the novelistic imaginations*, with the reporting of strange adventures, great exploits, and golden regions, where marvels mixed with the vastness and the unknown of those countries. (47; emphasis mine)[69]

In Tapia y Rivera, under European influences, there is a preponderance of exoticized images of the foreign woman: the sultana and the heavenly Arabian beauty, but also the trans-cultured body of the exotic Andalusian woman and the Greek bodily ideal of the nymph. In addition to those we also find Herculean warriors (Taínos) and Castilian heroes (Cid-Salazar). Also important are imaginary transfers of the indigenous protagonists to Europe and the mirroring against their European counterparts, for example Guarionex as a knight: "Guarionex translated to Europe and educated to feudal customs would have been, obeying his passionate and valiant heart, a completely *noble and accomplished cavalier*" (40; emphasis mine).[70] The female characters experience the same kind of transfer, when Tapia y Rivera imagines Loarina as a European and reflects the "wild woman" in a "cultivated lady," who strategically manages her feelings: "A similar struggle in Loarina's heart was natural, who ... felt herself blush at the knowledge that her desire was driving her to love another; *because the beautiful savage was not the cultured lady of our times*" (42; emphasis mine).[71]

Transfers of philosophical ideas, then, especially in the French-speaking Caribbean, are represented as failed, whereas in the Spanish-speaking Caribbean they fall on fertile soil, as shown by the case of Heredia in the previous chapter. Literary and aesthetic models, often exoticized, are also shown as successful transfers there. And yet, although the reception in the two colonial spheres is

---

[69] "Estas ideas, por otra parte, eran muy naturales y propias en la juventud distinguida de su época, pues aún estaba en pie el caballeresco edificio que levantó Enrique I de Alemania, y que aún no había derribado con su implacable pluma, el más grande y singular de los satíricos. Libre la península ibérica del dominio musulmán con la toma del baluarte granadino, el espíritu aventurero y belicoso de los españoles, encontraba un nuevo terreno más vasto a su ejercicio, que el que podía ofrecerles la Flandes y la Italia; así que no era de extrañar que la juventud ardorosa, acudiese en tropel a las tierras nuevamente halladas, en *donde mil empresas quiméricas se hacían lugar en las imaginaciones novelescas*, con la relación de extrañas aventuras, de grandes proezas, y de doradas regiones, en que los prodigios se mezclaban a lo vasto y desconocido de aquellos países."
[70] "Guarionex trasladado a Europa y educado a usanza feudal, habría sido, obedeciendo a su corazón apasionado y valiente, todo *un noble y cumplido caballero*."
[71] "Natural era una lucha semejante en el corazón de Loarina, que ... sentía rubor al conocer que su veleidad la impulsaba a amar a otro; *porque la hermosa salvaje no era la culta dama de nuestros tiempos*." I thank Johanna Abel for this reference.

III.5 The In-Between and the Figure of the Mulatto

> From the heights of their privilege, the whites shower contempt down onto the mulattos, men molded by their blood. These latter, humiliated by their inferiority, cast the hatred of envy towards their fathers and take revenge on the blacks for the degrading shade of skin to which they are heir. The Negroes, for their part, recognizing the superiority of the whites and rejecting the pretentions of the colored class, conspire against the first because they are the masters and despise the second because they aspire to become so. (Levilloux 14)[72]

A constant struggle around attributions of ethnic identity can be seen in Levilloux. There is no conversation that does not include a determination of skin color. The mulatto Estève insists that he and the white Creole Edmond are both Americans: "we are two American shrubs on the soil of Europe, far from our beautiful sky" (25).[73] And yet, in spite of the strong definitional drive towards clear attributions, there nevertheless remains a kind of latent uncertainty. At one point, for instance, free and unfree mulattos are described as two different groups. Estève, as a mulatto himself, observes: "When he left, he was old enough, he had had reason enough to observe and remember the superiority that the free mulattos and mestizos assumed, especially in relation to the blacks" (27).[74] From the point of view of the blacks, the mulattos are sometimes pitied, and recognized as being located in the *in-between:* thus, the herbal healer Iviane, for instance, has sympathy for Estève. And the concept of the nation, interestingly enough, has something to do with that: "'Me possessed by God alone,' retorted the old woman. 'You mulatto, me Negress. Nation of mine is large in a large country. You not have a nation, you'" (104).[75]

---

[72] "Du haut du privilège les blancs laissent tomber le mépris sur les mulâtres, hommes pétris de leur sang. Ceux-ci humiliés de leur infériorité, lancent à leurs pères la haine de l'envie et se vengent sur les noirs de la nuance dégradante d'épiderme dont ils sont héritiers. De leur côté les nègres reconnaissant la supériorité des blancs, repoussant les prétentions de la classe de couleur, conspirent contre les uns parce qu'ils sont maîtres, et haïssent les autres parce qu'ils aspirent à le devenir." On this aspect in Levilloux see also Meyer-Krentler, "El Bois-Caïman."
[73] "nous sommes deux arbustes américains sur le sol de l'Europe, loin de notre beau ciel."
[74] "A son départ il était assez âgé, il avait assez de raison pour avoir observé et gardé souvenir de la supériorité que les mulâtres et les métis libres affaictaient sur les noirs surtout."
[75] "'Moi possédée de Dieu seul,' répliqua la vielle. 'Vous mulâtre, moi negresse. Nation à moi est grande dans un grand pays. Vous pas avoir une nation, vous.'"

The only way to avoid the stigma of the word *mulatto* is to flee. "Then, let us go away, leave the Antilles, flee to France or to the American continent. Then there will be no more terrors, we will be free, free from the tyranny of a word, mulatto" (110).[76] Estève feels torn in both directions. From Paris, he writes back to his father:

> My father ... why did you separate me from my country? Why did I not grow upon the soil that witnessed my birth? Why this vain and fatal education which must cause my misery? It is in vain that my learning, my knowledge shall raise my ambition; the whites will reject me; my peers, wounded by my superiority, will envy me. It will be a light that is shut up inside me and which will only better illuminate the horror of my isolation. (28)[77]

Maynard de Queilhe depicts the mulattos very critically. They are usually the ones who break the rules of the *Code Noir*. After free men of color (*hommes de couleur libres*) had received political and civil rights in 1831, it is they who pose the greatest danger of sedition, in his opinion. They become increasingly disrespectful:

> Most of the time, they were ridiculous or odious. As the price of their insolences, they were beaten with a cane. ... Protected by the night, they would cover the walls with vile placards, on which they did not blush to insult and threaten the most honorable existences in the country. ... They ceased to salute the wives and daughters of their masters or former masters. Their songs resounded with the word freedom, which has never been a good sign. (Maynard de Queilhe I:161)[78]

In *Les amours de Zémédare et Carina*, the mulatto Dérima is depicted as being on the side of slavery. This is not all that surprising, since a large proportion of the mulattos themselves owned slaves.

---

76 "Ensuite, partons, quittons les Antilles, fuyons en France ou sur le continent américain. Alors plus de terreurs, nous sommes libres, libres de la tyrannie d'un mot mulâtre."
77 "Mon père ... pourquoi m'as-tu éloigné de mon pays? Pourquoi ne me suis-je pas développé sur le sol qui m'a vu naître? Pourquoi cette vaine et fatale éducation qui doit faire ma misère? C'est en vain que mon savoir, mes connaissances élèveront mon ambition; les blancs me repousseront; mes semblables, blessés de ma supériorité, m'envieront. Ce sera une lumière enfermée en moi et qui ne sait que mieux éclairer l'horreur de mon isolement."
78 "Ils étaient la plupart du temps ridicules ou odieux. Pour prix de leurs insolences, ils se faisaient rompre de coups de canne. ... A la faveur de la nuit, ils couvraient les murs de placards infâmes, où ils ne rougissaient pas d'insulter et de menacer les existences les plus honorables du pays. ... Ils ne saluaient plus les femmes et les filles de leurs maîtres ou de leurs anciens maîtres. Leurs chansons retentissaient du mot de liberté, ce qui n'a jamais été bon signe."

The free man of color would certainly be treated the worst if he dared to declare himself against the white men. The slaves, having shaken off the yoke of their masters, would be properly subjugated by the enormous forces that would be easily sent from Europe.[79] ... After the victory, the free men of color, no longer able to be useful and having proven themselves dangerous, would all be massacred and that would be done, I say, with justice.— Does anyone suppose, for that matter, that the slave, who does not want to be subject to white men, whose superiority he nevertheless recognizes, would prefer men of color, descended from Whites, envied and detested by the Negroes? (Prévost de Sansac 170f., cited in Corzani II:36)[80]

This mulatto speaks like a free man and, in the process, defends all of the values of the colonial society.

In contrast to these examples from the French-speaking Caribbean, mulattos in texts like *Sab* and *Cecilia Valdés*, from the Spanish-speaking Caribbean, are much more often presented as positive figures, possessing a cohesive, integrative force. The texts are marked by the way in which the concrete designation of color already conveys an *in-between* that has no clearly definable place in the social structure. What all the texts have in common is the uncertainty, or even impossibility, of positioning the mulatto.

III.6 The Island Function, or between Nature and Culture

"Altogether, there are times when I envy you, you a poet exiled in a sunny land, an exile which Ovid would have loved, in that beautiful Martinique which you have described so admirably" (Hugo, *Letters* 56).[81] These words are from a letter written by Victor Hugo in 1835 to his writer colleague Louis de Maynard de Queilhe, who had set out shortly before from Paris for Martinique, his island of origin.

---

79 He is referring here to Leclerc's expedition to Saint-Domingue.
80 "L'homme de couleur libre serait certainement le plus maltraité, s'il osait se déclarer contre les hommes blancs. Les esclaves, ayant secoué le joug de leurs maîtres, seraient proprement subjugués par les forces immenses qu'on enverrait facilement d'Europe. ... Après la victoire, les hommes de couleur libres ne pouvant être utiles et s'étant rendus dangereux, seraient tous massacrés et ils le seraient, je le dis, avec justice.—Supposera-t-on d'ailleurs que l'esclave, qui ne veut pas être soumis à des hommes blancs, dont il reconnaît cependant la supériorité, lui préférait des hommes de couleur, sortis des Blancs, jalousés et haïs par les Nègres?"
81 "Il y a des heures où je vous envie, vous poète exilé sous le soleil, exil qu'Ovid eût aimé, dans cette Martinique que vous avez si admirablement peinte" (Hugo, *Bug-Jargal* 69).

"But for me, to abandon my homeland. ... Why does there exist an island named Martinique? Why am I here instead of elsewhere?" (Maynard de Queilhe I:43)[82]—this is the plaint of Marius, the hero of Maynard de Queilhe's *Outre-mer*, when he has to return from England to the island of his birth. The novel was written only a few years after the exchange of letters cited above. Here we see how various the values are that can apparently be easily projected onto the colonial Caribbean islands.

In the novel *Eugène de Cerceil ou les Caraïbes* (Eugène de Cerceil or the Caribbean) (1824), by J.H.J. Coussin (Guadeloupe 1773–1836), we find an island metaphor that is strongly oriented towards isolation and exile. It refers to the feeling of being banished into the distance, far from any civilization or cultural possibilities. The author writes about himself in the preface:

> Living far from the literary world, on an island in the American archipelago and in the midst of the wild places that he was trying to describe, he could not resort to the advice of enlightened and straightforward friends who would perhaps have taught him to think even more negatively than he is already inclined to do of these ramblings of his spirit. (Coussin I:xxiii)[83]

It is significant that the island is located in an American archipelago. And Coussin adds in a footnote:

> Although learning and literary knowledge are rather rare in the country where this work was composed, the author would be wanting in gratitude if he did not declare here that certain persons, to whom (long after having written this Preface) he had sent copies of his manuscript, had given him good advice from which he profited. (ibid.)[84]

Thérèse Bentzon's *Yette. Histoire d'une jeune créole* (Yette. The history of a young Creole woman) (1880) also shows, right from the beginning, that the thematic introduction to the plot can only work by passing through the most exotic island

---

[82] "Mais, moi, abandonner ma patrie. ... Pourquoi existe-t-il une île appelée Martinique? pourquoi suis-je ici plutôt qu'autrepart?"

[83] "Vivant loin du monde littéraire, dans une île de l'Archipel Américain, et au milieu des sites sauvages qu'il a essayé de décrire, il n'a pas eu la ressource de recourir aux conseils d'amis éclairés et francs qui lui auroient peut-être appris à penser encore plus désavantageusement qu'il n'est porté à le faire de ces élucubrations de son esprit."

[84] "Quoique le savoir et les connoissances littéraires soient assez rares dans le pays où cet ouvrage a été composé, l'auteur manqueroit à la reconnaissance, s'il ne déclaroit ici que quelques personnes, auxquelles (long-temps après avoir écrit cette Préface) il a communiqué son manuscrit, lui ont donné de bons conseils dont il a profité."

depictions.⁸⁵ The novel's "frictional" features are particularly evident (cf. Ette, "Eine Literatur ohne festen Wohnsitz"), but it also suggests a clear ethnographic reading, like some literary Caribbean texts:

> All travelers who have visited the Antilles and sailed along the steep coastline of one of our most beautiful colonies, Martinique, remember the picturesque look of the sugar plantations, between the double blue of the sky and the sea, the factory smokestacks, the farm buildings, and the Negroes' huts covered in straw, sheltered from the tropical sun by the disheveled foliage of the coconut palm trees. (279)⁸⁶

Unlike later understandings of the Caribbean, the nineteenth-century conceptions of the islands share the idea of exile and isolation. Any positive island imaginaries derive from the most exotic notions. And because the island is generally only "tolerated," as a way station, it is also a part of an *in-between* that is symptomatic of writing in and about the nineteenth-century Caribbean.

This imagery of isolation and exile in connection with islands can be found in the French Caribbean in particular. In Galván's *Enriquillo*, instead of an explicit confrontation with insularity, we find individual descriptions of landscapes as idyllic and perfectly planned by nature. The European traveler's descriptions of euphoria over nature are matched in Fray Bartolomé de las Casas's enthusiasm. They are inscribed in the established, quasi-religious, European tradition of that time of admiring nature as an aesthetic work of art. Las Casas is an intellectual traveler who ecstatically devours the exotic landscape.

> Las Casas, endowed with an exquisite sensibility, a fervent admirer of the beautiful, felt his mind transported on wings of the purest and most religious enthusiasm, contemplating the rich variety of lacquers and hues with which provident Nature has decorated the fertile, rugged soil of Hispaniola. He paused, like a child, showing signs of amazement and joy, now at the majestic sight of the far-off mountain range, now at the view of the wide plains or at the feet of the erect mountain that reached its crest, bushy with pines and *baitoas* [an indigenous tree]. Everything was a motive for ecstasy for the impressionable traveler, who eloquently expressed his admiration, wanting to share it with his companions; they, however, not as rich in artistic sentiment, or maybe poor in imagination or lyricism, remained

---

85 Thérèse Bentzon (actually Marie Thérèse Blanc, France 1840–1907) was a French journalist, novelist, and a longtime contributor to the *Revue des deux mondes*. She traveled through the Caribbean and, in addition to her novels, wrote articles about Caribbean literature and social conditions.
86 "Tous les voyageurs qui ont visité les Antilles et longé le littoral escarpé d'une de nos plus belles colonies, la Martinique, se rappellent l'aspect pittoresque des habitations sucrières dont on aperçoit, entre le double azur du ciel et de la mer, la cheminée d'usine, les bâtiments d'exploitations et les cases à nègres couvertes en paille qu'abrite contre le soleil tropical le feuillage échevelé des cocotiers."

with stoic cold in front of the superb spectacles that electrified the graduate. (Galván, *Enriquillo*, notes 249 f.)[87]

Thus, the nature that is present on the islands is made into a *pars pro toto* in the functionalization of the island as metaphor. This suggests both a dissociation from the center and a break with the colonially established bipolar axis.

In Juan Francisco Manzano's *Autobiografía*, nature, in the sense of the natural environment, is not depicted romantically. It only appears as a medicinal resource for lightening the depressive state of his soul, in the context of walks that are prescribed to him or when he is supposed to go hunting and fishing with his doctor on his masters' lands as a way of recuperating. But it is always domesticated culture that is his undoing, as in the case of the geranium. Culture appears in the context of drawing and writing, among other places. Manzano is given drawing lessons early on, along with the masters' children; he proves to be very talented, but then he is forbidden to continue after he draws a witch copulating with the devil. At that point his father throws his drawing materials into the river. His father plays the harp and is a part of the contemporary black musician culture, classical ensembles that play at the masters' baptisms and parties. His mother also acts as a vehicle of culture, having been chosen by her mistress to be educated in particularly civilized skills and having internalized courtly customs. Manzano, therefore, is the product of a cultured family home, and his parents made sure that he did not consort with the black slave children who did not belong to their household. But because access to "(written) culture" was, however, denied him (with bans on writing, drawing, and speaking), he transposes his abilities into orality, incessantly reciting poems, sayings, prayers, verses, and psalms and even entering into imagined dialogues with objects such as tables and chairs. Manzano speaks of the "notebook in his imagination" (*cuaderno en la imaginación*) where he kept his poems and could retrieve them when he needed them for improvisations. His verbal giftedness earns him

---

[87] "Las Casas, dotado de sensibilidad exquisita, ferviente admirador de lo bello, sentía transportada su mente en alas del más puro y religioso entusiasmo, contemplando la rica variedad de esmaltes y matices con que la próvida Naturaleza ha decorado el fértil y accidentado suelo de La Española. Deteníase como un niño haciendo demostraciones de pasmo y alegría, ora al aspecto majestuoso de la lejana cordillera, ora a vista de la dilatada llanura, o al pie del erguido monte que llevaba hasta las nubes su tupio penacho de pinos y baitoas. .... Todo era motivo de éxtasis para el impresionable viajero, que expresaba elocuentemente su admiración, deseoso de compartirla con sus compañeros; los cuales, no tan ricos de sentimiento artístico, o más pobres de imaginación y lirismo, permanecían con estoica frialdad ante los soberbios espectáculos que electrizaban al Licenciado."

the epithets of "speaker" (*parlero*) and "gift of the gab" (*pico de oro*, literally "golden beak").

In Alejandro Tapia y Rivera's *La palma del cacique*, the natural world of the islands functions as a mirror of the characters' mental state, illustrating their melancholia and despair. The "wild" culture of the chieftains corresponds to an "intelligence" of the rain forest: "the pleasant and enormous, though uncultivated, intelligence, like the eternally green forests" (54).[88] Indigenous thinking is staged, in the novel, as literature, from the point of view of the Euro-Creoles.[89]

The opposition between nature and culture is treated as a much more clearly polarized division in the literature of the French Caribbean than in the Spanish texts. This corresponds to a different function that is served by islands in the two colonial spheres: the island imagery of exile and isolation that is frequently found in the French Antilles—from the mouth of the plantation-owning oligarchy that chose to settle there—is barely to be seen in the Spanish Caribbean.

III.7 Between Trans-Tropical Dimensions: Xavier Eyma and the Philippines

Xavier Eyma, a Martinican writer who mostly traveled between Saint-Pierre (on Martinique), Paris, and New Orleans and who was a proponent of slavery, was concerned with influencing the debates in New Orleans in such a way that the southern states of the United States did not also abolish slavery, as had already been done in the French colonial empire in 1848. His descriptions of transfers of ideas and experiences, descriptions that unfold over an immense body of narrative and essayistic work, move across multiple colonial axes over the area of the entire French, but also Spanish, colonial realm. In his essay *La vie aux États Unis* (Life in the United States), for instance, he compares cock fights in Cuba with cock fights in Mexico and in Manila (280). The line connecting Cuba, Mexico, and the Philippines is one that he simply takes for granted. "Cock fights are as popular in Cuba as they are in Mexico and Manila. They take place on Sunday afternoons in the villages in the interior of the island" (274).[90] Eyma compares plantation owners in Cuba with plantation owners in Louisiana just as naturally:

---

[88] "la inteligencia, aunque inculta, amena y gigante, como las selvas siempre verdes."
[89] I am grateful to Johanna Abel for comments on Manzano, and Tapia y Rivera.
[90] "Les combats de coqs sont aussi populaires à Cuba qu'au Mexique et à Manille. C'est l'après-midi du dimanche qu'ils se donnent dans les villages de l'intérieur de l'île."

> I must say that the planters of the island of Cuba are without contest the noblest hearts in the world. The southern planters of the United States make up a charming population. Many of them are rich, all of them are hospitable, quite a few are intelligent, enlightened, and sensitive; but they do not surpass the Cuban planters in refinement, in intelligence, or in wealth. As for their fortune, it is doubtful whether one could find more affluent men anywhere in the world than the most affluent of the Cuban planters. (267)[91]

What is striking is how open Eyma is towards the Spanish colonial regime, which he praises for being able to hold onto Cuba, the "ever-faithful" island (*La siempre fiel*); in fact, he even seems to be holding up Spanish colonialism as a model for the French colonial empire (266). Eyma thinks within colonial systems, but he definitely compares their cultures with each other, including their political cultures. The French Creole upper class is interconnected, as he sees it, very tightly across the most varied regions of the world. Thus, for instance, he expresses himself very sympathetically towards the Louisiana Creoles, and also compares the French "Creole race" around the world with the Anglo-Saxons. Writing about New Orleans, almost a divided city, he remarks: "There is more than political antipathy today, there is an absence of social sympathy between the Creole race and the Anglo-Saxon race" (47).[92] Eyma takes similar global conceptions of regional relationships as the basis for his novel *Le roi des tropiques* (The king of the tropics). He does not differentiate here among the various Caribbean islands, nor between the Caribbean and the area around it: he considers the tropics as one zone. Ette has pointed out that the tropics constitute *at the same time* a center and a transitional space, both the center of the globe and the threshold to another world that is familiar to Europeans: a shifting figure that is constantly being reformulated and both artistically and cartographically redrawn within the Western pictorial tradition.

While the examples of Levilloux and Maynard de Queilhe suggest that transfers take place on a one-dimensional, bipolar axis between the mother country and the colony, transfers take on a definitely multidimensional character in Eyma. He takes as his frame of reference not only the Caribbean periphery but goes far beyond that, including the Philippines as well. The fact that Manila

---

[91] "Je dois dire que les planteurs de l'île de Cuba sont incontestablement les plus nobles cœurs du monde. Les planteurs du Sud, aux Etats-Unis, forment une population charmante. Beaucoup sont riches, tous sont hospitaliers, plusieurs sont intelligents, éclairés et délicats; mais ils ne surpassent point les planteurs cubains en raffinement, en intelligence et en richesse. Quant à la fortune, il est douteux qu'on puisse rencontrer au monde des hommes plus opulents que les plus opulents des planteurs cubains."

[92] "Il y a plus que de l'antipathie politique aujourd'hui, il y a absence de sympathie sociale entre la race créole et la race anglo-saxonne."

was subject to Spain's rule and influence for several centuries is due to its strategic position on the naval route between the American continent and Asia, especially China. The silver trade route, which was especially booming before the nineteenth century, meant that Spanish trade galleys kept arriving in the Philippines, bringing not only precious metals and luxury goods from Asia but also cultural goods. Thus, a close relationship developed between the Philippines and Mexico, which was also reflected in literary production and was a contributing factor to the close connection between Philippine typography and that of the Spanish viceroyalty. Many of those who began their literary career in the Philippines received the opportunity to present their intellectual work in Mexico. This included the Dominican Francisco Blancas de San José, the father of book printing in Manila; Dr. Don Antonio de Morga, the governor of the Philippines, judge of the royal high court of Mexico und president of the high court in San Francisco de Quito; Don Diego de Camacho y Ávila, first the archbishop of Manila and later the bishop of Guadalajara; and Diego de Gorozpe, born in Puebla, a monk and later the bishop of Nueva Segovia (in the Philippines) (Laslo 9).

Eyma's openness to the Philippines does not, however, mean that he therefore questions the colonial status quo. On the contrary, he affirms France as a colonial power everywhere that he can. France, very much in the spirit of the civilizing mission (*mission civilisatrice*), was successful in implementing the spread of its colonial and cultural influence, although Eyma does regret the abolition of slavery, seeing it as a grave mistake, and seems to want to turn back the wheels of time.

What we see happening on the literary level in Eyma is the focus of a current scientific paradigm in the more recent publications of Ottmar Ette, where he programmatically argues for a further conceptual opening of Caribbean research beyond the Atlantic and for the integration of the Pacific archipelago into the research on nineteenth-century hemispheric transfer processes. From the very beginning, the perception of the Caribbean islands involved a trans-archipelagic island fiction, given that Columbus, taking his cue from Marco Polo, invented America as Asia. It was not until the end of the nineteenth century that the Cuban José Martí and the Philippine José Rizal first destroyed the fiction of the colonial kaleidoscope, which had held sway since Marco Polo, and understood their archipelagoes as translocal worlds whose whirlwinds would eventually do away with the colonial systems. Ette describes the Caribbean archipelago as a fractal world that shares a "translocalized local diversity" with other archipelagic zones of tropical consumer goods. This approach should ultimately lead to a more radically dynamic understanding of the Caribbean in a global context and according to vectorial modals (cf. Ette, "Le monde transarchipélien").

III.8 Between Literature and the Natural Sciences

There was a great deal of interest in the natural world of the Caribbean islands in the nineteenth century, from two sides: on the one hand as a wild, romantic, and paradisiac setting for literary works, and on the other as the object of research for explorers.[93] Following Rousseau, literature in general became enthusiastic about landscape descriptions; on top of that, there was the contemporary trend of literary exoticism, which expressed itself, among other ways, in the portrayal of the luxuriant vegetation of the tropics and other unfamiliar displays of nature. But at the same time, the Caribbean archipelago was a destination for geographic and other scientific expeditions exploring the flora, fauna, geological features, and suchlike.

A closer look, however, reveals that these two realms can by no means be examined in such isolation from each other as it might at first appear. There were numerous areas of cross-fertilization and reciprocal transfers, transfer processes that decisively shaped both genres in the nineteenth century. In the foreword to his novel *Eugène de Cerceil ou les Caraïbes*, J.H.J. Coussin refers to the aesthetic value of the landscape descriptions in the scientific works written by explorers, who helped to initiate the development towards a lyrical enjoyment and literary processing of nature:

> The passion for natural history that became so strong in late-eighteenth-century France also served to increase the taste for the picturesque. Botanists and geologists, especially, visited deserts that were unknown to the whole world. ... The imagination of these travelers, friends of the sciences, was able to find in these hitherto unexplored sites a charm that several of them succeeded in bringing into their writing. Truly sensitive men were fascinated by this kind of beauty, which had been neglected for so long; the others pretended to love it, because it was fashionable; and from that time on, it was the custom of almost all travelers who aspired to the reputation of being men of taste to turn aside from their path to go admire precipices, waterfalls, caves, and desert scenes of which in the past no one would have ever thought to dream. (Coussin I:iv–v)[94]

---

[93] I am grateful to Marion Schotsch for crucial conceptual suggestions and research for this and the following section.

[94] "La passion de l'histoire naturelle qui se développa avec force en France vers la fin du 18ᵉ siècle, servit aussi à augmenter le goût du pittoresque. Les botanistes, les géologues surtout visitèrent des déserts ignorés de tout le monde. ... L'imagination de ces voyageurs, amis des sciences, sut apercevoir dans ces sites jusqu'alors inexplorés, un charme que plusieurs d'entre'eux réussirent à faire passer dans leurs écrits. Les hommes véritablement sensibles se passionnèrent pour ce genre de beautés si longtemps négligées; les autres firent semblant de les aimer parce que c'étoit la mode; et depuis lors, ce fut l'usage de presque tous les voyageurs, qui aspiroient à la réputation d'hommes de goût, de se détourner de leur chemin, pour aller ad-

The contagion between the literary and the scientific contemplation of nature took place just as much in the opposite direction as well. Contemporary novels very often included long passages referring to natural science and sometimes sounding like treatises. In the novel *Les amours de Zémédare et Carina* (1806), Prévost de Sansac uses a visit by natural researchers as the excuse for a digression about the geological composition of the island of Martinique:

> After they left Mr. le J***, our travelers went to visit Mount Pelée; this mountain, its surroundings, and in fact the entire island presents undeniable vestiges of volcanic eruptions. Nowhere on Martinique does one see a primitive mountain, their formation only dates, if one judges by the materials composing them, from the era of the violent convulsions of nature, long after the creation of the world. „I establish this opinion," says Mr. Tamony, „based on the very small quantity of topsoil that covers them and the fact that their interior does not contain any of those immense blocks of hard rock that one finds in almost all mountains in other parts of the world. The only granite to be found consists of very small, rolled pieces, and only at the edge of the ocean, which could make one think that it had been brought there." These naturalists had observed that in some places, the layer of topsoil was barely more than six inches thick, and that it is followed by a layer of pumice stone about a foot thick; that after that, there is another layer of topsoil, eight to ten inches high and stripped of any vegetative capacity, which was certainly removed from it by the action of the blazing pumice stones that suddenly covered it during the last eruption. Then there is a second layer of pumice stones that came after that, which was followed by a bed of loamy soil, dyed by red iron oxide; underneath that, one found true pozzolana, which the inhabitants of Saint-Pierre found it useful to use in building. Mr. Tamony complained of not having been able to collect more than a very small amount of important minerals: flood basalt, calcinated hornfels containing pieces of feldspar, some volcanic garnets, pyroxene, and the substances that one finds the most often in volcanic countries. He had some very light pumice stones, all of whose interstices were filled with mica flakes of the most beautiful golden color. He showed Mrs. Sainprale some ferruginous sands of various qualities, containing some very pretty microscopic crystals; but the purest and finest, he said, can be found in abundance along the seashore, in the town where they have the boat building. He also had some beautiful pieces of ocher of all colors (91 f.)[95]

---

mirer des précipices, des cascades, des grottes, des scènes de désert enfin, auxquelles personne ne s'avisoit de songer autrefois."

[95] "De chez M. le J***, nos voyageurs furent visiter la montagne Pelée; cette montagne, ses environs et même toute l'île entière, offre des vestiges irrécusables d'éruptions de volcans. On ne voit nulle part, à la Martinique, de montagne primitive, elles ne datent leur formation, si on en juge par les matières qui les composent, que de l'époque de violentes convulsions de la nature, très postérieures à la création du monde. 'J'établis cette opinion, dit M. Tamony, sur la très petite quantité de terre végétale qui les recouvre, et que leur intérieur ne contient aucun de ces blocs immenses de pierre dure et autres, qu'on retrouve dans presque toutes celles des autres parties de la terre. Le granit ne se trouve qu'en très petits morceaux roulés, et sur le bord de la mer seulement, ce qui pourrait faire croire qu'il y a été apporté.' Ces naturalistes avaient observé que

The passage I have cited here in detail shows that the elements of the scientific description of nature and of the fictional plot of the novel can barely be kept separate any more. The description of reality is transferred to the fictional project, producing an effect that Ottmar Ette ("Eine Literatur ohne festen Wohnsitz") describes as friction and which can be found particularly often in travelogues and biographies.

In the context of the Caribbean, however, it is not only descriptions of nature that are affected by the phenomenon of "friction"; it also extends to other realms of the scientific registration of the world, for example early ethnological studies, which will be more closely looked at in the next chapter, with the help of selected journals. At this point, I want to cite a further passage from Prévost de Sansac's novel as an example, a passage titled "Observations by the Priest of Gros Morne on How to Recognize Character through the Study of Physiognomies" (*Observations du curé de Gros-Morne sur les moyens de reconnaître le caractère par l'étude des physionomies*) and in which physiognomy and the study of temperament are entered into in depth. Many contemporary geographers and ethnologists took for granted that conclusions about the people's character could be drawn from the shape of the face and head:

> Physiognomy often has its home in the eyes; one rarely sees someone with black eyes who is habitually indolent and lazy, those who are usually have blue eyes; with blue eyes, tenderness is more energetic; very clear eyes are rarely lacking in order and clarity in the spirit; confident eyes do not love anything, no matter what they might say; damp eyes are very loving, and wide-open eyes love everything—Eyes whose liqueurs are blurred inspire mistrust; slitted eyes promise little spirit; eyes that are large and shining tell me that they are animated by a healthy soul; those that start out of the head make one fear stupidity and malice; deep-set eyes sometimes belong to an envious and treacherous man; if they are

---

dans quelques endroits, la couche de terre végétale n'avait guère plus de six pouces d'épaisseur, qu'elle est suivie d'une couche de pierre-ponce épaisse d'un pied environ; qu'après celle-ci, vient une autre couche de terre végétale, haute de huit à dix pouces, dénuée de toute faculté végétative, qui lui a sans doute été enlevée par l'action des pierres-ponces embrasées qui la couvrirent tout à coup lors de la dernière éruption. Une seconde couche de pierres-ponces venait encore après, et elle était suivie par un lit de terre argileuse teinte par l'oxide rouge de fer; au-dessous on trouvait de la vraie pouzzolane, que les habitants de Saint-Pierre emploient utilement pour bâtir. M. Tamony se plaignit de n'avoir ramassé que très peu de minéraux importants; des trapps, des cornéennes calcinées qui contenaient des morceaux de feld-spath, quelques grenats de volcans, des pyroxènes et les substances que l'on trouve le plus fréquemment dans les pays de volcans. Il avait des pierres-ponces extrêmement légères, dont tous les interstices étaient remplis par des paillettes de mica de la plus belle couleur d'or. Il fit voir à Mme Sainprale des sables ferrugineux de diverses qualités qui contenaient de très jolis cristaux microscopiques; mais le plus pur et le plus fin se trouve, dit-il, en abondance sur le rivage de la mer, au bourg de la case des navires. Il avait aussi de très beaux morceaux docre de toutes les couleurs."

too close to each other, if they make the gaze fierce, then one should expect cruelty; the eyes of the distracted man look at you and do not see you, they imitate the preoccupation of the studious man while the mind thinks of nothing. (101)[96]

III.9 Digression: Sugar and Skin Color between Metropolis and Colonial Projection

There are two basic pillars to the nineteenth century's (anti-)slavery debates that reach back into the eighteenth century and which have to date received hardly any attention in studies of the literary presentation of these debates; these two pillars are sugar and skin color.[97] In the context of cultural studies debates over "things" as practical social strategies of appropriation (Ecker and Scholz; Latour; Daston), it is worth taking a look at these basic pillars and, especially, at the connection between them in the fragile in-between space of Caribbean experiences and attributions of identity. Travelogues discursivized and (re-)contextualized the circulation of novel goods and things that were foreign to Europeans and carried it to the European metropolises (see Leonard and Pretel). Two travelogues in French, in which the knowledge of foreign things intersects in a very concentrated way, were particularly influential: Jean-Baptiste Labat's *Nouveau voyage aux isles de l'Amérique* (New voyage to the islands of America) (1722) und Guillaume-Thomas François Raynal's *Histoire philosophique et politique des établissements et du commerce des européens dans les deux Indes* (Philosophical and political history of the establishments and trade of Europeans in the two Indias) (1770). Using an analysis of these two texts as a starting point, in this digression I will examine the chronological development of cultural forms of rep-

---

[96] "Le siège de la physionomie se trouve fréquemment dans les yeux; on voit rarement quelqu'un avec des yeux noirs être indolent et paresseux par habitude, ceux qui le sont ont les yeux bleus; chez les yeux bleus la tendresse est plus énergique; des yeux bien nets manquent rarement d'ordre et de netteté dans l'esprit; les yeux certains n'aiment rien, quoi qu'ils puissent dire; les yeux humides aiment beaucoup, et les yeux fort ouverts aiment tout – Les yeux dont les liqueurs sont brouillées inspirent de ta défiance; les yeux bridés promettent peu d'esprit; des yeux bien fendus et brillants me disent qu'ils sont animés par une âme saine; ceux qui sortent de la tête font craindre la bêtise et la méchanceté; les yeux enfoncés appartiennent quelquefois à un homme envieux et perfide; s'ils sont trop rapprochés l'un de l'autre, s'ils rendent le regard farouche, on doit s'attendre à de la cruauté; les yeux de l'homme distrait vous fixent et ne vous voient pas, ils imitent la préoccupation de l'homme studieux, tandis que l'esprit ne songe à rien."
[97] An exception is Boren, who also includes missionary Christian theology in his analysis. For the following remarks cf. Müller "Vom 'Genuß der Dinge, die wir so weit herholen ...'."

resentation of sugar and skin color as "things" into the middle of the nineteenth century. To what extent are the discourses for and against slavery connected to the exotic resource of sugar, as a consumer good, and to skin color as an exclusionary strategy of appropriation, in Labat's and Rayal's depictions? Looking at Labat's[98] major work will reveal strategies with which foreign things are made present, in this case the way in which sugar is presented as a local medium of exchange. It refers, in particular, to the conversion of basic foodstuffs and other imported goods into sugar:

> In addition, our house was in debt to the tune of nearly seven hundred thousand pounds of sugar and had no credit anymore: these debts had been contracted by the poor housekeeping of the monks who had mismanaged their affairs, by the exorbitant spending of the priests who took whatever they wanted from the merchants and paid them with a sugar note, which was at that time the common currency of the islands, to be drawn on the plantation. ... This loss kept us from producing the quantity of sugar that we would have been able to produce. ... Besides, it was only raw sugar, disparaged for its poor quality, and which the war had reduced to such a low price that a hundredweight was only worth fifty or sixty sols, whereas food and other commodities from France were at an excessive price. A barrel of flour cost fifteen hundred pounds of sugar; a barrel of salted beef the same; a barrel of bacon two thousand five hundred pounds; a wine keg cost three thousand pounds and sometimes more; all the sugar that we could produce added up to barely thirty thousand pounds, on which we had to maintain the Negroes, the livestock, the mill, and the other expenses of a plantation and feed the monks who were there. (Labat [1722] I:114–16)[99]

---

[98] Jean-Baptiste Labat (Paris, 1663–1738) entered the Dominican order in 1684 and set out as a missionary to the West Indies in 1694. There he owned a plantation where he kept slaves and burned rum. Later, he was named as the general procurator for his order's mission in the East Indies, and from there he returned to Europe in 1705. His travelogues from the Antilles are very vividly written and were highly popular in Europe. His six-volume work *Nouveau voyage aux isles de l'Amérique* was published in Paris in 1722.

[99] "D'ailleurs notre maison était endettée de près de sept cent mille livres de sucre et n'avait plus aucun crédit; ces dettes avaient été contractées par la mauvaise économie des religieux qui avaient mal gouverné leurs affaires, par les dépenses exorbitantes des curés qui prenaient chez les marchands tout ce qui leur plaisait et les payaient avec un billet de sucre qui était en ce temps-là la monnaie courante des îles à prendre sur l'habitation. ... Cette perte nous empêchait de faire la quantité de sucre qu'on aurait pu faire. ... D'ailleurs ce n'était que du sucre brut, décrié pour sa mauvaise qualité, et que la guerre avait réduit à si bas prix, que le cent ne valait que cinquante ou soixante sols, pendant que les vivres et les autres denrées de France étaient à un prix excessif. Le baril de farine coûtait quinze cent livres de sucre; le baril de bœuf salé autant; le baril de lard deux mille cinq cent livres; la barrique de vin trois mille livres et souvent davantage; tout le sucre qu'on pouvait fabriquer chez nous allait à peine à cent trente mille livres, sur quoi il fallait entretenir les Nègres, les bestiaux, le moulin et les autres dépenses d'une habitation et nourrir les religieux qui y étaient."

Thanks to sugar, the French colonies of the Caribbean established themselves as productive spaces of consumption. Trading establishments expanded and exports to Europe, in particular, flourished.

> This town has grown a great deal because the considerable quantity of cocoa, sugar, and cotton that is produced in these quarters, and particularly on Gros Morne peak, has attracted a large number of merchants and a quantity of ships, especially from Nantes, which make commerce flourish there and which find a guaranteed and prompt market for all the merchandise that they bring there from Europe. (I:336)[100]

The sugar trade between the Caribbean colonies and the French metropolis is staged in Labat as a strategy of creating presence. He gives the inhabitants of the island the advice that they should only exchange sugar for money, preferably on the spot, in the colonies, but to always use it themselves as a means of payment:

> The last piece of advice that I would give a resident is to sell his sugars and his other commodities for hard cash or for well-backed promissory notes, and not to pay for what he buys with anything other than sugar or some other thing originating from his plantation. This is the secret to enriching oneself. ... It is even better to sell to the islands for cash or for promissory notes than to send goods to France, because the freight charges, the entry tariffs, the tares, the barrels, the companies' claims, the storage fees, and the commissions take away most of the profit and sometimes even part of the capital, leaving the owner for a long time in a state of anxiety over the fate of his goods. (Labat [1742] IV:221 ff.)[101]

Labat also describes sugar, as a "thing," in relationship to French culture, of which it is a part in spite of its foreignness. In the *Nouveau voyage aux isles de l'Amérique*, it is presented not just as the dominant product of the Antilles, simultaneously a commodity and a means of payment, but also as, for European

---

100 "Ce bourg s'est beaucoup augmenté, parce que la quantité considérable de cacao, de sucre, de coton que l'on fabrique dans ces quartiers-là, et surtout au gros morne, y ont attiré bon nombre de marchands et quantité de vaisseaux, particulièrement de ceux de Nantes qui y font fleurir le commerce et qui trouvent un débit assuré et prompt de toutes les marchandises qu'ils y apportent d'Europe."
101 "Le dernier avis que j'aie à donner à un habitant est de vendre ses sucres et ses autres denrées en argent comptant ou en lettres de change bien assurées, et de ne payer ce qu'il achète qu'en sucre ou autre chose provenant du fond de son habitation. C'est le secret de s'enrichir. ... Il vaut mieux encore vendre comptant aux îles ou en lettres de change que d'envoyer les effets en France, parce que le fret, les entrées, les tares, les barriques, les droits des Compagnies, le magasinage, les avanies et les commissions emportent le plus clair du profit et quelquefois même une partie du capital et laissent le propriétaire pendant longtemps dans l'anxiété du sort de ses marchandises."

readers, a kind of metonymic stand-in for the Caribbean colonies: their economic importance and position in the world is contained in sugar, as is their otherness, which is particularly expressed in the linkage of sugar and skin color.

A further example of Labat making foreign things present is the reification of skin color, inasmuch as it is skin color that determines the amount of head tax that must be paid to the king:

> The king's dominion in the islands consists of the right to impose a head tax which all white men and free, indentured, or enslaved black men pay from the age of fourteen years until sixty. This entitlement is for one hundred pounds of actual raw sugar per year, for those who produce it, and six francs for those who do not. It is the masters who pay for their indentured or enslaved servants. One pays another one percent of all the sugar that one delivers for the right to weigh it oneself. ... All of the white Creoles, that is those born in the islands, and generally all the white women, are exempt from the head tax as well as slaves, servants, or indentured servants of the clergy, of the former lords, owners of the islands, and their representatives. (Labat [1722] I:242ff.)[102]

Sugar and skin color, as foreign things, remain in constant relation with each other, as the tax, which is determined along skin color lines, is paid by the plantation owners in sugar. Labat describes the two as inseparably connected within the universe of plantation slavery: "it was absolutely necessary to have slaves, unless one wanted to discontinue the work of the sugar factories" (Labat [1742] IV:419).[103] Even in the slave trade itself skin color becomes a criterion, that is to say it undergoes a reification. In Africa one paid in bars of crude iron, guns, powder, and cowries from the Maldives (IV:428 ff.),[104] while in the An-

---

[102] "Le domaine du roi dans les îles consiste dans le droit de capitation que tous les hommes blancs ou noirs libres, engagés ou esclaves payent depuis l'âge de quatorze ans jusques à soixante. Ce droit est de cent livres de sucre brut effectif par an, pour ceux qui en font ou de six francs pour ceux qui n'en font point. Ce sont les maîtres qui payent pour leurs domestiques engagés ou esclaves. On paye encore un pour cent de tout le sucre qu'on livre pour avoir le droit de le peser chez soi. ... Tous les blancs créoles c'est-à-dire, nés dans les îles, et généralement toutes les femmes blanches sont exemptes du droit de capitation aussi bien que les esclaves, serviteurs ou engagés des religieux ou des anciens seigneurs, propriétaires des îles et leurs représentants."

[103] "il était absolument nécessaire d'avoir des esclaves, à moins de discontinuer le travail de la sucrerie." Cf. also Labat's description of the blacks' huts on a hill behind the sugar factory (Labat [1722] I:114).

[104] "they are paid in bars of iron, rifles, powder, bullets, canvases, paper, light fabrics and other goods, and especially in 'bouges,' shells from the Maldive Islands that are used as common currency all along the coast" ("on les paye en barres de fer, fusils, poudre, balles, toiles, papier, étoffes légères et autres marchandises, et surtout en bouges, des coquilles des îles Maldives qui servent de monnaie courante dans toute la côte").

tilles, on the other hand, it was sugar that was used as a means of exchange: "I bought twelve [slaves], who cost me five thousand seven hundred francs, which I had to pay in raw sugar" (IV:419).[105]

Sugar is very frequently perceived in relation to skin color and is, as a result, exotic, foreign, and near all at the same time. On the one hand, it is a coveted commodity; on the other hand it is necessarily bound up with slavery and therefore with distinctions between colors of skin. In Labat's *Nouveau voyage* it is constantly shown that, given the Western privileging of spirit over matter, sugar can at first arouse the appearance of immediacy because the separation of subject and object, of the perceiving I and the sensual world of things, causes the things that are located on the object side, as distinct from consciousness, to appear to be moved, governed, and appropriated by consciousness. This almost paradoxical relationship of radical division between person and thing on the one hand and their simultaneous dependency on each other in all realms of the cultural and social production of meaning is constitutive of the representation of sugar in Labat (cf. Ecker and Scholz 10).

Although the primary mode of existence for things in a consumer society is as goods, these attributions of value are also relevant beyond the discourse of goods. The reduction of value to an exchange value is only one aspect of the ways in which things acquire meaning, because in addition to their material value there can be a symbolic or ideal value that is often the dominant force in giving them meaning, both personal and collective (cf. Ecker and Scholz 12). It is worth taking a look here at the relationship between skin color and sugar as a condition for the Haitian Revolution. Even though the Haitian Revolution could not have been anticipated from a cultural historical standpoint, Guillaume-Thomas François Raynal's travelogue communicates a way of reading eighteenth-century Caribbean constellations that is steeped in ambivalence and prepares the ground for long-lasting categories of perception built on this ambivalence to assert themselves; in the year 1770, a six-volume work was published anonymously in Amsterdam under the title *Histoire philosophique et politique des établissements et du commerce des Européens dans les deux Indes* (Philosophical and political history of the establishments and business of the Europeans in the two Indias), which was disseminated and attracted attention throughout Europe. The following editions were expanded to include texts by several authors, the most famous of them being Diderot. His contributions were far more uncompromising in their anti-colonialism than the more moderated and

---

[105] "j'en achetai douze [esclaves], qui me coûtèrent cinq mille sept cens francs, que je devois payer en Sucre brut."

conciliatory tones of the original text, written by Raynal. When the final version of the text appeared in 1780, this time under Raynal's name ("a kind of mini-*Encyclopédie* of colonialism's political, intellectual, and social effects on Europe" [Pagden 118][106]), it was banned by the censor. In "The Extinction of Difference," Anthony Pagden sums up the key findings on Raynal:

> Raynal himself was a moderate reformer, a man who, as Frédéric Grimm put it, advocated positions that were "more in keeping with conventional politics than with justice." Later, in 1785, Raynal also wrote an *Essai sur l'administration de St. Domingue* (Essay on the administration of Saint-Domingue) in which, although he did suggest reforms, he espoused neither the liberation of the slaves nor the abolition of the slave trade. (116)[107]

In this essay he expresses moral outrage, as many others also do, over skin color as a distinguishing feature and over the evil that follows from it, slavery, which he calls "the terrible right of the stronger" (*le droit terrible du plus fort*) (Raynal, *Histoire philosophique* 13), but he also claims that abolishing it would not be politically acceptable. For Raynal, slavery is a manifest evil, an absurdity, that as a social practice denies the human being the one inalienable right that is a person's own, namely "self-ownership" (*propriété de soi*) and therefore also denies "the specific character of a human being." For slavery, as the prominent abolitionist Frossard argued to the National Assembly in 1793, not only made humanity into a thing, in other words a commodity, but it also valued humans according to their physical strength, the very quality that is the least essential to human identity, thereby representing "the greatest insult to our nature" (Pagden 125).[108]

---

106 "eine Art Mini-*Encyclopédie* über die politischen, intellektuellen und gesellschaftlichen Auswirkungen des Kolonialismus auf Europa".
107 "Raynal selbst war ein gemäßigter Reformer, ein Mann, der, wie es Frédéric Grimm formulierte, Auffassungen vertrat, die sich 'mehr mit herkömmlicher Politik als mit Gerechtigkeit vertrugen'. [...]. Später, im Jahre 1785, schrieb Raynal auch einen *Essai sur l'administration de St. Domingue*, in dem er zwar Reformen vorschlug, aber weder für die Freilassung der Sklaven noch für die Abschaffung des Sklavenhandels eintrat." As Ottmar Ette sums up Raynal's position: "In spite of all of the contradictions and ambivalences that ... compromised the effectiveness of the *Histoire des deux Indes*, Raynal and his famous work were nevertheless the symbols of a liberation from colonial oppression." ("Allen Widersprüchen und Ambivalenzen, welche die Wirkung der *Histoire des deux Indes* [...] beeinträchtigten, zum Trotz, standen Raynal und sein bekanntes Werk doch symbolhaft für eine Befreiung aus kolonialer Unterdrückung.") (Ette, "Figuren und Funktionen des Lesens" 590).
108 Condorcet, in his 1781 *Réflexions sur l'esclavage des nègres* (6 ff.), also specifically pointed to the legal objectification of slaves: even a contract worker, who in some sense had sold himself into slavery, had really only sold the right to the use of his work and was, in his relationship to his master, bound by public rather than private law. The slave, on the other hand, was nothing

Raynal and his co-authors of *Histoire ... des deux Indes* respond to this radical objectification of the African slaves by referring to skin color, which they recognize as the central justification for this inhuman treatment. In the manner of the late Enlightenment, they present skin color as a foreign thing that needs to be examined as a scientific object, freed from its old interpretive connections, and newly explained. Skin color is described as a value-free physiological phenomenon:

> This color comes from a mucous substance that forms a kind of network between the epidermis and the skin. This substance, which is white in Europeans, brown in olive-skinned peoples, and dotted with reddish spots in blond or red-headed peoples, is blackish in the Negroes. (Raynal, *Histoire philosophique* VI:52 ff.)[109]

Science, they point out, has not yet found a clear explanation for the varying skin colors of humanity, because skin color is a complex thing: "Our organs are so weak, our resources so short, our studies so distracted, our life so agitated; and the object of our research is so vast!" (VI:58)[110] Thus, the climate is often mentioned as an important factor influencing skin color, in connection with the thought that skin color might possibly change over a period of generations in a new environment:

> The coloring of Negroes is the result of the climate, the air, the water, the foodstuffs of Guinea, and it changes when you take them to other countries. The children that they procreate in America are less black than those who gave birth to them. After each generation, the difference is more noticeable. It could be that after a number of generations one would no longer be able to distinguish the men who have come from Africa from those of the countries to which they had been transplanted. (VI:57)[111]

---

but a legal matter (a *res*), exactly as in Roman law, and was therefore entirely dependent on the "whim of his master" (Pagden 126).

109 "Ce coloris vient d'une substance muqueuse, qui forme une espece de rézeau entre l'épiderme et la peau. Cette substance qui est blanche dans les Européens, brune chez les peuples olivâtres, parsemée de taches rougeâtres chez les peuples blonds ou roux, est noirâtre chez les negres."

110 "Nos organes sont si foibles, nos moyens si courts, nos études si distraites, notre vie si troublée; et l'objet de nos recherches si vaste!"

111 "Le coloris des nègres est l'effet du climat, de l'air, de l'eau, des alimens de la Guinée, c'est qu'il change lorsqu'on les conduit dans d'autres nations. Les enfans qu'ils procréent en Amérique sont moins noirs que ceux dont ils ont reçu le jour. Après chaque lignée, la différence est plus sensible. Il se pourroit, qu'après de nombreuses générations, on ne distinguât pas les hommes sortis d'Afrique, de ceux des pays où ils auroient été transplantés."

By no means could the dark coloring of the skin be traced back to any chemical processes of decay, because after all the physiological organization of the Negroes is "just as complete ... as in the whitest of human species" (*aussi parfaite ... que dans l'espece d'hommes la plus blanche*) (VI:54). The conventional essentializations of skin color, with their negative value judgments, are flatly rejected, as can also be seen from the ironic treatment of the religious discourses about the original sin of the Africans:

> Theology, after having made a race of men guilty and unhappy through Adam's fault, now makes a race of men black to punish the fratricide of his son. It is from Cain that the Negroes are descended. If their father was an assassin, it must be admitted that his crime is being cruelly expiated by his children; and that the descendants of the peaceful Abel have thoroughly avenged the innocent blood of their father. (VI:53)[112]

Pagden points out that it is, paradoxically, the slave trade itself that ties together the two main themes of the *Histoire des deux Indes*, namely traveling/migration and trade. After the discovery of America, slavery, which until then had been a product of warfare, now became a branch of trade instead (130). And the *Histoire* looks just as critically at traveling and the circulation of foreign things and consumer goods that is bound up with it, sugar being the preeminent example:

> Does our true happiness require us to enjoy the things that we fetch from so far away? ... Can the advantages it brings us in goods make up for the loss of the citizens who leave their fatherland and who perish either through illnesses that seize them while they are traveling or through the climate when they arrive? ... What firm bonds can tie us to a possession from which we are separated by an immeasurable space? (Raynal and Diderot 186–187)[113]

Diderot in particular, in the passages written by him in the *Histoire des deux Indes*, opposes the swelling stream of goods when he writes that the diversity and quantity of objects that are served to the spirit and the senses have splintered men's emotions and weakened the energies of all sensations (cf. Pagden

---

112 "La théologie, après avoir fait une race d'hommes coupables et malheureux par la faute d'Adam, fait une race d'hommes noirs, pour punir le fratricide de son fils. C'est de Caïn que sont descendus les negres. Si leur pere était assassin, il faut convenir que son crime est cruellement expié par ses enfants; et que les descendants du pacifique Abel ont bien vengé le sang innocent de leur père."
113 "Erfordert unser wahres Glück den Genuß der Dinge, die wir so weit herholen? ... Kann das, was er an Waren bezieht, mit Vorteil den Verlust der Bürger ersetzen, die sich von ihrem Vaterland entfernen, um entweder durch Krankheiten, die sie auf der Reise ergreifen, oder durch das Klima bei ihrer Ankunft umzukommen? ... Durch welche festen Bande kann mit uns eine Besitzung, von welcher uns ein unermeßlicher Raum trennt, verbunden sein?"

134 ff.). The voyages and the long-lasting sea journeys, he wrote, had impoverished the morals and imagination of all Europeans and, what was worse, had increased their tolerance for the suffering of others, represented by the lasting symbol of the enslaved African. Diderot was, for this reason, also firmly convinced that only a revolution, under the leadership of a new "black Spartacus," could hope to open the eyes of the European colonial world to the misdeed that it had committed—in retrospect, this sounds like an advance announcement of the Haitian revolutionary leader Toussaint Louverture (135).

Considering sugar and skin color as things reveals a new perspective on cultural forms of representation from and about the Caribbean: by focusing on the two pillars represented by sugar and skin color, we can read the Caribbean as a place in which the American culture of presence and the European culture of the senses collide. Sugar and skin color are protagonists in these continental encounters. While sugar functions above all as a medium of exchange and a consumer good in Labat, in Raynal sugar and skin color, in the context of a prehistory of the Haitian Revolution, function as the constitutive pillars of the constitution of the subject in the context of the (anti-)slavery debate. Following the Haitian Revolution, we can determine that in literary as well as in ethnological representations of sugar, it always acts as a counterbalance to the French metropolis's concept of culture. In Paris, the colonial center, it is impossible for sugar as a thing to escape the standards of commodity valuation: as soon as sugar is transferred from the Caribbean to Europe, it belongs there to a new economy of meaning and value and its original meanings are pushed into the background (Ecker and Scholz 12).

The look we have taken at Labat and Raynal has, however, also shown that sugar and skin color always take on a life of their own. As Susanne Scholz has shown in relation to objects in modernity (Ecker and Scholz 11 ff.), sugar and skin color also produce a surplus of meaning in whatever environment they are in—whether it is the Caribbean or Paris—that leads to their constantly being revaluated, restructured, and inserted into new meanings or to their producing new meanings. Sugar and skin color function as projections or as alter egos, whether of a colonial master or of a chronicler (in other words, of those who own them or desire them), and yet they produce a surplus of materiality or tangibility that is not absorbed in the service of the subject (11). This can be seen, for example, in the reification of skin color in the nineteenth century, in the context of new Caribbean ethnic mixtures as a utopian project, in a quotation from the *Revue des Colonies* that circulated from 1834 to 1842 and will be discussed in greater detail in the next chapter:

> From these whites, from these blacks, from these reds, there will be founded a mixed race of Europeans, Africans, and Americans, which within several generations and through various interminglings will arrive, by way of brown, caramel, plum—dear sir, orange-ish—at a pale yellow, lightly coppered. All of these singularities, all these marvels of civilization that elevate and interest our heart and our spirit, are more or less near. (*Revue des Colonies*, July 1836, 20 ff.)[114]

Here (dark) skin color, as a foreign thing that made the separation between European colonial masters and African slaves obvious to eighteenth- and nineteenth-century Europeans, deploys its potential to overcome this very distinction and dissolve the hierarchy that is attached to it. In the color-rapture of all the possible shades of skin the aesthetic "singularities" show the way to the "marvel of civilization," understood both ethically and ethnically, of a Caribbean society without racial differences.

---

114 "De ces blancs, de ces noirs, de ces rouges, il se fondera une race mélangée d'Européens, d'Africains et d'Américains, qui en quelques générations et au travers des croisements divers, arrivera, par le brun, le carmélite, le prune—monsieur, l'orangé, à un jaune pâle, légèrement cuivré. Toutes ces singularités, toutes ces merveilles de civilisation qui élèvent et intéressent notre cœur et notre esprit, sont plus ou moins prochaines."

IV Processes of Ethnological Circulation

Even for the Enlightenment, which established the principle of critique, including self-critique, Europe was not simply the center of the world but in fact the embodiment of humankind. The tide only began to turn with European Romanticism: that epochal change, which has often been noted, has to do with the fact that the classical forms of knowledge, based on the concept of representation, were replaced by a new way of organizing knowledge (cf. Foucault 217; Matzat 86; Küpper 64–82).[1] One of the expressions of that change is the emergence of ethnology, which was indispensable for the colonial situation (cf. Fink-Eitel 211).[2] The encounter with the other, with the foreign, always points back to the mediating subjectivity of the observer (Hölz 11, referring to Wolfzettel).

Scholarship, with its new infrastructure, was not only influential in consolidating France's discourses of imperialism but also gave the Napoleonic overseas interlude a cultural dimension, which had a much more lasting impact than did the actual political dominion. (In Spain, on the other hand, there was no corresponding reorganization of the foundations of knowledge.) The great Parisian institutes of teaching and learning, which were established by Napoleon, contributed to the development of archeology, linguistics, historiography, oriental studies, and experimental biology. Novelists often refer to the academically driven discourse about the overseas possessions.[3]

The establishment of ethnology as a new form of knowledge led to an intellectual atmosphere that legitimized and, in fact (unlike earlier, eighteenth-century formulations of the noble savage), promoted a great variety of discourses about the Other. Scholarship and the sciences understood themselves, at this

---

[1] I am grateful to Hafid Derbal for important insights for this chapter on ethnology and the three ethnological journals. Although I particularly emphasize non-European Romanticism, it should be noted that the Enlightenment, too, can only be understood with reference to its non-European dimensions. Some of the important studies on the ethnographic discourse that was developing in France in the second half of the eighteenth century and the turn to 1800 include Chappey; Copans and Jamin; Duchet, *Anthropologie et histoire*; Duchet, *Le partage des savoirs*; Ette, "Réflexions européennes"; and Lüsebrink, *Das Europa der Aufklärung* 10 ff. (Exiled) Jesuits also made very important contributions to the development of ethnographic knowledge, both about South America and about the transcultural space of the Caribbean, in the second half of the eighteenth century; see Lüsebrink, "Missionarische Fremdheitserfahrung"; Tietz and Briesemeister.
[2] Fink-Eitel relies here on Foucault. Abbé Raynal and Cornelius de Paux are also important to the new forms of representing the Other. Cf. Ette, *Alexander von Humboldt* 74 ff.
[3] This is of course true not only with respect to the Caribbean but also in talking about Africa, possessions in the East, etcetera; see for example Balzac's *The Magic Skin* and *Cousin Betty*, as well as section III.8 of the present book, on frictionality.

point in time in Europe, as "simultaneously both the driver and the means of European expansionary politics" (Ette, *Alexander von Humboldt* 49).

As a backdrop for the following observations about the reception of ethnological knowledge from the Caribbean, allow me first to sketch a panorama of the contemporary racial discourse in France and Spain. The Parisian journals *Revue des Colonies* (Colonial review), *Revue des deux mondes* (Review of the two worlds), and *Revue encyclopédique* (Encyclopedic review) are representative of the negotiation of colonial questions within specific Caribbean discourses at a point in time at which Paris operated as a privileged center for the circulation of knowledge. All three were founded between 1820 and 1830. While the *Revue des Colonies* and the *Revue encyclopédique* each enjoyed only a short heyday, were highly specialized, wrote for a very limited public, and were rather quickly discontinued, the *Revue des deux mondes*, a more establishment-oriented publication, continues to this day.

In terms of their content, all three of the journals address questions of cultural scholarship, which are not clearly categorized because this scholarship was only just beginning to be divided into its later specialties. The themes that appear include ethnology, colonialism, literature, literary history, and culture. In the first half of the nineteenth century, a number of periodicals appear in France that survived for only a short time. The only reason for my choice of the three named here is that they primarily communicate Caribbean transfer processes.

Because very little research has been done, I have chosen the aspects that I wanted to look at inductively. In the case of the *Revue des Colonies* and the *Revue encyclopédique*, colonial questions are the main concern of the journals, and in those cases, therefore, I chose topics that seemed particularly relevant to the illumination of colonial transfer and circulation processes and questions of conviviality. In the case of the *Revue des deux mondes*, on the other hand, I look at entire articles that stand as witnesses to early Caribbean literary historiography. The focus, though, in all three cases, is on the staging of questions that are relevant to this study, rather than on an examination of the publications as such.

The fact that Spain has no such array of publications at that point in time speaks for itself. Through an examination of the wide variety of themes that appear in the French publications, I would like to pursue the question of the degree to which the capacity to integrate the Other, which has been postulated for France, was indeed expressed.[4] It is key to note that this promotion of integra-

---

4 On the concept of integration, particularly this aspect of it, please compare Lüsebrink's comment that "integration refers to forms of cultural and social adaptation to a dominant culture, in which, at least in the transitional phase, important identity-constituting elements of the original

tion was in fact also disseminated by the media that were critical of colonization. The question of a median position between bipolarity and multirelationalism is equally important. And finally, I want to ask the question of whether and how these periodicals dealt with questions of conviviality.

IV.1 "Labeling People": Discourses of "Race" in France and Spain

In his 1976 study of the "end of natural history," Wolf Lepenies shows how in the aftermath of the Enlightenment, there was a gradual sense of time and chronology that established itself within scholarly thinking, a sense that developed into historical thinking. He makes it clear that the discovery of the perspective of time took place in the disciplines that we now consider to be the natural sciences. This can be seen in a particularly explosive manner in the transition from classical natural history to modern biology: the breakneck pace of the growth in the number of known animals and plants made a new organization of knowledge necessary in the second half of the eighteenth century, and as a result the previous system, with its multiplicity of catalogues and tables, most of them organized alphabetically, was restructured. It was not until a historical understanding of nature had arisen, connecting the individual species with their temporal development, that it was possible to organize biological knowledge in a concise and lucid way. Long before Darwin, then, a chronological understanding of nature had developed according to which the history of a scientific object was what determined its classification. However, the end of natural history cannot be imagined without the non-European dimension (Ette, "Europäische Literatur[en]" 262), which occasioned intense debates in the first half of the nineteenth century, nowhere more energetically carried out than in Paris, the privileged center of the circulation of knowledge (cf. Ette, *Alexander von Humboldt* 115).

As Michel Foucault explains in *The Order of Things*, the entire modality of seventeenth- and eighteenth-century classical knowledge was based on the classification of species. As Europeans pushed further and further into the Pacific and the African interior, even when it was more a question of establishing trading posts than setting up colonies, new contacts were established and new subjects of classification arose. Martin Staum's study *Labeling People*, the results of

---

culture, such as language, ritual, and dress codes, are preserved." ("Mit Integration sind Formen kultureller und sozialer Anpassung an eine dominante Kultur gemeint, bei der jedoch zumindest in einer Übergangsphase wichtige Identitätselemente der Ausgangs- und Herkunftskultur erhalten bleiben, wie Sprache, Rituale und Kleidungscodes.") (*Interkulturelle Kommunikation* 130).

which inform my observations in the following, shows that as time went on, there was a tendency to consider the new subjects more through the grid of biological determinism than according to their degree of cultural "backwardness" or their "savagery." This point of view also definitely served to give a "scientific" justification to slavery:

> Fully developed classification of humans by skin and colour emerged only among the naturalists of the late eighteenth century. Ordering "races" by superiority could serve to assuage guilt about slavery, although even anti-slavery authors generally believed in racial hierarchy and African inferiority. (Staum 8)

Between 1800 and 1850, strictly physical criteria definitely prevail. And now that there was the unavoidable nature of "race," there was no longer any way around labeling. These classifications, however, did not necessarily mean that the characteristics and abilities of individual peoples were considered to be fixed and unchangeable. Many eighteenth-century European philosophers (including Smith and Turgot) turned away from the myth of the "noble savage," which had been used as a contrast to European imperfection. They assumed that all populations went through the same life cycle, eventually arriving at higher levels of development (ibid.).

IV.1.1 The Development of Anthropology in France

The eighteenth-century classification of people according to their external characteristics can also be seen in the specific social context of France. At that time, dress codes and consumer preferences were in transition. This made it hard to distinguish social origins and classes. The rich bourgeoisie could now imitate the aristocracy, and boundaries that had once been visibly marked were now obscured. The revolution, which definitively abolished all explicit dress codes and rules about who was and was not allowed to wear certain decorations, only exacerbated the existing trends.[5] In this situation, such things as the interpretation of the shape of the human head as a way to find appropriate employees or even suitable marriage candidates took on even greater importance. In this era of social upheavals, of global economic rivalries, and of an increasing tendency to label people, there was growing interest in the emerging human sciences (cf. Staum 9 ff.). People were interested in determining the laws of human behavior.

---

[5] On the subject of fashion transferences, see Gertrud Lehnert's studies, for example "Des 'robes à la turque.'"

It is against this background that the establishment of a variety of scientific societies should be seen, beginning with the *Société de Géographie de Paris* (SGP; The Paris geographical society), in 1821, which was constituted of active explorers, theoretical geographers, and linguists.[6] The society's expressed goal was to dominate the entire rest of the world through French economic intervention. The SGP helped to develop theories of the hierarchies of populations, also with the goal of legitimizing French dominion over them (cf. Staum 11). Starting as early as the eighteenth century, geographers and explorers developed "retardation models" and a necessary and unavoidable sequence of developmental steps leading from savagery to civilization. Europeans were supposed to support the "childish" species and help them in becoming "adult" (cf. 86):

> Such an argument foreshadowed the ideology of assimilationism prominent throughout the 19th century in French imperial theory. The French mission was to lead non-Europeans to civilization. By means of the French language, Christianity, its associated morality, and superior science and technology, the French would develop the intellectual and moral faculties of the colonized. (86–87)

Sometime after 1830, a much smaller group, the *Société phrénologique de Paris* (SPP; The phrenological society of Paris) was established, dealing with the science of the skull. This group claimed that intelligence and character could be determined based entirely on the shape of the skull (cf. 11). A variety of measurements were used to identify developed and underdeveloped areas of the brain. One result of this was that the social mobility of some individuals was restricted and that some races were considered to have only limited intellectual capacities, across the board. Most phrenologists were essentially agreed that the various "species" could be educated, but opinions were often clearly expressed that for certain ethnicities, there were definite predetermined limits set by their brains and the shape of their skulls. Almost all of these theorists placed the Africans, or "Negroes," on the bottom rung of the hierarchy. But phrenology gained only limited recognition among the scientific, medical, and intellectual leaders of the time, and as a result, it was never able to be transformed into an experimental psychology (cf. 12).

In 1839, the physicist William Frédéric Edwards brought together a group of geographers and linguists to form the *Société ethnologique de Paris* (SEP; Ethnological society of Paris). The declared goal of this group was to collect, coordinate, and publish material in order to make known the various human races

---

6 On natural geography see also Lüsebrink, *Das Europa der Aufklärung* 11.

that are or were spread across the earth.[7] To this end, the SEP asked readers and travelers a series of questions about the physical characteristics, language, religions, customs and mores, traditions, and the influence of the soil and the climate among various peoples of the earth. This was for the explicit purpose of studying human variety and evaluating the potential for improvement of the various races. Thus, they undermined the theory that had traditionally held in France, namely that all subjugated peoples should be considered to be as educable as French citizens (cf. Staum 11 f.).[8]

These three societies (the SGP, the SPP, and the SEP) shared an interest in the question of the potential of individuals and races for development; none of the societies, however, was internally monolithic. They mirrored the three broad trends that Staum detects in France. First, there were those who wanted to bring European civilization to non-Europeans and assimilate them, making them French citizens. Second, there were those who advocated European leadership but believed that because of "racial inequality" no assimilation or equality would ever be possible, only at the most an approximation. And third, there were those who held the European race to be far superior and the other races and peoples in no way capable of learning or improvement; this group as a result also had no qualms about European dominion and exploitation (Staum 188). The more exploration and classification was undertaken, the greater the tendency became to claim that some races were either "incapable of becoming civilized" or else only "capable of becoming civilized" with European help:

> The alleged disparities within the human species, combined with commercial or strategic motivations, provided a synergy between theories of race and projects of empire. In this fashion scientific studies of ethno-geographers gave aid and comfort to French expansion even before the heyday of imperialism and the distinctive Third Republic version of the civilizing mission. (120)

Although the shock of the 1848 revolution broke up both the SPP and the SEP, the ethnologists' discourses provided the basis for physical anthropology, which had its base in the *Société d'anthropologie de Paris* (SAP; Anthropological society of Paris), founded in 1859 and led by Paul Broca (Staum 12). The interpretation of cranial shapes therefore became an essential research object for anthropologists.[9] And although leading physicists and physiologists denounced phre-

---

[7] I use the term "race" here as it was used in contemporary discourses.
[8] Cf. the first part of Louandre's article on societies, focusing on Paris.
[9] The *Musée National d'Histoire Naturelle* (MNHN; National museum for natural history) provided an important institutional basis for anthropological studies and also played a role in the academic establishment of French anthropology that should not be underestimated. However, al-

nology in the eighteen-forties, it remained "active" through the end of the nineteenth century and formed a part of regular long-term experiments carried out by the SAP (Staum 81). And finally, it should not be forgotten that phrenology, which claimed scientific validity for its cranial measurements, paved the way for theoreticians like Arthur Graf von Gobineau and Houston Stewart Chamberlain, who made a pseudoscientific racism socially acceptable in wide bourgeois and intellectual circles.

As early as the beginning of the nineteenth century, the French had articulated a kind of civilizing mission, and the strictly hierarchically conceived monogenism or, alternatively, the rigid polygenism that could be noted starting in the middle of the century hinted at the brutal forms that imperial politics would take by the end of the century, rejecting the assimilation of the colonized and downgrading them to second-class human beings.

IV.1.2 The Development of Anthropology in Spain

We know very little about the history of how anthropology emerged in Spain, and the research on it has been sparse.[10] In general, we can note that naturalist anthropology in the French style appeared only very late in Spain. It is true that there were ethnographic and anthropological investigations being carried out in the first half of the nineteenth century, but not on behalf of or in the context of any institutionalized anthropology. Everything that took place in Spain in the direction of anthropology was based on impetuses coming from its northern neighbor and needs to be seen in connection with the work of French researchers.

The explicitly biologically racist anthropology that was fundamental to the second half of the nineteenth century was just making its first appearance in the first half of the century. A short article by Francisco Antonio Beavides, entitled "Historia física del hombre" (Physical history of man), provides an indication. It carries no publication date, but Elena Ronzón places it in the late eighteen-forties. In the article, the author refers to taxonomic problems and the question of human races and their classification and characteristics (Ronzón 174). Ronzón points out how foundational this study is, and that it was the forerunner of later Darwinist developments. Looking at where anthropological examinations originating in Spain set their focus, the lack of any nineteenth-cen-

---

though various academics were already addressing issues of racial theory, there was no officially named anthropology professorship until 1855 (Staum 125–126).
10 I am indebted to Ana Mateos for important insights on anthropology in Spain.

tury contributions from or about the Caribbean is striking, while Africa, especially northwest Africa, including Morocco and Algeria, make a strong showing. Ronzón highlights three representatives of Spanish anthropology in particular: Vicente Adam, Francisco Fabra Soldevilla, and José Varela de Montes (Ronzón 173). Adam's 1833 publication *Lecciones de Antropología* (Lessons in anthropology) is a work of philosophy, of moral philosophy in particular. He subscribes to Locke's empirical line as well as to the sensualist empiricism of Cordillac and the French *idéologues*. There is, however, no ethnographic information to be found in his work. Fabra Soldevilla (1778–1839), who wrote *La filosofía de la legislación natural fundada en la antropología* (1838; The philosophy of natural legislation, based on anthropology), studied medicine in Montpellier and wrote the procedural rules for the Academy of Natural Sciences, which were approved in 1835. Although he assigned human beings to the natural sciences and regarded them to be the object of study of those sciences, he remained an anti-Darwinist (Ronzón 220) and was particularly interested in demonstrating the limits of the natural scientific examination of human beings. Varela de Montes (1796–1868) wrote his *Ensayo de Antropología* (1844; Essay on anthropology) from a medical perspective. His idea of a "unity of humankind" involves a critique of the naturalist and zoological perspective on species (Ronzón 267).

In 1864 Dr. Velasco, who was influenced by the positivistic and naturalist school, founded the *Sociedad Antropológica* (Anthropological society) in Madrid (ibid.). The declared goal of this society, which published its own journal of ethnology, was the classification of the human species and diversity, for which it used data from a variety of sources, including the various peoples of Spain and of the Caribbean. For this purpose, the society asked the respective provincial governors to collect skulls and bones. This analysis was mostly dominated by the biological approach (273). In Sevilla, in 1871, another society was established, the *Sociedad de Antropología* (Society for anthropology), founded by Antonio Machado Nuñez, a professor of natural history. However, this society only existed until 1875 (Ronzón 296).

As I have already mentioned, the African continent was the preferred location for Spanish anthropological research; I think, therefore, that it would be advisable in this context to take a look at Spanish colonialism in Africa. In 1436 the Portuguese Alfonso Goncalves explored the coast of the Sahara and bought slaves from the Sahrawi people (Pedraz Marcos 28). To make peace in the region, however, the Catholic kings outlawed the slave trade on the Saharan coast in 1497 (19). The attitude of the Bourbons towards their African possessions bordered on indifference until the reigns of Ferdinand VI and Carlos III, who, in concert with the Moroccan king Mohamed Ben Adballa (1757–1790), tried to use a variety of treaties to strengthen the relationship between the two monarchies

(34). In 1778, with the Treaty of El Pardo, Portugal relinquished sovereignty over the islands Fernando Poo (which became known in the nineteenth century for the deportation of political prisoners from Cuba) and Annobón to Spain. Also in 1778, the first Spanish expedition set off for the Gulf of Guinea with the goal of establishing support bases on the islands and to create, there as well as on the African mainland, a commercial footing for the shipment of slaves to the Americas.

The travelers who undertook these nineteenth-century expeditions to Africa are interesting from an ethnographic point of view, because they collected data and documents and described the lives of the other peoples they encountered. One of these is Domingo Badía, alias Ali Bey, from Barcelona (1767–1818), who in 1801 presented plans to Godoy, the Spanish prime minister, for a trip to Africa for both political and scientific purposes. José María de Murga, better known as the *Moro vizcaíno* (the Vizcainian Moor), must be mentioned here. He did anthropological research in North Africa, in particular in Morocco, and his contributions to our knowledge about the world of the Berbers and Jews of the Maghreb are very important, especially his 1868 travelogue *Recuerdos marroquíes* (Moroccan memories) (Ronzón 83). Both Badía and Murga claimed to be Moroccans and to belong to some remote Arab ethnic groups in order to make their contacts with local peoples easier. In 1868, another Spaniard, Manuel Iradier Bulfi (1854–1911), with the society that he had founded in 1868 named *La viajera* (The traveler; the society's name was later changed to *La exploradora* [The explorer]), neared the coasts of the Gulf of Guinea, where the Spaniards owned some islands that enabled them to penetrate into the interior of the country (Ronzón 88). During his expedition, Bulfi took notes in the fragmentary form of a daily journal, in which he commented on not only geographic but also ethnographic data. He was convinced that his observations would be able to serve as a guide for future researchers. In 1876, he founded the *Sociedad geográfica* (Geographic society) and one year later, in 1877, the *Asociación Española para la exploración del África* (Spanish association for the exploration of Africa). In the very first year of its founding, this latter society commissioned the Catalan Joaquín Gatell (1826–1879), who maintained contacts with the French geographical society, to explore Africa, specifically to investigate the inner coastal areas of the western Sahara. He then wrote *Manual del viajero explorador en África* (Manual for the exploring traveler in Africa).

Given the parlous situation of early ethnological research in Spain and how little it concerned itself with the Caribbean as an object of research, it should not be surprising that in the following, looking at French and Spanish colonialism from a comparative perspective, I pay much greater attention to France.

IV.2 The *Revue des Colonies* as a Transfer Medium Within a French-Speaking Colonial Diaspora

"The colonies in general know the great principles of philanthropy only in theory as of yet; of liberty in action, nothing. The suffering and oppressed classes make demands and fight without ceasing, always without success" (Duke Bryant 251). In her noteworthy examination of the *Revue des Colonies* and the early role it played in the French diaspora, Duke Bryant highlights these opening sentences.[11] The tenor of this first issue of the journal, published in Paris in July of 1834, sets the tone for the reports and debates that appeared in this unusual periodical over the eight years of its existence. One of its foremost goals was to "group together" the problems and injustices to which people of color living in the French colonial world were exposed and to give them "the greatest publicity" (*Revue des Colonies* July 1834, cited in Duke Bryant 251). With Cyrille Bissette, a mulatto from Martinique who functioned as a semi-official representative in Paris of the free nonwhite population (*hommes de couleur*)[12] in the colonies, at its helm, the journal was the first French periodical that was produced by a person of color for people of color. The magazine had the objective of addressing all issues that concerned the French colonies, and it focused on themes such as slavery, racial prejudices, and social inequalities in the French colonies. In concentrating on these thematic areas, the magazine brought the contours of a particular kind of black diaspora to light (Duke Bryant 251). But the editorial team did not envisage publishing for an exclusively black and mulatto readership; the first issue announced that the journal, in addition to its ethnic and social

---

11 Duke Bryant's research, on which I rely here, provided important information and context, especially on the *Revue des Colonies*'s understanding of the diaspora. I am grateful to Stephan Eberhard for important suggestions on my engagement with Duke Bryant's and Bongie's research. Cf. also Müller, "La *Revue des colonies* comme média de transfert."

12 The term "people of color" or "colored people" usually refers to both free and enslaved mulattos, in other words people of mixed African and European ancestry. In the context of the ethnological periodicals, however, the term *hommes de couleur* (people of color) is primarily used as a legal concept from civil law, referring to free people with at least one African ancestor. The category includes both the freeborn and former slaves, and can indicate either purely African or mixed-race individuals. "Free people of color" can therefore also designate dark-skinned free people. Contemporary publications use a mixture of phrases: usually *hommes de couleur (libres)*, but also *gens de couleur (libres)*, *nègres*, *noirs*, and *mulâtres* ("[free] men of color" as well as "[free] people of color," "Negroes," "blacks," and "mulattos"). I will be using the terms "people of color" or "mulattos" or, especially in the context of the ethnological journals, *hommes de couleur* (the adjective *libres* [free] is implied), since these are the terms that appear most frequently in the contemporary literature.

themes, would address the "political, intellectual, moral and industrial interests of colonists of one and the other color" (*Revue des Colonies* July 1834, 4; cf. Duke Bryant 252). Although its editor-in-chief, Bissette, was a free mulatto living in Paris, neither the intended audience nor the themes of the *Revue des Colonies* were concentrated exclusively on mulattos (Bongie, "C'est du papier?" 443).

The second main concern of the journal, after the demand for equal rights for different ethnic groups, was staying true to the connection with France, the mother country. The *Revue des Colonies* was a decisive supporter of the equality of *hommes de couleur* within the French community. One important aspect of this was including African topics in news reporting, thus declaring the continent to be a politically relevant place (253). Duke Bryant talks about how the *Revue* advanced the idea of a diaspora with two homelands—Africa, the place of origin but without the logical consequence of return, and France, which offered a place of exile for *hommes de couleur*—thus connecting the past and future of people of color in the French colonial realm. The *Revue des Colonies* provided an identity-shaping function for people of color within the French-speaking world. Its most prominent goals were the attainment of comprehensive French political and civil rights; the abolition of slavery; and an attempt at a historiography with black, often African, heroes, in order to promote the liberation of the oppressed races (ibid.). The way that Africa was handled in the *Revue des Colonies* brings up new questions about the use of the concept of the diaspora and provides an example of an intellectual connection between the Antilles and Africa that predated the négritude movement by almost a hundred years (ibid.).

Even though the *Revue des Colonies* never had a very large number of subscribers, it received a great deal of close attention. The magazine circulated in four British West Indian colonies, three French colonies, British Mauritius, French Mauritius (La Réunion, formerly Île Bourbon), French Senegal, and Haiti. The journalists from the French colonial empire addressed a wide variety of topics, but the contributions from the British colonies mostly dealt with the consequences of the abolition of 1834. These reports, in turn, contributed to the emancipation movements in the French colonies (Duke Bryant 259 f.).

The explicit goal of the *Revue des Colonies* was in equal parts patriotic and humanist. Its aim was to change the social order of the colonies while safeguarding the material interests and personal security of the owners. The connection between the colonies and the mother country was also to be solidified (*Revue des Colonies* July 1836, 3): the magazine claimed that ignorance in the mother country about the population of the Caribbean led to the "false" belief that France could not hold onto the colonies. This false idea was explained by the fact that until that point, the population had only been known through descriptions provided by the slave owners, which leads to a criticism of the so-called sugar aristocracy:

> The debris of the colonial aristocracy still came to France to saunter around and to consume there, with fruitless expenditures, the products of a labor that was poorly appreciated two thousand leagues away. There were only three things that were known of the colonies: sugar, coffee, and the white Creoles. The first two were what made it possible to tolerate the third. (4)[13]

What is particularly telling is that knowledge about the colonies is judged to be inadequate. The authors of the *Revue des Colonies* claim for themselves a "neutral perspective" on the colonies. They are proud of having promoted emancipation to the best of their abilities: "We have pushed the chariot of emancipation with all of our strength, we have maintained a constant and impartial scrutiny of colonial society, and there are now other tasks we must still fulfill. The foremost of these is to make the colonies known more intimately to France" (6).[14] The achievements and capacities of which the "black and colored races" are considered capable are particularly emphasized. Haiti is especially foregrounded; France should finally be given an introduction to the history of this country, about which false ideas have prevailed:

> Seeing the enormous step that has been taken by a society of slaves abandoned to themselves, prey to civil war and foreign war for 25 years, one will conceive that under the enlightened protection of France, the colonies could peacefully arrive at a social revolution, that they possess all the elements of the strongest and most intelligent society if these elements are combined justly and moderately. (6)[15]

As a first, preliminary conclusion, we can state that insofar as the *Revue des Colonies* is a transfer medium per se, it is worth paying particular attention to. What

---

[13] "Les débris de l'aristocratie coloniale venaient encore parader en France et y consommer dans de stériles dépenses les produits d'un travail qu'on appréciait mal à deux mille lieues de distance. On ne connaissait des colonies que trois choses; le sucre, le café et les créoles blancs. Les deux premières fesaient supporter la troisième."

[14] "Pour nous, qui avons poussé de tous nos efforts au char de l'émancipation, qui avons incessamment porté un regard scrutateur et impartial sur la société coloniale, d'autres devoirs nous restent à remplir. Le premier de tous, c'est de faire connaître plus intimement les colonies à la France."

[15] "En voyant le pas immense qu'a fait une société d'esclaves abandonnée à elle-même, en proie à la guerre civile et à la guerre étrangère pendant 25 ans, on concevra que, sous la protection éclairée de la France, les colonies peuvent arriver pacifiquement à une révolution sociale, qu'elles possèdent tous les élémens de la société la plus forte et la plus intelligente, si ces élémens sont combinés avec justice et avec mesure."

is important for our questions is that the declared goal of equality can only work within the French commonality. Here we can also see clearly what we already concluded with respect to literature in the opening chapter, namely that an abolitionist stance is not necessarily accompanied by a questioning of the colonial status quo. Looking at the debates about inclusion and exclusion that took place in the first half of the nineteenth century, we can say that the gravitational force of French colonialism is not just an inclusive force, but also very much an integrative one.

Paris was the nodal point for the *Revue des Colonies*; in comparing it with the literary texts, however, a change in direction should be noted. Knowledge from the colonies came together in Paris and was reorganized, and also redistributed, by the *Revue*. Readers from Guyana, for instance, could thus learn about cultural practices in Senegal. The interpretation given by cultural studies, so far unchallenged, that négritude was the first black movement that used the common colonial center of Paris as a way to become aware of its own collective history, definitely needs to be revisited.

IV.2.1 The Critique of Slavery and the Civilizing Mission

Ogé-Barbaroux, the state prosecutor for the Île Bourbon and one of the editors of the *Revue*, points out how important the magazine was for slave uprisings on distant colonial possessions south of Africa, such as Bourbon (now La Réunion): "When the *Revue des Colonies* circulated among the inhabitants, all classes of society were agitated" (*Revue des Colonies* III.x, 400, cited in Bongie, "'C'est du papier?'" 447[16]). Ogé-Barbaroux stresses the magazine's heavily abolitionist agenda, starting with the picture of a black man lying in chains that graced the cover (under which the question "Am I not a man and your brother?" appeared), and goes on to say that reading it gives one the impression that the necessary measures—namely ending colonial ownership and instituting a sudden and complete restructuring of the social order—should be implemented immediately, without delay, precautions, preparations, or reparations. Although Ogé-Barbaroux's opinion that the *Revue*'s precepts were subversive of the existing order was not necessarily shared by his co-editors, the effect on certain readers may very well have been subversive. Reactions to slave uprisings, for instance, often refer to the *Revue*'s distribution and reception in the colonies themselves,

---

[16] Unfortunately, I did not have access to these earlier issues of the *Revue des Colonies*, so I rely on Bongie's extensive citations in "'C'est du papier?'".

even though its greatest influence was in Paris, where it elicited a series of polemical discourses and complaints even though its readership was in fact very limited (Bongie, "'C'est du papier?'" 447).

In an 1837 article that reproduces the speech by Ogé-Barbaroux cited above and includes Bissette's responses to it, Bissette denies the accusation that he and his staff had called for rebellion and "endeavored to turn the colonies completely upside down": he calls such accusations baseless and says that in the three volumes of the *Revue* there were no signs anywhere, from the first line to the last, of any such impulses (ibid.). Bissette's comments suggest that the "social revolution" that the *Revue* was encouraging was intended to take place on the basis of negotiation, and the constant calls for such a revolution were based on an unshakable belief in the effectiveness of legal reform and moral reeducation. This understanding of revolution grew out of a revaluation of past revolutionary violence as the basis of a society in which peaceful coexistence was now possible. The *Revue* understood the French Revolution as its source, and the Declaration of the Rights of Man in Society was set down at the beginning of the journal's first issue (ibid.). While commenting on the Declaration, Bissette notes that "no matter what happens, in these principles—sown throughout Europe by the French Revolution, by its republican and imperial armies, and throughout the entire world by its books—there is a virtuality that no one will ever succeed in quashing" (*Revue des Colonies* III, 8, cited in Bongie, "'C'est du papier?'" 447–48). The French Revolution was accompanied by "virtual" dynamics of truly global dimensions, as the Haitian Revolution all the way on the other side of the Atlantic confirmed. In his 1836 retrospective of the *Revue's* achievements over its first two years of publication, Bissette notes this fact: "The Haitian Revolution, despite the massacres of the Cap, just like the French Revolution, despite the September massacres, created a new people and rendered hallow the principles of justice and humanity" (*Revue des Colonies* III.i, 4, cited in Bongie, "'C'est du papier?'" 448). Bissette cites the Haitian Revolution as a revolutionary model from which one can learn in a postrevolutionary age.

In his decisive rejection of the project of colonial independence, which he considers ridiculous and connects with the interests of the white oligarchy, Bissette emphatically proclaims his preference for a "peaceful fusion as opposed to any and all insurrectionary movements" (*Revue des Colonies* I.iv, 33, cited in Bongie, "'C'est du papier?'" 448) and maintains an image of France, the mother country, as "the necessary arbitrator of all colonial problems" (*Revue des Colonies* III.x, 397, cited in Bongie, "'C'est du papier?'" 448) while repeatedly expressing his disappointment at the lack of social progress in the colonies. He not only stresses the necessity of education in the colonies but also addresses leading mulatto figures of the New World, such as Bolívar, Pétion, and Boyer, who had the opportunity "to imbibe the noble and generous ideas for which they would fight with such bravery and success," adding that

> we, children of France, do not have to wish for a Bolívar who would come and deliver us from the foreign yoke. France is too dear to us, its beneficial effects too precious, and its protection too necessary for us to indulge in ideas that are hostile toward her. In the domination of those who govern over us and who falsely interpret the wishes of France we see only isolated undertakings, and not the faithful expression of the intentions of the *mère-patrie*. (*Revue des Colonies* I.ii, 6, cited in Bongie, "'C'est du papier?'" 448–49)

The pages of the *Revue* are full of such professions: revolution is necessary, but violence can and must be prevented. This is to be achieved through the virtuous administrative bodies of the colonial "parent." Bissette's postrevolutionary and antirevolutionary conception of assimilation and his belief in the omnipotence of the metropolis are positions that are well known in twentieth-century French Caribbean politics. As Bongie notes, these positions can be mapped almost exactly onto Aimé Césaire's enthusiastic support for the departmentalization of the islands of Martinique and Guadeloupe in 1946 (Bongie, "'C'est du papier?'" 449).

The abolition of slavery, in the spirit of the French Revolution, was the *Revue*'s most pressing concern from the very beginning and one of its founding ideas. The magazine was heavily inspired by the abolition in the British colonial realm:

> Let us also say that even if the French are not always the first to arrive in terms of revolution, they go more directly and farther when they have been shown the way. Mental activity turned towards overseas questions. People studied this world, so different from the European world. And from this day of surprise, the abolition of slavery was pronounced. It was at that moment that the *Revue des Colonies* published its first issue. The bill to emancipate blacks was about to go into effect. (*Revue des Colonies* July 1838, 5)[17]

Over and over, we find very clear statements in favor of the abolition of slavery:

> An association had been formed that was respectable because of the men who composed it and because of its goal. This association was the association for the abolition of slavery,

---

[17] "Disons aussi que si les Français n'arrivent pas toujours les premiers en fait de révolution, ils vont plus droit et plus loin quand on leur a montré le chemin. L'activité des esprits se tourna vers les questions d'outre-mer. On étudia ce monde si différent du monde européen. De ce jour de surprise, l'abolition de l'esclavage fut prononcée. C'est à ce moment que la Revue des Colonies publia son premier numéro. Le bill de l'émancipation des noirs allait être mis à exécution."

and we will allow ourselves here to remember, happily, that this association, announced by the *Revue des Colonies*, was constituted shortly after the publication of our first issue. (ibid.)[18]

Bissette was often described as the first advocate for complete and immediate equal rights in France's July Monarchy. Even without taking into account the highly problematic positions ("reactionary," "rightist," and "populist") that Bissette embraced later, during the Second Republic, his self-identification as a (mulatto) *homme de couleur libre*, a free person of color, and his intense loyalty to the French mother country which in 1833 legitimized that identification, nevertheless also contained a reservation, which we can describe (following Bongie) as a certain identification with "blackness" (Bongie, "'C'est du papier?'" 443).

The colonial aristocracy is often criticized in the *Revue*'s articles, and in particular there are warnings against the preservation of the system of slavery, because it would only cause social tensions to heighten. Slavery, which has been accepted for far too long, these articles write, are thoroughly destroying the colonies: "France understood that the soporofic speeches of the colonist aristocrats had hidden an enormous, inevitable, and impending danger: inevitable, if the social relations of the colonies were not changed" (*Revue des Colonies* July 1838, 5).[19]

The *Revue des Colonies* sometimes deals very sarcastically with political positions from the "other camp." Charles Dupin, the minister of the navy, for instance, receives this ironic criticism—he only wants the slaves to continue to be whipped because he loves them so much:

> Yesterday it was Mr. Charles Dupin of the navy; today it was Mr. Charles Dupin the representative of the colonists; tomorrow it will be Mr. Charles Dupin the professor of arts and crafts; the day after tomorrow it will be Mr. Charles Dupin of the Institute. ... Those poor slaves! Mr. Charles Dupin loves them, and if he wants their kidneys to continue to be caressed with bamboo beatings, it is because he loves them!!! (*Revue des Colonies* July 1836, 44–45)[20]

---

18 "Il s'était formé une association respectable par les hommes qui la composaient et par son but. Cette association était celle de l'abolition de l'esclavage; et il nous sera permis ici de rappeler avec bonheur que cette association, annoncée par la Revue des Colonies, se constitua peu de temps après la publication de notre premier numéro."
19 "La France comprit que les discours endormeurs des aristocrates colons lui avaient caché un danger immense, inévitable et prochain; inévitable si l'on ne changeait les rapports sociaux des colonies."
20 "Hier c'était M. Charles Dupin, le marin; aujourd'hui c'était M. Charles Dupin le délégué des colons; demain ce sera, M. Charles Dupin le professeur des arts et métiers; après-demain ce sera,

It is noted with amusement that the advocates of slavery, in other words the political opponents of the authors of the *Revue des Colonies*, write under constantly changing pseudonyms to make it seem as though there are more of them than there actually are and to give the (false) impression that there is a substantial elite of French writers speaking out against the emancipation of the blacks. The *Revue du XIXe siècle* is also ridiculed as being five hundred years behind its times:

> The partisans of slavery are not numerous but they have found an excellent way to multiply themselves. Our readers will remember the ingenious metamorphoses of Mr. Granier, a native of Cassagnac. This great writer sometimes signed his articles Granier, and sometimes de Cassagnac, and then Mr. P.L.M., and later Mr. three stars; and the aristocrats of the colonies said: you see that the elite of French writers is coming out against the emancipation of the blacks! Today the Count of Mauny, who found these masquerades to be to his taste, begins a new chapter of metamorphoses. After having written to *Le Temps* under his own name, Mr. de Mauny has disguised himself the way that Cassagnac did and has changed himself into a subscriber to the *Revue du XIXe siècle*, which would do better to call itself *Revue du XIVe siècle*. (*Revue des Colonies* November 1836, 216)[21]

De Mauny was a well-known conservative aristocrat who was at odds with the ministry newspapers and the government, who were trying to change the social order in the colonies as carefully as possible. It was therefore not the colonial governments but rather individual plantation owners who wanted to impose a pro-slavery attitude because of their economic interests. Elsewhere, the Aristotelian justification of slavery is ironically examined and connected with the polemical critique of a "white" Christian doctrine of salvation.

> Slavery is divine; God created mankind to serve and to be sold in the market; God created blacks to cultivate sugarcane while being beaten; God created women in order to defile them eternally through concubinage; God created masters and through the torture that

---

M. Charles Dupin de l'Institut. ... Ces pauvres esclaves! M. Charles Dupin les aime, et s'il veut que l'on continue à leur caresser les reins à coups de bambou, c'est qu'il les aime!!!"

21 "Les partisans de l'esclavage ne sont pas nombreux; mais ils ont trouvé un excellent moyen de se multiplier. Nos lecteurs se souviennent des ingénieuses métamorphoses de M. Granier, natif de Cassagnac. Ce grand écrivain signait ses articles tantôt Granier, tantôt de Cassagnac, puis Mr. P.L.M., puis M. trois étoiles; et les aristocrates des colonies disaient: Vous voyez que l'élite des écrivains français se prononce contre l'émancipation des noirs! Aujourd'hui M. le comte de Mauny, qui a trouvé ces mascarades de son goût, commence un nouveau chapitre de métamorphoses. Après avoir écrit au journal le Temps, sous son nom, M. de Mauny prend un déguisement à la Cassagnac et se métamorphose en un abonné de la Revue du XIXe siècle, laquelle Revue ferait mieux de s'appeler Revue du XIVe siècle."

slaves suffer Jesus Christ died for us, owners of human beings. Jesus Christ came to teach the human race the greatest of all crimes! (263)[22]

The discourses justifying slavery or its abolition are integrated into apologetic discourses and counterdiscourses. Another line of argumentation runs as follows: mankind is compelled to work because of its fall from grace, and slavery only forces work on people so that humanity can develop further. Christianity, however, could replace slavery. Its mission is to end slavery and to continue the journey of humanity. A new relationship is added to the one existing between master and slave, namely that of Christian to Christian. It follows that slavery and Christianity represent the two greatest achievements known to the history of humankind. One of them submits human beings to the will of human beings, while the other submits the slaveholder to the will of God. One of them leads from the state of savagery to the state of barbarism, while the other leads from barbarism to civilization. The task of one of them was to introduce work into the world and the task of the other is to abolish slavery (*Revue des Colonies* January 1837, 305).

In our time, when the observance of human rights has become the standard of social progress worldwide, this line of argumentation may be convincing. But it is an open question whether the Christian argument would have been effective at that time, in secularized post–French-Revolution society.

Nell Irvin Painter has drawn attention to the fact that the issue was often either proving or disproving that white supremacy was willed by God. One can find this kind of religious discourse in, for instance, the writings of the black United States abolitionist David Walker (1785–1830). Painter describes him and the eighty-page treatise that he published in 1829 entitled "David Walker's Appeal: In Four Articles, Together with a Preamble, To The Coloured Citizens of the World, but in Particular, and Very Expressly, to Those of the United States of America"[23] (Painter 118–121). Walker also published the first black newspaper in the United States, *Freedom's Journal*, in which he reported on the Haitian Rev-

---

22 "L'esclavage est divin; Dieu a créé les hommes pour servir et pour être vendus au marché; Dieu a créé les noirs pour cultiver la canne à sucre à coups de bâton; Dieu a créé les femmes pour les souiller éternellement par le concubinage; Dieu a créé des maîtres et Jésus-Christ est mort du supplice des esclaves pour nous, possesseurs d'hommes. Jésus-Christ est venu enseigner au genre humain le plus grand de tous les crimes!"
23 Excerpts can be found at Walker, *David Walker's Appeal* (http://www.pbs.org/wgbh/aia/part4/4 h2931 t.html). The full version is Walker, *Walker's Appeal* (http://docsouth.unc.edu/nc/walker/walker.html).

olution. He was highly respected among the black population of Boston, where he spent the final years of his life.

In his treatise, he condemns the hypocrisy of Christian whites and describes the history of blacks from Egypt to Haiti, calling the Haitians brothers ("our brethren Haytians"). Walker, who was a very committed Christian, condemned African nature-worshiping religions and appealed to Christian doctrine. He argued that murder was a part of the nature of the whites, and prophesied that white Christians would receive divine punishment for their treatment of blacks. Although he died of tuberculosis just a year after the publication of his text, his work continued to be discussed through the end of the American Civil War, and we can therefore assume that his discourse gained currency in abolitionist circles not only in the United States but also beyond.

This very same religious tenor that is found in Walker's work can also be seen in the *Revue des Colonies*, where reports are continually published in which blacks are described as good Christians. The ability to convert to Christianity is equated with the ability to become civilized.

Alongside the basic message of the *Revue des Colonies*, which is the critique of slavery, the thought of the civilizing mission is also very present. The critique of slavery and the idea of the need to civilize peoples are therefore apparently not mutually contradictory. Thus, the journal introduces the work of the nuns of the Sisters of Saint Joseph, an order of nuns who maintain hospitals, schools, and other social institutions in Guyana. Here, too, the debate over abolition is an implied theme: six hundred Africans who had been "liberated" from the hands of slave smugglers by French warships had been given into the care of the nuns.[24] An article describes how "conscientiously" they are being integrated into Cayenne.

> The six hundred blacks who were entrusted to Sister Javouhey [the leader of the order of nuns] and her ladies are the ones that slave smugglers had gone to find in the Gulf of Benin and that our war vessels that cruise against the slave trade had taken away from the slavers. These blacks, therefore, were brought together in government workshops, they had been tamed and cleansed. They were put to work on the roads of the colony, on a few local drainage projects, at sweeping the roads of Cayenne, on various public works projects, and above all on agriculture. A few young people were drawn from these workshops who showed more abilities than the others, and they have been much more useful than one could possibly have hoped. (*Revue des Colonies* July 1836, 19)[25]

---

24 It was often the case that while the slave trade was forbidden, slavery itself was allowed.
25 "Les six cents noirs confiés à la soeur Javouhey et à ses dames sont ceux que le commerce interpole avait été chercher dans le golfe de Bénin, et que nos bâtimens de guerre en croisière contre la traite, ont enlevés aux négriers. Ces noirs ont donc été réunis en ateliers du gouverne-

There is also the matter of the conversion of these slaves to Christianity and the representation of the nuns as the "white" mothers of these black offspring, whom they educate in moral and social questions and lead to civilization. The nuns are represented as raising beautiful, young, black men, educated for the achievements of civilization and culture. In the light of France's demand for civilization, the work of the nuns is praised as being a contribution to progress, to the further development of civilization and culture, and to the joining together of the races, a contribution that happens through religion and the Gospel. The connection between the Christian idea of mission and the cultural expectation of civilization is clearly articulated: "We shall see, ... under the standard of the cross, tribes of Caribs receiving the benefits of civilization from the hand of Sister Javouhey and the hands of the Sisters of Saint Joseph" (20).[26] Because the blacks have been held to decent and meaningful work and made familiar with Christianity, their integration into French society appears to have been successful. It is significant, however, that they continue to be seen as objects of the nuns, who do not seem to be concerned with their political equal rights.

For the most important question of the time as well, the question of being for or against abolition, the same thing is true of the *Revue des Colonies* that we have already established for the literary media: philanthropic discourses arise in the center and the aristocratic plantation owner classes on the islands try to refute them. Unlike with literature, however, in the case of the *Revue* the transfer that takes place is exponentially multiplied, turning into a circular structure that is interrupted in many places, because many of its editors come from the colonies but, inspired by the center's discourses that are critical of slavery, express themselves from that center and put their ideas into worldwide circulation. Here, too, the editors' social background, so different from that of the white plantation owners and writers, may very well play a decisive role. While a protagonist such as Marius, from *Outre-mer*, is staged as moving in one direction only, the *Revue* has a multirelational dissemination. But because its center, with its civilizing mission, is tremendously powerful, unlike the situation in the Spanish colonies, that center is affirmed around the globe; on the colonial level, there continues to be a bipolar structure. The fact that the affirmation of the colonial status quo can simultaneously coexist with the critique of slavery indicates that for the

---

ment, ils se sont apprivoisés, assainis. On les a employés aux chemins de la colonie, à quelques desséchemens locaux, au balayage des rues de Cayenne, à divers travaux publics, et surtout à la culture des vivres. On a tiré de ces ateliers quelques jeunes gens qui montraient plus de dispositions que les autres, et ils sont beaucoup plus utiles qu'on ne pouvait l'espérer."

26 "Nous verrons ... sous l'étendard de la croix, des tribus de Caraïbes, recevoir de la main de la soeur Javouhey et de celles des soeurs de Saint-Joseph, les bienfaits de la civilisation."

expression of political positions the category of an in-between is also necessary, just as was so characteristically the case for Caribbean literary attempts at positioning.

IV.2.2 Whiteness in the In-Between: The Colonist, the Parisian Aristocrat, and the Creole Way of Life

But what does the *Revue des Colonies* tell us about the forms of representation of the white population in the colonies? Because the literature of the time, as we have seen, is the expression of a white Creole upper class and, precisely in its descriptions of other ethnic groups, expresses certain things about being white, it is now particularly interesting to see how being white is perceived from a mulatto perspective. In the following I will introduce a few kaleidoscopic snapshots of the *Revue* in order then to filter out, through this inductive process, a higher-level representation of whiteness.

One important topic is the complaint of press censorship. Criticism is explicitly directed at the colonial aristocracy and the newspaper *Courrier de la Guadeloupe* and, more concretely, at Cicerón, the Count de Mauny, and Louis de Maynard de Queilhe. Maynard de Queilhe is especially relevant here because of his colonialist novel *Outre-mer*. We find the sarcastic remark:

> If we had to analyze the eloquence of the gentlemen of the colonial councils in detail, our *Revue* itself would not be equal to the task even from now until several years in the future. Therefore we must restrain our admiration for the last masterpiece which has just arrived from the general council of Guadeloupe: make way for Guadeloupean eloquence! (ibid. 42)[27]

This remark is an introduction to a letter from the colonial council to Governor Arnous, which is annotated, in places ironically and sarcastically; or rather, more specifically, the self-representation of the colonists as men of worth (*hommes de bien*) is put into perspective. In one place, the colonists are reported as saying: "The government wants respect for all interests and for order; for work and security: that is what THE MEN OF WORTH OF THE METROPOLIS AND THE

---

27 "S'il fallait analyser en détail l'éloquence de Messieurs des conseils coloniaux, notre Revue elle-même, ne suffirait pas d'ici à plusieurs années. Force nous est de restreindre notre admiration, au dernier chef-d'oeuvre qui nous vient d'arriver du conseil général de la Guadeloupe: place à l'éloquence guadeloupéenne!"

COLONISTS THEMSELVES WANT" (ibid.).²⁸ In a strategic rhetorical move, the *Revue*'s authors explain that precisely because the colonists are comparing themselves to men of worth, the conclusion must be that they cannot claim that description for themselves. They are mockingly described as "outstanding overseas Frenchmen" whose sugarcane is more important to them than is France:

> These excellent overseas Frenchmen, these Frenchmen of Guadeloupe, who will tell you that France should perish rather than our sugarcane; these excellent Frenchmen have not left any doubt. They have said: men of worth and ourselves. No more discussion is possible. Unless these gentlemen want to claim that their address to Governor Arnous says exactly the opposite of what they think. That is indeed another explanation which might seduce some readers of the *Courrier de la Guadeloupe*, but most of them will say: Yes, that's exactly it; MEN OF WORTH AND THE COLONISTS THEMSELVES. (ibid. 43)²⁹

While these two groups taken together, the colonists as the white ruling class in the colonies and the *hommes de bien* as a prerevolutionary ideal, represent an ironic representation of outdated aristocratic self-staging, there is another class whose stock is appreciating, namely that of progressive whites, who are depicted as being definitely sensitive and critical of slavery but nevertheless defend French colonialism. Thus, in a speech that was discussed in the *Courrier de la Guadeloupe*, Cicéron declares how concerned he is with the well-being of about twenty black men from Dominica who had sought refuge on Guadeloupe. There is also apparently a bounty of 1,485 francs on the head of each of these runaway slaves. Cicéron explains that the slaves who had arrived in Guadeloupe had been so badly treated on Dominica that they would soon wish to return to slavery in the French colonies. On the island of Antigua there had been a tragic event: escaped slaves from Guadeloupe had been arrested, put in chains, and sentenced to work on the road gangs. The population that was free lived in complete misery, he goes on, and the black Frenchmen suffered from that even more than did the native population. Some of the refugees had apparently asked to re-

---

28 "Le Gouvernement veut le respect de tous les intérêts, l'ordre; le travail et la sécurité: c'est aussi ce que veulent LES HOMMES DE BIEN DE LA MÉTROPOLE ET LES COLONS EUX-MÊMES."
29 "Ces excellens Français d'outre-mer, ces Français de la Guadeloupe, qui vous disent périsse la France plutôt que nos cannes à sucre; ces excellens Français n'ont laissé place à aucun doute. Ils ont dit: Les hommes de bien et nous-mêmes. Plus de discussion possible. A moins que ces Messieurs ne prétendent que leur adresse à M. le gouverneur Arnous, dit tout le contraire de ce qu'ils pensent. C'est encore là une explication qui peut séduire quelques lecteurs du Courrier de la Guadeloupe, mais le plus grand nombre dira: Oui, c'est bien cela; LES HOMMES DE BIEN ET LES COLONS EUX-MÊMES."

turn to Guadeloupe since life in French slavery was still better than freedom in the British colonies.

Following this question, there is a clarification of the implements that are used: in the article "De la peine du fouet" (On the pain of the whip), the whites, as opponents of abolition, and the use of the whip are criticized (*Revue des Colonies* October 1836, 145–146). But the issue is also raised of whether blacks can even be "civilized" at all, which is a question that the advocates of slavery answer with a vehement no, though the gentlemen would be happily willing to try it in exchange for the payment of a horrendous sum:

> When Mr. Mauguin, Mr. Dupin, Baron Charles, and Mr. Granier from Cassagnac come to lull us to sleep with their weighty homilies, what conclusion do these great statesmen reach? That the blacks are slaves because they have no intelligence, no morality, and no love of work, and that they are incapable of acquiring these qualities. It is only after having shown that it is not possible to raise the morale of the blacks that all of the defenders of slavery come so far as to say: well, go ahead and try, but definitely do not start anything until you have given us 250 million in advance. (ibid.)[30]

The other is existentially necessary as a way to reassure oneself. Thus, the criticism is made that everyone talks about instilling morality in the slaves, but that that morality will always be in question so long as the whip is still in use:

> We would not be surprised to see Mr. Mauguin appear before the forum to ask for a law that would establish the slave masters as the teachers of their slaves; and Mr. Mauguin, who has a very lively disposition, is perfectly capable of asking for this law with a whip in his hand! As for us, we ask for a law, a decree, an ordinance (it does not matter much to us which!) that would cause a terrible torture to disappear from the colonial laws. Emancipation will not begin to become a truth until the whip has been taken out of the hands of a slave owner. (146)[31]

---

30 "Lorsque M. Mauguin, M. Dupin, Charles le baron, M. Granier, natif de Cassagnac, viennent nous endormir de leurs pesantes homélies, quelle est la conclusion de ces grands hommes d'état? que les noirs sont esclaves parce qu'ils n'ont ni intelligence, ni moralité, ni amour du travail, et qu'ils sont incapables d'acquérir ces qualités. Ce n'est qu'après avoir démontré qu'il y a impossibilité de moraliser les noirs, que tous les défenseurs de l'esclavage en viennent à dire: essayez, pourtant; mais surtout ne faites rien sans nous avoir préalablement donné 250 millions."

31 "Nous ne désespérons pas de voir M. Mauguin venir demander à la tribune une loi qui nomme les maîtres instituteurs de leurs esclaves; et M. Mauguin qui est d'un naturel très vif sera bien capable de demander cette loi, le fouet à la main! Quant à nous, nous demandons une loi, un décret, une ordonnance (peu nous importe!) qui fasse disparaître des lois coloniales un horrible supplice. L'émancipation ne commencera à être une vérité, que lorsqu'on aura ôté le fouet des mains d'un possesseur d'esclave."

Yet another, different form of representation can be found in the article "Esquisses de moeurs créoles—par un créole de Cayenne" (Outlines of Creole Mores—By a Creole from Cayenne). It is a travelogue by a young Creole from France who was born and grew up in Guyana and is now visiting his country of origin again after a long absence (*Revue des Colonies* December 1836, 253–261). He sets off for the plantations where he used to live and describes his impressions. The account originally appeared in a different newspaper (*Temps*), and it is interesting to note the ways in which this article's emphases differ from the usual areas of focus that appear in the *Revue des Colonies*. Thus, the author describes the slaves' rituals and their spiritual connection with nature, especially with the stars, whereas articles in the *Revue* otherwise tend to emphasize the successes of missionary work among the slaves:

> the songs become clearer and clearer; and when the sun appears, with that brilliant majesty with which it always surrounds itself in the equatorial regions, every Negro strikes the wave with his wide paddle and, lifting his eyes to the heavens, utters a long and noisy hurrah, as if to salute the day star. All of those unhappy slaves who are forcibly baptized keep the memory of the idolatry that they practiced in Africa and continue to love the sun as a benevolent divinity. (254)[32]

He depicts the work of the slaves and remembers how brutally they were treated. He praises the advantages of steam machinery, which have meant that fewer women are needed in order to complete the work. And he also discusses the private life of the blacks:

> The colonists of Cayenne grant their slaves what they call Negro Saturday. The slave works from Monday morning until Friday night for the master, but he can use Saturday to cultivate the little garden that he has been given where a few banana trees and potatoes grow. ... In the city, the slave laborers work for themselves on Saturday and Sunday; they use all of the money that they earn to buy themselves clothes and hats of varnished leather. ... On the plantations, the Negroes more rarely have savings, and if so they are less considerable; nor do they share the passion of the city dwellers for adornment. (256)[33]

---

32 "les chants deviennent de plus en plus distincts; el lorsqu'apparaît le soleil, avec cette éclatante majesté dont il s'environne toujours dans les régions de l'équateur, chaque nègre frappe l'onde de sa large pagaie, et, levant les yeux au ciel, pousse un hourra long et bruyant, comme pour saluer l'astre du jour. Tous ces malheureux esclaves, que l'on baptise par force, conservent le souvenir de l'idolâtrie qu'ils pratiquaient en Afrique, et aiment encore le soleil comme une divinité bienfaisante."

33 "Les colons de Cayenne accordent à leurs esclaves ce qu'ils appellent le samedi nègre. L'esclave travaille depuis le lundi matin jusqu'au vendredi soir pour le compte du maître; mais il peut disposer du samedi pour cultiver le petit jardin qu'on lui a donné et où croissent quelques bananiers et des patates. ... A la ville, les esclaves ouvriers travaillent pour leur propre compte le

The slaves' self-interest is kindled because they are working their own piece of land. It seems to the author that they are better off than they used to be in his childhood.

The way that the representation of whiteness is perceived, which is often formulaic, becomes relativized through a kaleidoscopic look at a variety of excerpts from *Revue* articles. There is no longer any recognizable attribution, simply because of the complicated processes of geographical circulation. Thus, it becomes impossible to draw any clear lines between the colonist, as a plantation owner, and the man of worth (*homme de bien*), as a Parisian aristocrat. It is just as impossible to categorize a Creole from Guyana who returns to Cayenne after a long residence in Paris and who sees himself as obviously Creole, but is not perceived that way by others in Cayenne. As we have already seen on the literary level in the context of the categories of nation/fatherland/exile in Gómez de Avellaneda and the Countess of Merlin, the practices of denominating whiteness, which had seemed socially uncontestable, are relativized here. And here, again, it would seem that Caribbean productions cannot manage without the category of the in-between; it is not particularly surprising that this happens at the same time that the clear colonial center is maintained.

IV.2.3 Whiteness in Haiti

Unsurprisingly, the Haitian Revolution and, even more so, its consequences were an important topic in the *Revue des Colonies*. An article entitled "Haiti. Principe de sa constitution" (Haiti. The principle of its constitution) appeared under the simple byline of "a Haitian" (*Revue des Colonies* September 1836, 97–100). The article is a defense of the Haitian constitution, particularly of one law that caused a great deal of heated debate at the time. The law states that no white person, of any nation whatsoever, could ever enter Haiti as a master (*maître*) or property owner (*propriétaire*) (98). The article asks for understanding of this kind of exclusion of whites: racial prejudices, it says, will only be overcome when Europe can see that the black race has found its way out of the harshest slavery on its own power and has been able to constitute itself through its own nature:

---

samedi et le dimanche; ils emploient tout l'argent qu'ils gagnent à s'acheter des vêtemens et des chapeaux en cuir vernissé. ... Dans les habitations, les économies des nègres sont moins considérables et plus rares; aussi ne partagent-ils pas la passion de ceux de la ville pour la parure."

> It would be a great mistake to see nothing in this basic law but an expression of hatred towards whites. There is something higher in it than a feeling of vengeance or of anger: there is faith in the future of a country and the firm desire to establish its foundations on a new principle, new at least to Europeans. Haiti's lawmakers wanted to show that the country is just as capable of preserving as it is of conquering. If this demonstration has become necessary, they are not the ones to be blamed for that necessity. Racial prejudice will never be totally abolished until Europe sees the black race, which has emerged from the severest slavery by its own efforts, organizing itself through its own ingenuity and building up after having destroyed. (98)[34]

The author tries to explain that there is no alternative to this law, as well as describing the scope of such a law. He begins with the colonists' belief that the blacks are slaves and deserve that lot; that they belong to an inferior race and are therefore not capable of ever founding a civilized society. But now that the world has seen, in Haiti, a country that is shaping and civilizing itself with no outside help, this syllogism, far more meaningful than any theory for or against slavery, will usher in a new era in human societies. The example of Haiti, he writes, is of importance far beyond the country's borders:

> Haiti's lawmakers were guided by the interest of the entire black race. Haiti has stipulated for the whole of Africa. The example that its lawmakers wanted to give to the world is of such great significance that they should not have been held back by the fear of proclaiming a law that may have been unjust in its principle but was necessary and required by all the considerations that motivate society. (98–99)[35]

The noble motives for the exclusion of whites are therefore by no means to be confused with hatred or the desire for vengeance; it is necessary to be tolerant with the young nation, which has had to assert itself against Europe's intellectual and material dominance, and after all, the principle of exclusion in France it-

---

34 "On se tromperait fort si on ne voyait dans cette loi fondamentale qu'une expression de haine envers les blancs. Il y a quelque chose de plus élevé qu'un sentiment de vengeance ou de colère: il y a la foi dans l'avenir d'un pays et la ferme volonté d'en établir les bases sur un principe nouveau, du moins pour les Européens. Les législateurs d'Haïti ont voulu montrer que la nation était aussi bien capable de conserver que de conquérir. Si cette démonstration était devenue nécessaire, ce n'est pas à eux qu'il faut en imputer la faute. Le préjugé de race ne sera totalement aboli que lorsque l'Europe verra la race noire, sortie par ses seules forces du plus dur esclavage; s'organiser par son seul génie, édifier après avoir détruit."

35 "Les législateurs d'Haïti ont été guidés par l'intérêt de toute la race noire. Haïti a stipulé pour l'Afrique tout entière. L'exemple que ses législateurs ont voulu donner au monde, est d'une si grande portée, qu'ils ne devaient point être retenus par la crainte de proclamer une loi, injuste peut-être dans son principe, mais nécessaire et commandée par toutes les considérations qui servent de mobile à la société."

self had only disappeared with the French Revolution (less than fifty years earlier). In summary, the author explains: "The French people, who have done so much for the cause of humanity, should have enough experience to understand that sometimes one must separate the end from the means and that necessity does not always impose the fairest law" (100).[36]

Among the store of items published in the *Revue des Colonies*, it is also worth noting a satirical play about Haiti, with the not very informative title "Dramatic Proverb," which is set in the Department of the Navy and was published in the *Revue* in its entirety, all five scenes. The five characters are: Mr. Saintileurre (director in chief of all the colonies, whose name is constantly being distorted in the play in order to demonstrate his opportunistic and "ridiculous" manner); a black man (his name is only revealed in the course of the play); a mulatto (his name is never given at all); a man named Thé(-au-d'or) Baboule (a play on Theodore and tea-of-gold; he is sarcastically described as a humanitarian who wants to improve the world); and a baron. The whole thing takes place in Saintileurre's office, where the portraits of a large number of colonists and their lobbyists are displayed; the subjects of the portraits are all named in the play. One painting is described in which the colonists are shown asleep in the council:

> In the faces of the various characters, one can even see that this sleep is of a prodigious nature, and so concentrated that one would be tempted to believe that each of these honorable sleepers is carrying in his pocket a copy of *Outre-Mer*, by Mr. Louis de Maynard de Queilhe, a gentleman of Quercy. (*Revue des Colonies* September 1836, 137)[37]

The theme of the play is Haiti; Thé Baboule is applying to Saintileurre to become the new governor in order to save bankrupt Haiti. Another issue that comes up a great deal is the difficulty of how to deal now with the freed slaves and the mulattos. Saintileurre has no idea what he should call them. They are no longer blacks, but they are also not whites. The baron is called to bring some clarity to the situation, but because of his stutter he cannot produce any. The mulatto and the black man end up having to disappear again, more or less helplessly. The climax of the play involves Saintileurre telling the baron, full of sarcasm

---

36 "Le peuple français qui a tant fait pour la cause de l'humanité doit avoir assez d'expérience pour reconnaître qu'il faut quelquefois séparer le but des moyens et que la nécessité n'impose pas toujours la loi la plus juste."
37 "On voit même à la figure des divers personnages que ce sommeil est d'une nature prodigieuse, et tellement concentré qu'on serait tenté de croire que chacun des honorables dormeurs porte dans sa poche un exemplaire d'*outre-mer*, par M. Louis de Maynard de Queilhe, gentilhomme de Quercy."

and with a stutter of his own, that he has no choice but to have recourse to irony. Unambiguous categories of skin color do not appear to work anymore, and yet skin color continues to be a constitutional function. It is probably not a coincidence that in this example we are dealing with a literary and concretely dramatic form of representation, which has a different and greater range of the un-sayable available to it than do journalistic texts.

IV.2.4 The Transcolonial Dimension

A piece entitled "L'Espagne, sa révolution, son influence sur l'abolition de l'esclavage colonial" (Spain, its revolution, its influence on the abolition of colonial slavery; *Revue des Colonies* August 1836, 49–54) discusses the Spanish Revolution and its influence on the abolition of slavery. The role of a great Spanish nation, where progress cannot be stopped, is emphasized. The political developments in Spain, which are challenging the power of the aristocracy, cannot but have effects on the Spanish colonies. If Spain is not willing to act skillfully and fairly, it will not be able to keep its remaining colonies, and the Caribbean islands will follow the example of those nations that are already independent:

> The combined efforts of a few philanthropists and a few ambitious men, calling masters and slaves to arms without distinction, shook off the yoke of the metropolis, and the African and the Indian, held in servitude until then, became free citizens and proved from that point on, on the battlefields and in the council rooms, that glory and liberty were priceless goods to them, as they are to all human beings. The current rulers will certainly ... not expose themselves to the loss of Havana and Puerto Rico in addition. Through adept and just policies, they will take care ... to preserve for their fatherland these rather important remnants of their enormous American empire, which they are threatened with losing if they act unskillfully or unjustly. (52)[38]

It is notable that the *Revue des Colonies*, a body that is critical of colonialism, invokes Spain as a model for France. This passage is particularly interesting from a rhetorical standpoint, because it is ostensibly addressed to Spain, encour-

---

[38] "Les efforts réunis de quelques philanthropes et de quelques ambitieux, appelant aux armes, les maîtres et les esclaves sans distinction, secouèrent le joug de la métropole, et l'Africain et l'Indien, jusqu'alors tenus en servitude, devinrent citoyens libres et prouvèrent depuis, sur les champs de bataille et dans les conseils, que la gloire et la liberté étaient pour eux des biens inappréciables, comme pour tous les êtres humains. Certes, les gouvernans actuels ... ne s'exposeront pas à perdre encore la Havane et Porto-Rico. Par une politique habile et juste, ils s'occuperont ... de conserver à leur patrie ces débris assez importans de leur immense empire d'Amérique, et qu'ils sont menacés de perdre s'ils sont inhabiles et injustes."

aging it to leave France behind in matters of colonial politics; the actual addressee, however, is France. Spain is credited with having a political head start and is called on to embrace a pioneering role in terms of social progress as well:

> We repeat that there is only one adroit and just policy that the Spanish government can pursue that will guard against the loss of the islands of Cuba and Puerto Rico. ... It must follow the example of England and, like England, proclaim the principle of the abolition of slavery, as a consequence of the abolition of the slave trade; it is necessary, by this great act of justice, to bind this mass of little islands to the metropolis in gratitude, these islands who never stopped looking towards Jamaica and Haiti, from where they expected their deliverance. Their gratitude and the productions of liberty will greatly make up to you for the curses of a few planters. Do not imitate France, and because you are ahead of that country on the political path, anticipate it in social progress as well and leave it shamefully behind, enduring the insults and outrages of a handful of colonists who want to impose on it the freedom of commerce and on whom France does not have the courage or the dignity to impose the liberty of humankind! (53)[39]

Rather than France's example, it is instead England's model that Spain should follow, and abolish slavery. Here, the intra-Caribbean dimension plays an important role: once the Spanish Caribbean islands have also abolished slavery, the authors hope, the isolation of the remaining two slave-holding societies, namely Guadeloupe and Martinique, will lead to a change in conditions there as well:

> Once again, follow England's example and do not imitate France; and when, in the Gulf of Mexico, Martinique and Guadeloupe alone still contain a handful of masters and a population of slaves, the times will be close to arriving and the destinies close to being fulfilled for these two islands. (54)[40]

---

39 "Nous le répétons, il n'y a qu'une politique habile et juste de la part du gouvernement espagnol qui peut préserver la perte des îles de Cuba et Porto-Rico. ... Il faut suivre l'exemple de l'Angleterre et proclamer comme elle le principe de l'abolition de l'esclavage, conséquence de l'abolition de la traite; il faut par ce grand acte de justice rattacher par la reconnaissance à la métropole cette masse d'ilotes qui ne cessaient d'avoir les yeux tournés vers la Jamaïque et vers Haïti d'où ils attendaient leur délivrance. Leur reconnaissance et les productions de la liberté vous récompenseront largement des imprécations de quelques planteurs. N'imitez pas la France, et puisque vous la devancez dans la carrière politique, devancez-la aussi dans le progrès social et laissez-la honteusement en arrière, subissant les injures el les outrages d'une poignée de colons qui veulent lui imposer la liberté du commerce, et auxquels elle n'a pas le courage et la dignité d'imposer la liberté de l'homme!"
40 "Encore une fois, suivez l'exemple de l'Angleterre, et n'imitez pas la France; et lorsque dans le golfe mexicain, la Martinique et la Guadeloupe seules renfermeront une poignée de maîtres et une population d'esclaves, les temps seront bien près d'arriver et les destinées bien près de s'accomplir pour ces deux îles."

In an article entitled "Sur les derniers évènemens de l'île de Cuba et sur l'importance politique de cette colonie" (On the most recent events on the island of Cuba and on the political importance of the colony; *Revue des Colonies* February 1837, 334–337), the importance of the island of Cuba for control over the entire Caribbean is emphasized. A "racist" sentence at the end warns that England, like all great powers, has an interest in this strategic position. It is important to prevent England, at any cost, from gaining more room to maneuver: "The existence of the Spanish race in North America is an important guarantee for us; we must therefore, with all our might, prevent the invasions of the English race" (337).[41] In support of this view, the British colonies, where the abolition of slavery had only negative effects, are invoked as an example. Agriculture, industry, and trade, the author writes, came to an almost complete standstill, and the British colonists were threatened with complete ruin. The British balance of trade is represented as negative too, which is in stark contrast to the positive report by Governor Smith on production figures (*Revue des Colonies* July 1836, 21–25). As a result then, people should learn from the consequences of abolition in other colonies and be patient, because the preparations for liberation require a lot of time and definitely not hasty legislation: "the civilizing of peoples is the product of the times even more than it is the product of the lawmakers" (*Revue des Colonies* August 1836, 67).[42] It is noteworthy that a periodical that campaigns so unambiguously for abolition also allows voices to be heard that clearly identify the disadvantages of the liberation of slaves.

But there are definitely other voices coming out of the British colonial realm as well: in yet another issue, the abolition that has already taken place on the islands of Jamaica, Saint Christopher, and Tobago is recounted as a success story. A letter from the Moravian Brothers praises the positive effects of the abolition of slavery, albeit as it has to do with church attendance. In various places in Jamaica the crush of former slaves coming to church was so great that many of them had (unfortunately) had to be sent home. In addition, there was an urgent desire to become literate: "Everywhere one sees a vivid desire being manifested to hear the word of God and to learn how to read" (*Revue des Colonies* July 1836, 27).[43] This positive depiction of the consequences of abolition stands in contrast

---

41 "L'existence de la race espagnole dans l'Amérique du Nord est pour nous une garantie nécessaire; nous devons donc, de tous nos efforts, empêcher les envahissemens de la race anglaise."
42 "la civilisation des peuples est l'oeuvre des tems bien plus encore que celle des législateurs."
43 "Partout on voit se manifester un vif désir d'entendre la parole de Dieu et d'apprendre à lire."

to the great skepticism of the plantation owners, who had a variety of reservations, including some to do with the harvest itself: "There were also some doubts about the results of the harvest, but these doubts resulted as much (or more) from the vague fears of the planters as from any ill will on the part of the blacks" (29).[44] In order to reassure the plantation owners, English-language reports are translated that show the great benefits produced by the abolition of slavery, which had already occurred in the British colonies.

In another issue, the biography of the Englishman Thomas Clarkson appears. Clarkson's battle for abolition is recounted, including how he tried to work for abolition outside his own country, for instance in Germany:

> The abolition of the slave trade by the English parliament in 1807 was the reward for all these efforts. But once he had achieved this result, Clarkson was far from considering his work as being done. He wanted all the nations of the world to end the trade, and in order to bring them to that position he went to the 1818 conference at Aix-la-Chapelle where the sovereigns of Europe had gathered. (*Revue des Colonies* October 1836, 160)[45]

Although the comparative examination of Spanish, French, and English colonialism does not produce any exciting insights on the level of a differentiated view of the various colonialisms, it does illustrate in yet another way France's unshakable self-containedness, which is only further affirmed by looking outside itself.

---

[44] "on a aussi manifesté quelques doutes sur les résultats de là récolte, mais ces doutes venaient tout autant, et même bien plus, des craintes vagues dés planteurs que d'aucune mauvaise volonté de la part des noirs."

[45] "L'abolition de la traite par le parlement anglais en 1807 fut la récompense de tant d'efforts. Mais ce résultat obtenu, Clarkson fut loin de considérer son œuvre comme accomplie. Il désirait que toutes les nations du monde missent fin à la traite, et pour les y amener, il se rendit en 1818 au congrès d'Aix-la-Chapelle, où les souverains de l'Europe étaient réunis."

IV.2.5 The Intra-Caribbean Dimension

What kinds of knowledge transfers took place between the islands themselves? To what extent did the *Revue des Colonies* serve as an intra-Caribbean medium of communication? Because the printing presses and other official media were controlled by the colonial centers, there continues to be a dearth of historiographical light shed on the intra-Caribbean processes of circulation, which are mostly attributed to subversive actors who have left little behind in the way of written evidence. The following article excerpts should give an indication of the extent to which the *Revue des Colonies* played a mediating role here.

First, with respect to Guyana and the question of the possible emancipation of the black population: in August 1836, the *Revue des Colonies* printed a speech by de Choisy, the governor of Guyana, that was given before the colonial council and addressed particularly to the plantation owners, entitled "Guiane—Conseil Colonial—Discours de M. de Choisy, gouverneur, à l'ouverture de la session de 1836" (Guyana—colonial council—speech by Mr. de Choisy, governor, at the opening of the 1836 session; *Revue des Colonies* August 1836, 60–64). One can see how de Choisy has adapted his tone to his audience: he shows understanding for the defensive attitude of the colonists, who had not wanted to change "things" too quickly, but at the same time he points out that the time has come to make concessions, because all of France desires emancipation and it is up to them to protect their interests. He also emphasizes this "time for concessions" by pointing out that the king is very willing to accommodate the colonies with investments:

> Nevertheless, gentlemen, we will not deny it, the time for concessions has arrived. The great question of emancipation, the terror of colonists, the chimera caressed by the metropolis, is now the order of the day; all of France desires it and calls for it with all its wishes, without calculating its probable results. The blacks, worked on by ideas of independence ... come from near and far to claim rights founded in principle on the liberty of the human race. ... In this state of affairs, caught between the philosophical ideals of the mother country and the much more pressing demands of the slaves, the colonists will feels as though it is time to make an appearance and to calm the irritated spirits by wise and gradual concessions that can accommodate both the current interests of the owners and the future of the blacks. (62)[46]

---

[46] "Cependant, Messieurs, nous ne le dissimulons pas, le tems des concessions est arrivé. La grande question de l'émancipation, terreur des colons, chimère caressée par la Métropole, est à l'ordre du jour; la France entière la désire et l'appelle de tous ses voeux, sans en calculer probablement tous les résultats. Les noirs, travaillés par des idées d'indépendance ..., viennent réclamer à leur loin des droits fondés en principe sur la liberté du genre humain. ... Dans cet état de choses, placés entre les idéalités philosophiques de la mère-patrie et les réclamations bien

The council's reply is also reproduced in the journal, under the title "Adresse du conseil en réponse au discours du gouverneur" (Response by the council to the governor's speech; 64–68). The colonists (no author is named) make it clear that they do not intend to give in to what are in their view the dangerous utopias of emancipation. They insist that they continue to be open to suggestions for improvement as long as these are desirable and feasible, but that the time is not ripe for innovations and that the slaves are not yet ready for freedom.

> We have walked and we will still walk towards all desirable and possible improvements. But as you yourself recognize, Mr. Governor, the time has not yet come for us to embark on a career of innovations. We can safely say, in spite of the assertions of our detractors, that the men that a few innovators are busying themselves about, without knowing them, are not up to the benefits that people want them to enjoy. (65)[47]

In the same issue, after Guyana, Cuba is also addressed, along with the question of whether it should follow Haiti's example and declare its independence. Two possible models of how independence could be achieved are discussed: either through an agreement between the colonists and the blacks, the way it was done (though the comparison is a little off) in Peru, Mexico, and Chile; or through violent and "happy" uprisings by the blacks—to the great terror of the slave owners who presume to hold property rights over other human beings— as was done in Saint-Domingue (52–53).

For the English-speaking Caribbean, the island of Barbados comes under consideration particularly often, usually under the aspect of issues of missionization. For instance, the article "Barbade: Mission des frères moraves" (Barbados: mission of the Moravian Brothers), reporting on the Brotherhood's mission work, includes particular mention of the positive results of emancipation: "The emancipation of the Negroes there has produced nothing but happy results so far" (71).[48]

The focus returns to Guyana again, which traditionally receives a prominent position in the *Revue des Colonies* because of its position on the continent and as

---

plus pressantes des esclaves, les colons sentiront qu'il est tems de prendre un paru et de calmer les irritations par des concessions sages, graduées, qui puissent concilier et les intérêts presens des propriétaires et l'avenir des noirs."

47 "Nous avons marché, nous marcherons encore à toutes les améliorations désirables et possibles. Mais, ainsi que vous le reconnaissez vous-même, monsieur le gouverneur, le temps n'est pas venu pour nous de nous lancer dans la carrière des innovations. Nous pouvons le dire avec assurance, malgré les assertions de nos détracteurs, les hommes dont quelques novateurs s'occupent sans les connaître ne sont pas à la hauteur des bienfaits dont on voudrait les faire jouir."
48 "L'émancipation des nègres n'y a produit jusqu'à présent que d'heureux effets."

a bridge to a trans-tropical zone. Here, again, the main topic of the Caribbean, namely abolition, cannot be avoided. At one point, Bissette rebukes M. Ursleur, a mulatto member of the colonial council in Cayenne, for being "the only man of color" in Cayenne who is acting against "common sense" by refusing to support abolition. He claims to be able to prove that the nonwhite population in Cayenne categorically protests "against this kind of treason from a man who so forgets all morality and all modesty that he conspires against his own race and his own family, in honor of that most miserable of aristocracies, that of [the color of] skin" (*Revue des Colonies* September 1836, 117, cited in Duke Bryant 261). Here it becomes clear that Bissette is not only working towards the abolition of slavery but that he had connected the topic of abolition so closely with that of the construction of identity of people of color that support for the status quo became monstrous and unthinkable. Bissette also distinguishes here between race and skin color, considering blacks and mulattos to be one and the same race in spite of the difference in the color of their skin (ibid.).

In his *Notice sur la Guyane* (Bulletin about Guyana), Catineau-La-Roche, a royal commissioner and responsible for the development of Guyana, includes a revealing plan about how Guyana should be colonized. The plan refers to the commission report of 1822, which advises against colonizing Guyana, but Catineau-La-Roche argues that Guyana could in fact very well be colonized but that one only has to go about it "correctly."

> In order to succeed in a matter as complicated as colonization, no matter what the environment is in which one undertakes it, a great deal of care and foresight are required: the care given to the details is the principal means to success, and it is because of having neglected this that France has experienced as many setbacks as it has undertaken colonizations. ... I suppose that the colonization is undertaken and carried out by the government alone: what population could it send to Guyana? Its agents, no matter what recommendations the government makes to them, will consider the new colony as a cesspool into which they will hurry to send the least pure population, and Guyana will receive nothing but the dregs. I would suggest, however, that an association of a hundred property-owning families, for example, would have a particular interest in sending honest and hard-working men to the new colony: the best choices will be made and it will be easy to make them because each family will have only a small number of people to choose. (7–8)[49]

---

[49] "Pour réussir dans une affaire aussi compliquée que l'est une colonisation, quel que soit le climat sous lequel on l'entreprenne, il faut beaucoup de soins et de prévoyance: les soins donnés aux détails sont les principaux moyens de succès, et c'est pour les avoir négligés que la France compte autant de revers que de colonisations entreprises. ... Je suppose que la colonisation soit entreprise et conduite par le gouvernement seul: quelle population pourra-t-il envoyer à la Guyane? Ses agens, quelques recommandations qu'il leur fasse, regarderont la nouvelle colonie comme un égout dans lequel ils se hâteront d'envoyer la population la moins pure,

The guiding principle of the *mission civilisatrice*, the civilizing mission, is portrayed here in a particularly trenchant manner with respect to "uncivilized" Guyana. The emphasis on the superior workforce rounds out the racial prejudices that have been established: "Supposing that each white worker does nothing but the tenth part of the work of a Negro, who barely works, that is to say, he only works one hour a day if the Negro works ten" (15).[50]

In discussing the intra-Caribbean dimension I refer to transfers, between the islands, of knowledge regarding the main themes of the Caribbean of that time: abolition, the colonial status quo, racial discourses, and missionization. It becomes clear that these topics are handled differently to some extent and that what is happening between the islands is not so much that there is a net of solidarity being stretched across them as that each island is critically eyeing the others to see how they are dealing with discourses from the colonial centers. The perception of the other is filtered and, thanks to this publication, is directly reflected back to the metropolis. The capacity for integration, not to say inclusion, goes so far that even obvious topics are not negotiated in the immediate neighborhood but always via the center.

IV.2.6 The Transfer of Ideas

IV.2.6.1 The Reception of the Haitian Revolution: *Le Chevalier de Mauduit*

In the play *Le Chevalier de Mauduit* (The knight of Mauduit), by Bauvais Lespinasse, which was printed in the *Revue des Colonies* in its entirety, the first part recounts the background of the slave uprisings in Haiti, more specifically the power struggles that took place on October 30, 1790 and almost led to a civil war. The account tells of two governments that exist in opposition at that time in Saint-Domingue: on the one side the governor general, the count de Peynier, and his followers, who wear white hats (which is the king's color); and on the other side the red-hatted followers of the national assembly, including the colonists, who are full of enthusiasm for the progress that they expect will follow the revolution and at the same time are vehemently opposed to any creation of equal

---

et la Guyane ne recevra que des rebuts. J'admets au contraire qu'une association de cent familles propriétaires, par exemple, ait un intérêt particulier à envoyer dans la nouvelle colonie des hommes honnêtes et laborieux: les meilleurs choix seront faits, et il sera facile de les faire tels, car chaque famille n'aura qu'un petit nombre de personnes à choisir."

50 "En supposant que chaque ouvrier blanc ne fasse que la dixième partie du travail d'un nègre, qui ne travaille guère, c'est-à-dire, qu'il ne travaille qu'une heure par jour, si le nègre en travaille dix."

footing and emancipation for the mulatto (for whom Lespinasse uses the term "yellow" [*jaune*]) and black population: "The provincial assembly of the West and all the white property owners shared the views of the general assembly, because they feared that if one portion of the African race achieved emancipation it would carry the rest along with it, which would mean the loss of their immense possessions" (*Revue des Colonies* October 1836, 166).[51] The free blacks and mulattos therefore follow de Peynier and his colonel, Mauduit. The power struggle intensifies and the assembly convenes to hold its meeting, but when the assembly's followers try to take over the gunpowder store and to connect with the mutinous crew of the ship Léopard, de Peynier intervenes and sends Colonel Mauduit to dissolve the assembly, fight against the efforts towards independence, and protect the king's property. Up until this point, de Peynier and Mauduit are described as positive and "fair," while the assembly is described as being underhanded.

Mauduit storms the assembly and wins. When the assembly notices what a great danger Colonel Mauduit and de Peynier represent, they try to arm the free blacks and mulattos to fight on their side, but these latter remain true to the king, because they hope that the dissolution of the assembly will lead to their emancipation (169). Soon, however, the free blacks and mulattos realize that they cannot expect any true emancipation from Mauduit and de Peynier. The break happens when they receive their hats: these are not white, as they expected, but a whitish yellow. The hats are taken as an affront and refused, and this in turn angers Mauduit. Taking the May 28th decree that guarantees to all property owners over twenty-five years old the opportunity to be a part of the colonial assemblies, he tears it up in front of their eyes, saying: "and now we shall see ... who will protect you, you band of g. ...!" (170).[52] The conflict ends without damage when the members of the assembly take flight on the ship Léopard, and Saint-Domingue narrowly escapes a civil war. But the conditions remain anarchistic; no authority is recognized there anymore.

Seven months after the flight of the members of the assembly, two ships full of soldiers land in Port-au-Prince; the soldiers are supposed to help Mauduit's "white hats" (de Peynier has been replaced by Rouxel Blanchelande in the meantime) to restore order (*Revue des Colonies* November 1836, 206–211). On the way, however, the soldiers have been convinced to join the "red hats" instead. Particularly notable here is the figure of Madame Martin, a woman descri-

---

51 "L'assemblée provinciale de l'ouest et tous les propriétaires blancs partageaient les vues de l'assemblée générale; car ils craignaient, qu'une portion de la race africaine arrivant à l'émancipation, n'entraînât l'autre avec elle, et de là, la perte de leurs biens immenses."
52 "et nous verrons maintenant, ... qui vous protègera, bande de g. ...!"

bed as masculine and strong, who now wants to convince Mauduit's white soldiers to change sides as well. She convinces Schelec, one of Mauduit's young soldiers, to win his squadmates over to the reds too, and he succeeds. Now he is supposed to go to Mauduit and offer him a red hat. Mauduit learns of this plan and sees his end approaching. He dies a "hero's death" by consciously walking into a trap. His beauty is described in detail (*Revue des Colonies* December 1836, 245–248). He calmly dresses in front of the mirror, knowing that he will soon be murdered. Some of the soldiers and officers remain loyal to him. His courage is portrayed very dramatically. It is Schelec who deals him the first blow, and then he is torn "into a thousand pieces" by the other sabers. Very macabre and harsh scenes are described, including the way in which Madame Martin carries the news of Mauduit's death through Port-au-Prince. The text mourns Mauduit's loss as that of a great man:

> In Mauduit, the colonial government lost the most resolute support of its authority, which, now handed off from city to city, was destined to become empty of any substance. As for the colony, it had lost a man of order, of great talent, of steadfast activity, who would have been able to render it real services if his beliefs had been on the right side. (248)[53]

Schelec soon dies as well: "Three months after Mauduit's death, it became known in Port-au-Prince that Schelec had been hanged in the United States: the people added that it was 'for having boasted of his magnificent acts'" (248).[54]

Unlike the previous literary example from Haiti, which dealt with questions of the dividing line in skin color, the *Chevalier Mauduit* belongs to the group of Haitian literary texts that are characterized by the fact that their representation of the Haitian Revolution is mainly limited to a depiction of the revolution's chaotic conditions (see chapter III). The fact that the emphasis is primarily on how the revolution took place is important for the view of the Haitian Revolution on a global scale. Much like in the literary texts, the event itself is not given any universal revolutionary importance.

---

[53] "Le gouvernement colonial perdait en Mauduit le plus ferme soutien de son autorité qui, dorénavant promenée de ville en ville, ne devait plus être qu'une nullité. Quant à la colonie, elle perdait un homme d'ordre, de grand talent, d'une activité persévérante, qui eût pu dans la circonstance lui rendre de véritables services, s'il avait été de meilleure foi."

[54] "Trois mois après la mort de Mauduit on sut au Port-au-Prince que Schelec avait été pendu aux Etats-Unis: 'pour s'être vanté de ses belles actions' ajoutait le peuple."

IV.2.6.2 The Transfer of Ideas from the Metropolis to the Colonies

The transfer of theories from the metropolis to the colonies, which is essentially established as the only possible direction for colonial transfers, was considered highly problematic by white Creoles, as we can see from a speech by M. Cicéron to Guadeloupe's colonial council, printed in the *Revue des Colonies* (October 1836, 151–154). France, he claims, had mistakenly followed foreign models, in particular that of England, and thereby jeopardized the future of the white plantation owners. Cicéron criticizes the new 1833 colonial laws as too restrictive, compared to the laws of 1790. At that time, the National Assembly had been conscious of the special position of the colonies and had taken into consideration that in countries that were so far from the metropolis, other customs and mores prevailed than in France:

> In 1790, the National Assembly, for reasons of justice and equity, had endowed the colonies with a broader representation than that of April 24, 1833. It took into consideration the fact that countries that were located two thousand leagues from the metropolis had customs and habits that were different from those in France; by reason of their exceptional status, they had the right, in their assemblies, to pass laws and regulations that were in harmony with their situation, laws and regulations that were then subject to royal agreement. (154)[55]

The epistolary duel between the Count de Mauny and the *Courrier Français* (the French Mail) is illuminating on the subject of the exchange between the metropolis and the colonies (*Revue des Colonies* October 1836, 171–177, "Polémique de Journaux" [Newspaper controversy]). The exchange would seem to indicate that the *Courrier Français* was well-established in France, and that it took a negative attitude towards the colonists. The argument has three parts: it begins with an article that appeared in the *Courrier Français*; in response, the Count de Mauny wrote a letter of complaint, which was also printed; and finally, the *Courrier Français* gave a response to de Mauny's letter.

The writer of the article in the *Courrier Français* accuses the plantation owners of concealing the true conditions in the colonies, claiming that their motives for rejecting the emancipatory ideas coming out of the mother country are purely economic:

---

55 "L'assemblée nationale, en 1790, par des considérations de justice et d'équité, avait doté les colonies d'une représentation plus large que celle du 24 avril 1833. Elle n'ignorait pas que des pays, situés à 2,000 lieues de la métropole, avaient des mœurs et des habitudes différentes de celles de la France; en raison de leur exceptionnalité, elles avaient le droit, dans leurs assemblées, de voter les lois et réglemens en harmonie avec leur situation, lois et réglemens qui étaient soumis à la sanction royale."

> The colonies have always sought to deflect public attention from these possessions, over which they rule arbitrarily, ... in such a way that the important questions that concern them escape the knowledge of the metropolis. In addition, the discussions of the colonial councils on the question of sugar and the language used by the newspapers of Île Bourbon and Guadeloupe in talking about the intentions of the metropolis with regard to slavery also make it easy enough to suspect what arguments they would use to reject the intervention of the legislature and the government on this subject. (171–172)[56]

On October 14, 1836, the Count de Mauny replies that Martinique guaranteed the freedom of the press and that it was in the active interest of the colonial council to advocate for its positions. On the subjects of slavery and the freedom of trade, he expresses himself as follows:

> The question does not seem to merit such supreme contempt given that what is proposed would cause a loss to the metropolis's maritime trade, just for Martinique, of eighty to a hundred million, and that in invoking the ringing names of liberty and humanity they are inciting insurrection, arson, and murder; it is natural enough that, on a question in which the colonists are defending civilization against the state of savagery, one should know who is going to decide it. (175)[57]

De Mauny thus summarizes once again the arguments of the anti-abolitionist colonists against the metropolis's attempts at reform: the emancipation of the blacks would lead to considerable economic losses, to uprisings (in other words: to the loss of the privileges of the white property-owning class), and to the downfall of (French) civilization.

Following the Count de Mauny's letter, the *Courrier Français* printed another statement of its own, clearly expressing how hypocritical and dishonest de Mauny's words appear. This critical assessment can be explained by the fact that while the Count de Mauny affirms the ideas of 1789, he sees problems in their concrete implementation in the colonies. Thus, the failure of the transfer

---

56 "La division des colonies a toujours cherché à détourner l'attention publique de ces possessions qu'elle régit arbitrairement, ... de manière que les questions importantes qui les concernent échappent à la connaissance de la métropole. Au surplus les discussions des conseils coloniaux sur la question des sucres, et le langage des journaux de l'île Bourbon et de la Guadeloupe, sur les intentions de la métropole, relativement à l'esclavage, laissent assez soupçonner, par quels argumens on repousse l'intervention de la législature et du gouvernement sur ce point."
57 "La question ne semble pas mériter un si superbe dédain, lorsqu'on propose de faire perdre au commerce maritime de la métropole, pour la Martinique seulement, de 80 à 100 millions, et qu'en invoquant les noms sonores de liberté et d'humanité, on excite à l'insurrection, à l'incendie et à l'assassinat; il est assez naturel que dans une question où les colons défendent la civilisation contre l'état sauvage, on sache qui la décidera."

from the center to the colonies that is represented so often in literary texts finds a counterpart in some of the articles in the *Revue des Colonies*.

IV.2.7 Programmatic Fusion

The word that best encapsulates the *Revue*'s revolutionary project is "fusion": as expressed in its foreword, the *Revue* was founded with the goal of influencing public opinion through "an always sensible and straightforward, but vigorous and never timid, discussion of the causes, whatever they might be, that are hindering the desirable fusion of the colonies' various peoples" (*Revue des Colonies* I.i, 3, cited in Bongie, "'C'est du papier'" 449).[58] It wants to break down the racial segregation that structures colonial society. This is shown particularly clearly in Bissette's article on the English colonies: "De l'émancipation des esclaves, considérée comme premier élément du progrès social aux colonies" (On the emancipation of slaves, considered as the first element of social progress in the colonies; *Revue des Colonies* I.vii, 3–14; cf. Bongie, "'C'est du papier'" 449). In that article, he notes that "production and material prosperity are moving ahead there and, in a very limited number of years, the fusion of the black and white races will turn these lands ... into a country enjoying civil and political liberty and equality" (*Revue des Colonies*, I.vii, 3–4, cited in Bongie, "'C'est du papier'" 449). Although fusion is connected here with the project of assimilation into the mother country, the ideal of fusion is not identical to the idea of assimilation that was circulating in Parisian circles at that time. On the contrary: as Bongie points out, the idea of fusion is primarily concerned with the formation of a Caribbean society with its own customs ("'C'est du papier'" 450).[59] In the article "De la fusion des deux races aux colonies et des causes qui la retardent" (On the fusion of the two races in the colonies and on the causes that are delaying it; *Revue des Colonies* I.vi, 3–7; cf. Bongie, "'C'est du papier'" 450), most likely written by Bissette, the creation of a post-racial "shared homeland" is also advocated, a homeland that would be both a part of France and different from it:

---

[58] This subchapter rests primarily on Bongie's foundational analysis of the first editions of *Revue des Colonies*, to which I did not have access. Therefore, if it seems that I reproduce Bongie's argument here to an unusually extensive degree, this is only because such elaborate quotation constitutes an important cornerstone for the overall understanding of my book's argumentation.

[59] More than a century later, the Barbadan poet and cultural historian Kamau Brathwaite analyzes the development of such a Caribbean society in his pioneering study of processes of creolization. Cf. Bongie, "'C'est du papier'" 450.

In effect, it is impossible that, once legitimate grievances have been satisfied, resentments assuaged, the playing-field leveled out, the oppressors disarmed and punished, in a word, equal rights proclaimed and adequately protected by the public authorities, it is impossible, we say, that the white and black populations in the colonies should not fraternize and join together, in everybody's best interests, to work the land in common, their shared homeland today, in which a better organization of labor and the development of an eminently social feeling of the fraternity of man will turn it for them into a homeland that is as beloved as it is free, industrious and prosperous. (*Revue des Colonies* I.vi, 3, cited in Bongie, "'C'est du papier'" 450)

Bongie points out that a demand like this could only appear inadequate, and yet in its motivational rhetoric it opens a way to a different future and in doing so fulfills a function much like that of today's many calls for creolization and hybridity. The concept of "fusion" may very well appear to be an unjustifiable simplification, and it may seem appropriate to rewrite it as "(con)fusion," which, according to Bongie, would be a more chaotic way of being with others, a more complex and disturbing version of what Glissant characterizes as relationalism (Bongie, "'C'est du papier'" 450). And yet this kind of post-colonial transcription should not lead us to ignore this nineteenth-century colonial precedent; instead, it forces us to recognize its lasting presence in the form of a trace that, once noticed, directs our attention to the conceptual boundaries of these contemporary conceptions of intercultural mixing—métissage, creolization, and the like—with which it is genealogically linked (ibid.).

Any defense of the idea of fusion also needs to address questions about constructions of identity: how will the old identities be distinguished from each other once they have been fused with each other? For Bissette, an ideally fused Martinican identity is not characterized by the disappearance of the old racial identities ("white/brown/black") but rather by a productive restructuring of the relationships among the three "classes." The "brown" mulatto, the prime example of the complete dissolution of old ("white/black") identities into a new one, is therefore seen as just one possibility among the "multiple populations" of the colony, although it is decidedly privileged, as a middle category that can facilitate the "desirable fusion of the diverse populations of the colonies" (451). Bissette uses the redefinition of this intermediate space[60] as a channel between "white" and "black" (as opposed to a barrier that divides the two categories from each other) and to call into question the divide-and-conquer strategy of colonial discourse that in countless ways insists on the difference of the "mulatto subject" in order to more effectively carry out and maintain its

---

60 Bongie uses the term "third space," but I prefer "intermediate space."

own power. Though the mulatto is also unchallenged as a (racial and social) category in the *Revue*, Bissette nevertheless often shows his sharp awareness of the contingent nature of colonial identities and of the language with which colonial discourse attempts to "naturalize" these historically created identities; he speaks, for instance, of "this magic word, *homme de couleur*, a word by means of which they have been banished to the fringes of civilization" (*Revue des Colonies* I.iii, 10, cited in Bongie, "'C'est du papier'" 451). Bissette recognizes that such identities are inventions, a fact that becomes ever more obvious in the case of "this magic word" because, as he shows, the 1833 law actually abolished the legal category of the *homme de couleur*, so that all those who had up until then been united in that phrasing were now turned into colorless citizens of the mother country (Bongie, "'C'est du papier'" 451).

Thus, according to Bongie, the *Revue*, in that it is in fact produced by so-called *hommes de couleur*, is a posthumous enterprise, written into a language that demystifies attributions of identity. Bongie points out that nothing better clarifies the dubiousness of a politics of identity than the paradox of the literature of these *hommes de couleur* in the year 1834 (451f.).

Bissette, of course, cannot be summed up in just this one posthumous identity; the "we" that he uses in the *Revue* includes not only the concept of an *homme de couleur* but also, depending on the context, of a Frenchman, a Martinican, a mulatto, and a person of African heritage. His reflections on "this magic word," which illustrate the baselessness of colonial discourse (if not of language in general), are part of what might be the decisive strategy of his work in the *Revue*, which is equally significant for postcolonial revisionism: Bongie describes this strategy as a demystified, and essentially even deconstructivist, critique of colonial (mis)representations: this critique identifies colonial discourse, as it is written down in governmental documents, legal decisions, literary texts, newspaper articles, and so on, as a systematic kind of what the *Revue* refers to as the "denaturing" of reality (452). This critique entails an interest in the problem of stereotyping and in the way in which literary conventions result in the representations of historical facts, an interest that expresses itself in a highly interesting way, as set forth in the discussion of the phrase *hommes de couleur*. Bongie shows how Bissette, by repeatedly exposing the gap between colonial discourse and reality, adopts a rhetorical practice that is widespread among many representatives of this generation, namely romantic irony, which "reminds us of the double nature of language (life), which cannot mean or be what it says" (ibid.).

Let us take a brief look at a historical event to which the first issues of the *Revue* paid a great deal of attention, and in Bissette's reporting of which this problematization of (colonial) speech played a central role. The incident was one that Bissette sarcastically called the "*great revolution* of Grand'anse," an uprising presumably led by mulattos that took place in Martinique in December of 1833 and ended in the sentencing to death of dozens of people (although this sentence would finally be lightened a few years later) (cf. 452). As Bissette repeatedly argues, in order to create outrage and moral panic, the white Creole elite transformed a simple demonstration into a mulatto conspiracy to crush the white population of the island and seize its possessions. In indicating the ways in which "the public prosecutor's office in Martinique is laboriously giving birth to what it calls the *insurrection* of Grand'anse" (cited in ibid., 453), he also provides detailed reports of the violent oppression (including the murder of militia members) that followed this "uprising" and heavily criticizes the government's unwillingness to pursue the authors or perpetrators ("*les auteurs ou fauteurs*") of these bloody and arbitrary saturnalia as well as its willingness to ignore "incontrovertible facts," which

> give proof for the hundredth time to the *métropole* of the systematic oppression of the "colored" classes, the daily provocations directed against them, the persistent denial of all their rights in defiance of the laws that grant these rights to them—all those facts, in short, that show the events of Grand'anse in a true light [*qui donnent aux événemens de la Grand'anse une véritable couleur*]. (*Revue des Colonies* I.i, 15, cited in Bongie, "'C'est du papier'" 453)

Such facts, he claims, are "omitted, dissimulated, if necessary denied, and in all cases excused" (ibid.) by the governmental media. The colonies officially presented France with one hundred and seventeen conspirators, supported by a three-hundred-page indictment, but on closer inspection, trivial offenses had been blown out of proportion into a plot:

> What will be shown to the colonies, to France in the accounts—official and authentic, as everyone knows—of the *Moniteur* will be *one hundred and seventeen conspirators* appearing in court under the weight of a 300-page indictment, all accused of conspiracy plot, for that is exactly what the government of Martinique needs, and each then charged in particular with having *plundered* two jugs of tafia and two jugs of rum from Seguinol's; or some soap, candles, and a curry-comb from *Desmadrelles's*; or a bottle of genever from *Lereynerie's* (pages 85–86 of the court decision). And all that printed up by the government of the colony in 200 pages, pompously entitled, by the most ignorant of magistrates, *Insurrection de la Grand'anse*. (*Revue des Colonies* I.i, 15–16, cited in Bongie, "'C'est du papier'" 453)[61]

---

[61] "Ce qu'on montrera aux colonies, à la France, dans les relations officielles et authentiques, comme on sait, du *Moniteur*, ce sera *cent dix-sept conspirateurs* comparaissant sous le poids d'une accusation de 300 pages, accusés tous de complot, car il en faut bien un au gouvernement de la Martinique; puis prévenus chacun en particulier d'avoir *pillé deux pots de taffia et deux pots de rhum chez Seguinol*; ou chez *Desmadrelles*, du savon, de la chandelle, une étrille de cheval; ou chez *Lereynerie*, une bouteille de genièvre (pages 85 et 86 d'arrêt de renvoi). Et tout cela

In this illustrative passage, Bissette shows how colonial history is supposedly "faultily written" (by the *auteurs* and *fauteurs*) and how it achieves its deceptive appearance of "weightiness." The supposedly "authentic" and "official" knowledge that appears in a governmental organ such as the *Moniteur* becomes the object of an ironic knowledge ("as everyone knows"), which is ready to believe in the questionable existence of the one hundred and seventeen "conspirators" and their act of "plundering." The fact that such words only represent the empty signs of power, which lack any real referent but nevertheless construct a brutal reality, is underscored by the emphasis put upon them. Thus, the repetition of a word like "conspirator" empties it of its meaning; the emphasis put on colonial names such as "Seguinot," "Desmadrelles," and "Leyreynerie" (whose establishments were "robbed") fulfills a similar function, by way of metonymic associations: could these italicized family names, and the authority to which they allude, be as baseless as the other italicized words in the text? Could the justification for them be as empty of substance as the nonsensical title *Insurrection of Grand'anse?* These are the sorts of questions that are raised by Bissette's ironic interrogation of individual words (453f.). By repeatedly undermining the authority of the colonial discourse and showing it in its true (in other words false) "colors," he supplements this ironic critique with a reverse discourse when, a few lines later, he refers to "the permanent conspiracy against the rights and personal security of the 'colored' population, the permanent insurrection of the whites against the laws of the *métropole*" (*Revue des Colonies* I.i, 16, cited in Bongie, "'C'est du papier'" 454).

This kind of deconstructive irony, of which there is a great deal in the pages of the *Revue*, along with Bissette's far-reaching unmasking of the omissions, concealments, denials, and justifications of (a particular variety of) the colonial discourse, deserve more attention in the context of French-language Caribbean literary history and cultural critique than they have so far received. The fact that Bissette's work for the *Revue* has not been looked at more closely, in spite of its obvious contributions, which would otherwise have certainly given it a place in the Afro-American canon, is of course at least partially due to his ambiguous positioning, which I have referred to as his (non-)identification with blackness; that, however, is something that no mulatto in the French colonies at that time could have avoided. It could also have something to do with the increasingly religious and conservative rhetoric that Bissette used in the years following the *Revue*'s decline—years that were marked by his "superhuman efforts"

---

imprimé par le gouvernement de la colonie à 200 pages, intitulé pompeusement, par le plus ignorant des magistrats, *Insurrection de la Grand'anse*."

in the service of the abolitionist cause (Bongie, "'C'est du papier'" 454). However, one could argue that, in an important respect, such "anomalies" make him not a less but in fact a more valuable person for the understanding of the complexity of a nineteenth-century Afro-French identity, and that in his alternately biting and conciliatory treatment of the relationships between Martinique and the mother country, he fits very well into Paul Gilroy's description of those black writers whose peripatetic lives and regime-critical political observations can only disappoint and frustrate any absolutist understanding of racial cultural forms (Gilroy, *The Black Atlantic* 21; see Bongie, "'C'est du papier'" 455).

In fact, the intermediate space of the *homme de couleur* that a mulatto writer like Bissette "officially" occupies is not just a colonial product but anticipates our own world of global intercultural entanglements, a world that, as Gilroy puts it, escapes from the "ruthless simplicity of undifferentiated racial essences as a solution to growing divisions inside black communities" (ibid.). Positioned between conformity and critique, Bissette's writings are reminiscent of a double identity—simultaneously colonial and postcolonial, white and black, French and Martinican—which demands to be read, above all, neither positively nor negatively but rather, exclusively, with the highest degree of ambivalence. Nowhere is the necessity of such an ambivalent reading more evident than when we look at the bitter rivalries that developed in the early eighteen-forties between Bissette and his colleague Victor Schœlcher, the man who will later be glorified as *the* conqueror of slavery in the French colonies. It is in this apotheosis that Bongie finds the main cause of the ongoing neglect of Bissette in our current revisionist times, which pride themselves on rehabilitating marginalized figures of the past (455).

IV.3 Haiti and the *Revue encyclopédique*

IV.3.1 The *Revue encyclopédique* and Colonial Questions

"But all this surprising progress, achieved in the space of a quarter century, these oh-so-lovely hopes offered to the entire world by the Haitian nation: must we abandon them?" (*Revue encyclopédique* 25, January 1825, 113).[62]

---

[62] "Mais ces progrès si étonnans, conquis dans l'espace d'un quart de siècle, ces espérances si belles données par la nation haitienne au monde entier, faudra-t-il y renoncer?" In my remarks on the *Revue encyclopédique*, I rely on Yves Bénot's foundational article "Haïti et la 'Revue encyclopédique,'" published posthumously. See also Lüsebrink's important analysis of Antoine Métral in "Transfers culturels."

The prestigious *Revue encyclopédique*, which first appeared in Paris in 1819 and continued through the early months of 1835, was a monthly that was archived in bound volumes every trimester. This periodical was a gathering place for a group of oppositionists who were against the Restoration and used the *Revue* as a place to conduct their discussions. The paper was headed by Marc-Antoine Jullien, who in Year II after the French Revolution, at the age of 17, was a special envoy for the Public Health Committee (*Comité de Salut Public*) in eastern France and in Bordeaux; since that high point of revolutionary fervor, however, the Jacobinist Robespierrian's convictions had softened somewhat (Bénot 99).

In many ways, Jullien's new *Revue encyclopédique* fit into the pattern of *Décade* or the *Revue philosophique, littéraire et politique* (1794–1807), one of whose founders, Jean-Baptiste Say, was also active in this new group, as was the scholar Louis-Mathieu Langlès. A certain Guadet, a nephew of Coquerel, the representative from Gironde, was also involved, as was the nephew of Helen Williams, who had run a salon during the revolution. Among the many contributors to the *Revue encyclopédique*, it is also worth mentioning Louise Swanton Belloc, the geographer Edme-François Jomard, author of *Études géographiques et historiques sur l'Arabie*, Adolphe Blanqui, the economist Alexandre Moreau de Jonnès, and, a particularly frequent contributor, Jean Charles Léonard de Sismondi (Bénot 99). The largest number of articles were written by the two very well-known intellectuals Abbé Grégoire, the former bishop of Blois; and Jean-Denis Lanjuinais.[63] They only started publishing in the *Revue enyclopédique* in 1822, after their own journal, the *Revue religieuse*, was no longer allowed to appear. In Grégoire's case, at least, he had been in contact with Jullien as often as possible from the *Revue encyclopédique*'s beginnings (cf. Bénot 99). Grégoire's presence in this group is an indication that issues involving slavery and the slave trade, as well as questions having to do with newly independent Haiti, which so characterized that time, took a central position at the journal. The group held its meetings in the form of monthly dinners, which are reported on in the *Revue encyclopédique* in 1827. Friends who were visiting Paris at the time were often invited to these meetings, including such visitors as Haitian parliamentarians or Osage Indians from the United States (100).

Most of the *Revue encyclopédique*'s writers advocated a parliamentary system; even though some of them, including Grégoire, were still deeply and staunchly Republican, they would have been satisfied with a constitutional mon-

---

[63] Up through 1827, Abbé Grégoire's contributions consist of around fifty pieces, signed "G." On Grégoire, cf. Lüsebrink, "'Négrophilie," and Lüsebrink, "Aufklärerisches Erkenntnispotential."

archy on the English model (cf. Bénot 100). And though they all believed that a parliament should be elected, that in no way means that universal suffrage was one of their primary demands. They insisted on the freedom of the press as long as the press did not call for revolt and political violence; they believed in the effectiveness of public education; and they admired the constitutional model of the United States. When Sismondi began a vigorous attack on slavery in the *Revue encyclopédique*, he had to deal with a large number of counterarguments from his opponents, many of them with heavily racist tendencies.

Politically, the journal's writers were liberal, and quite a few of them were also economically liberal. Jean-Baptiste Say set the tone, even though Sismondi attempted a few times to contradict him. The belief in progress based on the role of the state being reduced to a minimum is visible at all levels. The group was interested in the progress of knowledge and the development of technology. The *Revue encyclopédique* reported on the state of the press, of education, of knowledge, and of technology in the various regions of the world that its correspondents were able to get to. The bulk of its publications consisted of book reviews, including comments from the authors (ibid.). As had been true earlier at *Décade*, the prevailing attitude involved the rejection of slavery and the constant denunciation of the slave trade. Nevertheless, abolition was only thought of in terms of a gradual change; revolutionary uprisings were to be avoided. The fight for an effective implementation of the ban on the slave trade was of paramount importance, not only to the *Revue encyclopédique* but also to the *Société de la Morale Chrétienne* (Society for Christian morality), whose director was none other than Coquerel (also a contributor to the *Revue encyclopédique*, as we have seen) and of which Jullien himself was also a member (101).

As for Haiti, its colonial status was one of the central issues for France's domestic and foreign policy (cf. Bénot 101). Although the *Revue encyclopédique* had as one of its stated objectives not to interfere in current politics, its preoccupation with Haiti took on not just an ideological but also a political aspect.

IV.3.2 Colonialism and Pan-African Ideas

In its October 1820 and October and November 1824 issues, the *Revue encyclopédique* reports on Jean-Pierre Boyer's requests to the United States to organize the emigration of free blacks from there to Haiti. At the same time, it criticizes the actions of the American *Sociéte de Colonisation* (Colonization Society), which is in the process of creating the foundations for a nation that will later be called Liberia. Boyer rightly observes that the section of the African coast that has been chosen is not a desert—that there are long-established African peoples already living there. Boyer considers those peoples to be "barbarians" and is of the opinion that it would be in the interest of the "already civilized" blacks from the United States to settle in a developed country, such as Haiti, instead. Jonathas Granville, a veteran of Napoleon's armies who had returned to Haiti after 1815, reported very extensively on Boyer's efforts for the *Revue encyclopédique*.

The *Revue encyclopédique* itself, however, was very interested in the colonies of Liberia and Sierra Leone, which were just being established in Africa; the *Revue* considered them to be where the vanguard of civilization was to be found. The general line taken by the *Revue encyclopédique* can be found in an introductory article by Sismondi from 1825:

> We will not mention at all the colonies that are destined to spread civilization across the vast continent of Africa and which, starting from the Cape of Good Hope and from Sierra Leone, will, little by little, carry light and virtue into the interior in order to repair Europe's longstanding crimes. (*Revue encyclopédique* 25, January 1825, 37, cited in Bénot 107)[64]

The *Revue encyclopédique* is not anti-colonial; even when it sometimes criticizes colonization, it is mostly because it is considered too expensive (cf. Bénot 108).

Haiti is not only a challenge to the political fabric of France and of the world. For the *Revue encyclopédique*, it is a successful model for contradicting all those who consistently disparage everything black. The arguments of the proponents of slavery were still being put forward loudly and indiscriminately at that time. In 1822, the *Revue encyclopédie* answered them that the Haitian government could serve as a model for old Europe (cf. ibid.). Haiti is the living proof that all human beings, including blacks and mulattos, have the same intellectual capacities, so that they develop and perfect themselves, which for Enlightenment thinkers and, later, for the *idéologues* was an essential part of human existence.

Like Haiti, Sierra Leone, too, contributed to an optimistic view of the situation and of the future of the blacks. In a July 1822 article on the subject of Sierra Leone, Coquerel argues against those who in "treatises on physiology" or "in some political publications" allege the blacks' "intellectual inferiority" or their "supremacy of the senses over thought." Instead, he writes, "whenever the unhappy slaves achieve freedom, the qualities of intelligence follow," and in a footnote he cites Grégoire's book *De la littérature des nègres* (On the literature of the Negroes):

---

[64] "Nous ne parlerons point des colonies destinées à répandre la civilisation sur le vaste continent de l'Afrique et qui, du cap de Bonne Espérance et de Sierra Leone, porteront peu à peu dans l'intérieur la lumière et la vertu pour réparer les longs forfaits de l'Europe."

Wherever they have been freed, they have shown a very pronounced taste for ingenious industry. With an indubitable success they have cultivated the arts and literature; ... their heart has opened, just like our own, to the sublime impressions of the beautiful and the right. These are the facts. (*Revue encyclopédique* 15, July 1822, 24)⁶⁵

In a piece by Sismondi entitled "Review of the progress of peoples in the last 25 years" (*Revue des progrès des peuples dans les 25 dernières années*), which is the opening article for the January 1825 issue, the praise given to Haiti appears to be a provocation to the advocates of slavery but also to the learned "physiologists" who support racial ideology with seemingly scientific theories. In order to understand it more clearly, allow me to cite from it here somewhat at length:

> The path that was taken by the new Haitian nation, in Saint-Domingue, in this quarter of a century, is a more triumphant subject for all of humanity. That is where the sons of Africa have proven that they are men, that they deserved to be free, that they knew how to appreciate light and virtue. A frightful crime by the Europeans transported the Africans to the islands of the Americas; a series of crimes continued to keep them in slavery there and made them ferocious; if they also committed crimes in breaking their chains, the responsibility for that rests entirely on those who forged them. As long as slavery endured in Saint-Domingue, immorality and ignorance were proportional to the absolute deprivation of liberty. ... Since Haiti has been free and the Negroes have been their own masters, their zeal for learning has been even greater than their zeal to free themselves. A quarter of a century has been enough to transform those who were considered livestock into human figures in a civilized nation, where there are schools opening everywhere, where thought is making rapid progress, where every year brings a noticeable improvement in customs in spite of the climate, where crimes are rare, where justice is served promptly and impartially, where agriculture, industry, and commerce prosper, where the population has doubled even in the middle of the terrible wars which brought and followed emancipation. This is what some Negroes have been able to do in twenty-five years. (*Revue encyclopédique* 25, January 1825, 37)⁶⁶

---

65 "Partout où on les affranchit, ils ont montré un goût très prononcé pour une ingénieuse industrie. Ils ont cultivé avec un succès non douteux les arts et la littérature; ... leur cœur s'est ouvert tout comme le nôtre aux sublimes impressions du beau et du juste. Voilà les faits."
66 "La carrière parcourue par la nouvelle nation haïtienne, à Saint-Domingue, dans ce quart de siècle, est pour l'humanité entière, un plus beau sujet de triomphe. C'est là que les fils de l'Afrique ont prouvé qu'ils sont des hommes, qu'ils méritaient d'être libres, qu'ils savaient apprécier la lumière et la vertu. Un crime effroyable des Européens transporta les Africains dans les îles de l'Amérique; une suite de crimes les y maintint dans l'esclavage et les rendit féroces; S'ils commirent aussi des crimes en brisant leurs chaînes, la responsabilité en pèse tout entière sur ceux qui les avaient forgées. Tant que l'esclavage dura à Saint-Domingue, l'immoralité et l'ignorance furent proportionnelles à la privation absolue de liberté. ... Depuis qu'Haïti est libre et que les nègres sont leurs propres maîtres, leur ardeur pour s'instruire l'a emporté encore sur leur ardeur pour s'affranchir. Un quart de siècle a suffi pour transformer ceux qu'on regardait comme un

It is not hard to recognize that along with Sismondi, the *Revue encyclopédique* has been true to its ideological goals: the journal believes in the possibility of development for all human beings, and in particular also for blacks, when historically based barriers have been lifted. This Enlightenment optimism was typical of early-nineteenth-century liberalism. Sismondi could of course not know what kind of socio-economic conditions Haiti's development would have to suffer under until the present day. He attempts to see Haiti's independence not just as the result of a revolution by chained slaves but also as a universal event. Because the Haitian Revolution proclaims, under the eyes of the entire world, that these blacks, whom the "physiologists" had wanted to assign to lower levels of humanity, in fact possess full legitimacy as human beings. To use Buffon's terminology, the revolution confirms the fundamental equality of "all varieties of the human species" (cf. Bénot 109).

The fact that Sismondi took this stand was all the more important because the *Revue encyclopédique* did not always articulate its position as clearly as Grégoire was able to do at that time in *De la noblesse de la peau* (On the nobility of skin). Other writers also felt as though Haiti's example was a challenge that pushed them to state their position. Thus, for instance, in an 1825 issue of the *Revue encyclopédique*, Garnier reviewed a book by an obscure contemporary philosopher by the name of Dunoyer, titled *L'industrie et la morale considérées dans leurs rapports avec la liberté* (Industry and morality considered in their relationship to freedom). Garnier refuted Dunoyer's thesis by appealing to Haiti's success story, which by this time was twenty-five years old: "This is obviously contradicted by the facts, because today the blacks of Haiti are more intelligent than the copper-skinned people of Tierra del Fuego" (cited in Bénot 110).[67]

No less a writer than Benjamin Constant himself weighed in in the *Revue encyclopédique* in 1825. Although he allows that there is a grain of truth in Dunoyer's system of racial differences, he warns against giving too much importance to these differences. "Power is only too ready to see its own capricious and voluntary excesses as the simple result of the laws of nature" (Constant

---

bétail à figure humaine en une nation civilisée, chez laquelle des écoles s'ouvrent de toutes parts, où la pensée fait des progrès rapides, où chaque année apporte dans les mœurs, en dépit du climat, une amélioration notable, où les crimes sont rares, où la justice est rendue avec promptitude et impartialité, où l'agriculture, l'industrie, le commerce prospèrent, où la population a doublé au milieu même des guerres terribles qui ont accompli et suivi l'émancipation. Voilà ce que des nègres ont su faire en vingt-cinq ans."

67 "Or ceci est évidemment contredit par les faits; car les noirs d'Haïti sont aujourd'hui plus intelligents que les cuivrés de la Terre de Feu."

59).⁶⁸ He, too, refers to the example of the blacks of Haiti: they "have become very reasonable legislators, well-enough disciplined warriors, and statesmen who are as able and polished as our diplomats" (ibid.).⁶⁹ And here he takes on the role of Enlightenment spokesman again, arguing against Dunoyer to say that all races are capable of being perfected. His attitude towards racial ideology permeates his purely political attitude: "Let us allow the physiologists to deal with the primitive differences that will sooner or later be overcome by the perfectibility with which the entire species is gifted; and let us beware of giving politics the weapon of this new pretext for inequality and oppression" (ibid.).⁷⁰ Constant guessed very early on what it can lead to when differences between the human races that have supposedly been scientifically proven are called on as a justification for political and social exclusion. Others at the *Revue encyclopédique* were more restrained: in the next issue, for instance, Paganel refers to an article by Bory de Saint-Vincent in the *Dictionnaire classique d'Histoire Naturelle*, seeing no problem in the fact that the author distinguishes among fifteen different races.

In conclusion, we must ask whether the French liberals were, in the end, helpful to Haiti's cause in any way. And even more important is the question of the extent to which the slaves' victory and the independence of their new nation served the cause of progress in France and around the world. C.L.R. James insists that the popular uprising helped the French Revolution to finally gain long-term significance: the abolition of slavery sent a signal of liberation to all of humanity. At the same time, independent Haiti became a first dam against the rising tide of racial ideologies and of racism in general—or, in Grégoire's words, a lighthouse that proclaims universal equality and brotherhood from afar: because it was not for themselves alone that they won freedom.

From the point of view of the French liberals, who were surely not in a position to analyze the socio-economic process to which Haiti was subject, it was absolutely necessary to draw a picture of the country that accorded with the progressive vision of the entire human race. Seen in the context of world history, this vision is not wrong (cf. Bénot 112). There has indeed been progress, and it has to be a help for other people and other regions of the earth. Seen in this light, the

---

68 "Le pouvoir n'est que trop disposé à représenter ses propres excès capricieux et volontaires comme une suite des lois de la nature."
69 "sont devenus des législateurs fort raisonnables, des guerriers assez disciplinés, des hommes d'état aussi habiles et aussi polis que nos diplomates."
70 "Laissons les physiologistes s'occuper des différences primitives que la perfectibilité dont toute l'espèce est douée surmonte tôt ou tard; et gardons-nous d'armer la politique de ce nouveau prétexte d'inégalité et d'oppression."

Haitian Revolution, which probably cost the most human life, finally did achieve its universal value.

IV.4 Literary Transfer Processes in the *Revue des deux mondes*

The *Revue des deux mondes* is an anthology dealing with politics, administration, and customs, which was first published in Paris in 1829 and is an important journal to this day. Its fundamental guiding principles are described in the magazine's first and second issues as follows: extended travels will be undertaken in order to describe different regions. Everything that is poetic, everything that aims to provide brilliant representations, and every astute reflection on a topic will be given particular care and attention in its pages, but there will be no claim to complete coverage of the specificities of local administration, the civil and political organization of the country, or its financial, industrial, and agricultural resources (in order to address that sort of question, one would have to become involved in deeper and more particular studies, and a collection like that is still not available). All of the journal's co-editors, the introduction continues, are familiar with foreign countries; all of them have lived in such countries for a long time, some of them even fulfilling important offices there, and because of these experiences they are able to make their observations from the outside, without personal involvement. Thus, the *Revue des deux mondes* will be able to claim the merit of historical innovation. The journal will definitely be open to new and unusual observations about customs and traditions and about the religious practices and the character of foreign nations. The habits of a people have often provided the necessary background for understanding their laws, and for this reason the *Revue* will include a large quantity of strange (and largely unpublished) information (Tessonneau 183).

IV.4.1 Gustave d'Alaux: First Attempts at a Haitian Literary Historiography

Very little is known about Gustave d'Alaux (see also Müller, "*La littérature jaune*"). According to Léon-François Hoffmann (*Littérature d'Haïti* 259), d'Alaux is the pseudonym of Maxime Raybaud. The only texts we have of his are his literary reports, appearing from 1850 through 1852 in the prestigious Parisian *Revue des deux mondes* (cf. Tessonneau 183). Among other things, d'Alaux published a series of articles on Haitian literature, which he divided into three parts: "Negro Customs and Literature"[71]; "Yellow Literature I"[72]; and "Yellow Literature II."[73] These literary historical articles include the first examples of Haitian literature from the early stages of the revolution, manuscripts that have largely been lost and are to this day not reconstructable in their original form (cf. Tessonneau 184). D'Alaux, whose main focus is Dupré (who lived under King Henri Christophe, but about whom we have no other information at all), rates him very highly both as a poet and as an actor ("La littérature jaune II"). Unfortunately, d'Alaux's articles are all somewhat incoherent and lacking in rigor. He jumps constantly from one theme to another and never provides a close analysis or any clear conclusions. In the following, therefore, I will be using an inductive approach to develop and explain the main themes of his thought.

IV.4.1.1 *Littérature jaune:* Between Francophilia and Plagiarism

As I have already shown in my introductory chapter, a dialectic involving the imitation of the mother country's cultural forms of representation is very characteristic of Haiti's literature. The affirmation of political independence and the cultural imitation of French Romanticism do not seem to be mutually exclusive. In describing the context of the newly emerged Haitian literature, which he calls "yellow literature" (*littérature jaune*), d'Alaux starts right off by saying that plagiarism (or what he calls an "imitative aptitude") is an essential feature of Haitian literature.

---

[71] Of this literature, d'Alaux says: "in its rudimentary or latent state, this literature is essentially Negro, whereas the other, that which is printed, makes its home in the class of color. The first borrows its expressions from the Creole dialect and African body language, the other takes them almost exclusively from French" ("cette littérature à l'état rudimentaire ou latent est essentiellement nègre, tandis que l'autre, celle qui s'imprime, a pour foyer la classe de couleur. La première emprunte ses expressions au patois créole et à la mimique africaine, l'autre les demande presqu'exclusivement au français") ("Les mœurs et la littérature nègres" 264; cf. Tessonneau 184).

[72] "La littérature jaune I." D'Alaux also speaks of "black politics" (*politique noire*) and "yellow politics" (*politique jaune*) as well as of an "antagonism that divides the mixed-blood or yellow caste from the black caste" ("antagonisme qui divise la caste sang-mêlée ou jaune et la caste noire") (*Revue des deux mondes*, new period, series 1, vol. VIII, 1850, 775). The term "yellow" (*jaune*) is in fact characteristic of that time. In her study of literature and colonialism, Martine Astier Loutfi points out that in all of the literature of this time the term "Algerian" refers to Europeans living in Algeria, just as "Indochinese" or "African" refers to white colonizers in those respective places. The colonized are called "the Arab," "the yellow," "the Negro" (79). Cf. also Tessonneau 184.

[73] "La littérature jaune II."

> With very few exceptions, the freemen of earlier days, whether yellow or black, in whom the young nation's literary initiation was accomplished had received only an elementary instruction; the social upheaval that suddenly connected them with the rights, the interests and the passions of Republican France also delivered them up defenseless against the intellectual influence of this new context, and the prodigious memory and imitative aptitude with which Creole organizations are endowed facilitated this contagion; ... at the very moment of the definitive break with France, the literate minority was already well enough trained to be able to return to the good literary sources on its own. ("La littérature jaune I" 939).[74]

D'Alaux leaves no doubt that these "good sources" come from France. This is the first time that he mentions Dupré: "In a doubly rare distinction, both for the times and for a man whose mind was saturated with French tragedy, Dupré is, above all, Haitian; whether drama or comedy, his plays are exclusively devoted to national events or characters" (943).[75]

Next, d'Alaux describes a play that he says is one of Dupré's most celebrated, whose theme is the conflict between the old colonial customs and the relative Puritanism that was created by freedom. The play is about an English merchant who wants to marry a young black woman. In spite of the work her mother puts into convincing the girl to make a decision in favor of wealth and prosperity, the girl ignores the old merchant. D'Alaux welcomes this imitation of Molière as a good idea because he is of the opinion that the simple audience is more receptive to comedy than it would be to a serious thematization of its living conditions, which, given that the audience is without previous artistic experience, it would find boring and tasteless.

> Dupré was imitating or guessing at Molière, who, often engaged in equally brutal facts, ... does not turn up his nose at finding his way out of them through buffoonery. ... Even if a fraction of the spectators already shared some of the delicate feelings of a European public, the majority had no idea of it whatsoever and would therefore have found nothing dramatic, only something suppressed and coldly vulgar, in the serious depiction of a thing that

---

74 "Sauf de très rares exceptions, les anciens libres, tant jaunes que noirs, par qui s'est accomplie l'initiation littéraire de la jeune nationalité, n'avaient reçu qu'une instruction élémentaire; le bouleversement social qui vint brusquement les associer aux droits, aux intérêts, aux passions de la France républicaine, les livra donc sans défense à l'influence intellectuelle de ce nouveau milieu, et la prodigieuse mémoire, l'aptitude imitatrice dont sont douées les organisations créoles facilitèrent encore la contagion, ... au moment de la rupture définitive avec la France, la minorité lettrée était déjà assez exercée pour pouvoir remonter d'elle-même aux bonnes sources littéraires."
75 "Mérite doublement rare et pour l'époque et chez un homme dont l'esprit était saturé de tragédie française, Dupré est, avant tout, Haitien; drame ou comédie, ses pièces sont exclusivement consacrées aux évènemens ou aux caractères nationaux."

had already been as generally accepted as positional prostitution. ... I am disposed to believe that there is more of chance than of calculation in this discovery; at the same time, however, I believe I also glimpsed in the same play a scene reminiscent of Beaumarchais, half laughs and half tears. (944)[76]

D'Alaux ends this first part with a summary, before introducing the second part of his account of "yellow literature": "If, twenty years ago, journalism contributed to turning the country's writers away from the theater, it did, on the other hand, produce serialized literature which, after feeling around in sterile imitations of French literature, finally reinserted itself into the realm of local customs" (967).[77]

D'Alaux devotes himself not only to discussions of literature but also to depictions of society. Thus, in "Yellow Literature II," he ridicules the behavior of noble ladies and gentlemen who try to imitate English and French style. He mentions that the ladies and the gentlemen both adopted Parisian fashion, but sometimes with a delay of several decades, and then were under the impression that they were dressed just like their contemporaries in the French capital. The model of the French *gentilhomme* was a big part of this, as were English phrases and terms such as *how do you do* and *sportsmen* ("La littérature jaune II" 1055).

One interesting thing that d'Alaux does is to look at advertisements placed in Haitian magazines, because they provide telling evidence of what passes for chic in Port-au-Prince. Thus, for example, a grocer and seller of sweets advertises "with the sanction, approval, and support of all the high authorities: ambassadors, legal advisers, etc." and recommends his chewing tobacco "to the particular attention of gentlemen" (1055).[78] D'Alaux then refers to another advertisement and finally sums up, commenting on the two together:

---

76 "Dupré imitait ou devinait Molière, qui, souvent engagé dans des données tout aussi brutales ... ne dédaigné pas d'en sortir par l'issue de la bouffonnerie. ... Si une fraction des spectateurs partageait déjà toutes les délicatesses d'un public européen, la majorité n'en avait pas la moindre idée, et n'eût trouvé délors rien de dramatique, rien que d'effacé et de froidement vulgaire dans la peinture sérieuse d'une chose aussi généralement accepté que la prostitution des placemens. ... Qu'ils y ait dans cette trouvaille plus de hasard que de calcul, je suis disposé à le croire; J'ai cru cependant entrevoir dans la même pièce une scène à la Beaumarchais, moitié rire, moitié larmes."
77 "Si le journalisme contribua, il y a vingt ans, à détourner du théâtre les écrivains du pays, il a produit, en revanche, la littérature de feuilleton, qui, après de stériles tâtonnemens dans le domaine de l'imitation française, a fini par se rejeter dans celui des mœurs locales."
78 "sous la sanction, approbation et appui de toutes les hautes autorités; ambassadeurs, jurisconsultes, etc."; "à l'attention particulière des gentilshommes."

Another one addresses himself particularly to gentlemen, offering to refurbish their old clothing "without the most intimate friend being able to recognize that these are restored clothes." Here, then, is a grocer who knew how to take advantage of the weakness of shoppers, and here is a clothes cleaner who ought to write the Haitian novel of manners. (ibid.)[79]

The suspicion of plagiarism and France's function as a role model are clearly named by d'Alaux when he writes that Haitian writers adopted the development of the French school, but with a certain time lag (1067). The distinct differences between the French poetry of 1800 and of 1840 (a time that d'Alaux describes as completely isolated for Haitian intellectuals, because of the Revolution) can also be seen in Haitian literature in an (almost) parallel way:

> While Chanlatte's opera is, for the most part, nothing but a serious and confident parody of the most famous naïveties of our own librettos, still here and there we find one or two pieces that are worth no more and no less, finally, than the many couplets that we have here trimmed to the pattern of *"Partons pour la Syrie"* or *"Vice Henri IV."* (1067)[80]

It is telling that on the one hand, the isolation of intellectuals in this time period is stressed while, on the other, the emphasis is on the fact that during this time the developments of French literature were imitated, though with a certain delay. These opposite tendencies correspond to the underlying tenor of d'Alaux's remarks, making it impossible, given the parlous state of the research, to present any coherent positioning or analysis of the time period.

The article also briefly mentions Milscent, who published his stories in the *Abeille Haytienne* (The Haitian bee), based in Port-au-Prince.[81] D'Alaux expresses his astonishment at the fact that Milscent apparently writes well: "The most noticeable thing about his tales is a certain sober, easy, polished elegance that one

---

[79] "Un autre s'adresse spécialement aux gentlemen pour leur offrir de remettre les vieux habits à neuf, 'sans que l'ami le plus intime puisse reconnaitre que ce sont des habits restaurés.' Voilà un épicier qui savait prendre les chalands par leur faible, et voilà un dégraisseur qui devrait écrire le roman de mœurs haïtien."

[80] "Si l'opéra de Chanlatte n'est presque partout que la sérieuse et confiante parodie des plus célèbres naïvetés de nos livrets, on y rencontre pourtant çà et là un ou deux morceaux qui ne valent ni plus ni moins, en somme, que les nombreux couplets taillés chez nous sur le patron de 'Partons pour la Syrie' ou de 'Vice Henri IV.'"

[81] The mulatto Jules Solime Milscent (1778–1842) was a Haitian storyteller, poet, and politician who was educated in France and was one of the founders of the periodical *L'Abeille Haytienne* in 1817. He worked for several Haitian governments and was a member of the constitutional commission; he died in an earthquake in 1842.

would hardly expect to find among the tangled and untidy shoots of this wasteland of a literature" (1067).[82]

About Coriolan Ardouin, d'Alaux writes: "If I quote him repeatedly, it is because, once again, this is the first true poet that I have encountered here, and he is a completely unexpected poet, because his name has not yet been defiled—a rare happiness for him—by the crushing admiration of the Negrophiles" (1072).[83] D'Alaux uses Ardouin's early death as a justification for the fact that the poet had hardly had time to create a body of original work. At the same time, d'Alaux makes it clear that he admires Ardouin and emphasizes that what interests him in his poetry is more the person of Ardouin himself:

> In his lost echoes of Millevoye and Lamartine, where, one will say, is the originality? Where is the local cachet?—In truth, I have not even looked for them there. Coriolan Ardouin had not yet had the time to ask the nature around him for impressions; his poetry remained essentially intimate to the end, and if it only finds notes that have already been heard, it is because apparently the heart beats about the same in Port-au-Prince and in Paris. In a word, my claim here was to present a poet, and not Haitian poetry. (1074)[84]

There are, however, frequently places where d'Alaux's apparent ambivalence[85] towards non-whites comes into play, for instance when he writes: "Negro wisdom, which had later so well judged liberal scruples, ... even more picturesquely characterized the candid and enthusiastic security of the Negrophile" (1079).[86]

---

82 "Ce qu'on remarque surtout dans ses fables, c'est une certaine élégance sobre, aisée et correcte qu'on ne s'attendrait guère à trouver au milieu des pousses enchevêtrées et désordonnées de cette littérature en friche."
83 "Si je multiplie les citations, c'est qu'il s'agit, encore une fois, du premier véritable poète que je rencontre ici, et d'un poète entièrement imprévu; car son nom,—rare bonheur pour lui,—n'a pas même été défloré par l'écrasante admiration des négrophiles." Coriolan Ardouin (1812–1835 [or, according to other sources, 1836 or 1838]) was a Haitian poet who modeled himself on classicism and was influenced by Delavigne and Lamartine. Orphaned at an early age, he died soon after the death of his wife, whom he had lost after only five months of marriage.
84 "Dans ses échos perdus de Millevoye et de Lamartine, où est, dira-t-on, l'originalité? où est le cachet local?—En vérité je ne les y ai même pas cherchés. Coriolan Ardouin n'avait pas encore eu le temps de demander des impressions à la nature extérieure; sa poésie est restée jusqu'à la fin essentiellement intime, et si elle ne trouve que des notes déjà entendues, c'est qu'apparemment le cœur bat à peine près de même à Port-au-Prince et à Paris. J'avais, en un mot, la prétention de montrer ici un poète et non pas la poésie haïtienne."
85 We can call this an apparent ambivalence because it becomes clear that for d'Alaux there is absolutely no contradiction in describing non-whites as uncivilized and "wild" and at the same time expressing his admiration for their literature.
86 "La sagesse nègre, qui, plus tard, avait si bien jugé les scrupules libéraux, ... caractérisait d'une façon plus pittoresque encore la candide et enthousiaste sécurité de négrophile."

After the death of King Christophe, d'Alaux reports,[87] the generation of historians who had been educated in the French environment came to an end with Juste Chanlatte. Hérard Dumesle marked the beginning of the second generation that had to learn and figure everything out itself, since there was always a lack of French books. Here d'Alaux keeps returning to the great historical work *Voyage au nord d'Haïti* (Voyage to the north of Haiti), lamenting that it had not appeared a good ten years later, "when the literary breath of France had already refined and ripened the author's talent" (1083).[88]

The last page of this article is dedicated to Linstant,[89] who could, according to d'Alaux, "have been honorably situated among the European publications" if his pieces had not been signed "Linstant (Haïti)." D'Alaux presents two of Linstant's works: *Essais sur les moyens d'extirper les préjugés de couleur* (Essays on the means of eradicating color prejudices, 1842) and *L'Émigration européenne dans ses rapports avec la prospérité future des colonies* (European emigration in its connections with the future prosperity of the colonies, 1850). About the first of these two, d'Alaux writes:

> Color prejudice, which, after having bounced step by step from the master to the slave, then climbed back again from the Negro to the mulatto, from the illiterate to the literate Negro: this, in fact, is the germ of and the bloody foreword to Haitian history, this history which begins with Toussaint's massacres and ends with the massacres of Soulouque. (1085)[90]

All of the sections of the article confirm that the imitation of French Romanticism is an essential feature of Haitian literature. But what does the metalevel of literary historiography tell us? Because the primary texts are not unavailable to us, this would seem to be an unresolvable problem. Nevertheless, what is certain is that literary creativity on Haiti cemented the idea of France's inclusive power and the bipolar relationalism of French colonialism. This is because even in a state that has gained its independence, the effects of earlier mechanisms of integration still survive.

---

87 D'Alaux sarcastically asks God for forgiveness for slandering the "Negro tyrant of the Cap."
88 "quand le souffle littéraire de la France avait déjà épuré et mûri le talent de l'auteur."
89 Linstant had won an essay contest, organized by Grégoire, that was intended to save the "honor of the black race."
90 "Le préjugé de couleur, qui, après avoir rebondi de gradin en gradin du maître à l'esclave, est remonté du nègre au mulâtre, du nègre illettré au nègre lettré, voilà bien, en effet, le germe et comme le sanglant avant-propos de l'histoire haïtienne, de cette histoire qui commence aux massacres de Toussaint pour aboutir aux massacres de Soulouque."

IV.4.1.2 Haitian Rulers as Despots

In his articles on Haitian literature, but especially in the two-part article on "yellow literature," d'Alaux also sketches a picture of an uneducated, superstitious, brutal tyrant, which is how he sees Haiti's rulers. He puts the following words, for example, into Emperor Dessalines's mouth:

> I am, I been (I have been), that white language! Dessalines says disdainfully, using a proverbial phrase that serves to this day to express the Negro's ironic disdain for French conjugation (1); us no need that! for whites, need (you need) rifles with powder, not talking paper. ("La littérature jaune I" 939)[91]

According to this passage, Dessalines scorns the word—including the written word—with which certain agreements were made. In dealing with white people, a gun is enough for him—naked violence. D'Alaux pursues this contempt for written culture further: the title of the first section, "Renaissance inconnue" (Unknown renaissance), is derived from the fact that with the Haitian Revolution, and on Dessalines's orders, literature was largely "destroyed." As a result, the educated minority had trouble keeping up to date intellectually.

> [Dessalines's company of grenadiers] went from house to house strangling our unhappy compatriots and lacerated and threw into the streets all the books that they found. Not satisfied with suppressing "talking paper," the emperor was about to do away with schools when he was killed in the interest of enlightenment; but the evil had been done, and the group of those who were literate remained limited, for lack of books, to its first representatives, themselves reduced to ruminating the heavy intellectual pasture that they had picked up bit by bit in the philanthropic clubs, Jacobin newspapers, and Thermidorian tragedies. (ibid.)[92]

---

[91] "Je suis, j'été (j'ai été), ça parole blancs! dit dédaigneusement Dessalines par une locution proverbiale qui sert aujourd'hui encore à exprimer l'ironique dédain du nègre pour la conjugaison française (1); nous pas bisoin ça! avec blancs, ifaut (il faut) fisils avec la poudre et non papier parlé." In the footnote, d'Alaux explains that in Creole grammar, verbs only have one or two modes; taken together with his Creole quotations, this would seem to indicate that even if he did not speak the language perfectly himself, he at least had a sound understanding of it.

[92] "[La compagnie de grenadiers de Dessalines] allait de maison en maison égorger nos malheureux compatriotes lacérait et jetait dans les rues tous les livres qu'elle découvrait. Non content de supprimer le 'papier parlé,' l'empereur allait supprimer les écoles, lorsqu'on le tua dans l'intérêt des lumières; mais le mal était fait, et le groupe lettré resta limité, faute de livres, à ses premiers représentants, eux-mêmes réduits à ruminer la lourde pâture intellectuelle qu'ils avaient ramassée par bribes dans les clubs philanthropiques, les journaux jacobins et les tragédies thermidoriennes."

The entire article makes it clear that there is an important connection between literary production and the ruler under which it is created. It is evident from the various examples and descriptions of rulers not only which time period and which part of Haiti are under discussion but also the way in which these rulers influenced the country's productions. Understandably, d'Alaux judges Pétion, who had been the president of the mulatto republic in the south of Haiti since 1807, much more favorably than he does King Christophe, under whose regime of terror everyone suffered as much as under Dessalines.

> Président Pétion was very anxious to renew the chain of civilization that had been so suddenly broken by the Negro emperor. ... Around Christophe, on the other hand, whose despotism had given a fabulous impetus to production and who wanted to organize education as violently as he had organized work, it was terror that created the void. Our emigrants experienced a very natural repugnance at going to fill university positions in a country where being French was equivalent, almost as surely as under Dessalines, to a death sentence. (939–940)[93]

D'Alaux talks, as well, about Dupré staging another "mania" or "illness" of the Haitian rulers, namely that of decorating themselves with all sorts of medals (940–941). Dupré also provides the model for the despotic combination of mutually contradictory political principles that d'Alaux diagnoses in Haiti. In the second section of "La littérature jaune I," d'Alaux briefly introduces a play by Dupré in which the irony consists of the fact that someone refuses to feed his horses, so that the question arises as to why one would own horses if one does not want to feed them. Soulouque behaves in a similarly contradictory way:

> It is Soulouque who cried all in the same breath: long live liberty! long live the empire!—having himself consecrated and drugged at one and the same time—imprisoning, deporting, or ruthlessly shooting any deputy or senator that he suspected of parliamentarism but obstinately maintaining his parliament. (945)[94]

---

93 "Le président Pétion avait fort à cœur de renouer la chaîne civilisatrice si brusquement rompue par l'empereur nègre. ... Par contre autour de Christophe, dont le despotisme avait imprimé une impulsion fabuleuse à la production, et qui prétendait organiser l'instruction aussi violemment que le travail, c'est la terreur qui créa le vide. Nos émigrans éprouvaient une répugnance bien naturelle à aller remplir des cadres universitaires d'un pays où le titre de Français équivalait, presque aussi sûrement que sous Dessalines, à un arrêt de mort."
94 "C'est Soulouque criant tout d'une haleine: vive la liberté! Vive l'empire!—se faisant sacrer et droguer à la fois,—emprisonnant, déportant ou fusillant sans pitié tout député ou sénateur qu'il soupçonne de parlementarisme, mais conservant avec obstination son parlement."

In the third section of the article, d'Alaux makes a leap to talk about opera under King Christophe, who had created for himself not only a court but also a royal music academy and a royal theater. The librettist was the count de Rosiers, named Juste Chanlatte (the brother of Desrivières Chanlatte, who was responsible for grammar and printing under Pétion). D'Alaux presents an opera by Cassian, a Haitian, entitled *La partie de chasse du roi* (The king's hunting party). In this case, d'Alaux refers explicitly to plagiarism from Molière (952); in addition, he summarizes the play, act by act. The entire section is devoted to this one opera, in which Christophe plays the leading role and is portrayed as a good and just king. "The king of Negro opera, who is named 'the good Henri' as in the French opera, is no more nor less a person than Henri Christophe, who was staged along with the most important members of his court" (952).[95]

After this, d'Alaux gives an account of a scene that he sees as characteristic of the entire play. Here are some excerpts from the dialogue:

> COMMANDER: ... Haiti is no longer in its political adolescence; in founding a throne, a representative monument to its dignity and a certain guarantee of its rights, it has offered an authentic proof of its physical and moral virility. Glory be to the Almighty who has stretched out a helping hand to the persecuted innocent!
>
> EVERYONE: Glory to the Almighty!
>
> COMMANDER: Long live Henri, that benevolent hero, whose immortal arm, after having reconquered our rights, founded the edifice of our political strength on unshakable foundations!
>
> EVERYONE: Long live Henri!
>
> COMMANDER: Eternal hatred to France!
>
> EVERYONE: Eternal hatred to France! (953)[96]

---

[95] "Le roi de l'opéra nègre, qui s'appelle, comme dans l'opéra français, 'le bon Henri,' n'est ni plus ni moins qu'Henri Christophe, lequel était mis en scène avec les principaux personnages de sa cour."

[96] LE COMMANDANT: ... Haïti n'est déjà plus dans son adolescence politique; en fondant un trône, monument représentatif de sa dignité et sûr garant de ses droits, elle a donné une preuve authentique de sa virilité physique et morale. Gloire soit au Tout-Puissant qui a tendu une main secourable à l'innocent persécuté!
TOUS ENSEMBLE: Gloire au Tout-Puissant!
LE COMMANDANT: Vive à jamais Henri, ce héros bienfaisant, dont le bras immortel, après avoir reconquis nos droits, a assis l'édifice de notre consistance politique sur des bases inébranlables!
TOUS ENSEMBLE: Vive à jamais Henri!
LE COMMANDANT: Haine éternelle à la France!
TOUS ENSEMBLE: Haine éternelle à la France

D'Alaux mentions, without providing any further details, that one verse is addressed to the despots, and explains that this means the French (955) and that in this way there is a connection being made repeatedly between Haiti's King Henri Christophe (the First) and France's King Henri the Fourth, although, as already mentioned, the Haitian Henri, unlike the French one, is consistently shown as just and good. D'Alaux recounts the plot of the opera with a hint of irony, ending with the explanation that in real life, Christophe's actions are the exact opposite. For instance, in one scene, Christophe disappears during a hunt. His two companions, two dukes, become worried when he fails to appear. D'Alaux points out here that in real life these two would be dancing for joy (956), because Christophe had many of them put to death simply because he had dreamed of them, and they therefore had to live in constant fear. In the play, Christophe reappears laughing, explaining that his horse had slipped and that he had almost died. Here, again, d'Alaux briefly describes what would have really happened in such a case: the horse would have been beaten and whoever was responsible for that section of road would have been punished. "In the opera it is always the opposite [of what would have happened in reality]: Christophe jokes about his accident with a cheerful charm" (957).[97]

The second and third acts of the play are about a family named Bayacou, which is planning a wedding and with whom Christophe is involved. The most interesting thing about this is the way that d'Alaux insists that the Christophe in the play does not correspond to the true Christophe. He makes his point with drastic comments, remarking for example that in the play, Christophe does not have anyone shot one morning for a change (958). He supports his portrayal of Christophe by mentioning a work by the historian Hérard Dumesle that explains how Christophe, unlike in the theatrical productions, forced his mingling with the public and coerced the homage of his subjects.

> On one of these tours, where [Christophe] was accompanied by the English admiral Sir Hom Popham, he ordered the cultural inspectors to collect, at the gates of their houses, the unfortunates, the price of whose sweat he devoured. Having taken this measure, he acted like someone who had to rise very early, as if to dodge the eager homage of a people who adored him; but the noise of the horses and carriages warning the Royal Dahomets [Christophe's agents] to prepare the unfortunates who had thus been stationed after having already rendered forced labor all the day long; awakened with beatings, the cry of "Long live the king!" came to die on their lips. (960)[98]

---

97 "Dans l'opéra c'est toujours l'opposé: Christophe plaisante avec une gaieté charmante sur son accident."
98 "Dans une de ces tournées, où il [Christophe] était accompagné de l'amiral anglais, sir Hom Popham, il ordonnait aux inspecteurs de culture de rassembler aux barrières des habitations les

On the subject of the "fictional" Christophe character in Chanlatte's play, d'Alaux then also points out: "And one should not suspect either irony or hidden advice in this audacious counterpart to the true Christophe" (961).[99] He therefore uses this section about the opera at Christophe's court to describe the image of the Haitian despot.[100] The play that he has introduced to us with Christophe in the leading role serves, in a way, as a complete idealization and therefore an antithesis to the real ruler. The only way to explain this positive representation of the despot in the opera is that in King Christophe's time there was very strict censorship in Haiti to which writers had to submit. Thus, in a footnote, d'Alaux cites the historian mentioned above, Hérard Dumesle: "One day, after having had a pregnant woman cruelly punished for picking a mango from that orchard, he had them open her breast to see whether the embryo had tasted the fruit" ("La littérature jaune I" 961n2).[101] We have to ask to what extent these stories are true and to what degree the conflict between the two Haitis of that time contributed to defamations of the rulers of both the governments. For d'Alaux, at any rate, this story substantiates his picture of Christophe and of the Haitian despot in general, because at the end of his critique of Christophe he draws a connection between Christophe and d'Alaux's own contemporary Soulouque (also known as Faustin the First), who was a match for Christophe in brutality and vengefulness.

> If I insist on these details about customs, it is because they are still of interest today. This concert of congratulatory sentimentality that arose around the Caligula of the small Cap court was nothing but the anticipated image of what is happening today around the new Negro tyrant—with the only difference, however, that Soulouque's flatterers are responding much less to fear than they are to the illusions of an interest which they do not well understand. People of color have imagined that in exalting the good and magnanimous Faustin

---

malheureux dont il dévorait le prix de leur sueurs. Cette mesure prise, il avait l'air de partir fort avant le jour comme pour se dérober aux hommages empressés d'un peuple qui l'adorait; mais le bruit des chevaux et des voitures avertissaient les royals-Dahomets de préparer les malheureux ainsi mis en station après un travail forcé durant tout le jour; éveillés à coup de bâton, le cri de 'vive le roi!' venait expirer sur leurs lèvres."

99 "Et qu'on ne soupçonne ni l'ironie ni le conseil détourné dans cette audacieuse contre-partie du véritable Christophe."

100 It is interesting to note that a number of European, and especially French, philosophers of the eighteenth and nineteenth centuries used the description of an Oriental despot as the antithesis of a virtuous European ruler. In d'Alaux's case here, then, this is a conscious depiction of the Haitian despot but at the same time, surely unconsciously, a positive depiction of his own ruler.

101 "Un jour, après avoir fait cruellement châtier une femme enceinte qui avait cueillie un mango dudit verger, il lui fit ouvrir le sein pour voir si l'embryon avait gouté le fruit."

the First, they will end up giving him a taste for that goodness and magnanimity, ... far from it, Souiouque's vanity only makes him complacent in a situation where he adds to the pleasures of vengefulness and cruelty the honors of clemency. Faustin the First will end up, which is the worst thing, taking his own magnanimity seriously, because it is in the African character, I repeat, to pair the most incompatible facts, sentiments, and ideas, all in very good faith. Christophe, who was nevertheless much more enlightened than Souiouque, Christophe himself even got to the point of believing himself the most sensitive man in his kingdom, and no one wept or was moved more easily than he was. (962)[102]

In part two of "La littérature jaune," d'Alaux writes that next to the *Abeille Haytienne,* he found the most accounts from this time in Dumesle's *Voyage dans le nord d'Haïti* (Travel to the north of Haiti). His judgment of Dumesle's work is that it is essentially a history of the barbarities from the first revolution through Christophe's reign ("La littérature jaune II" 1068).[103]

D'Alaux then introduces another poet, named Darfour, who gave Pétion and Boyer the opportunity to put out a newspaper. But because he published texts that were critical of the government, Boyer had him executed (1070). D'Alaux writes that this shows that even under the republican president, Haiti was very far from actually being able to enforce the achievements of the French Revolution.

D'Alaux goes on to talk about metaphors and proverbs that refer to the reigns of Dessalines, Toussaint, and Boyer. He mentions the fate of the French soldiers who had to stay behind in hospitals, and of the "unhappy" colonists, men, women, and children, who had trusted Dessalines's invitation, emphasizing the depiction of Dessalines as a beastly despot. Dessalines's hate-filled out-

---

102 "Si j'insiste sur ces détails de mœurs, c'est qu'ils ont encore un intérêt d'actualité. Ce concert de louangeuse sensiblerie qui s'élevait autour du Caligula de la petite cour du Cap n'était que l'image anticipée de ce qui ce passe aujourd'hui autour du nouveau tyran nègre—à cette différence près toutefois que les flatteurs de Souiouque obéissent bien moins encore à la peur qu'aux illusions d'un intérêt très mal entendu. Les gens de couleur se sont imaginé qu'en exaltant tout le bon, le clément Faustin 1er, ils finiront par lui donner le gout de la bonté et la clémence, ... la vanité de Souiouque ne peut au contraire que se complaire à une situation où il cumule, avec les plaisirs de la vengeance et de la cruauté, les honneurs de la clémence. Faustin Ier finira, qui pis est, par prendre sa clémence au sérieux, car il est dans le caractère africain, je le répète, d'accoupler de très bonne foi les faits, les sentiments, les idées les plus incompatibles. Christophe, bien plus éclairé pourtant que Souiouque, Christophe en était lui-même venu à se croire l'homme le plus sensible de son royaume, et personne ne pleurait, ne s'attendrissait plus aisément que lui."
103 Hérard Dumesle (1784–1858) was a Haitian poet and politician. As a mulatto, he was in Jean Pierre Boyer's opposition. His volume *Voyage dans le nord d'Haïti* appeared in 1824, after Christophe's death. It is questionable whether his defamatory statements, including the barbaric story about the pregnant woman, have a basis in reality.

bursts against whites in general and the French in particular allow for no ambiguity whatsoever.

> Dessalines ... gave Charairon's task to Boisrond-Tonnerre, saying: "That's it, *Mouqué*, that's it I want! It's white blood my need." [D'Alaux's footnote clarifies: "That's it, sir, that is exactly what I want. It is the blood of white people that I need!"] The next morning, at the moment of the ceremony, they had to break down Boisrond-Tonnerre's door, who was dead drunk by this time, and on his table they found ... this proclamation, which was the signal for six weeks of massacres, a proclamation that, among other things, caused Dessalines to say: "These generals who have guided your efforts against tyranny have not yet done enough. ... The name 'French' still darkens our country!" This is the same inspiration, and probably also the same barrel of tafia, from which the *Mémoires* also came. (1081)[104]

D'Alaux follows this by a presentation of *La géographie de l'île d'Haïti* (The geography of the island of Haiti, 1832) by Alexis-Beaubrun Ardouin (1796–1849, Coriolan Ardouin's brother), calling it "the only truly irreproachable work produced by the second literary generation" (1083).[105] D'Alaux regrets a little that Haitian literature tends to idealize or even glorify its rulers, and therefore suggests that a new history be written: "There is an entire history to be rewritten there" (1084).[106] Then, finally, he turns to issues of contemporary relevance: Soulouque (emperor since 1849, publicly crowned in 1852) is faced with the question of reestablishing civilization in Port-au-Prince or else potentially being annexed by pirates:

> The cry of civilization is nothing but the echo of an ardent patriotism here. Will this cry be spontaneously repeated in Port-au-Prince? Or will Soulouque prefer to wait until he is vomited out by the ports of some annexionist pirate running the coastlines between Cuba and Puerto Rico? That is the entire question. (1085)[107]

---

104 "Dessalines ... chargea Boisrond-Tonnerre de la besogne de Charairon, en lui disant: *C'est ça, Mouqué, c'est ça même mon vlé! C'est sang blanc mon besoin* [Footnote: C'est cela, monsieur, c'est cela même que je veux! C'est du sang de blanc qu'il me faut!]. Le lendemain matin, au moment de la cérémonie, il fallait enfoncer la porte de Boisrond-Tonnerre, cette fois ivre mort, et l'on trouva sur sa table, ... cette proclamation qui fut le signal de six semaines de massacres, proclamation qui faisait dire entre autres choses à Dessalines: 'Ces généraux qui ont guidé vos efforts contre la tyrannie n'ont point encore assez fait. ... Le nom français lugubre encore nos contrées!' C'est de la même inspiration et probablement du même baril de tafia que sont sortis les Mémoires."
105 "le seul travail véritablement irréprochable qu'ait produit la seconde génération littéraire."
106 "C'est là, en un mot, toute une histoire à refaire."
107 "Le cri de la civilisation n'est ici que l'écho d'un ardent patriotisme. Ce cri sera-t-il spontanément répété à Port-au-Prince? Soulouque aimera-t-il mieux attendre qu'il soit vomi par

D'Alaux's critique is of the barbaric circumstances themselves, but also has to do with the connection between the political regime and cultural production. It is not the Haitian Revolution that ever appears as the point of reference, but rather the French Revolution. There is not even an indirect reference to the Haitian Revolution as a result of the French Revolution. An efficient French colonial model is communicated in the person of d'Alaux, a model that glorifies France as a cultural nation with the power to broadcast its message and a capacity for integration. In spite of the value, not to be discounted, of providing contemporary snapshots of Haitian social critique, the deeper dimensions of d'Alaux's remarks have to do with their reference back to a French self-understanding. Even when racial discourses are not explicitly alluded to, the term "yellow literature" alone is a testimony to an external perception that makes the existential dimension of a denomination of skin color into *the* decisive categorical criterion.

IV.4.1.3 The Conditions for Intellectual Work in Haiti

If, in reading d'Alaux's reports, we pay attention to his attitude towards Haitian intellectuals, there are two striking points: first, his careful analysis of the conditions under which they live and work, including a focus on the "despotic" and uneducated behavior of their rulers, as just described in the previous sections; and second, the fact that his understanding includes a certain amount of admiration for these intellectuals who manage to produce literature in spite of the obstacles. They often formed groups that would meet in the cities in Masonic lodges: "These lodges ... turned into small literary meetings, veritable schools of mutual education, to which each one brought his contribution of reflections and reminiscences in the form of dissertations, toasts, stories, dramatic essays, songs, or funeral orations" ("La littérature jaune I" 941).[108] Some of these textual productions were able to appear in various newspapers under Pétion. In his evaluation of Haitian literature, d'Alaux takes the external circumstances seriously and points out that the level of Haitian literature has risen since 1825, the year in which France recognized Haiti's sovereignty.

---

les sabords de quelque pirate annexionniste courant des bordées entre Cuba et Puerto-Rico? Là est toute la question."

108 "Ces loges ... devinrent de petites réunions littéraires, de véritables écoles d'enseignement mutuel, où chacun apportait, sous forme de dissertations, de toasts, de fables, d'essais dramatiques, de chansons ou d'oraisons funèbres, son contingent d'élucubrations et de réminiscences."

We should not smile: measured not by its absolute value but by its spontaneity, by the obstacles that it has had to overcome, by the relative aptitudes that it has brought into play, this naive literature would in itself be a very interesting object of observation; however, it did not stop there. The ordinance with which Charles X recognized Haitian independence, stipulating as it did special advantages for the trade between us, reestablished, in 1825, the intellectual current that the revolution of 1803 had severed, and since then the literary level in Haiti has constantly risen. (942)[109]

What d'Alaux sees, then, is on the one hand a completely new beginning since the revolution, when the French intellectual elite had been either driven out or murdered and their books had been withdrawn from circulation; and on the other hand a revival through the normalization of contacts between Haiti and France. He considers these connections to be of the greatest importance because in his opinion, the large differences between the various works can be explained by the respective time periods in which they were written: "These preliminaries were indispensable for an equitable appreciation of the writers of all kinds—whether playwrights, poets, historians, or journalists—that our former colony has produced so far." (942)[110]

In the last section of "La littérature jaune I," d'Alaux draws the connection to the Haiti of his own time and tries to foresee how Haitian literature and the form in which it is presented will develop. He is interested not only in the writers and actors but also the audience. After Charles the Tenth had lifted the intellectual isolation that Dessalines had ordered, d'Alaux writes, Haiti's writers recognized that they were twenty years behind and were forced to admit that they were now considerably below the level of even the simplest French playwrights (963). D'Alaux explains the "infrastructural" problems that existed in Haiti: although there were still three theaters in Port-au-Prince in 1841, they were all closed within a few weeks because too many people were opposed to them; in addition to that, there was a shortage of good, self-confident actors who did not just simply withdraw entirely from the theater world after their first newspaper review (964). D'Alaux also points out that the operas and plays he describes

---

109 "Ne sourions pas: mesurée non à sa valeur absolue, mais à sa spontanéité, aux obstacles qu'elle a dû vaincre, aux aptitudes relatives qu'elle a mises en jeu, cette naïve littérature serait à elle seule un très intéressant sujet d'observation; elle ne s'est pas d'ailleurs arrêtée là. L'ordonnance par laquelle Charles X reconnaissait l'indépendance haïtienne, en stipulant des avantages spéciaux pour notre commerce vint rétablir, en 1825, le courant intellectuel que la révolution de 1803 avait rompu, et depuis lors le niveau littéraire haïtien s'est constamment élevé."
110 "Ces préliminaires étaient indispensables pour une équitable appréciation des écrivains de tous genres,—auteurs dramatiques, poètes, historiens, journalistes,—qu'a produits jusqu'à ce jour notre ancienne colonie."

only represent one part of the Haitian intellectual movement. But, he says, there are three components that are missing: a literature (of manners), the poets, and the historians. Oddly, d'Alaux considers there to be too much material for writers to work with. In addition, there appear to be tensions between the colored people who have had a French socialization and the "Africans."

> This literature must overcome many obstacles in order to emerge in Haiti, and the greatest of these is the proximity and abundance of the materials that are offered to it. In this tedious work of fusion which has, for half a century, pitted the almost-French minority of mixed-bloods against the numerical preponderance of Africans, and the Negro reminiscences of these last against incessant naive counterfeits of European civilization, everything must be eccentric and heavily accented. ("La littérature jaune II" 1048)[111]

D'Alaux continually alleges plagiarism, which is of course intended as a criticism, but he regrets the fact that many of the new Haitian writers are not personally acquainted with France and considers that they should definitely remedy this shortcoming: "Unfortunately, most of the writers of the new generation did not know France except through hearsay, while others had only brought back with them a few memories of school days, such that the shadow often lacked truth." (1049)[112] He concedes that, due to their social position and their knowledge of the country, they are in a good position to write about the customs and mores of their country, but he does see a danger: if they write critically, they could incur the enmity of the *ghion* and *saint* sects (ibid.).

D'Alaux sees a further difficulty in the fact that there is no clear market for Haitian books, since on the one hand very few people can read, and on the other, those who can prefer French books. Thus, theater remains an important medium:

> In summary, as we can see, it is not the elements that are missing from the future Haitian novel of manners. What is lacking is the readership. A book of this nature would certainly not find an audience, in our former colony, of more than three or four hundred readers, and novel by novel, these readers would prefer to buy our own, which combine an easily explainable superiority of form with the recommendation, very important for that country,

---

111 "Cette littérature a de nombreux obstacles à vaincre pour se faire jour en Haïti, et le principal de tous, c'est la proximité et l'abondance même des matériaux qui lui sont offerts. Dans ce pénible travail de fusion qui met, depuis un demi-siècle, aux prises la minorité presque française des sang-mêlés avec la prépondérance numérique des Africains, et les réminiscences nègres de ceux-ci avec d'incessantes et naïves contrefaçons de la civilisation européenne, tout doit être excentrique et fortement accentué."
112 "Malheureusement la plupart des écrivains de la nouvelle génération ne connaissent la France que par ouï-dire, d'autres n'avaient pu en rapporter que quelques souvenirs de collège, de sorte que l'ombre manquait souvent de vérité."

of a European blessing. The few attempts of this kind that have been made by the writers of Port-au-Prince have therefore, until now, had no place to go but to the local newspapers, and the insufficient frequency with which these papers appear and the short existence of most of them[113] make any lengthy work impossible. The theater, which substitutes for readers the much more numerous category of listeners, is, once again, the true local outlet for the Haitian literature of manners. (1064–1065)[114]

IV.4.1.4 Essentialist Attributions as a Source of Inspiration

D'Alaux's admiration for this intellectual work, including its engagement with customs and traditions, is full of contradictions. His reporting on local practices is sometimes admiring and sometimes condescending, and even while he is praising the activities of the intellectuals he at the same time accuses them of plagiarism, sometimes in the tone of a scolding father. These contradictions also surface in his descriptions of the locals. On the one hand, d'Alaux refers to "Negro wisdom" and makes it clear how much creativity and potential there is in the former colony, but on the other hand he repeatedly depicts the locals as "uncivilized," uneducated, and observing some "bestial" customs.

In the context of the aforementioned destruction of books, d'Alaux explains that French books were not burned, but only "shredded," so that in fact some fragments of them were able to be saved, which the educated could then use as a source of information. He credits this salvage, among other things, to the superstitious reverence of the blacks:

> I said that the colonists' books had been lacerated and not burned; the Negresses' superstitious veneration for "talking paper" and the more positive solicitude of the country's grocers had, therefore, saved some fragments of the books, sometimes even entire volumes,

---

113 In a footnote, d'Alaux explains that between 1812 and 1842, a good twenty newspapers in Haiti gradually disappeared because their subscribers no longer had the money to subscribe.
114 "En résumé ce ne sont pas les éléments, on le voit, qui manquent au futur roman de mœurs haïtien. Ce qui lui manque, c'est le public. Un livre de cette nature ne trouverait certainement pas à s'adresser, dans notre ancienne colonie, à plus de trois ou quatre cents lecteurs, et, roman pour roman, ceux-ci préféreraient acheter les nôtres, qui joignent à une supériorité de forme bien explicable la recommandation capitale pour le pays d'une consécration européenne. Les quelques essais de ce genre qu'ont fait les écrivains de Port-au-Prince n'ont donc eu jusqu'ici pour refuge que les journaux de l'endroit, et l'insuffisante périodicité de ces feuilles, la courte existence de la plupart, interdisant toute œuvre de longue haleine. Le Théâtre, qui substitue, aux lecteurs la catégorie beaucoup plus nombreuse des auditeurs, le théâtre est encore une fois, le véritable débouché local de la littérature de mœurs haïtienne."

which the literate or those who wanted to become so then took to collecting with a veritable passion. ("La littérature jaune I" 941)[115]

D'Alaux goes on to describe how everyone who owned a book was then visited by pregnant women, who wanted to find names for their unborn children in these books, and he gives various examples of names that are intended to elicit hilarity from his readers.

Among other things, d'Alaux also describes a comedy, written by an anonymous author, that was published in the newspaper *Abeille Haytienne* under the title *Le Physicien* (The doctor). There are a few interesting aspects to this play, involving the conflict between modern science and African superstition, communicated via a conversation between a doctor and his servant. The doctor explains to his assistant that superstition is only useful to a small number of charlatans: "Magic, or sorcery, is only the abusive use that a few malicious or self-interested frauds make of certain discoveries or knowledge that are part of physics" ("La littérature jaune I" 949).[116] D'Alaux writes about this text that critiques of superstition were only able to be published in written form (not, however, performed), because books themselves were under the protection of superstition: "This could, at most, be written, thanks to the inviolability enjoyed by 'talking paper' among the illiterate class of the 'papa-loi' [voodoo priests] and their adepts" (950).[117]

Nevertheless, d'Alaux sees hope in the new generation of writers, such as Dupré and his literary descendants, and in their works and productions. It is precisely in a country where superstition and illiteracy reign, he writes, that literature has the great task of advancing the process of civilization.

> Plays like those that Dupré wrote, reproducing national situations and characters that everyone would recognize, punctuated, even, with Creole proverbs and sayings that make them doubly clear and interesting, such plays would not only be the quickest method of civilization for a country whose masses cannot read, most of whose priests are nothing but copies of voodoo sorcerers, and where the vanity of appearances is the only spur to work: in addition, they would be guaranteed financial successes. The taste for dramatic

---

115 "J'ai dit que les livres des colons avaient été lacérés et non pas brûlés; la superstitieuse vénération des négresses pour le papier parlé et la sollicitude plus positive des épiciers du pays en avaient donc sauvé de fragmens, parfois même des volumes entiers, que les lettrés, ou ceux qui voulait le devenir se mirent à collectionner avec une véritable passion."
116 "La magie ou la sorcellerie n'est que l'abus que quelques fourbes méchans ou intéressés font de certaines découvertes ou des connaissances qui appartiennent à la physique."
117 "Cela pouvait à la rigueur s'écrire, grâce à l'inviolabilité que dont jouit le 'papier parlé' dans la classe illettrée des papa-loi et de leur adeptes."

imitation and effects has been pushed to a frenzy among the Negroes and manifests itself there in all its forms; witness their magical and religious ceremonies where, as we have said elsewhere, a powerful instinct for stagecraft is deployed. (966)[118]

D'Alaux presents two stories, by an anonymous author, that appeared in the Haitian magazine the *Républicain* (Republican),[119] which he uses to demonstrate Haitian customs and practices. The first story (which is untitled) is about an upcoming wedding between two young people, Marie and Alexandre. Over the course of the story, it becomes clear that the two are sister and brother, and d'Alaux expresses surprise that the characters in the story talk about that very straightforwardly, as though it were commonplace and normal: "Marie is Alexandre's sister. These innocent young ladies philosophize quite simply about incest. Let us make some tragedies out of it!" ("La littérature jaune II" 1051).[120] The mother of the two young people goes to the priest and arranges the wedding. D'Alaux explains what would be surprising to European readers as deriving from local practices:

> One might suspect the author of having wished to amass monstrosities and improbabilities, as if on a bet; but, once again, we are in a different world here, and if we remember how the Haitian clergy are recruited, the casuistry of the "good priest" in no way negates local color (1052).[121]

The second story, titled "Comment peut-on être meilleur fils?" (How can one be a better son?), is about a young man who is taking care of his sick mother and, in the process, neglects his work in the fields. At the same time, however, over the

---

118 "Des pièces à la façon de Dupré, reproduisant des situations et des types nationaux qui seraient intelligibles pour tous, émaillées même de dictons et de saillies créoles qui en doubleraient la clarté et l'intérêt, ces sortes de pièces ne seraient pas seulement le plus prompt moyen de civilisation pour un pays où les masses ne savent pas lire, où la plupart des curés ne sont que la doublure des sorciers vaudoux, et où la vanité du paraître est le seul stimulant du travail: elles auraient encore un succès assuré d'argent. Le goût de l'imitation et de l'effet dramatiques est poussé jusqu'à la fureur chez les nègres et s'y manifeste sous toutes les formes, témoin leurs cérémonies magiques et religieuses, où se déploie, nous l'avons dit ailleurs, un puissant instinct de mise en scène."
119 This magazine was the successor of a magazine called *L'Union*.
120 "Marie est la sœur d'Alexandre. Ces innocentes demoiselles philosophent tout bonnement sur l'inceste. Faites en donc encore des tragédies!"
121 "On pourrait soupçonner l'auteur d'avoir voulu accumuler ici, comme par gageure, les monstruosités et les invraisemblances; mais nous sommes encore une fois dans un monde à part, et, pour qui voudra bien se rappeler comment se recrute le clergé haïtien, la casuistique du 'bon curé' ne pèche nullement contre la couleur locale."

course of a year, he collects the food, chickens, and other things necessary for the feast that will take place at the funeral. In secret, he prays for his mother to die soon. But when the time has come, he turns his prayers around in the opposite direction:

> On awakening, however, that same cry now resounded like a death knell in the depths of his conscience, and, with that swift change in impressions that characterizes the Negro, passing from brutal indifference to tenderness, he goes looking for his mother, begging the Virgin and all the saints to help him find her safe and sound. (1054)[122]

D'Alaux observes that such attitudes can also be found among us, but then he quickly relativizes that thought, explaining the barely comprehensible emotional contradictions as a result of the influence of the blacks in Haiti.

> We could find, among us, a similar type: that of the peasant who begrudges the remedies for his dying father more than those for his ailing ox; but the serious and so sincerely naive accumulation of this sordid hardness, with all the prodigalities that are included in the family religion in the colonies, the contrast between these parricidal impatiences with sincere pretentions to filial sentiment, this is what is essentially characteristic of the Negro. (ibid.)[123]

Following these two stories, d'Alaux introduces Ignace Nau, or rather, without going into Nau's work, d'Alaux explains that this author shows how the "life of the Negroes" is constantly suffused with miracles (ibid.).

The first section of "La littérature jaune II" ends with the court hearing of a lawyer by the name of Mullery (who is also mentioned in d'Alaux's article "La littérature nègre"), who also owns one of the few newspapers, the *Revue des Tribunaux* (Court review). What d'Alaux sketches out here is a court (and therefore, also, a court system) that is not to be taken seriously, where some of the participants fall asleep and some of the proceedings are disturbed by voodoo processions in front of the court (1062–1063).

---

[122] "Au réveil, ce même cri retentit cependant comme un glas de mort au fond de sa conscience, et passant, avec cette mobilité d'impressions qui caractérise le nègre, de l'indifférence bestiale à la tendresse, il se met à la recherche de sa mère, suppliant la Vierge et les saints de la lui faire retrouver saine et sauve."

[123] "On pourrait trouver chez nous un type approchant: celui du paysan qui plaint plus les remèdes à son père mourant qu'à son bœuf malade; mais le cumul sérieux et si sincèrement naïf de cette sordide dureté avec toutes les prodigalités que comporte aux colonies la religion de la famille, le contraste de ces impatiences parricides avec de sincères prétentions au sentiment filial, voilà qui est essentiellement nègre."

D'Alaux devotes the second section of this article to poetry, declaring that there are only a very few isolated poets in Haiti, because, of the small number of educated people, only a small fraction has dedicated itself to poetry. A further problem, he says, is the almost complete absence of female readers, whom he judges to be very important for the reception of poetry. In addition, many of the potential poets can only survive the struggle for daily bread by giving themselves over to alcohol. Thereupon, d'Alaux draws a picture of the Haitian attached to alcohol, among whom the poets are also counted:

> Worn out and harassed by this fruitless daily struggle with the preoccupations of a life full of hard work, to which there are neither those intellectual pleasures that every center of civilization offers to both rich and poor, nor the encouragements of fame that are distributed far away from them, to act as a counterbalance, most Haitian poets end up by abandoning the ink bottle for the tafia bottle, and that is where, alas! they find their best poems. (1066)[124]

On the last pages of d'Alaux's article, finally, the quotations, almost self-explanatory, begin to pile up. Their particular social situation—including the revolution, the tensions between blacks and whites, and the division of Haiti into north and south—was in d'Alaux's opinion an important source of inspiration for the writers in Christophe's court:

> The hatred of the whites, the cynically stupid bias that means burying all abominations committed by blacks under the flowers of sentiment and idyll, the violent accusations exchanged between the two governments in Port-au-Prince and in Cap-Haïtien, the theory of the equality of whites and blacks or even of the physiological and civilizational superiority of the black over the white, have provided to the writers of Christophe's court the material for a relatively large number of writings of a more or less historical form and content. (1081–1082)[125]

---

124 "Usés et ennuyés par cette inféconde lutte de tous les jours avec les préoccupations d'une vie besogneuse, auxquelles ne font contre-poids ni ces jouissances intellectuelles que tout centre de civilisation offre au pauvre comme au riche, ni les encouragemens de la renommée qui se distribuent trop loin d'eux; la plupart des poètes haïtiens finissent par abandonner la bouteille à l'encre pour la bouteille de tafia, et ils y trouvent, hélas! leurs meilleurs poèmes."
125 "La haine des blancs, le partis pris cyniquement niais d'ensevelir sous les fleurs du sentiment et de l'idylle les abominations commises par les noirs, les violentes accusations qu'échangeaient les deux gouvernemens de Port-au-Prince et du Cap, la théorie de l'égalité des blancs et des noirs, voir celle de la prééminence physiologique et civilisatrice du noir sur le blanc, ont fournie aux écrivains de la cour de Christophe la matière d'assez nombreux écrits de forme et de fond plus ou moins historiques."

In his seemingly neutral descriptions of the contemporary Haitian cultural landscape, d'Alaux mostly relies on the prefabricated conceptions of what is specifically Haitian that were circulating in France at that time. Positive and negative stereotypes take turns in his evaluation. Because he is working with models of exoticism, his approach can be seen as an effort at self-reassurance. The work of transfer here is therefore a double one: first, the preformulated concepts he uses distort his ethnographic lens, but then those same concepts are translated back to the metropolis in a process of acculturation. D'Alaux's articles in the *Revue des deux mondes* were primarily aimed at a French audience in the colonial center, for whom a confirmation of the success of the French cultural model was a key concern. Given how incompletely Haiti's early literary products have been preserved, his remarks provide very valuable insights into social constellations and various networks of connection. It is obvious that relationships with the literary production of the former French mother country are asymmetrical; the fact that Francophilia can sometimes turn into plagiarism is only perpetuated by an interpretation that exaggerates the gravitational force of French culture. In spite of the political freedom and the possibilities of entering into a multirelational connection, a bipolar model appears to have continued to prevail even after the recognition of Haiti in 1825. However, we should not ignore the possibility that d'Alaux's outlook is also heavily influenced by a sense of compensation connected with the loss of Haiti.

In what follows, we will continue to address the French perspective, but this time as it concerns its Spanish neighbor.

IV.4.2 Charles de Mazade: "La société et la littérature à Cuba"

In mid-nineteenth-century France, Charles de Mazade was considered an important historian of Spain. Given the comparatist nature of the central question of this study of Spanish and French colonialism, it may be productive to look at how Cuba's literary production was perceived in France, the mother country of its neighboring colonies. Not for nothing is an entire article in the *Revue des deux mondes* devoted to this topic. In the article, Mazade introduces Cuban society as well as some of its writers, along with their works (as the title of his article, "La société et la littérature à Cuba" [Society and literature in Cuba] makes clear), and there are some aspects of Mazade's piece that are worth noting. Early in the text, he makes an interesting comment about the contemporary acceleration of knowledge transfer: "What is newer and more peculiar to our century is that the multiplicity of connections, the electrical rapidity of communications allow us to watch, in a manner of speaking, what is being done or tried in every latitude" (1018).[126] This comment about the simultaneity of global process could fit seamlessly into today's diagnoses of globalization, and it explicitly emphasizes yet again the phenomenon, detailed by Ottmar Ette, of historical phases of accelerated globalization, which this study has, implicitly, already repeatedly confirmed. It is probably no accident that it was in 1851 that Mazade made this comment, right at the transition from the second to the third of the phases discerned by Ette; for this third phase, Ette emphasizes the "changed meaning of time as a factor," and this is the phase in which the gaze of the global stage is turned to the "American double continent" where, in the progressive second half of the nineteenth century, a new high point is ushered in (Ette, *Weltbewusstsein* 27). For the purposes of our investigation, it is very important that the transfer of knowledge between the Caribbean islands and the colonial powers happened relatively quickly; the importance of the connection between France and both the French and Spanish islands was particularly pronounced.

Mazade's reflections show how Cuba can be a literary model for the entire Caribbean. Other important topics include the Haitian Revolution and the Latin American liberation movements along with their repercussions and possible influences on the region. In addition, he wants to issue a warning about the Anglo-Saxon "danger" that might take over power in Cuba. The context of the opium war points up the ambitions to power of the two great Anglo-Saxon powers. At some points, Mazade also makes disparaging remarks about North America. He refers repeatedly to the Countess of Merlin, a "thinking woman" (*femme d'esprit*), documenting her influence on the intellectuals of the time. Mazade describes her three-volume travelogue *La Havane* (1849), which I introduced and discussed in section III.2.1, as follows:

> possessing a lively and penetrating observation and dedicated chiefly to describing the life and customs of Cuba, but its ingenious and familiar form in no way disguises the serious questions that are stirring at the foundations of Cuban society, and which constitute its originality. (Mazade 1019)[127]

Mazade also refers frequently to the relationship between Cuba and Spain as a colonial power. Although Cuba is largely economically independent, politically

---

126 "Ce qui est plus nouveau et plus particulièrement propre à notre siècle, c'est que la multiplicité des rapports, la rapidité électrique des communications nous font assister pour ainsi dire à tout ce qui se fait ou se tente sous toutes les latitudes."
127 "d'une observation vive et pénétrante, consacré surtout à décrire la vie et les mœurs de Cuba, mais dont la forme ingénieuse et familière ne déguise nullement ces graves questions qui se remuent au fond de la société cubanaise et constituent son originalité."

it continues to be tied to Spain, he points out, adding that the best thing would be for it to remain so in perpetuity, in order to prevent Anglo-Saxon dominion over this island in the heart of the Caribbean, the "queen of the Antillean archipelago" (1034). He analyzes Cuba's political, climatic, and social situation: "These conditions and tendencies can be naturally deduced from the traditions of this political regime of which we were speaking, the seduction of the climate, the coexistence of the slave races alongside the free race, and the diverse nuances of the Creole population itself" (1020).[128] The influence of the Countess of Merlin can be clearly seen in Mazade's description of the system of slavery, specifically when he describes the gentle and paternal traits of the slave owners. Nevertheless, he also points out: "But it must also be noted that this protection is extended to the slave as an inferior and degraded race: it is in no way in the name of human equality. The feeling of the white man's superiority maintains all of its power in their practices towards the blacks" (1024).[129] Mazade's evaluation of Cuban literature is double-edged. On the one hand, he finds Cuba's literature lacking in historical depth and significance, but on the other he finds there an impressive power of imagination (and he also notes that the Cuban poets' love for Cuba can turn against Spain):

> In the works of the Cuban poets, as in the social milieu in which those works are produced, there is more imagination than depth, more outer sparkle than power, more grace than moral character, more movement than cohesion. One Cuban critic says that it is the literature of a country without history and without monuments, gifted with a poetic nature and abundant in marvelous scenes, where the sciences and the fine arts have barely begun and where the spectacle of Europe's intellectual movements has the fascinating prestige of distance. One trait that is common to all of these overseas poets is their unassailable love for their dear Cuba—a love that, for some of them, turns into a kind of conspiracy against Spain. (1027)[130]

---

[128] "Ces conditions et ces tendances se déduisent naturellement des traditions de ce régime politique dont nous parlions, de la séduction du climat, de la coexistence des races esclaves à côté de la race libre, et des nuances diverses de la population créole elle-même."

[129] "Mais, qu'on le remarque, c'est à titre de race inférieure et dégradée que cette protection s'exerce sur l'esclave: ce n'est nullement à titre d'égalité humaine: Le sentiment de la supériorité du blanc garde toute sa puissance dans les mœurs vis-à-vis du noir."

[130] "Il y a en général dans les œuvres des poètes cubanais comme dans le milieu social ou elles se produisent, plus d'imagination que de profondeur, plus d'éclat extérieur que de puissance, plus de grâce que de caractère moral, plus mouvement que de cohésion. C'est, dit un critique cubanais, la littérature d'un pays sans histoire et sans monumens, doué d'une nature poétique et abondante en scènes merveilleuse, où les sciences et les beaux-arts naissant à peine, et ou le spectacle des mouvemens intellectuels de l'Europe a le prestige fascinateur de la distance. Un trait commun à tous ces poètes d'outre-mer, c'est l'amour inviolable de la chère Cuba—amour qui chez quelques-uns se transforme en une sorte de conjuration contre l'Espagne."

The voyages of discovery and adventure during the conquests, in Mazade's eyes, constitute important sources for the great potential of Cuban literature. This supply of literary material makes up for the lack on the civilizational and cultural level. Though some claim that Cuba could not produce any poetry because the island has no memories or traditions, this, writes Mazade, is only partially true, because the entire dramatic and moving history of the first settlers in these regions is, after all, nothing short of a wonderful "fabric of tradition" (1033).

An important concern for Mazade is warning against the Anglo-Saxon influence on Cuba, which could lead to the English actually taking possession of the island. For this reason, he calls on the white population to attend to social equilibrium and to continue to develop, building on the progress that has already been achieved. "This is an appeal addressed to the white population to fortify, with a civilizing element, this ill-balanced society. ... The most essential kinds of progress for Cuba are both obscure and practical, in every moment, in the laws, in the customs, in the intellectual and moral education" (1035).[131]

This French historian's wish, finally, is that Cuba remain Spanish so that it can become a modern, independent society. The idea of the civilizing mission, so firmly entrenched in France, is simply transferred, with an astonishing assumption of straightforwardness, to the neighboring Iberian Peninsula and its possibilities for retaining colonial power. This is also why Mazade's comparatist perspective on the Spanish neighbor owes less to a comparatist colonial perspective than to his preoccupation with the important reference point of culture and civilization.

I would now like to take a look at the Countess of Merlin, who also has a say (a different kind than in her travelogue) in the *Revue des deux mondes*, where her text became an almost canonical monument to the critique of abolitionism.

IV.4.3 The Countess of Merlin: "Les esclaves dans les colonies espagnoles"

In this article about slavery in the Spanish colonies, the Countess of Merlin, who has already been introduced, provides a highly complex model for the critique of abolitionism. She repeats, in multiple places, that slavery is not a good thing, but adds that it is nevertheless, given this evil and chaotic world, certainly desirable:

---

[131] "C'est un appel adressé à la population blanche pour fortifier d'un élément civilisateur cette société mal équilibrée. ... Les progrès les plus essentiels pour Cuba sont des progrès obscurs, pratiques et de tous les instans, dans les législations, dans les mœurs, dans l'éducation intellectuelle et morale."

> Nothing could be more just than the abolition of the slave trade; nothing more unjust than the emancipation of the slaves. ... Nevertheless, if one reflects that while the Africans are now condemned to slavery, they were previously destined to be killed or devoured, one no longer knows which is the blessing and which is the cruelty. (Condesa de Merlín, "Les esclaves" 735)[132]

Slavery is still better than falling victim to cannibalistic Africans, she writes. She does acknowledge that the British have prohibited the slave trade, but at the same time blames them for having done too little to combat the local (immoral) practices in their African possessions. If their humanitarian attitude were genuine, they would, as the world's greatest colonial power, have to take on the task of acting as educators in Africa, "to go to teach the savage tribes in Africa, whether by persuasion or by force, that one must respect human life and liberty" (736).[133] There are a few indications that she deplores slavery, for instance, her statement that "one of the saddest consequences of slavery is the degradation of material labor" (741).[134] In other words, interestingly, her reservations have to do not with enslavement as such but with the devaluation of physical labor that is connected with it.

The Countess of Merlin's comments on the subtle differences between Europeans and Creoles are also illuminating. She repeatedly describes the caring, paternal manner of the Creole slave owners, while showing the European slave owners as frequently mistreating their slaves. Europeans who bring the expectations of their own country with them to Cuba feel an exaggerated pity for "the Negro," she writes, but then the stupidity of the slaves makes them impatient, and because the poor Negroes do not understand them, the Europeans come to the conclusion that the Negroes are a kind of beast, and therefore begin beating them like animals.

Large parts of the Countess of Merlin's article are devoted to describing Cuba's legal system, which protects the slaves. The status of the slaves is therefore better, she concludes, than that of the freed slaves, who must look after themselves. Thus, some slaves turn down the liberation that is offered to them, because the meaning of the word "freedom" is unclear to them and they value material well-being over independence. And the fact that the slaves

---

[132] "Rien de plus juste que l'abolition de la traite des noirs; rien de plus injuste que l'émancipation des esclaves. ... Cependant, si l'on réfléchit qu'alors comme maintenant les Africains condamnés à l'esclavage ont été préalablement destinés à être tués et dévorés, on ne sait plus où est le bienfait, ou est la cruauté."

[133] "d'aller en Afrique apprendre aux tribus sauvages, soit par la persuasion, soit par la force, que l'homme doit respecter la vie et la liberté des hommes."

[134] "Une des plus tristes conséquences de l'esclavage, c'est d'avilir le travail matériel."

in Cuba are well treated by the descendants of the Spaniards is due most of all to the Gospel:

> The Spaniard, deeply and sincerely attached to his belief, has undergone this influence both in his laws and in his practices, and it is to the application of the precepts of humanity, charity, and fraternity imposed by the Gospel that the slave here owes most of the blessings that are accorded to him. (749)[135]

The black slaves fare decidedly worse in the eyes of the Countess of Merlin, who offers the entire spectrum of the usual stereotypes in her characterization of them:

> The Negroes and Negresses who work inside the house are allowed to use their free time for other work on their own account; they would profit from this favor more if they were less lazy and vicious. Their habitual idleness, the ardor of the African blood, and the unconcern that results from the absence of responsibility for their own fate engender in them the most disordered practices and habits. (751)[136]
> One of the sources of profit for the Negro is stealing. It is rare to find faithful ones, and, for people lacking in principles, the reason is very simple, it is impunity. (753)[137]

More surprising are the characteristics attributed to the Creoles (*criollos*), a term that in the Countess of Merlin's usage refers not to the descendants of the Spanish colonizers but to slaves who were born in the colonies: "Most of the slaves who are dedicated to domestic housework were born on the island: they are called *criollos*. Their intelligence is more developed than that of the Africans and their aspect is frank and familiar" (756).[138] The author is amazingly blithe in reaching judgments and assessments that she has no way of testing scientifically but can only justify with a "gut feeling." It may in fact be the case that she

---

135 "L'Espagnol, profondément et sincèrement attaché à sa croyance, a subi cette influence dans ses lois comme dans ses mœurs, et c'est à l'application des préceptes d'humanité, de charité et de fraternité imposés par l'Évangile, que l'esclave doit ici la plupart des bienfaits qu'on lui accorde."
136 "Les nègres et négresses destinés au service intérieur de la maison peuvent employer leur temps libre à d'autres ouvrages pour leur propre compte; ils profiteraient davantage de cette faveur s'ils étaient moins paresseux et moins vicieux. Leur désœuvrement habituel, l'ardeur du sang africain, et cette insouciance qui résulte de l'absence de responsabilité de son propre sort, engendrent chez eux les mœurs et les habitudes les plus déréglées."
137 "Une des sources de profit du nègre est le vol. Il est rare d'en trouver de fidèles, et, pour des gens dépourvus de principes, la raison est toute simple, c'est l'impunité."
138 "La plupart des esclaves réservés au service intérieur des maisons sont nés dans l'île: on les appelle criollos. Leur intelligence est plus développée que celle des Africains, et leur aspect franc et familier."

had experience with a few *criollos* who were notably capable, but were they for that reason "more intelligent"? Could their aptitude not be very easily explained by the fact that they were already socialized within the household as slave children? It becomes clear how contradictory her argumentation is in part when, elsewhere, she gives a fundamental denunciation of slavery:

> Thus, the state of being a prince in Africa is worth less than that of being a slave in our colonies.
> This does not mean that slavery is a desirable state: God preserve me from thinking that! I confine myself simply to drawing from this an irrefutable conclusion; and that is that the benefits of civilization and of good institutions can correct even slavery, making it preferable to an independence that is stripped of all material benefit and always exposed to the caprice and brutality of the strongest. (756)[139]

The Countess of Merlin goes into great detail in discussing the reasons for the differences between whites and blacks in terms of capacity for work and resilience. She contrasts the low spirits of "the Negro" with the energy of white workers:

> One fact struck me. Every time that I saw the Negro tasked with the same work as the European day laborer and that I compared the labors of the two, I found, in the first, effort, fatigue, and dejection, and in the second gaiety, vigor, and courageous intelligence. Where did this disadvantage of the African race come from if it is indeed, as one says, stronger than ours? Must it be attributed to the climate? But the Negroes were born under the burning sun of Africa. Is it due to their stupid ignorance, which adds to the difficulties of the work, or to their indolence, which puts them to sleep? (757)[140]

One thing she sees as highly problematic is the fact that the black slaves do not have the habit of dealing confidently with all kinds of work; no matter how robustly a slave might be built, this is a disadvantage he cannot overcome. He might be able to run, jump, and tame wild beasts, but he abhors the regular,

---

139 "Ainsi, l'état de prince en Afrique ne vaut pas celui d'esclave dans nos colonies.
Ceci ne veut pas dire que l'esclavage soit un état désirable: Dieu me préserve de le penser! Je me borne seulement à tirer de ce fait une conséquence incontestable; c'est que les bienfaits de la civilisation et des bonnes institutions corrigent même l'esclavage, et le rendent préférable à l'indépendance dépouillée de tout bien-être matériel, et toujours exposée au caprice et à la brutalité du plus fort."
140 "Un fait, m'a frappée. Toutes les fois que j'ai vu le nègre chargé du même travail que le journalier européen, et que j'ai comparé les deux labeurs, j'ai trouvé, chez le premier, effort, fatigue, accablement, et chez l'autre gaieté, vigueur et courageuse intelligence. D'où vient ce désavantage de la race africaine, si elle est, comme on le dit, plus forte que la nôtre? Faut-il l'attribuer au climat? Mais les nègres sont nés sous le soleil brûlant d'Afrique. Est-ce à leur stupide ignorance, qui augmente les difficultés du travail, ou à l'indolence, qui les endort?"

practical, peaceful work that is the fruit of culture and civilization.[141] In some places the Countess of Merlin even calls the slaves savages and refers to groups of them as hordes.

As in just about all discussions of the culture of the blacks, there must of course also be a reference to Haiti. According to the Countess of Merlin, the colored people of Cuba, who are more privileged and happier than the mulattos of Saint-Domingue, would never think of imitating the rebellious slaves of the Haitian Revolution. On the contrary, they are always ready to fight against slave revolts. They are proud of the liberal laws that allow them to move close to the white caste, and they therefore try to distance themselves completely from the degraded black race.

The author ends by asking about the possible consequences of abolition, assuming that no one could actually wish for the kind of legal and civil equality that, according to her, would end in "mixed marriages":

> Let us suppose, furthermore, that by a miracle, the moral education of the freed slaves, developing all of a sudden, led them to a love of work. ... Within a constitutional political system, in a country governed by equitable laws, would they not then be able to claim a share in the same institutions? Would you accord them all your rights, all your privileges? Would you make them your judges, your generals, and your ministers? Would you give them your daughters in marriage? (767)[142]

From her point of view, then, it is completely consistent that she finally argues for the preservation of the system of slavery, for the good of the slaves:

> At any rate, you do have one other way to improve the lot of the slaves: rigorously maintain the abolition of the trade in slaves; the masters will watch over the fate of their slaves with greater care, because they will represent a property whose value will increase, and what has not been achieved in the name of humanity will be accomplished because of self-interest. (769)[143]

---

[141] On the overall issue of humans and animals in the Caribbean, cf. Meyer-Krentler, *Die Idee des Menschen*.
[142] "Supposons encore que, par un miracle, l'éducation morale des esclaves affranchis, se développant tout à coup, les amenât à l'amour du travail. ... Sous un régime politique constitutionnel, dans un pays gouverné par des lois équitables, ne pourraient-ils pas réclamer le partage des mêmes institutions? Leur accorderiez-vous tous vos droits, tous vos privilèges? En feriez-vous vos juges, vos généraux et vos ministres? Leur donneriez-vous vos filles en mariage?"
[143] "D'ailleurs, vous avez encore un moyen d'améliorer le sort des esclaves: maintenez rigoureusement l'abolition de la traite; les maîtres veilleront avec plus de soin sur l'esclave, propriété dont la valeur augmentera, et ce qui n'aura pas été obtenu par l'humanité sera dû à l'intérêt."

In fact, this last argument shows what the issue is for the Countess of Merlin. The slave trade should be abolished, but not slavery in Cuba. Although the number of slaves is high enough, people will then make sure that they increase. Thus she also describes how well pregnant slaves are treated, so that they will give more "manpower" to the plantation. She compares these slaves with pregnant peasant women in Europe and once again comes to the conclusion that slaves could never have greater social status or better living conditions than they do in Cuba.

We have already developed an understanding of the Countess of Merlin's situation as one that is characterized by writing in the in-between; we can further extend this understanding to include the ambivalence of her political attitude. She persists in aristocratic thought patterns that reject philanthropic ideas, but at the same time she is not consistent in upholding her pro-slavery attitude. At any rate, her representations are communicated as the result of highly complex circulations which can neither be reduced to a bipolar colonial model nor result in a productive multirelationality. She wants to assume that she can assign Spain a gravitational force that is comparable to that of France, and she appropriates a mode of speaking that bypasses reality. The fact that the Countess of Merlin was not taken seriously by Cuba's intellectual elite, such as Félix Tanco, for example, is also attested to by the mockery of such writers as Reinaldo Arenas (cf. Ette, "'Traición, naturalmente'"; Ette, *La escritura de la memoria*; Méndez Rodenas, *Gender and Nationalism* 231). But one can also readily imagine that her opinions would have been received quite differently by the readers of the Parisian *Revue des deux mondes*.

IV.4.4 Lerminier: "Des rapports de la France avec le monde"

Within the context of the decisive question of the outward reach of French culture, the 1836 article by the historian Eugène Lerminier (1803–1857) that repeatedly extols France's exceptional position in the world promises fascinating insights. Although Lerminier does not refer to the Caribbean—1836 being a time when the exploitation of Africa was at its height—his text is nevertheless very useful, because he clearly depicts France's self-image and its missionizing idea. Lerminier's extremely noteworthy theses therefore deserve to be explained in detail here. Lerminier begins with a short history of France; he sees his country as having two main characteristics:

> There are two thoughts that have alternately preoccupied France: establishing its territory and developing its genius. Sometimes it debates at home, with its own children, the ideas

whose solution and truth it seeks; sometimes it occupies itself with spreading both its ideas and its power to the outside. (326)[144]

While advocating understanding among peoples, he emphasizes France's leadership role, because France, he writes, is the most vital of the modern nations:

> But France has already lived a great deal; and if it has nevertheless succeeded in remaining young; if, being both old and new, it has an abundant past and at the same time a long future; one can envy the good fortune of those writers who will, several centuries from now, trace the annals of France. (329)[145]

France's favorable geographical position has predestined it, in Lerminier's telling, to be in contact with the world. The Atlantic is its connection to America, the Mediterranean its conduit to Africa and the Near East. As for Spain, "the Pyrenees separate it from the Iberian Peninsula, which [France] would never dream of conquering but only wants to guide into the paths of the new civilization" (330).[146] Lerminier is so convinced of France's mission that he reinterprets Napoleon's wars of conquest as defensive wars that were necessary in order to spread the modern ideas of the French Revolution throughout Europe: "When, at the end of the last century, France had to resist all of Europe, it necessarily had the instinct to oppose it with its principles and to launch at it, in the middle of its bombs, also its passions and its ideas" (332).[147] Since France is almost synonymous with the progress of humankind, Lerminier can justify French imperialism as the logical (and beneficial) consequence of this pioneering role.

> The thing is that the law of France is always to march forward; not that France does not share this admirable necessity with the rest of the human race, but it seems to satisfy the need more vigorously than do the other peoples. One would have to say that France is in more of a hurry to arrive, to reach a goal. ... Today, in this first quarter of the nineteenth

---

144 "Deux pensées ont tour à tour préoccupé la France: constituer son territoire et développer son génie. Tantôt elle débat chez elle, avec ses enfans, les idées dont elle cherche la solution et la vérité; tantôt elle s'emploie à répandre au dehors et ses idées et sa puissance."
145 "Mais la France a déjà beaucoup vécu; et si néanmoins elle est restée jeune, si, à la fois vieille et nouvelle, elle a un abondant passé et en même temps un long avenir, on peut envier la fortune des écrivains qui, dans plusieurs siècles, traceront les annales françaises."
146 "les Pyrénées la séparent de la Péninsule hispanique qu'elle ne saurait songer à conquérir, mais seulement à guider dans les voies de la civilisation nouvelle."
147 "Quand à la fin du siècle dernier, la France dut résister à toute l'Europe, elle eut nécessairement l'instinct de lui opposer ses principes, et de lui lancer, au milieu de ses bombes, ses passions et ses idées."

century, France must be concerned with three things: its progressive spirit, its continental grandeur, and its universal influence. (334)[148]

Thus, it is only consistent for this new discourse to consider the most recent conquests not as an attack but as progress:

> In addition, Europe's moral situation no longer permits war with the sole goal of an enlargement, a conquest. Moral interests are too tightly connected to positive results for the principles and ideas not to intervene among the causes that would make men take up arms. But France must always cultivate the thought and the love of its continental grandeur; it must also carefully maintain its military spirit and not allow anything that could weaken or depreciate it. (335)[149]

France can only be compared with ancient Rome. But while Rome was oppressing other peoples, France wants to come into contact with other peoples in order to spread its ideas. At the end, it becomes clear yet again what significance the conquest of Africa had for France and why its focus is directed there:

> France having found its Indies in Africa, it no longer has to concern itself with positive conquests on other coasts but only with the care of carrying its commerce and its name everywhere. In a century, there will have to be a France of the East; and then everywhere, on all the seas, among all the peoples, the name and the influence of France. Here is an ambition that is not like that of old Rome but which honors and serves humanity. (337)[150]

France's influence must be dominant on this continent, for the good of all humankind. In order to be recognized by other peoples, France needs to interest

---

[148] "C'est que la loi de la France est de marcher toujours, non qu'elle ne partage cette admirable nécessité avec le reste du genre humain; mais elle semble y satisfaire plus vivement que les autres peuples. On la dirait plus pressée d'aboutir, d'arriver à un but. ... Aujourd'hui, à ce premier quart du XIXe siècle, la France doit avoir souci de trois choses: de son esprit progressif, de sa grandeur continentale, de son influence universelle."

[149] "Au surplus la situation morale de l'Europe ne permet plus de guerre dans le but unique d'un agrandissement, d'une conquête. Les intérêts moraux sont trop étroitement unis aux résultats positifs, pour que les principes et les idées n'interviennent pas parmi les causes qui feraient prendre les armes. Mais la France doit toujours cultiver la pensée et l'amour de sa grandeur continentale; elle doit aussi entretenir avec soin son esprit militaire et ne rien permettre qui puisse l'affaiblir ou le déprécier."

[150] "La France en Afrique ayant trouvé ses Indes, elle n'a plus à se préoccuper de conquêtes positives sur d'autres côtes, mais seulement du soin de porter partout son commerce et son nom. Dans un siècle, il doit y avoir une France d'Orient; et puis partout, dans toutes les mers, chez tous les peuples, le nom et l'influence de la France. Voilà une ambition qui ne sent pas la vieille Rome, mais qui honore et sert l'humanité."

itself in their history and culture, because that will only strengthen the interest in France that is already present:

> Carelessness must be banished and ignorance dispelled; we must take an interest in the movements of peoples, learn about their connections, their history, their geography, to understand that because France is so well regarded in the world, it must respond with a constant attention. (341)[151]

IV.5 Conclusion

In and of themselves, as mediums of transfer, all three of the magazines we have talked about here, the *Revue des Colonies*, the *Revue encyclopédique*, and the *Revue des deux mondes*, set multirelational processes of circulation in motion. Because the departmentalization of fields of knowledge has not yet been clearly defined, the magazines can be located in the context of a young ethnology but can finally also go far beyond that—mostly thanks to the many literary texts— to connect to universal dimensions. The section on racial discourses that precedes the discussion of the newspapers is intended to serve as a foil for introducing contemporary societies in Paris, the center, that were concerned with classifying the Other. The fact that knowledge from the Caribbean played no important role in basic discussions about phrenology, etcetera, may be quite surprising, especially given the density of material in the reception of the Caribbean among the three magazines. The explanation for this surely has to do with the fact that their editors' involvement with racial discourses was more implicit than explicit. What most of the articles in these magazines have in common is that the wrestling over attributions of identity is a constant underlying theme but that any positioning of that theme is only possible in an in-between space, if at all. These magazines constitute an indispensable element in the sketching of the cultural processes of circulation in colonial and postcolonial constellations, processes that are, as a whole, difficult to delineate. Yet even though clear categorizations are impossible, political programs and colonial mechanisms can certainly be recognized. On this level, the inclusiveness of the French cultural model proves itself in spite of the multirelational patterns of movement.

The *Revue des Colonies*, unusual as it is and the furthest of the three from the establishment, run by mulattos and critical of slavery, explicitly advocates a

---

151 "Il faut bannir l'insouciance et dissiper l'ignorance; il faut s'intéresser aux mouvemens des peuples, connaître leurs rapports, leur histoire, leur géographie, comprendre que, puisque la France est si fort regardée du monde, elle doit lui répondre par une attention constante."

French model of integration. The *Revue encyclopédique* has a unique status because of its short life and its explicit concern with Haiti, which sheds light on one variety of economic transfer. The literary historical articles of the *Revue des deux mondes*, with its wide range of interests, represent the pioneering French role on all levels. The following chapter will look more closely at this pioneering role and examine canonical literary texts in terms of their imperial dimension. Given the previous investigations, it is certainly to be expected that this will reveal asymmetrical relationalities, especially in the interaction with Caribbean literatures. But we will still need to determine the extent to which the reciprocal effect that is inherent to every form of relationality will be articulated here.

V The Imperial Dimension of French Romanticism: Asymmetrical Relationalities

V.1 Towards Madrid or Paris?

> I read the episode of Atala, and the two of them [María and the sister of Efraín], admirable for their immobility and abandon, heard pouring from my lips all of that melancholy collected by the poet to "make the world weep." ... María, hearing my voice, uncovered her face, and thick tears rolled down it. She was as beautiful as the poet's creation, and I loved her with the love that he imagined. ... Oh! My soul and María's were not just moved by that reading: they were overwhelmed by foreboding. (Isaacs 88)[1]

This text, from the circum-Caribbean country of Colombia, was written by Jorge Isaacs, a resident of Colombia's Cauca Valley but the son of a Jamaican father. The scene excerpted here, from his novel *María* (1867), which became a Latin American best seller shortly after its publication, illustrates a phenomenon that is paradigmatic for nineteenth-century Latin American and Caribbean literatures, namely the explicit orientation towards French Romanticism, in this case in the form of the favorite books of the protagonists of narrative texts. What is the context of this intensive reception of French Romanticism in the middle of the tropics?

Most Caribbean authors spent varying amounts of time in the colonial centers of their respective mother countries. Here a difference emerges between the writers of the French and Spanish colonies. For the inhabitants of the French Caribbean colonial sphere, time spent in Paris appears to have been a self-evident prerequisite for the life of a writer. It was part of the ongoing pattern of life for the ruling white Creole class from Guadeloupe and Martinique, who had a monopoly on writing far into the nineteenth century, to have their children educated in France, ignoring the necessary consequence that this only strengthened the cultural underdevelopment in the colonial sphere, which continued to

---

[1] "Leía yo el episodio de Atala, y las dos [María y la hermana de Efraín], admirables en su inmovilidad y abandono, oían brotar de mis labios toda aquella melancolía aglomerada por el poeta para 'hacer llorar el mundo.' ... María, dejando oír mi voz, descubrió la faz, y por ella rodaban gruesas lágrimas. Era tan bella como la creación del poeta, y yo la amaba con el amor que él imaginó. ... ¡Ay! mi alma y la de María no sólo estaban conmovidas por aquella lectura: estaban abrumadas por el presentimiento." This example from *María* is given for the sake of illustration even though Isaacs, representing as he does a country that is "only" part of the Caribbean periphery, is not strictly speaking part of our corpus of writers and in fact does not even come from the Caribbean side of Colombia.

be afforded only economic, but no cultural, significance (cf. Bader 187; Gewecke, *Der Wille zur Nation* 92 ff.). This exclusive orientation towards Paris can also be seen in Haiti (and perhaps even more strongly there), which gained its independence so early.

For the authors of the Spanish Caribbean, there was a much greater variety available in choosing their place of exile: Gómez de Avellaneda and Hostos spent time in Spain, Heredia in Mexico, and Villaverde in the United States. There were of course also examples of self-imposed exile to Madrid, which was comparable to Paris and drew intellectuals eager for education and culture, such as Gómez de Avellaneda, who preferred the metropolis of their own mother tongue to the City of Light. Others, including Hostos, chose the capital of their mother country mostly for political reasons, advocating a redefinition of colonial connections (cf. Gewecke, *Der Wille zur Nation* 110). The Cuban Heredia took a far more radical position: inspired by the political climate in Mexico, which was already independent, he participated in a conspiracy against the Spanish crown.[2] Even though in what follows we will be searching for and developing dominant patterns of reception, and therefore also finally dominant patterns of movement, it still needs to be noted that since their inception, Caribbean literatures have always been "literatures without a fixed abode" (cf. Ette, *Writing-between-worlds* 126–156).

Under these circumstances, the differences in how writers positioned themselves literarily in the colonies (still or former) of France and Spain, respectively, is not very surprising. The homogeneous geographical tendency on the part of writers from the French colonies (still or former) to orient themselves towards Paris also has a literary counterpart, in which these writers integrate themselves into Paris's literary currents (cf. Bader 187). Writers driven by revolutionary motivations—such as Heredia or Villaverde—who are more often writers from the Spanish than the French Caribbean, are also much more likely to be affected by the problematics of the in-between: from a distance and from the outside in, they inscribe their literature and themselves in the struggle for a political and, in part, also cultural emancipation, whereby they often are forced to the sobering recognition, on their return to the Caribbean, that they are not really at home there anymore either and are now perceived as foreigners by their countrymen as well (cf. Gómez de Avellaneda, *Sab*, ed. Servera 38).

As we have seen, an extended stay in Paris was taken for granted in the intellectual circles of the Antillean upper classes. And how were they integrated

---

[2] He thematizes exile very explicitly, for example in his "Hymn of the Exile" ("Himno del desterrado").

there? Were their works read and received critically? The most variegated forms of transatlantic exchange could be found in Paris; it is for instance known that Chateaubriand had a mistress from Martinique, who is supposed to have been an important source of inspiration for his *Le génie du Christianisme* (The genius of Christianity). Some intellectuals maintained direct exchanges: we can for instance document direct influence by Chateaubriand on Coussin and by Hugo on Levilloux and Maynard de Queilhe (Toumson I:69).

V.2 The Dominant Reception of French Romanticism

In spite of the very different reasons they had for leaving their respective islands, what unites the literary texts of all of these writers is an orientation towards contemporary European currents. Which of these currents, exactly, are used as models? In 1843, Tanco denounces Zorrilla, Espronceda, Bretón de los Herreros, and all of contemporary Spanish literature as imitations of foreign ideas and texts (cf. Wogatzke 100). We can compare this to the various scenes in which France is glorified in Levilloux's novel *Les créoles ou la Vie aux Antilles*. As we saw earlier, on their departure from the French mainland, Edmond and Estève run through all of the benefits that they have received there: scholarship, the "elevation of the soul," a new moral existence (Levilloux 32; cf. Wogatzke 201). This exaltation of the mother country is further emphasized by the fact that the conservative French-language writers like to contrast the primitive Spanish conquerors with the white colonial masters of French background, who are represented as more sensitive, better educated, and living a finer life (Wogatzke 312). While Spanish colonialism is equated with the pursuit of material interests, the French colonial power is honored as having made its former colonies into true treasuries of national culture (132).

In most Spanish-language texts, a clear differentiation is made with Spain, in the sense of "you versus us"; Levilloux's protagonist, on the other hand, talks about "we, France" (*nous, la France*), for example (Levilloux 20). Becoming French means emancipation from the uncultivated life of slavery, but it can also be understood as a demand; Estève, from Guadeloupe, happily chooses death for the fatherland on the French battlefields, just like the protagonist of *Bug-Jargal*. These examples already make it clear that the texts of French Romanticism enjoyed a much more intensive reception than did those from

Spain. The influence of Lamartine, Chateaubriand, and Hugo is particularly significant.[3]

But even in the Spanish colonial possessions, France's Romantic intellectuals exert a formative influence. Thus Heredia's work as a translator (cf. Pagni) of Byron, Chateaubriand, and Lamartine marks a decisive step within the reception history and development of Romanticism in the Spanish-speaking Caribbean (on Chateaubriand reception see also Rössner 1710–1711, 1720–1721). In Madrid, Gómez de Avellaneda was involved with Antonio Ferrer del Río's magazine *El laberinto* (1843–1845), putting her in close connection with other Spanish Romantics, such as Gil y Carrasco, Hartzenbusch, and Carolina Coronado (Gómez de Avellaneda, *Sab*, ed. Servera 25). Nevertheless, her literary texts display a clearer connection with France.[4] As an archetype of the Romantic hero, Sab points to a social-Romantic reception of Hugo. Other protagonists of Gómez de Avellaneda's indicate the influence of Chateaubriand's *Atala* (1801) and of *Paul et Virginie*, by the pre-Romantic Bernardin de Saint-Pierre (1787).

Such successful representatives of Spanish Romanticism as Larra, Zorilla, and Duque de Rivas enjoy a much smaller reception than do their French role models, even among Spanish-speaking readers. To a very large extent, of course, this has to do with the omnipresent role of French literature in all of Europe. If Spanish intellectuals themselves were looking to French Romanticism as an inspiration, how could they then in turn convincingly serve as models for the literary upper classes of their own colonies?

What manifestations of Romantic models can we recognize in the Spanish Caribbean? Here we reach the limits of classification attempts based on historical eras, because the late reception of Romanticism in Latin America overlaps chronologically with the reception of Neoclassicism. The paradox of a positivist Romanticism was created in a syncretistic alliance between Enlightenment and Romanticism. Classicism and Romanticism were not seen by all authors as mutually exclusive opposites but, often, as complementary phenomena (cf. Wogatzke 95, reference to Cintier Vitier).

Gudrun Wogatzke has aptly detailed the attributes of the era, along with its own attempts at delineating its boundaries: the Cuban members of del Monte's circle, like del Monte himself, regard themselves as eclectics, taking whatever

---

[3] Thus the Haitian writer Jean-Baptiste Chenêt, for example, expressed himself as follows in his *Études poétiques* (Poetic studies): "Lamartine and Hugo are immortal gods: they have received my faith and I serve at their altars." ("Lamartine, Hugo, sont des dieux immortels: Ils ont reçu ma foi, je sers sur leurs autels.") (192, cited in Hoffmann, *Littérature d'Haïti* 99).

[4] It must of course also be taken into consideration here that in general, many of the Spanish Romantics were influenced by their French colleagues.

serves their goals from each of the poetological preceptions. Their positions vary gradually, but not substantially, and continue to be indebted to Romanticism. And yet none of them wants to be called a Romantic—no more than do their European colleagues—which leads to the kind of negative connotation that can be seen not only in the articles of such writers as Manrique and Mesonero but also in Suárez's *Colección de Artículos*, Villaverde's *El perjurio* (Perjury, 1837), as well as in Ramón Palma's "La Romántica" and Ramón Piña's "El romántico Anselmo," both of which appeared in 1838, in *El Album* and *La Siempreviva* respectively (Wogatzke 95).

V.3 Variations of Reception

The French Romantics who enjoyed the most frequent reception in the Caribbean colonies were those whose work dealt in some way with the New World.[5] This interest in the New World found various expressions; the two poles were exoticism (most prominently represented by Chateaubriand) and social utopianism (as seen most saliently in Hugo) (cf. Müller, "Chateaubriand und Hugo"). And yet in all of these authors, one can also detect a certain ambivalence towards the new, towards all of the change ushered in by the French Revolution. Even in Chateaubriand, in his *Memoirs from beyond the Tomb*, we can find himself positioning himself as in the well-known passage, already cited above, in which he finds himself "between two centuries as at the junction between two rivers; I have plunged into their troubled waters, regretfully leaving behind the ancient strand where I was born and swimming hopefully towards the unknown shores where the new generations will land" (5; see section II.3 above).[6]

This ambiguity finds a variety of receptions among Caribbean authors, reflecting as it does their own mixed feelings about an ancien régime that, while it still lived on in their world, was nevertheless facing its end, as must have been clear to most of them. What appears in the French authors with a hint of nostalgia is sometimes expressed among the plantation owners of the French Caribbean as sheer terror, fed even more by the cautionary tale of Haiti. The writ-

---

[5] This includes Chateaubriand, with *Atala*; Hugo, with *Bug-Jargal*; and Lamartine, with *Toussaint L'Ouverture*. This does not, however, mean that these were the only representations of the Other that Caribbean writers read. In Jorge Isaacs's *Maria*, for instance, the title character is a devoted reader of Lamartine's *Méditations*.

[6] "Je me suis rencontré entre deux siècles comme au confluent de deux fleuves; j'ai plongé dans leurs eaux troublées, m'éloignant avec regret du vieux rivage où je suis né nageant avec espérance vers une rive inconnue."

ers of the Spanish-speaking Caribbean, on the other hand, tend more towards the social utopian moments in their mainland French models, whether emphasizing abolitionism or separatism. The latter is rather rare before abolition actually takes place, which makes the priorities clear: the fight against the glaring social inequalities stood in the foreground, and it was only after that was addressed that national independence might in turn receive focused attention.

In the reception of Romanticism, especially French Romanticism, by Caribbean writers, we can distinguish five broad patterns:

1. The explicit reception of French Romanticism as an unfiltered glorification of France's national culture. Poirié de Saint-Aurèle, Xavier Eyma, J.H.J. Coussin, and Ignace Nau, for example, stand out with their hymnlike tributes to their French role models. Let us take Coussin here as a representative voice:

   > It was during this time that that immortal work appeared in which, aside from a vast erudition, the most exquisite sensibility can be found united with an imagination that may be the most brilliant which has ever appeared among humankind: it should be apparent that I am speaking of the Genius of Christendom. (Coussin I:xii)[7]

2. The reflection of the reception of French Romanticism in the reading habits of the protagonists of narrative texts; in most cases, this consists of a reading of Lamartine or Chateaubriand. The quotation from Isaacs's *María* that begins this chapter is an example of this.

3. The implicit reception of socially revolutionary Romanticism. This variation is mostly focused on Victor Hugo. His early work *Bug-Jargal*, for instance, was an important influence for Gómez de Avellaneda's *Sab*, which we will look at more closely in the next chapter.

4. A mediated orientation towards the French Romantics' images of the Other in the service of self-description: Prévost de Sansac, for example, explicitly uses Bernardin de Saint-Pierre's exoticizing South Sea landscapes as a model for his own description of Martinique: "Using the author of *Paul et Virginie* as an example, I wanted to seat the lovers that I celebrate at the seashore, at the base of crags, in the shade of coconut trees, banana trees, and flowering lemon trees" (Prévost de Sansac 17).[8]

---

[7] "C'est dans ces entrefaites que parut cet ouvrage immortel, où, indépendamment d'une vaste érudition, la sensibilité la plus exquise se trouve partout unie a une imagination la plus éclatante peut-être qui ait jamais paru parmi les hommes: on voit que je veux parler du Génie du Christianisme."

[8] "A l'exemple de l'auteur de *Paul et Virginie*, j'ai voulu asseoir les amants que je célèbre sur le rivage de la mer, aux pieds des rochers, à l'ombre des cocotiers, des bananiers et des citronniers en fleurs."

5. An evasive move into descriptions of nature: this kind of Romanticism, often based on portrayals by travelers to the New World such as Chateaubriand, is widespread among the *Béké* writers of the French Antilles. J.H.J. Coussin introduces *Eugène de Cerceil ou les Caraïbes* with an explanation of these literary escapist tendencies, which he himself then uses in his own novel: the horrors of the French Revolution and its aftermath result in a retreat from society that ends in a love of pure nature and leads to an increase in representations of nature, whether in words or in pictures.

> In France, the scenes of blood were allied with hideous corruptions of the heart, which remained after the scaffolds had disappeared. Vice showed itself everywhere with its face uncovered; virtue, pale and disheveled, covered its face and sought out wild retreats in which to hide itself where, trying to forget the crimes of men by contemplating the things of God, it soon found, in these eminently moral speculations, a pleasure that beautified to its eyes these savage places where it had taken refuge. The love of solitude increased daily as the human race became more unhappy. Thus, one can reasonably say that in France today, among the class of honest people, there is more love for the countryside than there was before the revolution; and that love naturally leads to a love of scenes of nature, represented either by the painter's brush or the colorful expressions of writers who know how to paint with words. (Coussin I:x–xi)[9]

V.4 Hugo as a Model

Victor Hugo's influence on the novels of Gómez de Avellaneda and Maynard de Queilhe is particularly clear. The mulattos Marius and Sab are romantic heroes par excellence. Marius is subjected to an existential duality that shows the imprint of Hugo, who was a friend of Maynard de Queilhe's. In his preface to *Cromwell*, Hugo touches on a deep ambivalence in human nature when he writes that everyone has two beings within themselves: one that is transient and bound to

---

9 "Aux scènes de sang, s'allièrent en France les hideuses corruptions du cœur qui restèrent après que les échafauds eurent disparu. Le vice se montra partout à front découvert; la vertu, pâle et échevelée, se voila le visage, et chercha pour se cacher des retraites agrestes, où s'efforçant d'oublier les crimes des hommes par la contemplation des choses de Dieu, elle ne tarda pas à trouver dans ces spéculations éminemment morales, un plaisir qui embellit à ses yeux les lieux sauvages où elle s'étoit réfugiée. L'amour de la solitude augmentoit journellement à mesure que l'espèce humaine devenoit plus malheureuse. Aussi peut-on dire avec fondement qu'il y a aujourd'hui en France, dans la classe des honnêtes gens, plus d'amour pour la campagne, qu'il n'y en avoit avant la révolution; et cet amour conduit naturellement à celui des scènes de la nature, représentées soit par le pinceau du peintre, soit par les expressions coloriées des écrivains qui savent peindre avec la parole."

drives, needs, and passions, and one that is immortal and ethereal, quickened by enthusiasm and dreams. He associates the first one with the earth and the maternal principle, while the second one constantly strives towards the heavens, its fatherland (cf. Maignan-Claverie 250). As I have already shown, in a different context (section II.2.3), the character of Longuefort in *Outre-mer* assigns a racist version of this doubled nature to the mulatto Marius (Maynard de Queilhe II:16).

While this example of Maynard de Queilhe's reception of Hugo has to do primarily with the basic metaphysical dimension of Romanticist writing, the literary debate over *Bug-Jargal* in del Monte's circle shows that the social revolutionary aspect also resonated strongly. In a letter to del Monte, Tanco y Bosmeniel writes:

> And what do you say to *Bug Jargal?* I would like us to use the style of that novel for writing among ourselves. Think about it. The Negroes of the island of Cuba are our poetry, and we must not think about anything else; but not just the Negroes but the Negroes with the whites, all mixed up together, and then to make up the paintings, the scenes, which must of necessity be infernal and diabolical; but also certain and evident. This emerged through our Victor Hugo, and all of a sudden we know what we are, painted with the truth of poetry, since we already know the sad misery in which we live through numbers and philosophical analysis. (Letter from Félix Tanco to Domingo del Monte, dated February 13, 1836, in Gómez de Avellaneda, *Sab*, ed. Cruz 46)[10]

Hugo's *Bug-Jargal* served as a model for many, and not just for Gómez de Avellaneda's *Sab,* where the book was the immediate source for her subject. Galván's hero, Enrique, like Bug Jargal, wants his rebellion to remain clean; he does not want to dirty himself with thoughts of vengeance, and so he lets the Spanish prisoners free: "Tell the tyrants that my Indians and I know how to defend our liberty; but we are not executioners nor evildoers" (Galván [Porrúa] 210).[11] The Dominican writer even intones a hymn of praise to the "great Hugo" in his novel (267; cf. also Wogatzke 573).

How can we explain this enthusiasm for Hugo, and especially for *Bug-Jargal* as a model? Wogatzke points to an important constellation, namely that Hugo's predominantly negative representation of the black and mulatto populations of

---

10 "¿Y qué dice V. de Bug Jargal? Por el estilo de esta novelita quisiera yo que se escribiese entre nosotros. Piénselo bien. Los negros en la isla de Cuba son nuestra poesía, y no hay que pensar en otra cosa; pero no los negros solos, sino los negros con los blancos, todos revueltos, y formar luego los cuadros, las escenas, que a la fuerza han de ser infernales y diabólicas; pero ciertas y evidentes. Nazca por nuestro Víctor Hugo, y sepamos de una vez lo que somos, pintados con la verdad de la poesía, ya que conocemos por los números y el análisis filosófico la triste miseria en que vivimos."
11 "Decid a los tiranos que yo y mis indios sabemos defender nuestra libertad; mas no somos verdugos ni malvados."

Saint-Domingue collides with his positive sketch of the black title character as well as the narrator's partially anti-racist statements, making for an unsettling ambivalence that cannot be resolved through a reference to the noble savage (Wogatzke-Luckow 122).

One of the things that can be seen in *Bug-Jargal* is the development of the self-description of the former plantation owners, who were still trying to reclaim their lost possessions and who furnished Hugo with subjective information about the historical events that took place in Saint-Domingue. In addition, Wogatzke stresses that the stereotypes that are represented in *Bug-Jargal* and that were then absorbed by these and other writers, over and over again, include not only the idealization of the monarchists and the disavowal of the mother country's revolutionaries, philanthropists, and abolitionists, but also the depiction of the Haitian revolutionaries as a horde of stupid, fanatical, barbaric butchers who had followed their baser instincts without any plans or goals and had assassinated innocent people, the elderly, women, and children and abused their mortal remains as trophies just to satisfy their bloodthirsty desires (ibid.). Some of them seized the moment to turn the slave rebellions to personal profit. The mulattos, in particular, are depicted as "ringleaders, as power-hungry, egocentric, demagogically adept manipulators of the ignorant black masses," who interpret freedom as liberty to indulge their own caprice. The previous masters, meanwhile, are shown as having been, on the whole, rather benevolent, strict, but loving fathers. And if, in exceptional cases, a master turned out to be a despot with a "heart of stone," then he was either a revolutionary or a foreigner, usually an evil Englishman or Spaniard (ibid.) Thus, it was not French slave traders who abducted Bug and his family and took them to Saint-Domingue but a Spanish trader who abused the family's friendship and trust to lure them onto the ship and then sell them as slaves in the Antilles. Wogatzke points out that most of the evil (ex-)slaves speak Spanish, or a Spanish Creole, which shows that they had been corrupted by an evil *Spanish* version of slavery. The use of Spanish here should definitely be understood as a criticism. This attribution of guilt relieves the benevolent French Creole gentleman of responsibility for the atrocities of slavery, which were never committed by him, the good white master, but always by someone else (123).

As a result, as a contrast to the above-mentioned stereotype, Hugo develops the model of a justified revolution, exemplified first of all by the representation of the evil "great white man" (*grand blanc*), which conflicts with the plantation owners' picture of themselves; secondly, by the "repentant racist"; and most of all, by the title character, who figures as a noble rebel, in the form of a leader of the Haitian Revolution (ibid.). In order to get Hugo's ideas across, Bug cannot be a hateful slave who has been ruined by slavery, nor can he suffer from the pathological results of the stigmatization of blacks, define himself through white racism, nor internalize its prejudices. He is proud and self-confident and symbolically breaks the whip, the scepter of the white plantation owners' power, "through altruism, not egotism" (124). Bug desires freedom and power for the sake of the good of the other slaves. He wants to reinstate the natural law that the whites overturned with slavery.

The mulattos, who are portrayed in a particularly negative way, manipulate the black masses while Bug Jargal, the royal black prince, avenges the horrors of the decadent plantation owners (Spanish aristocrats) and fights for coexistence with the humane (French) plantation owners with the help of the *congos* who are devoted to him—none of whom have been in the colony long enough to have been corrupted by Spanish slavery (Middelanis 25).

V.5 Chateaubriand as a Model

In J.H.J. Coussin's *Eugène de Cerceil*, the reference to Chateaubriand is both explicit and implicit. Chateaubriand's *Genie du Christianisme* is extolled multiple times:

> It was at this juncture that that immortal work appeared in which, aside from its vast erudition, the most exquisite sensibility can be found, united everywhere with what might be the most brilliant imagination ever to have appeared among humankind: it is clear that I am talking about the *Génie du Christianisme*. The author had traversed the deserts of the New World; he had studied the secrets of Divine Wisdom in the midst of unknown forests and on the banks of unknown rivers to which the earth's inhabitants had not yet even given names. Entering the lists to defend the Christian Religion against the calumnies leveled by bad faith and the imputations uttered by ignorance, he armed himself with all the touching arguments that a deep knowledge of nature can suggest in favor of God's cause and he sketched a series of paintings the like of which no work had ever before presented for human admiration. The desert scenes were the masterpieces of his brush. He knew how to show, in these uncultivated sites that owe everything to nature, ravishing beauties that are far superior to anything that can be offered by the countrysides of those cultivated countries where the landscape is almost nothing but what man prescribes it to be. (Coussin I:xj-xiij)[12]

---

[12] "C'est dans ces entrefaites que parut cet ouvrage immortel, où, indépendamment d'une vaste érudition, la sensibilité la plus exquise se trouve partout unie à une imagination la plus éclatante peut-être qui ait jamais paru parmi les hommes: on voit que je veux parler du Génie du Christianisme. L'auteur avoit parcouru les déserts du Nouveau-Monde; il avoit étudié les secrets de la Sagesse Divine au milieu des forêts inconnues, et sur les bords de fleuves ignorés auxquels les habitants de la terre n'avoient pas même encore donné des noms. Entrant dans la lice pour

Two pages later, Chateaubriand's *Atala* is named as a source:

> I was born on an island which may be one of the countries in the world that presents the most of these kinds of beauty. Often, in my youth, traversing the rough mountains of my native country and losing my way under the domes of the virgin forests that still largely cover it, I grieved that the sublime scenes that surrounded me had not yet met the poets nor the painters who would have tried to render them. When I read the description of the desert in *Atala*, I went into transports at finding again the scenes that I had so long admired just about alone. It is well-known that the men who inhabit the colonies, generally speaking, have but one single object in view: the desire to enrich themselves. These sublime scenes whose aspect caused me such a lively admiration were perceived with cold and indifferent eyes by most of those to whom it was given to contemplate them; or if these so beautiful tableaus sometimes stimulated their dormant sensibility, the emotion was weak and immediately evaporated. In the eyes of those who have given themselves over to it, the love of gold almost always pollutes the colors of the most magnificent landscapes. (xiiij-xiv)[13]

We could list several other examples here of the intensive reception of Chateaubriand by Caribbean writers. But the decisive question is why there was such a marked focus on the nobleman from Brittany. Quite a few writers experienced the French Revolution as a traumatic break in their lives. The lot of the aristocrat Chateaubriand was the deprivations and depressions of exile; some of his rela-

---

défendre la Religion Chrétienne contre les calomnies de la mauvaise foi, et les imputations de l'ignorance, il s'arma de tous les argumens touchans qu'une connoissance approfondie de la Nature suggère en faveur de la cause de Dieu, et il traça une série de tableaux, telle que jamais ouvrage n'en avoit encore présenté une semblable à l'admiration humaine. Les scènes de déserts surtout furent les chefs-d'œuvre de son pinceau. Il sut faire appercevoir dans ces sites incultes qui doivent tout à la Nature, des beautés ravissantes, bien supérieures à celles que peuvent offrir les campagnes de ces contrées cultivées, où le paysage n'est presque partout que ce que l'homme lui prescrit d'être."

13 "Je suis né dans une île qui est peut-être un des pays du monde qui présentent le plus de ces sortes de beautés. Souvent dans ma jeunesse, en parcourant les montagnes aspères de ma terre natale, et en m'égarant sous les dômes des forêts vierges qui la couvrent encore en grande partie, je m'affligeois que les tableaux sublimes dont j'étois environné, n'eussent point encore rencontré de poëtes ni de peintres qui eussent essayé de les rendre. Lorsque je lus la description du désert dans Atala, je retrouvais avec transport des scènes pareilles à celles que, depuis longtemps, j'admirois à-peu-près tout seul. On le sait; les hommes qui habitent les colonies, n'ont guère, généralement parlant, qu'un unique objet en vue; le desir de s'enrichir. Ces scènes sublimes, dont l'aspect me causoit une admiration si vive, étoient apperçues avec des yeux froids et indifférens par la plupart de ceux auxquels il étoit donné de les contempler; ou si ces tableaux si beaux stimuloient quelquefois leur sensibilité endormie, cette émotion étoit foible et s'évaporoit à l'heure même. L'amour de l'or salit presque toujours aux yeux de celui qui y est livré, les couleurs des plus magnifiques paysages."

tives were executed. And even the liberal Madame de Staël, for example, who had greeted the Revolution with great enthusiasm at the beginning, was soon confronted with the era's shadow sides (Kirsch 173). For our examination here, what is important is that what prompted the writing of novels by these authors was not so much their personal suffering as it was the consciousness of a homelessness in the no-man's-land between the sunken old world and a new one whose contours were still very indeterminate.

The world of objects, the landscape, animals, and vegetation were still mostly just backdrops in eighteenth-century literature. Chateaubriand's books about Indians marked the beginning of the French novel's position as a place where creative consciousness met nature, where the prejudices of the "civilized" were put aside so that the socially uprooted individual could create a new home in the cosmos. Karl Hölz (33) points out that the cultural openness towards the Other has different names depending on the mood and the situation. Civilized René, the hero of the story that bears his name, who seeks the alternative of a wild life among the Indians, experiences his cultural split as a double alienation. While as a Frenchman he is marginalized among the Indians, as a naturalized Indian he is put on trial before a war tribunal by the French, of all people, for disturbing the colonial order. And that is when a new dimension is added: under these constraints, his cultural exile is intensified into an in-between space of mutual exclusions, "without a homeland, between two homelands" (*sans patrie, entre deux patries*; Chateaubriand, *Les Natchez* 296, cited in Hölz 33). Later, René describes the resulting sorrow to his Indian wife, Celuta, as a double loss of culture and nature: "In Europe, in America, society and nature wearied me" (*En Europe, en Amérique, la société et la nature m'ont lassé*; ibid.).

Kirsch makes it clear that now, unlike in the eighteenth century, nature no longer offers a refuge. The intact world that Chateaubriand's René hopes to find among the Indians of North America is then destroyed by European influences and, not least, by the actions of the hero himself (Kirsch 174; cf. Chateaubriand, *René* [1802] and *Les Natchez* [1826]). In a Europe that denies all ties that have evolved, René's sensibility has lost its way into love for his sister, and his life with the Natchez is also a wrong track that pulls an entire people into the downfall of the problematic hero. The reason for this *mal du siècle*, this unease of the century, which makes any search for happiness illusory, lies in the hopeless displacedness of the self, which cannot find a shelter either in the past or in the future: "The Revolution, finally, did not make us masters either of ourselves or of the world. Which is why this metaphysical anguish has returned" (Barbéris 144; cited in Kirsch 174–175).[14]

It is the collapse of the old value system that pushed Chateaubriand to explore mythical primordial zones, but that collapse also encouraged a poetic engagement with the experience of inner and outer isolation. The more immediately the downfall of the ancien régime was experienced and felt, the more unavoidable was the retreat into isolation of the novel's subject. The depths of solitude made possible the resulting regenerating encounter with the natural world and with the myths that compensated the self for its loss by making it into the lord of creation (Kirsch 178). Given the dynamics of a society that was looking for just the right amount of connection to tradition and optimism for the future after the convulsions of the revolutionary age and the Napoleonic wars, the flight into the wilderness had to be followed by a return to civilization and a reflection on civilization's problems.

The Romantic drama of passions that is staged in *Atala* positions Chateaubriand in the context of an America that is underdeveloped in terms of civilization. The framework is provided by the history of the Natchez that he has planned, which he introduces in the foreword to the first edition as an "epic of natural humankind" (*epopée de l'homme de la nature*; *Les Natchez* [1826] 16, cited in Matzat 113). Looking at the spatial basis of the structure of the subject, we can see that the space of America is semanticized in three different ways. Matzat shows that it is marked by the juxtaposition of two different unspoiled forms of society, namely that of the "hunters" (*chasseurs*) and that of the "tillers of the soil" (*laboureurs*); on the other hand, especially for Atala and Chactas, it provides a space for exile outside of society (13). The first level of semanticization is the "hunters," the uncivilized, nomadic Indian tribes. It is no wonder that their way of life is represented with ambivalence. In Chactas's account of his imprisonment, the indigenous population, living close to a state of nature, is first celebrated, in Rousseauian fashion:

> Although I was a prisoner, I could not help, during those first days, admiring my enemies. The Muskogee, and even more so his ally the Seminole, breathes gaiety, love, contentment. His gait is light, his manner candid and easy. He speaks much and volubly; his language is musical and smooth. (Chateaubriand, *Atala* trans. Heppenstahl 10)[15]

---

14 "La Révolution, finalement, ne nous a réellement rendus maîtres ni de nous-mêmes ni du monde. D'où le retour de l'angoisse métaphysique."
15 "Tout prisonnier que j'étais, je ne pouvais, durant les premiers jours, m'empêcher d'admirer mes ennemis. Le Muscogulge, et surtout son allié le Siminole, respire la gaieté, l'amour, le contentement. Sa démarche est légère, son abord ouvert et serein. Il parle beaucoup et avec volubilité; son langage est harmonieux et facile" (Chateaubriand, *Atala* 40, cited in Matzat 113).

Later, however, as Chactas's execution draws near, the population's emotionless cruelty is lamented (Chateaubriand, *Atala* 52, cited in Matzat 113). This is consistent with Chateaubriand's affirmation in the foreword that, unlike Rousseau, he is no "fan of savages" (*enthousiaste de Sauvages*; Chateaubriand, *Atala* 19, cited in Matzat 113). Matzat, however, also points out that Rousseau himself in no way ignored the cruelty of earlier social orders.

In describing the second social level, the society of the "tillers of the soil," Chateaubriand again follows Rousseau's parameters. The mission founded by O. Aubry is characterized as "a touching blend of social life and the life of nature" (Chateaubriand, *Atala* trans. Heppenstahl 46).[16] Aubry is described as having succeeded in taking the roughness from the indigenous peoples, who had now become settled, while still allowing them to keep "that simplicity which produces happiness" (Chateaubriand, *Atala* trans. Heppenstahl 41).[17] Once again, what we are seeing here is that threshold state between nature and culture that Rousseau so celebrated. Using the social stages of "hunters" and "tillers of the soil," Chateaubriand continues the conceptions of nature and the utopian designs that were put forward by Rousseau and other Enlightenment thinkers.

The third way in which the American space is semanticized, however, acts in a completely opposite way (Matzat 114). The stylization of that space as a space of exile corresponds to the definitions (often motivated by Christianity) of the Romantic experience of otherness.[18] The protagonists of this third way are Chactas and Atala. The American natural world has become an exile, or a non-place, for them even before their love: for Chactas because he has been separated from his tribe members as a result of military conflicts; for Atala because, as a mestizo woman and a Christian, she is no longer able to feel a part of her people (ibid.) After their shared flight, as they wander through the wilderness alone and Atala, as "exile's daughter" (*fille de l'exile*), sings the song of her "absent fatherland" (*patrie absente*), they seem to be completely outcast. (Chateaubriand, *Atala* trans. Heppenstahl 31; Chateaubriand, *Atala* 58–59, cited in Matzat 114). This subject is treated to one last culmination in the epilogue, where the later fate of the Natchez is outlined. After the tribe has been killed off in battle with the French, the last survivors seek a new place to live. How, then, could

---

16 "Le mélange le plus touchant de la vie sociale et de la vie de nature" (*Atala* 71, cited in Matzat 113).
17 "Cette simplicité qui fait le bonheur" (*Atala* 67, cited in Matzat 113).
18 There is of course a corresponding expression of the Romantic experience of alienation to be found in Chateaubriand's claims about the "wave of passions" (*vague de passions*), even though the word "exile" is not used there (Matzat 114).

their lament be otherwise than "we are exiles, and we look for a place to settle" (Chateaubriand, *Atala* trans. Heppenstahl 74).[19]

Matzat concludes that the juxtaposition of these semanticizations points to a social-critical intention, in the tradition of the Enlightenment. The "hunters," for example, stand for the "well-being and the woes of the natural state," while the society of the "tillers of the soil" stands for a utopian reconciliation of nature and culture, thus serving as a model for a positive form of civilizational progress; the uprooted existence of Atala and Chactas, meanwhile, and even more so the later fate of the Natchez, indicate the negative effects of European colonization. And yet these social-critical implications are breached by the Romantic associations given to the theme of exile, which refers to an experience of estrangement that is not primarily historical but, rather, metaphysical, and is, as such, irrevocable. It is thus no coincidence that Caribbean writers, even in a situation of historical in-betweenness, were particularly open to a reception of Chateaubriand. And yet the in-betweenness of Caribbean literatures has its own particular character that is distinct from that of French Romanticism: someone like Chateaubriand still partakes of a universe in which the frame of reference is clear, but for nineteenth-century French literatures, that frame of reference has been breached in multiple ways. The transfer processes that make up the patterns of receptions are highly complex and thus cannot be reconstructed in a linear fashion.

Chateaubriand wrote the two stories *René* and *Atala* when, after turning away from Napoleon, he was seeking refuge in Catholicism from the new historical reality, which he now perceived as threatening. Even the Bourbon Restoration was not able to patch the break. With no hope of a return to the old order, he turned with renewed interest to the New World, where he had already traveled early on, shortly after the Revolution. He saw a perpetuation of the old ways in the social order that had been handed down there and identified it with the "noble savage," however incongruous it might seem to identify a slave living under a paternalistic master as "savage" or wild. All of this is of a piece with the depiction of a natural idyll that does not exist in France and that represents a state of nature, a God-given order, that still endures in spite of the fundamental change on the European continent, though it is "still," tendentially, being suppressed.

This perspective is taken as a model by many Antillean writers, who suppress their fear of the possible coming break with the system of slavery and concentrate on the natural beauty on their islands (cf. Hartog). While the French

---

19 "Nous sommes des exilés, et nous allons chercher une patrie" (*Atala* 59, cited in Matzat 114).

mother country has to provide for the perpetuation of the idyll, it is also from that same mainland that seditious ideas also come, so that the harmony and legality of the (colonial) order in fact must be demonstrated to the French themselves. The Caribbean is nature and France is culture, although this contrast need not necessarily lead to an antagonistic conflict but should rather be thought of as a mutual enhancement. The Europeans first have to convince themselves of the Caribbean harmony of the plantations by seeing it with their own eyes, in order to understand that this is not some system of oppression driven by the whites but rather a coexistence that best corresponds to the nature of both sides, that of the masters and that of the slaves. It is not the mother country that is imposing a foreign order; instead, this order is one that the inhabitants actually have to defend against the political ideas coming from Europe that lump all societies together. Wherever advocates of independence appear, they are emissaries of France's revolutionary ideas and they quickly recognize that their conceptions of the colonies have no basis in reality.

> In order to rectify ... his judgments and to initiate him ... into the splendors of this vegetation which has no peer in the world and to the spectacle of the activity of a plantation, of the expanse of the properties, and of the curious and original aspect of the relationships between master and slave, I decided to take him ... to one of the largest sugar plantations on the island. (Eyma, "Les Borgias Noirs" 118; cf. Wogatzke 164)[20]

Unlike the Spanish-speaking authors, the French-language writers depict nature that has been cultivated by mankind as an extension of the tropical idyll. The gardens and plantations are paradises created by human hands. Prévost, Maynard, and Eyma design a picture of tranquility that is intended to justify slavery (Wogatzke 164). The novels are primarily addressed to an audience made up of French readers on the mainland, whose revolutionary ideas are much more in need of subduing than the barely existing ones of the local population. However, even the abolitionists among the Antillean writers address themselves to France, since their efforts appear to find very little resonance in the population there at home.

---

20 "Afin de rectifier ... ses jugements et de l'initier ... aux splendeurs de cette végétation qui n'a pas sa pareille dans le monde, au spectacle de l'activité d'une habitation, de l'étendue des propriétés, du côté curieux et original des rapports entre le maître et l'esclave, je résolus de le conduire ... sur une des sucreries les plus considérables de l'île."

The Specific Situation in Haiti: The Primacy of Enlightenment

In Haiti, after a phase of partial rejection of the political and cultural manifestations of the former colonial ruler, the extremely varied attempts to define the country's own self-understanding as Latin America's first independent black state finally led back to acknowledging France's guiding role yet again: but this was the France of Enlightenment, not the France of Romanticism (Wogatzke 53). In the September 7, 1867 *Moniteur*, D. Delorme emphasizes that a civilization based on French Enlightenment ideals will gain a foothold:

> The civilization that we want to introduce into the country will enter there by way of public education. These are the lights, radiating in all directions, that will spread the sound notions of order, law, and progress in a society throughout the Republic. There could not even be any natural, profitable, and solid wealth without the clarities of mind that show the path to be followed, the means to employ, and the goal to achieve. (46)[21]

Over and over again, Delorme returns to the Enlightenment's metaphor of light, and with regard to the educational system, he writes that higher education must be developed as much in Haiti as it is in Paris (Brutus 231, cited in Wogatzke 53). In *Lettres créoles*, Raphaël Confiant and Patrick Chamoiseau (86) highlight this aspect. Bergeaud's title character, Stella, for instance, they write, is nothing other than a personification of freedom! At the end of the novel, they go on, this allegory supports the idea of a generous France that advances freedom in the world through the universal declaration of human and civil rights. They see the distinction between France as colonizer and conqueror, on the one hand, and France as mother of the arts, literature, and freedom, on the other —a distinction that appears banal today—as having existed since 1859 (cf. also Wogatzke 509).

---

21 "La civilisation que nous voulons introduire dans le pays y entrera par l'instruction publique. Ce sont les lumières qui, rayonnant de tous les côtés, répandront dans la République les saines notions d'ordre, de droit et de progrès d'une société. Il ne saurait y avoir même de richesse naturelle, profitable et solide, sans les clartés de l'esprit, qui indiquent la route à suivre, les moyens à employer, le but à atteindre."

V.6 The Reception of French Romanticism and Its Cultural-Hegemonic Consequences

Nineteenth-century Caribbean literatures and the literary production of French Romanticism cannot be considered in isolation from each other. Watson, writing about British Romanticism, reaches a similar conclusion:

> In the end, then, *Caribbean Culture and British Fiction in the Atlantic World* shows that realism and romance in the Caribbean context can not be easily disentangled, just as in the nineteenth century Britain and the West Indies were mutually constitutive rather than discrete entities. Again and again, the attempt to narrate the Caribbean from the point of view of plausibility, verifiability, and reason—realism, in other words—turns into the very forms it seeks to avoid: romantic narrative and its cognates, the gothic, the sentimental, and the melodrama. (Watson 6)

Watson notes that "the history of the Caribbean—which from the point of view of Britain is the history of vast wealth, success, and imperial centrality turning into impoverishment and marginality—is continually transforming itself into romance" (3). Does the same apply to French Romanticism as well?

In his classic text *Culture and Imperialism*, Edward Said asks about the hegemonic tendencies that were transported and carried into the colonial space through literature and culture. He is concerned with images and forms of representation that have to do with the Otherness of the non-European dominions and their residents and that develop a gravitational force that integrates that Other. This takes place by way of the propagation of Eurocentric categories and values that position the Other both inside and outside the circle of belonging at the same time, putting it in its place and thus culturally justifying sovereignty, in other words a biopolitics that gains even more power and consensus through the cultural filter and amplifier. Although Said's focus is English literature and its stabilizing function for the British Empire, he also provides a few examples of the expansion of French culture—which takes a very different form—into the colonial realm. Thus, for example, he refers to the ubiquitous use in literature of the figure of Napoleon, which, given the exotic stylization of the general and emperor's Corsican background and physiognomy, provides a figure of identification that could also, and especially, develop a particular cohesive power among the mulattos of the overseas dominions. He also refers to the mastery with which literature makes use of academic discourses on the Orient and Africa and has created a breadth of impact for specialized knowledge about the ethnically and culturally Other that is unthinkable within the English system that so strictly separates fields of knowledge. And yet, although Said's concerns are absolutely justified and his conclusions very insightful, the (potential) recipients of these hegemonic discourses finally appear in his writing only implicitly and remain nothing but objects. In the context of this study, on the other hand, I want to ask how both sides engage as *subjects* within the processes that establish cultural hegemony. And here, the Spanish-language Caribbean (and Latin American) literature of the nineteenth century appears to show that Spain lost its gravitational force as a colonial power and that its cultural hegemony was dissolved.

The complexity of functioning cultural hegemony can be seen in its capacity to integrate resistance, even in the very center of colonial power. The integrative figure of Napoleon that Said describes finds its counterpart, complex and broken in many ways, in the Haitian independence fighter Toussaint Louverture, in Lamartine's abolitionist drama of the same name (1850). The play begins at the moment in which Toussaint's rule holds out the prospect of a free, mixed-race society on Saint-Domingue for the first time. The liberator is celebrated by the people as a divine emissary. With the arrival of Napoleon, two leaders are juxtaposed, and Napoleon and his entourage appear as two-faced, morally corrupt figures.

> Thus, Lamartine succeeds in making Toussaint into the agent of his own anti-Bonapartism and to stylize his rejection of slavery; the result, however, is that the author has created a black Napoleon who unites in himself all of the positive values that are attributed to the white one by his apologists. (Middelanis 115)[22]

Even if this is just a small element of a much more global hegemonic discourse, this discourse, or rather this almost nonverbal form of representation, is reflected and reproduces itself even in the act of resistance.

The Spanish mother country played a much less important role in the independence literature of the Spanish-speaking Caribbean than did France. This can be traced back not only to Spain's cultural decline, which had already been going on for a long time, but also to the short phase of Napoleonic sovereignty and the direct inspiration of the ideas of the French Revolution for Latin America's political liberation movement.

What is particularly noticeable about the French imperial experience is that, in comparison to Spain, it possesses a much stronger coherence and cultural gravitational force. The idea of an overseas dominion—the extension beyond immediately bordering territories out to very distant lands—has a great deal to do

---

[22] "So gelingt es Lamartine, Toussaint zum Agenten seines eigenen Antibonapartismus und seiner Ablehnung der Sklaverei zu stilisieren; allerdings mit der Konsequenz, dass der Autor einen schwarzen Napoleon geschaffen hat, der alle positiven Werte, die dem weißen von seinen Apologeten zugeschrieben werden, in sich vereint."

with cultural projections and justifications and acquires a continuing validity through actual expansion, administration, capital investment, and engagement. In France's case, the imperial culture displays systematic features that can be summarized in the phrase "civilizing mission," which are largely lacking in Spain (cf. Said xix). The processes of colonialism went beyond the level of economic contexts and political decisions and were solidified by the authority and unchallenged competence of cultural assessments and the continued consolidation in literature on the level of national culture. Might one even go so far as William Blake, who proclaimed, in his comments on Reynolds's *Discourses* on British Imperialism, that "the Foundation of Empire is Art and Science. Remove them or Degrade them and the Empire is No more. Empire follows Art and not vice versa as Englishmen suppose" (cf. Said 13)?

With the exception of Haiti, there is a clear connection in the Caribbean between political and cultural dependence on France, the mother country. The texts produced by writers anticipate the political events or, more specifically, the achievement or non-achievement of independence. This phenomenon also provides the most important reference points for the different colonial relationship and the very severe detachment of the Spanish colonies from their mother country.[23]

V.7 Conviviality and Relationalism in the French Colonial Empire: A Transoceanic Comparison

With regard to the interplay that we have addressed in this chapter between the political and cultural dependence of the French-speaking colonies on France, the mother country (always also keeping Haiti in mind as the exception), it is worth taking a look, in closing, at a transoceanic comparison between the island landscapes of the Atlantic and of the Pacific. If we take the island landscape seriously as a topos of paradigm building in cultural studies,[24] then seeing a landscape means adjusting one's view of a piece of the visible world so as to see it as a virtual aesthetic image (Schmeling and Schmitz-Emans 22). Seeing a part of the world, in this case the ocean, as a landscape assumes a certain distance, as well as an aesthetic attitude that is to be distinguished from the attitude of practical usefulness. An island landscape, or seascape, can therefore only emerge as a his-

---

[23] This assumes a cultural theory that grants the decisive role to cultural hegemony as the legitimizing agency for the power relationship.
[24] For the following remarks cf. Müller, "Chorégraphies"; Müller, "Victor Hugo y Pierre Loti"; Müller, "Konvivenz und Relationalität."

torical phenomenon if the cultural preconditions are in place. Among these preconditions are, first and foremost, that the world no longer appears as a mythical stranger but rather as a space that humans can actively shape (ibid.). Because the subject-space relationship is constitutive for every kind of definition of landscape, the higher-level concept of space is a fundamentally dynamic concept. The marine landscape, as it is understood here—as a culturally and socially produced space—therefore inscribes itself in the semantics of spatial dynamics.

While I will be talking, in the following, primarily about questions of conviviality and relationality, we should remember that these paradigms have definitely been reflected on in the context of the Atlantic Ocean, unlike the case for the Pacific (cf. "Black Atlantic", "archipelagic thinking", etc.; see also ch. VII of this book). If we were to try to undertake a genealogical examination of this conceptual toolkit we would soon find ourselves back in the nineteenth century, for instance if we think about the fact that for any understanding of *Créolité*, it is absolutely necessary to engage with the system of the plantation society (Benítez Rojo, *La isla* 396, not present in English translation; see also Delle). But how, then, are these transatlantic categories developed and reflected in the Pacific? Given a similar colonial history, and in the context of ever more acute questions of globalization, it is imperative to take a look at this other oceanic dimension. What are the connections between transatlantic and transpacific knowledge? What do the main differences consist of, and what do they tell us in reference to colonial dynamics? In view of France's colonial presence in the Atlantic, on the one hand, and in the Pacific, on the other, it would seem promising to do a comparative investigation of the geopolitical dimensions of cultural forms of French-language representation. The effects of French colonialism are still very present in both of these regions: Martinique, Guadeloupe, and French Guiana have had the status of French overseas departments (*départements d'outre-mer*, or DOM) since 1946; French Polynesia, including Tahiti, is an overseas collectivity (*collectivité d'outre-mer*, or COM), sometimes referred to as an overseas country (*pays d'outre-mer*, or POM); and New Caledonia has the special status of a special collectivity (*collectivité sui generis*). Among other forces, there are two universities that still institutionalize France's cultural influence: Tahiti's University of French Polynesia; and the University of the French West Indies and Guiana (UAG), based in Schoelcher, on Martinique, and with branches in Guadeloupe and Guiana.

Against the backdrop of this colonial French mapping that spans the globe, I would like to look more closely at two representative examples that reflect, respectively, the transatlantic and the transpacific cultural and theoretical formations of landscape. The first is Victor Hugo's first book, *Bug-Jargal* (1818, or 1826), where I would like to look again at his representation of Haiti and connect it with other transatlantic works by the same author (*Paysages de la mer* [Sea landscapes], *Les travailleurs de la mer* [The Toilers of the Sea], "L'archipel de la Manche" [The archipelago of La Manche]); the second is Pierre Loti's novel *Le mariage de Loti* (Loti's marriage, 1870), which describes the autobiographical first-person narrator's encounter with Tahiti, an encounter that seems at first to be less politically motivated than Hugo's representation of Haiti. These two authors seem particularly appropriate for a comparison of Pacific and Atlantic literary landscapes because each of them has written several texts that, not coincidentally, center on the respective oceans. In Loti's case, the other relevant work is *L'île de Pâques. Journal d'un aspirant de la Flore* (Easter Island. Diary of a naval cadet on La Flore).

How are conviviality and relationality, as highly complex spaces, presented in literature in the context of the Atlantic and the Pacific? To what extent do the literary versions of the two oceans play a role in questions of conviviality? Because archipelagic thinking has established itself as a cultural studies topos for analyses of the present day (see chapter VII), the question arises as to how far the islands were already multiply linked in the nineteenth century, to an extent that has so far been underestimated. What role does the oft-cited strong gravitational pull of French colonialism play, along with the civilizing mission that is specific to it? Or, more concretely: how is the so-called "trans" staged in the literature that was produced during the colonial expansion? In an excerpt from Hugo's "La Mer et le vent" (The ocean and the wind) the power that he attributes to the Atlantic Ocean is vividly evoked:

> Marine appearances are so fleeting that if one observes them for a long time, the look of the sea becomes purely metaphysical; that brutality degenerates into an abstraction. It is a quantity that decomposes and recomposes itself. This quantity is expandable: it holds infinity. Mathematics, like the ocean, is an undulation with no possible stopping. The wave is vain like the number. It, too, needs an inert coefficient. It is meaningful by the reef as the number is made meaningful by zero. The ocean's flows, like numbers, have a transparency that allows the depths to be seen below them. They disappear, erase themselves, reconstruct themselves, do not exist at all in themselves, waiting to be used, they multiply themselves as far as the eye can see in the darkness, they are always there. Nothing allows us a vision of numbers like the view of the water. Above this reverie the hurricane soars. (Hugo, "La Mer et le vent" 17)[25]

---

[25] "Les apparences marines sont fugaces à tel point que, pour qui l'observe longtemps, l'aspect de la mer devient purement métaphysique; cette brutalité dégénère en abstraction. C'est une quantité qui se décompose et se recompose. Cette quantité est dilatable: l'infini y tient. Le calcul est, comme la mer, un ondoiement sans arrêt possible. La vague est vaine comme le chiffre. Elle a besoin, elle aussi, d'un coefficient inerte. Elle vaut par l'écueil comme le chiffre par le zéro. Les flots ont comme les chiffres une transparence qui laisse apercevoir sous eux des profondeurs. Ils

What we are dealing with here is a metaphysical dimension that was expressed by Pierre Georgel in the aphorism: "There is thus a kind of Hugolian 'oceanic paradigm'" (*Il existe ainsi une sorte de "paradigme océanique" hugolien* [13]). The collection of drawings that Hugo (who was both a writer and a painter) entitled *Paysages de la mer* (Sea landscapes) also fits into this paradigm.

While questions of conviviality in this text are not addressed so much on an ethnic and colonial level, in *Bug-Jargal* they play a central role, as we saw earlier in this chapter when we looked at Hugo as a role model: racist representations collide with the representation of the title character, Bug Jargal, and with some of the narrator's anti-racist statements, which in turn are contradicted by the strong stereotyping in the drawing of the characters, producing an unsettling ambivalence overall. Hugo depicts Haiti as an island that is in danger of losing the values of the French mother country. He examines the coexistence and potential relationality of the various ethnic groups that have happened to encounter each other and that have abandoned the positive conviviality that they used to have under the prerevolutionary colonial government. But what is key here is again the fact that France's strong influence and cohesive power can be traced back to its ability to integrate the colonial Other but also to transform itself in the face of the Other and thus to propagate an idea of apparently positive conviviality.

Atlantic thinking can also be seen in another of Hugo's texts, bearing the telling title *Les travailleurs de la mer* (*The Toilers of the Sea*):

> Nothing is more confusing than to behold the diffusion of forces at work in the unfathomable and boundless waste of waters. One seeks the object of these forces. Space always in motion, the untiring sea, clouds which are busily moving, the vast hidden effort,—all this agitation is a problem. What is accomplished by this perpetual trembling? What do these winds construct? What do these shocks build? These shocks, these sobbings, these howlings of the storm, what do they create? With what does this tumult occupy itself? The ebb and flow of these questions is as eternal as the tide. Gilliatt himself knew what he was about, but the agitation of the vast expanse confused and perplexed him with its unsolvable puzzle. Unconsciously to himself, mechanically, urgently, by pressure and penetration, and without any other result than being unconsciously and almost blindly dazzled,

---

se dérobent, s'effacent, se reconstruisent, n'existent point par eux-mêmes, attendent qu'on se serve d'eux, se multiplient à perte de vue dans l'obscurité, sont toujours là. Rien, comme la vue de l'eau, ne donne la vision des nombres. Sur cette rêverie plane l'ouragan." "La Mer et le vent," a metaphysical reflection on the forces of nature, was originally conceived as part of the novel *Les travailleurs de la mer*, and was included in the 1865 manuscript version of the novel, but was not published until 1911.

> Gilliatt, the dreamer, made the vast and useless labor of the sea subservient to his work. (*The Toilers of the Sea* 71)[26]

The political dimension and the ocean's waves enter into an indissoluble bond. The setting is the Island of Guernsey, in the English Channel, where Hugo lived during his exile, in the Hauteville House, and where he undertook extensive studies of the island's geography, nature, and population.

> Gilliatt climbed upon the Great Douvre. From this position he surveyed the vast expanse of ocean. The view toward the west was peculiar. A wall was rising from it. A great wall of cloud barred the expanse from side to side and was slowly ascending from the horizon toward the zenith. This wall, rectilinear, vertical, without a crevice in its entire height, without a rent in its outline, seemed as square as though laid out by rule and line. (*The Toilers of the Sea* 186)[27]

Antje Ravic Strubel points out that Victor Hugo had conceived of the *The Toilers of the Sea* as the last part of a trilogy presenting the three powers with which humans must wrestle. In *Notre-Dame de Paris* he dealt with the power of religion; in *Les Misérables* it was society that stood at the center. In the third part, it is nature that takes up a large part of the story and that, at the end, takes Gilliatt, the main character, back to itself, after he had formerly conquered nature. The fisherman renounces his love for Deruchette and the sea erases him, just like the sun erases his name from the snow (Strubel).

It appears as though a limited ability to express oneself is the necessary precondition for dealing with nature, which is essentially mute. Strubel also points out that Gilliatt's ponderous articulation stands in stark contrast to the mono-

---

[26] "Voir manœuvrer dans l'insondable et dans l'illimité la diffusion des forces, rien n'est plus troublant. On cherche des buts. L'espace toujours en mouvement, l'eau infatigable, les nuages qu'on dirait affairés, le vaste effort obscur, toute cette convulsion est un problème. Qu'est-ce que ce tremblement perpétuel fait? Que construisent ces rafales? Que bâtissent ces secousses? Ces chocs, ces sanglots, ces hurlements, qu'est-ce qu'ils créent? À quoi est occupé ce tumulte? Le flux et le reflux de ces questions est éternel comme la marée. Gilliatt, lui, savait ce qu'il faisait; mais l'agitation de l'étendue l'obsédait confusément de son énigme. À son insu, mécaniquement, impérieusement, par pression et pénétration, sans autre résultat qu'un éblouissement inconscient et presque farouche, Gilliatt rêveur amalgamait à son propre travail le prodigieux travail inutile de la mer" (*Les travailleurs de la mer* II:62).

[27] "Gilliatt monta sur la grande Douvre. De là, il voyait toute la mer. L'ouest était surprenant. Il en sortait une muraille. Une grande muraille de nuée, barrant de part en part l'étendue, montait lentement de l'horizon vers le zénith. Cette muraille, rectiligne, verticale, sans une crevasse dans sa hauteur, sans une déchirure à son arête, paraissait bâtie à l'équerre et tirée au cordeau" (*Les travailleurs de la mer* II:163; cf. Barnett 159).

logues of the waves, the descriptions of the rugged cliffs of Douvres in their eternal conflict with the water, and the lyrical moods in which Hugo captures the sea and the clouds. Gilliatt, who barely speaks a word in this novel and yet who is talked about most of the time, apparently opens up in the other, non-referential language, in that cyclical becoming and decaying of the plants, in the regularity of the tides and the storms. This will prove to be an advantage in his later death-defying struggle with the sea. The superstition that the population of Guernsey displays as much towards Gilliatt as it does towards, say, the weather, shows the degree to which he himself is perceived as a natural phenomenon. In his broad satire, Hugo mocks such mystifications, which cling to anything that deviates from the usual—even if Gilliatt's supposed witchcraft mostly consists of making the correct deduction from careful observations (ibid.).

In his essay "The archipelago of La Manche" (*L'archipel de La Manche*), which (like "La Mer et le vent" [The wind and the sea], quoted above) was planned as a kind of introduction to *The Toilers of the Sea*, but was then published individually in 1883, Hugo writes:

> The Atlantic wears away our coasts. The pressure of the current from the Pole deforms our western cliffs. This wall that shields us from the sea is being undermined from Saint-Valery-sur-Somme to Ingouville; huge blocks of rock tumble down, the sea churns clouds of boulders, our harbors are silted up with sand and shingle, the mouths of our rivers are barred. Every day a stretch of Norman soil is torn away and disappears under the waves.
> This tremendous activity, which has now slowed down, has had terrible consequences. It has been contained only by that immense spur of land we know as Finistère. The power of the flow of water from the Pole and the violence of the erosion it causes can be judged from the hollow it has carved out between Cherbourg and Brest. The formation of this gulf in the Channel at the expense of French soil goes back before historical times; but the last decisive act of aggression by the ocean against our coasts can be exactly dated. In 709, sixty years before Charlemagne came to the throne, a storm detached Jersey from France. The highest points of other territories submerged in earlier times are still, like Jersey, visible. These points emerging from the water are islands. They form what is called the Norman archipelago. (*The Toilers of the Sea* 5)[28]

---

[28] "L'Atlantique ronge nos côtes. La pression du courant du pôle déforme notre falaise ouest. La muraille que nous avons sur la mer est minée de Saint-Valéry-sur-Somme à Ingouville, de vastes blocs s'écroulent, l'eau roule des nuages de galets, nos ports s'ensablent ou s'empierrent. Chaque jour un pan de la terre normande se détache et disparaît sous le flot. Ce prodigieux travail, aujourd'hui ralenti, a été terrible. Il a fallu pour le contenir cet éperon immense, le Finistère. Qu'on juge de la force du flux polaire et de la violence de cet affouillement par le creux qu'il a fait entre Cherbourg et Brest. Cette formation du golfe de la Manche aux dépens du sol français est antérieure aux temps historiques. La dernière voie de fait décisive de l'océan sur notre côte a pourtant date certaine. En 709, soixante ans avant l'avènement de Charlemagne, un coup de mer a détaché Jersey de la France. D'autres sommets des terres antérieurement submergées sont,

This quotation makes it very clear that a submarine archipelagic dimension has already been envisaged here, but it is never productively implemented. While conviviality is definitely part of Hugo's project, his idea of relationality is lacking any kind of programmatic character. The representation of the Atlantic as a force of nature is linked to the social revolutionary element. It is only by looking at the revolutionary events in Haiti in 1804, in *Bug-Jargal*, and the force of nature represented by the ocean, in *Les travailleurs de la mer*, together that the overarching function of a cultural landscape of the Atlantic Ocean reveals itself; this cultural landscape does not, however, take in the cultural elements of the individual islands but is, instead, linked back to Paris, the colonial center, as its sole point of reference.

Pierre Loti, on the other hand (whose real name was Julien Vaud, 1850– 1923), writes in his travelogue about Easter Island: "the indigenous race is extinct, the island is now nothing more than a great solitude in the middle of the ocean, inhabited only by old stone statues" (Loti, *L'Île de Pâques* 32).[29] Loti arrived on Easter Island on January 7, 1872, as a lieutenant on the French warship La Flore. His description of the island, while it is dominated by the idea of isolation, is also marked by a striking sense that the island's relational character is significant. But the many-faceted relationships are not described as positive; instead, they are mentioned in a matter-of-fact way, and often used for static comparisons:

> Around me a sort of plaintive and lugubrious chant was being sung, the same notes repeated indefinitely, without stopping; the harmony, the rhythm, and the voices could not be compared with the most bizarre things we hear in Europe, and even the African woman's most audacious passages are still far from this ideal of savagery. (37)[30]

The character of the exotic is the dominant note in this text, in the form of an almost depressive underlying mood. It may therefore not be a coincidence that Loti's other novels and travelogues, some of which are surely better known, have met with very differing assessments in the research literature. Karl Hölz, on whose accounts I will rely in the following, emphasizes that Loti's position

---

comme Jersey, visibles. Ces pointes qui sortent de l'eau sont des îles. C'est ce qu'on nomme l'archipel normand" (*Les travailleurs de la mer* I:3).

29 "la race indigène s'est éteinte, l'île n'est plus qu'une grande solitude au milieu de l'Océan, habitée seulement par des vieilles statues de pierre."

30 "On chantait autour de moi une sorte de mélopée plaintive et lugubre, c'était sans cesse les mêmes notes indéfiniment répétées; l'harmonie, le rythme, les voix, n'avaient rien de comparable avec ce que nous entendions de plus bizarre en Europe et les passages les plus audacieux de l'Africaine sont bien loin encore de cet idéal de sauvagerie."

within the exoticizing literature and his contribution to contemporary colonial colonialism are questionable (158). Loti is undisputedly a part of the tradition of literary evasion as developed by Bernardin de Saint-Pierre, Chateaubriand, Fromentin, and on through Gautier and Baudelaire. Just as these authors make the unknown world into a site for the projection of their own wishes and fantasies—with such themes as dreams, nostalgia, and ennui—Loti, too, captures the exotic from the point of view of a subjective sensibility.

Hölz also points out that Loti did not equate exoticism with colonialism in his work. His heroes do not conform to the edifying pioneer spirit of the colonial conquerors, and Loti does not share the enthusiasm of expansionist colonial politics. On the contrary, he counters all arguments with which the politically doctrinaire seek to justify France's colonial rule (159). At the same time, however, it is probably not surprising that in spite of Loti's anti-colonial theses, his subjective exoticism does display the aftereffects of colonial appropriation. Even the very gaze that is turned towards the Other and uses that as an excuse for confirming one's own wishes or fears leads the object, with an imperial air, into the writer's own horizon of consciousness (cf. Hölz 161). It is an open question whether in this case we can even speak of a focus on the representation of conviviality.

In the novel *Le mariage de Loti* (Loti's marriage), the exotic love idyll between the first-person narrator, Harry, and the native beauty Rarahu, from the South Sea Island of Bora Bora, is intertwined with the experience of the ephemeral encounter with the Other. Rarahu, both in her physical and in her psychic constitution, definitely displays the characteristics that match the anthropological constants required by the colonial organizational scheme and by the hero (cf. Hölz 181). Her black eyes, her short, delicate nose, and her long, bushy hair, together with her "exotic languor" and the "coaxing softness" that the hero sees in her eyes, make her recognizable as the "perfect specimen of the Maori race" (*type accompli de cette race maorie*; Loti, *The Marriage of Loti* 16; *Le mariage de Loti* 53, cited in Faessel 137). It is just such ethnic and racial definitions that support the exoticizing vision. The narrator, following the dictates of the biological model of evolution, understands the so-called primitive races as destined for destruction in contact with civilization (cf. Hölz 181). The hero, with patriarchal patience, attempts to explain this cultural-philosophical truth to Rarahu's "childish intelligence": "I am thinking, my little pet, that on those distant seas are scattered many unknown islands; that they are inhabited by a mysterious race destined soon to perish; that you are a child of this primitive race"

(Loti, *The Marriage of Loti* 109).³¹ Rarahu, in frustration, confirms to the narrator that for racial reasons her fate is hopeless, but she contains that hopelessness in a sobered view of love that can only assure itself of the white man's sympathetic compassion in that moment (cf. Hölz 182).

Torsten König's reading of Loti points the way for the differentiation of Pacific studies with reference to the French colonial empire. He describes how *Le mariage de Loti* takes up the myth of the delicious island (*île délicieuse*) that Bougainville and Diderot created. Tahiti appears as the New Cythera, an island of love where young women are offered to foreign travelers and where the "noble savage" also survives in an effervescent nature (cf. König, "L'imaginaire géopolitique" 135). Loti continues the writing of this myth, evoking Western fantasies of the *vahiné*, the Tahitian woman. His fantasies are mixed with picturesque descriptions of a nature that offers everything in overabundance: the pleasurable tropics. He blends in elements of a tropical exoticism that was very much in fashion at that time—think of Baudelaire's *Fleurs du mal* (1857/1868) or Paul Gauguin's *Noa-Noa* (1897) (cf. König, "L'imaginaire géopolitique" 136).

After traveling to the Pacific in 1871 to 1872, Loti had an idea of the difficult living conditions in Tahiti. This experience probably provided the basis for his report on the sad results, for the native population, of the European invasion. Faced with the degenerate Tahitian society, he describes the disappearance of the pure, innocent wild Tahitian of the precolonial era. In his pseudo-ethnographic fiction, Loti openly criticizes colonialism from the point of view of an exoticism that takes on decidedly racist traits. *Le mariage de Loti* corresponds to a stage in Western thinking that wanted to assimilate the Other (cf. König, "L'imaginaire géopolitique" 136). Loti uses the words "Tahiti" and "Polynesia" to build a projection screen for European imaginations. His text is full of pointers to the isolation of the islands:

> Go far away from Papeete, whither civilization has not penetrated; where, under the slender coco-palms, the native Tahitian villages are strown, huts thatched with pandanus-leaves, on the very edge of the coral reef and the immense and solitary ocean. See the tranquil, dreaming hamlets, the groups of natives lounging at the feet of the great trees—silent, passive, and idle, feeding, as it would seem, on the cud of speechless contemplation. Listen to the utter calm of nature, the monotonous, eternal murmur of the breakers on the barrier reef; look at the stupendous scenery, the tors of basalt, the dark forests clinging to the

---

31 "Je pense, ô ma petite amie, que sur ces terres lointaines sont disséminés des archipels perdus; que ces archipels sont habités par une race mystérieuse bientôt destinée à disparaître; que tu es une enfant de cette race primitive" (*Le mariage de Loti* 138 and 134, cited in Hölz 181).

mountain's flank—and all this lost in the midst of a vast, immeasurable solitude—the Pacific. (Loti, *The Marriage of Loti* 33)[32]

What does this tell us about our examination of conviviality and relationality? Given the basic tenor of exoticism, the staging of any project of conviviality is only present at a higher level, if at all, namely in the affirmation of the impossibility of a coexistence of cultures within the processes of colonial appropriation, as König shows in his analysis.

This makes the constant staging of relationality all the more striking. Loti's Polynesia reveals itself as a phantasm of European-imagined worlds that are communicated as the geographic fictions of a closed and isolated territory deriving all of its legitimacy from France. The colonial system is based on the relationships between the colony and the colonized island and creates a geocultural imaginary that privileges these particular relationships (cf. König, "L'imaginaire géopolitique" 137). König emphasizes that various zones in the Pacific are perceived, on the one hand, as isolated islands, but that the neighboring islands and the presence of an archipelago also play a significant role. Thus, there are scattered indications of the bond among the islands:

> While very young, her mother had sent her away in a long canoe with sails which was making for Tahiti. She remembered nothing of her native island but the enormous and terrible central tor which towers up from it. The profile of that gigantic block of basalt, rising like a stupendous corner-stone from the bosom of the Pacific, remained in her mind as the only image of her native land. (Loti, *The Marriage of Loti* 13)[33]

---

[32] "Allez loin de Papeete, là où la civilisation n'est pas venue, là où se retrouvent sous les minces cocotiers,—au bord des plages de corail—, devant l'immense Océan désert,—les districts tahitiens, les villages aux toits de pandanus.—Voyez ces peuplades immobiles et rêveuses;—voyez au pied des grands arbres ces groupes silencieux, indolents et oisifs, qui semblent ne vivre que par le sentiment de la contemplation. ... Écoutez le grand calme de cette nature, le bruissement monotone et éternel des brisants de corail;—regardez ces sites grandioses, ces mornes de basalte, ces forêts suspendues aux montagnes sombres, et tout cela, perdu au milieu de cette solitude majestueuse et sans bornes: le Pacifique" (*Le mariage de Loti* 68–69, cited in König, "L'imaginaire géopolitique" 136–137).

[33] "Toute petite, elle avait été embarquée par sa mère sur une longue pirogue voilée qui faisait route pour Tahiti. Elle n'avait conservé de son île perdue que le souvenir du grand morne effrayant qui la surplombe. La silhouette de ce géant de basalte, planté comme une borne monstrueuse au milieu du Pacifique, était restée dans sa tête, seule image de sa patrie" (*Le mariage de Loti* 51).

The protagonist, however, always sees Tahiti from the perspective of France. Applied to all of Polynesia, this perspective can be explained by Papeete's role as the administrative center of the entire French-speaking Pacific.

The influence of Loti's cultural mapping of the Polynesian islands cannot be emphasized enough. At the beginning of the twentieth century, it was difficult to write about the Pacific without referring to Loti.[34] His literary version of Tahiti was paired with a relative silence from ethnography about this region of the world. There are only two ethnological studies of it before the end of the nineteenth century: Jacques-Antoine Moerenhout's *Voyage aux îles du Grand Océan* (Voyage to the islands of the great ocean, 1837) and Édmond de Bovis's *État de la société tahitienne* (State of Tahitian society, 1851) (see König, "L'imaginaire géopolitique" 138). As a result, the history of the cultural and social situation in Polynesia, the exchanges among the islands, and the economic and social networks of the precolonial era remained largely unknown in France. The few publications about the region always repeat the image of the islands lost in the ocean. Thus, for example, in 1908, the Swiss traveler Eugène Hänni writes: "Seeing the vast solitudes of the Pacific open in front of me, and thinking back to the tiny dimensions of the island that I had just left, I said to myself: After all, it is strange to live in such places, simple clumps of grass lost in the immensities of the ocean!" (Hänni 173, cited in König, "L'imaginaire géopolitique" 138).[35]

And yet, over and over in Loti's novel, there are examples of a connection among the individual islands of Oceania, even though the main, dominant connection continues to be the connection to the metropolis:

> Rarahu's mother had brought her to Tahiti, the big island, the queen's island, to make a present of her to a very old woman of the Apiré district to whom she was distantly related. This was in obedience to an ancient custom of the Tahitian race by which children rarely stay and grow up in the care of their mother. (Loti, *The Marriage of Loti* 13)[36]

---

34 Loti did not, however, invent the image of the sensual connection between the European man and the indigenous woman. Maximilien Radiguet, secretary to Admiral Dupetit-Thouars, published *Les Derniers Sauvages, la vie et les mœurs aux îles Marquises, 1842–1859* (The last savages, life and mores in the Marquesas Islands, 1842–1859) in 1860 (see König, "L'imaginaire géopolitique" 137).

35 "En voyant s'ouvrir devant moi les vastes solitudes du Pacifique et en songeant aux minuscules dimensions de l'île que je venais de quitter, je me disais: Tout de même, il est drôle d'habiter dans des endroits pareils, simples mottes de gazon perdues dans les immensités de l'Océan!"

36 "La mère de Rarahu l'avait amenée à Tahiti, la grande île, l'île de la reine, pour l'offrir à une très vieille femme du district d'Apiré qui était sa parente éloignée.
Elle obéissait ainsi à un usage ancien de la race maori, qui veut que les enfants restent rarement auprès de leur vraie mère" (*Le mariage de Loti* 51).

As for the omnipresence of the water, the following passage shows that the fundamental interwovenness has an existential character: "Rarahu and Tiahoui were a pair of careless, laughing little beings, living almost entirely in the waters of their brook where they leaped and sported like a couple of flying-fish" (Loti, *The Marriage of Loti* 19).[37]

In summary, we can say that the representations of the seascape or island landscape serve as indicators as to whether and to what extent the authors have freed themselves from the colonial and exoticist image of nature, producing texts that gradually decipher the land and its landscape anew, thus taking possession of it with their imagination and language. The treatment of the marine landscape in nineteenth-century colonial and postcolonial and often exoticist literature is revealing, because colonization also implied a linguistic and literary occupation. Landscapes were captured and made accessible to the "old" world through European conceptual patterns and patterns of imagery (see Blümig 11). For both Hugo and Loti, these seascapes act as an essential creative source for their writing: the ocean as poetic inspiration but also as a social challenge, with the implied possibility of human trafficking. At first glance, it would not seem as though the concepts of a *Black Atlantic* and a *Black Pacific*,[38] as discussed and used in the debates of current cultural theory, could have much relevance to nineteenth-century debates. And yet it will become apparent that certain of these current viewpoints (see chapter VII) were more present in the nineteenth century, in an underlying way, than has so far been assumed.

Oceania shows itself to be the invisible continent in Loti in that any point of reference is located in the metropolis. But it is significant that the islands' multiple interconnections are also thematized in his texts. There are always subtle hints that there must have been a lively exchange, much more so in Loti than in Hugo, who was definitely interested in reaching the French reading public and making the loss of Saint-Domingue—which had been the pearl in the crown of the French colonial empire—intelligible again. What the two authors have in common is that they both affirm France as the colonial power, with its cultural gravitational force, at every possible opportunity.

In placing conviviality at the center of his conceptual structures, Hugo anticipates the transatlantic theoretical developments that will play a role in the iden-

---

37 "Rarahu et Tiahoui étaient deux insouciantes et rieuses petites créatures qui vivaient presque entièrement dans l'eau de leur ruisseau, où elles sautaient et s'ébattaient comme deux poissons-volants" (*Le mariage de Loti* 56).
38 Think, for instance, of the phenomenon of *blackbirding*, very widespread in Oceania, where South Pacific islanders were conscripted into forced labor starting in the middle of the nineteenth century.

tity discourses of *Créolité* and other such movements two hundred years later. In the transatlantic context, the paradigm of conviviality can be traced back to a social romantic dimension that measures itself against the values of the French Revolution and in so doing undermines multirelational networks. For a long time, therefore, relationality was suppressed in the theoretical discourse. The idea of multiple connections and of underlying archipelagic structures will have to wait a long time to assert itself in the Atlantic region. In the Pacific, on the other hand, cultural theories take the opposite path: because of the exoticizing interpretation that is dominant here, every literary staging of a programmatic concept of conviviality is made obsolete, while elements of relationality are strongly present instead. In the nineteenth century, however, these have not yet been made productive: "In the middle of the Great Ocean, in a region where no one ever goes, there is a mysterious and isolated island; no land lies nearby and for more than eight hundred leagues in every direction, it is surrounded by empty and moving immensities" (Loti, *L'île de Pâques* xxx).[39]

---

[39] "Il est, au milieu du Grand Océan, dans une région où l'on ne passe jamais, une île mystérieuse et isolée; aucune terre ne gît en son voisinage et, à plus de huit cents lieues de toutes parts, des immensités vides et mouvantes l'environnent."

VI Transcaribbean Dimensions: New Orleans as the Center of French-speaking Circulation Processes

VI.1 France and Spain as Colonial Powers in Louisiana

Within the textual production of the Caribbean, our focus has so far been primarily on intra-Caribbean forms of representation, along with a reference to the transoceanic colonial dynamics between the Pacific and the Atlantic. I would now like to widen the radius of our attention, looking at the dimension of the Caribbean periphery and, specifically, at New Orleans as a privileged center of colonial circulation processes within the American hemisphere.[1] New Orleans turns out to be an exciting node for transfer processes, not just because both Spain and France had acted as colonial powers there, but because its early independence from France, compared to the inner Caribbean possessions, had other postcolonial consequences (see Ette and Müller, *New Orleans and the Global South*). How, for instance, are the relationships with the erstwhile mother country, France, articulated in the context of the United States? How do literary stagings use New Orleans as a bridge to link hemispheric constructions of America?

France's colonial power was able to establish a functioning colonial settlement in the Mississippi Delta, namely New Orleans, by the middle of the eighteenth century; after the end of the French and Indian War, however, conditions changed. In the 1763 Paris peace treaty, France gave up its possessions in what is now Canada to Great Britain and lost the Louisiana Territory to Spain. This meant that France now disappeared as a colonial power from the map of North America. It would be another four years, however, before Spain sent colonial officials to Louisiana. It was clear to the Spanish crown that they could keep the territory under their rule over the long term only if they could provide it with a sufficient number of Spanish settlers. But even though the population of New Orleans did indeed grow threefold during Spanish rule, colonization was only very partially successful (Möllers 48).[2]

In between the white upper class—which was made up of former French and newly arrived Spanish colonial officials, along with white plantation owners and traders who had moved from the West Indian islands—and the constantly growing number of slaves, there was a group of free people of color that established

---

1 For the following remarks, cf. Müller, "Writing In-Between."
2 Möllers's study provides the basis for the following summary of historical constellations.

themselves in the last decades of the eighteenth century (ibid.). The growing number of interethnic common-law marriages was accompanied by the Spanish colonial government's special legislation on manumission, which allowed slaves to earn their freedom with money that they earned with extra work outside of their regular work allotment. If an owner tried to set an unfair price, there was supposed to be the possibility of addressing that by having a court determine the price. Möllers points out that although this practice, called "restriction" (*coartación*) in the colonial regions controlled by Spain, did generally make the slaves less dependent on the favor and caprice of the owners, the process of buying one's freedom often turned out to be a very lengthy, costly, and dangerous process. Nevertheless, between 1769 and 1803, 1,490 slaves succeeded in buying their freedom in this way. Given that the total population of Louisiana in 1785 was very low, counting only 4,433 white residents, 9,513 slaves, and 907 free people of color, this number is significant (49).

Because the Spanish colonial government had taken over and continued the French black code (*code noir*) that had been introduced in Louisiana in 1724, freed slaves had exactly the same rights and privileges as all free colonial citizens of Louisiana (ibid.).[3] The fifty-four articles of the code address the rights and regulations affecting the slave population as well as the status of freedmen and freeborn colored people: the article that was decisive for the development of the free people of color outlawed marriage between white and colored residents of Louisiana, no matter what their social status. Extramarital relations between slaves and free people of color were also outlawed.

By the time the United States took over the territory in 1803, a multiethnic society had developed in Louisiana. The influences of the French and Spanish rule had undergone a hybridization with cultural elements from the slave population, immigrants from Haiti and from the Canary Islands lived right next to settlers from Germany and Switzerland, and all of these together contributed to a creolized society and culture that differed from the Anglo-Saxon culture of the other United States states and terrritories in important ways. And yet, in spite of the fact that the population drew from such multiethnic roots, the influence of French culture, in its widest sense, is clearly identifiable, and that led to the creolized society being perceived as French from the outside. But in fact, Louisiana's French-influenced society was marked by the contributions of many immigrant European cultures (53; cf. Smith and Parenton).

---

[3] The black code that was decreed in Louisiana in 1724 was a slightly modified form of the black code that had been enacted in 1685 for the colonial regions in the French Caribbean islands. Cf. *Recueils de Reglemens*.

Because of France's cultural dominance there, many free people of color went from Louisiana to Paris in the eighteen-thirties (cf. Fabre, *From Harlem to Paris*). Especially in the literary world, time spent in Paris was a requirement: B. Valcour and Armand Lanusse went there to study and Victor Séjour, Pierre Dalcour, and Louis and Camille Thierry spent a large part of their lives in France. None of them were either runaway slaves or abolitionists. They belonged to a colored elite that enjoyed a certain economic status in New Orleans.[4] Armand Lanusse, (1810–1868) for example, was the director of New Orleans's black Catholic school from 1852 to 1866. He established the *Album littéraire*, "a journal for young people, amateurs of literature," with Jean-Louis Marciaq, where they published poems and short stories (Fabre, *From Harlem to Paris* 11). Because the writers of the *Album littéraire* occupied such a marginal position in United States society, they looked outside its literature for alternative models and sources of inspirations. They felt closer to the French Romantics, especially Lamartine, Musset, and Béranger, than to any other group of writers.

VI.2 Caribbean Louisiana

In addition to its cultural orientation towards France, Louisiana was also perceived as being part of the Caribbean cultural world. Its geographic and cultural proximity to the Republic of Haiti fueled the fear among the white population of New Orleans and the surrounding sugar parishes that there might be imitators among the local slave population (see Johnson, *The Fear of French Negroes*). Two slave revolts in the parish of Pointe Coupée, in 1791 and 1795, made it clear that this fear was not unfounded. Although the revolts were both nipped in the bud, a possible connection to Saint-Domingue was revealed in the 1791 trial, when the supposed leader of the uprising, a colored man named Pierre Bailly, admitted that he had been waiting for instructions from Saint-Domingue (Möllers 75).

This danger of a violent slave rebellion, possibly instigated and planned by educated free people of color, which hung over the white population like a sword of Damocles, had troubled the Creole slave owners even before the United States took over the rule of Louisiana. But the population that had already set down roots and the new American governmental officials did not always see eye to

---

4 See Candlin and Pybus for examples of entrepreneurial free women of color in Britain's Caribbean colonies. Some of them were able to rise to dizzying heights of success; they exercised remarkable mobility and developed extensive commercial and kinship connections in the metropolitan heart of empire.

eye on how best to prevent the danger. It was agreed that any uprising would primarily arise among slaves from the West Indies, and that their influence in Louisiana should therefore be minimized, but there was no agreement on the consequences of a possible restriction of the labor pool.

From the beginning of the violent clashes in Saint-Domingue, but especially since 1803, white people of color had been fleeing to Cuba with their slaves, as had free people of color (80). When Napoleon's brother Joseph ascended the Spanish throne, there were violent conflicts in Cuba between followers of the Spanish king, Ferdinand VII, and former residents of Saint-Domingue who were loyal to France. From May 1809 to January 1810, 9,059 of these refugees sought asylum in Louisiana, including 3,102 free people of color. The total free population of the Orleans Parish grew from 17,001 in 1806 to 24,552 four years later. Of the main influx of refugees, which took place in 1809, 30 percent were white, 34 percent were free people of color, and 36 percent were slaves.

In addition to the dangers that the Antillean slaves might pose, William Claiborne (1775–1817, and first governor of the state of Louisiana 1812–1816) worried about a potential strengthening of the trans-Caribbean cultural network, which threatened to severely disturb the Americanization of the Orleans area (81). Discussions about possible uprisings referred again and again to the trans-Caribbean connection, which made it more than likely that the local slaves and free people of color would be "infected" (83).

I would like now to take a look at how the image of Louisiana's Creole society was translated into the contemporary literature and how the trans-Caribbean connections are described from a literary viewpoint,[5] using the example of two short stories (published in Paris and in New Orleans, respectively) and a literary-historical treatise (published in Port-au-Prince).

VI.2.1. Victor Séjour: "Le mulâtre" (The Mulatto, 1837)

Victor Séjour's story "Le mulâtre" appeared in the March 1837 issue of the *Revue des Colonies*. The narrator tells a story that he claims to have been told by an old slave named Antoine in the Haitian coastal town of Saint-Marc. It is the story of a young slave woman named Laïsa who, because of her beauty, is bought by a wealthy and influential 22-year-old plantation owner named Alfred. On her way to the plantation, sorrowing that she will be at Alfred's mercy, she discovers

---

5 See also Lowe, who describes this in a broader sense in *The Crosscurrents of Caribbean and Southern Literature*.

that the coachman is her brother Jacques, that the two of them have the same father, a slave named Chambo.[6]

Alfred, who has the reputation of being gracious to whites and pitiless and horrible to slaves, forces Laïsa to share his bed, raping her over a period of months. When Laïsa gets pregnant and her aversion to Alfred in no way lessens, Alfred loses interest in her and chases her away, along with her newborn son, whom she names Georges (he is the mulatto for whom the story is named). Alfred makes Laïsa swear never to tell the boy who his father is, saying that otherwise, he will kill him. Therefore, Laïsa promises Georges that he will learn the identity of his father only when he is twenty-five years old. Laïsa dies within the next few years and gives Georges a portrait of his father, which she asks him not to unwrap until he has turned twenty-five. Out of respect for his dead mother, he honors her request.

Georges and Alfred meet and, over the years, come to value each other. One day, Georges learns of a plot to murder Alfred and hurries to him in order to save him. Alfred, alarmed, thinks Georges's attempts to help him get to safety are part of the plot by the four murderers, and flees from him. Georges takes on the four intruders and kills them all, but he is severely wounded and for two weeks he hovers between life and death. Recognizing his mistake, Alfred sends for the best doctor there is to save Georges, his son.

At this point, Georges's wife is introduced into the story, a colored woman named Zélie with whom he has a two-year-old son. While Georges is wrestling with death, Alfred tries to seduce her with money. She resists, and so Alfred has her brought to his room. But she defends herself against his attempt to rape her and wounds him in the head. Knowing full well that she will be punished with death, she hurries to Georges in tears to tell him the story. A day before she is to be put to death, Georges begs Alfred to intercede and to save his wife, in gratitude for Georges having saved Alfred's life. But Alfred shows no emotion, and when Georges realizes that his pleas are going unheard, he begins to threaten Alfred and to reproach him for the attempted rape. Now he has to flee in order to escape death himself, but he threatens Alfred with revenge. Zélie is hanged, and Georges and his son find refuge among a group of runaway slaves.

Georges waits three years, until Alfred marries and has a child. Then Georges returns to Alfred. Shortly after the birth of the child, Georges sneaks into Alfred's bedroom, poisons Alfred's wife, and threatens to kill Alfred, who implores him to have mercy on him and to give his wife the antidote, which he holds in his

---

[6] I am grateful to Hafid Derbal for important comments that were helpful for this section and for the next one, on Joanni Questy.

hands. After the wife dies, Georges raises his hand to deal the death blow against Alfred, who in that moment says to him that he can now go ahead and kill his father. Georges takes out the portrait, recognizes his damnation, and takes his own life next to his father's dead body.

The story paints a picture of a terrible and unscrupulous slave owner. Antoine, the narrator, explains that Georges, on the other hand, actually has a good heart but that in the face of such injustice even just people become criminals. The story also shows that the "evil" characteristics of the slaves, or of the blacks and the colored people, are produced by this unjust system. Although the modern word "socialization" is not used, that is the process that is being described.

In Louisiana, unlike in texts from the Caribbean itself, references to Africa appear to be part of a pointed political agenda. Whether or not this has anything to do with the wars of secession, which are on the horizon, is unclear. When, at the beginning of the story, the white traveler arrives in Port-au-Prince, he greets a black man with a handshake:

> "Good day, Master," he said, tipping his hat when he saw me.
> "Ah! There you are … ," and I offered him my hand, which he shook in return.
> "Master," he said, "that's quite noble-hearted of you. … But you know, do you not, that a negro's as vile as a dog; society rejects him; men detest him; the laws curse him. …"
> (Séjour, "The Mulatto" 353)[7]

The relatively strong, though always asymmetrical, relationship with Africa becomes particularly obvious when the siblings meet each other and discover that they are in fact siblings.

> "What country are you from, Laïsa?"
> "From Senegal. …"
> Tears rose in his eyes; she was a fellow countrywoman.
> "Sister," he said, wiping his eyes, "perhaps you know old Chambo and his daughter. …"
> (Séjour, "The Mulatto" 355)[8]

---

[7] "—Bonjour maître, me dit-il en se découvrant.
—Ah! Vous voilà. … et je lui tendis la main, qu'il pressa avec reconnaissance.
—Maître, dit-il, c'est d'un noble Coeur ce que vous faites là …; mais ne savez-vous pas qu'un nègre est aussi vil qu'un chien …; la société le repousse; les homes le détestent; les lois le maudissent. …" ("Le mulâtre" 377).

[8] "—De quel pays es-tu, Laïsa?
—Du Sénégal. …
Les larmes lui vinrent aux yeux; il venait de rencontrer une compatriote.

Later, Georges encounters a group of runaway slaves: "'Africa and freedom,' Georges replied calmly, as he pushed aside the barrel of the rifle. ... 'I'm one of you'" (Séjour, "The Mulatto" 364).[9]

Although the city of New Orleans is not explicitly present in the story, the city's status as an intersectional node of the most varied processes of circulation has self-evident consequences that are echoed on many levels of the literary representation. Haiti is the scene of action, in a very natural way, without much leadup. The relationship to Africa is also portrayed in a much more straightforward way, and is treated much more positively, without a lot of throat-clearing, than is the case in the texts of the inner Caribbean: the texts of the Spanish-speaking Caribbean of that time are much more formulaic, while the French-language stories and novels try to draw clearer boundaries.

Inasmuch as an examination of intra-Caribbean transfer processes with an eye to colonial comparisons has to make the connection between the multirelationality of the Spanish colonial realm and the bipolarity of the French colonial realm, always taking into account the potential in-between, this in-between is even more dominant in New Orleans, which probably has to do with the fact that it had been politically detached from the French mother country decades earlier. It speaks for itself that "Le mulâtre" was never able to be published in New Orleans itself, because of new censorship laws that were passed in 1830, but that through its publication in the journal *Revue des Colonies*, which circulated throughout the Caribbean, it found a wide distribution and even a reception far beyond that, for instance in Guiana and some regions of Africa.

VI.2.2 The Return to Haiti. Joanni Questy: "Monsieur Paul" (1867)

In the eighteen-fifties, Louisiana's free people of color suffered severe racist persecution and as a result, many Creoles from Louisiana sought exile in France, Haiti, and Mexico. Fifty years after the wave of immigration from a Saint-Domingue shaken by civil war, a flood of refugees began to go in the other direction. On board the ship Laura, two hundred and fifty emigrants arrived in Port-au-Prince on July 25, 1860:

—Soeur, reprit-il, en s'essuyant les yeux, tu connais sans doute le vieux Chambo et sa fille. ..." ("Le mulâtre" 379).

9 "Afrique et liberté, répondit Georges sans s'émouvoir, mais en repoussant de côté le canon du fusil ... je suis des vôtres" ("Le mulâtre" 388).

We welcome the arrival of these new brothers. May their example be imitated by all those in whose veins African blood flows and who suffer from the vile prejudices of color all over America. May they all come join us to enjoy liberty and equality under the Haitian palms and help us to make of our beautiful country, fertilized by the generous blood of our fathers, the metropolis of the black race in the civilized world. (*Le Progrès. Journal Politique*, Port-au-Prince, September 8, 1860, cited in Duplantier 163)[10]

It was more than just a promise of freedom that lured the refugees from Louisiana to the black republic (Möllers 152).[11] Creoles of color in Louisiana felt a strong connection to Haiti; many of them were only two generations removed from ancestors who had immigrated from the erstwhile Saint-Domingue: in the first decade of the nineteenth century, the influx from Saint-Domingue had been so great (as we saw above) that the population of the city of New Orleans doubled in a year.

In 1867, the daily paper *La Tribune de la Nouvelle-Orléans* published a short story by Joanni Questy entitled "Monsieur Paul." Questy was a prominent poet and educator in New Orleans's Creole society who also wrote for the poetic anthology *Les Cenelles*, which I describe in greater detail below. In "Monsieur Paul," which is probably set around midcentury in New Orleans, the idea of the revolution's refugees and their descendants returning to Haiti is very important (Möllers 151).

After a visit to the theater, the protagonist (who remains nameless in the story, but whom I will call Joanni from here on) makes his way home. On the way, in the dark of the night, he encounters a man, Monsieur Paul, who asks him for a cigarette. They become friends and Monsieur Paul invites Joanni to visit him sometime in the following days. Joanni pays a visit to Monsieur Paul, who is obviously rich and has servants and slaves. But when Monsieur Paul sees Joanni, he cannot hide his perturbation, because in the daylight he recognizes that Joanni is black. The obviousness of his reaction is very embarrassing to Monsieur Paul, and he apologizes to Joanni. He clearly shows him that he does not actually have any problem with it and that skin color will not be an issue for their friendship. A few days later, Joanni receives a handwritten note from Monsieur Paul asking him to visit. At that meeting, Monsieur Paul reveals

---

10 "Nous nous félicitons de la prochaine arrivée de ces nouveaux frères. Puisse leur exemple être imité par tous ceux dans les veines desquels coule le sang africain et qui souffrent dans toute l'Amérique des vils préjugés de couleur. Que tous viennent se joindre à nous pour jouir de la liberté, de l'égalité sous le palmier d'Haïti, et nous aider à faire de notre beau pays, fertilisé par le sang généreux de nos pères, la métropole de la race noire dans le monde civilisé."
11 It should be added that very few of the refugees were able to integrate themselves well in Haiti, and most of them returned to Louisiana.

to Joanni that he is being required to draw up his will, because he will soon be fighting a duel with Ernest Day. He tells Joanni about his past and the fact that he had a black wife named Athénais (they had secretly received a blessing from a priest) and that he has two children with her. He explains at great length how important they are to him and how much he regrets the existing prejudices against people of different skin color:

> In order to secure for myself the peaceful enjoyment of the woman who loved me, I had our union secretly blessed by a priest—it was a marriage of conscience—I believed that his prayers would be like a rampart around my loves. The color prejudice, with its terrible reprobation, cannot stop me in my loving fanaticism. When I married Athénais, as God is my witness, my friend, I considered myself legitimately and eternally bound to her. (Questy, "Monsieur Paul")[12]

It is this love story that is the reason for the duel: his wife left him for Ernest Day. Filled with jealousy and the desire for revenge, Monsieur Paul has worked out a plan in case he dies on the following day: he has provided a legacy for his wife and the children, but he wants Joanni to hold onto it and only give it to them two years later. In this way he hopes to make Athénais deeply regret her unfaithfulness. He needs Joanni to be the executor of his estate in order to bypass the legal situation that would otherwise confiscate it and hand it over to some distant relatives in France:

> As soon as I die, they will be putting their seals on everything: your country's inflexible and tyrannical laws do not recognize the validity of my marriage: the French consul will certainly find some relative of mine, some lost heir in any old department of France, that is certain. (ibid.)[13]

There follows a key passage in the text (which also gives the connection to Haiti), in which Monsieur Paul once again shows his attitude towards blacks by asking Joanni to pay out a legacy to his slave Georges:

---

12 "Pour m'assurer la jouissance tranquille de la femme qui m'aimait, je fis bénir secrètement notre union par un prêtre—un mariage de conscience—croyait que ses prières seraient comme un rempart autour de mes amours. Le préjugé de couleur, avec sa réprobation terrible, ne peut m'arrêter dans mon fanatisme amoureux. Quand j'épousais Athénais, je prends Dieu à témoin, mon ami, je me considérais légitimement et éternellement lié à elle."
13 "A peine mort, moi, on posera les scelles partout: la loi inflexible et tyrannique de votre pays ne reconnaît pas la validité de mon mariage: le consul français me trouvera bien quelque parent, quelque héritier perdu dans un département quelconque de France, c'est bien sûr."

> You must not forget Georges! Here, take this, this scroll belongs to him, as well as this letter: you will read it together. Two thousand dollars in bills, that is my ... slave's inheritance. And a special recommendation: my friend, please send Georges to Haiti. He is valiant, young, intelligent, gifted with excellent qualities, and not superstitious, and he will make his way in that country. Georges has a love of liberty that could make a person tremble, do not forget that, my friend. (ibid.)[14]

The next day, Ernest Day is killed in the duel; Monsieur Paul sustains a severe head injury. The two white witnesses who were supposed to stand by him as his seconds abscond, indifferent to his plight and leaving him badly wounded and without any support. Instead, it is the two black men, Georges and Joanni, who take attentive and loyal care of him. After a few days of delusions, however, Monsieur Paul succumbs to his injuries. At this point, Madame Paul suddenly appears at his deathbed with a cry of despair. (It is interesting that she is not referred to here as Athénais but as *Madame Paul*.) In his will, Monsieur Paul explains that Georges is not his slave but his nephew, the son of his brother and of a slave woman, both of whom died shortly after Georges's birth. Georges does indeed emigrate to Haiti, at a time when the wars of secession are on the horizon:

> At the point at which we have arrived in our narrative, preparations were being made for war all over the country; the future Confederacy already had in its midst several states that had declared their separation from the Union. There was talk in New Orleans of being forced to defend slavery. He embarked on board the ship Laura, which was leaving for Port-au-Prince, and swore never to return to his country so long as the "peculiar institution" was still in effect there. (ibid.)[15]

After a few years of loneliness, Athénais ends up taking her own life. Her husband's will and banknotes are found in her dead hand. And although at the end of the story it has become clear that Monsieur Paul's affection for Georges was (also) based on familial ties, since he was not only his slave but also his

---

14 "Il ne faut pas oublier Georges! Tenez, ce rouleau-ci lui appartient aussi bien que cette lettre: vous la lirez ensemble. Deux mille piastres en billets, voilà l'héritage de mon ... esclave. Une recommandation spéciale: Mon ami, vous enverrez Georges en Haïti. Brave, jeune, intelligent, doué d'excellentes qualités, pas superstitieux, il fera son chemin dans ce pays-là. Georges a un amour de la liberté à faire trembler, n'oubliez pas cela, mon ami."
15 "Au point où nous sommes arrivés de notre récit, il se faisait des préparatifs de guerre dans tout le pays; la future Confédération du Sud comptait déjà dans son sein plusieurs états qui avaient déclaré leur séparation de l'Union. Il était question à la Nouvelle Orléans de devenir un défenseur forcé de l'esclavage. Il s'embarqua à bord de la Laura qui partait pour Port-au-Prince, et fit le serment de ne jamais revenir dans son pays tant que 'l'Institution particulière' y subsisterait."

nephew, Monsieur Paul's positive attitude towards blacks can nevertheless not be ignored: it can be seen in his undeniable love for his black wife and their two children and in his implied criticism of the church and other institutions that refuse to recognize that love.

Another interesting thing is the way Questy differentiates the characters of the individual figures in this text: Monsieur Paul is white, fatherly, and passionate; the narrator is black, loyal, reliable, and educated; Ernest Day is again white and, aside from the fact that he is Athénais's new lover, a relatively neutral figure; Athénais is black and occupies the position of the beloved; Georges is black, a slave, intelligent, loyal, unsuperstitious, and loves freedom; and the traders Jean Delotte and William Brewer are white, disloyal, and materialist. The way the characters are drawn is less racially stereotyped than in other texts. But a key point in terms of our main focus is the glorification of Haiti, which is presented as the Athens of the Caribbean, the center of the double American continent, when Georges is solemnly promised that he can go there. Port-au-Prince promises the future, it is a center of culture and education and is economically thriving. In French-language inner-Caribbean texts, on the other hand, Haiti either barely plays any role at all or else is touched on, marginally, as a way to induce fear. As we will see in section VIII.1, there are certainly discourses within the Spanish Caribbean that include Haiti in utopian visions of the Caribbean as a whole, but in those cases it is always presented as a role model in the racial struggle. What is particularly fascinating is how things are staged from the point of view of Haiti's own literary production: the unidirectional gaze towards France is radically called into question by literary representations such as "Monsieur Paul." Focusing on Haiti reveals to us, in condensed form, how we set transcultural knowledge formation "into relationship (and into motion) through comparison" (*durch Vergleich in Beziehung [und in Bewegung] setzen*; Ette, *Alexander von Humboldt* 152; cf. also section I.2.2. of this book).

VI.2.3 Joseph Colastin Rousseau: "Nos frères d'outre-golfe" (Our Brothers from beyond the Gulf)

In 1862, Joseph Colastin Rousseau published his "Souvenirs de la Louisiane" (Memories of Louisiana), an early example of the literary historiography of Louisiana's colored Creoles, in *L'Opinion Nationale*, an important Port-au-Prince-based newspaper. Rousseau, linked to Saint-Domingue by his familiy history, had only just arrived in Haiti from Louisiana. He describes the romantic poets of Louisiana, both black and white, as an unfortunate aggregation, bound by persecution and economic crisis.

It is no coincidence that Romanticism was so well-developed in Louisiana, considering that the question of the flows of refugees back to Haiti was a contemporary political issue that lent itself very well to literary representations. Thus, for instance, we have the following detailed description of the reception of the refugees from Saint-Domingue who went first to Cuba and then, in 1809, as a consequence of conflicts with royalist Cubans after the Napoleonic occupation of Spain (as we saw above), to Louisiana:

> In 1809, a remnant of the Haitian exiles who had been expelled from the island of Cuba were thrown onto the shores of Louisiana, as though sent by God to come and enlarge the small number of families of whom I spoke above [the free people of color]. Already brothers by blood, locked into the circle of fire of an inconsistent prejudice, this shared misfortune, sanctifying them by unifying them, inspired in them a pure and open sympathy; their children grew up under the same roof and new bonds of fraternity, arising from the situation, drew tighter every day, and all mixed up in the same fate, they were soon but one and the same single family. (*L'Opinion Nationale*, November 29, 1862, cited in Duplantier 158)[16]

Rousseau emphasizes the commonalities shared by the Haitians and the Louisianans and talks about "our brothers from beyond the gulf" (*nos frères d'outre-golfe*, Duplantier 165). He calls America's black and colored population blood brothers. He makes use of early pan-African ideas that were circulating in the Atlantic world at that time and pleads for greater solidarity among Creoles. He ends with the words "in order to inform all of the members of the larger community, as well as our brothers the Haitians—who are so close to our hearts—about the lives of our Haitian brothers: because there, when you say 'Louisianan,' it is as though you said 'Haitian'" (*L'Opinion Nationale*, December 27, 1862, cited in Duplantier 155).[17] He shows very clearly how the bonds of a Creole class were pulled together out of a hybrid and relational experience (Duplantier 155). Like the Creole upper class of Martinique and Guadeloupe, Louisiana's free

---

16 "En 1809 un débris d'exilés haïtiens expulsés de l'île de Cuba, furent jeté sur les plages de la Louisiane, comme envoyés de Dieu pour venir grossir le petit nombre de familles dont j'ai parlé plus haut [les gens de couleur libres]. Frères déjà par le sang, enserrés dans le cercle de fer d'un inconséquent préjugé, ce malheur commun, les sacrant en les réunissant, leur inspira de pures et franches sympathie; leurs enfans grandirent sous le même toit, de nouveau liens de fraternité, naissant de la situation, se resserrèrent chaque jour plus étroitement et, confondus dans le même sort, ils ne firent bientôt qu'une seule et même famille."

17 "afin de renseigner tous les membres de la grande communauté aussi bien que nos frères les Haïtiens—lesquels nous touchent de si près—sur l'existence de nos frères louisianais: parce que là-bas quand on dit: Louisianais, c'est comme si l'on disait Haïtiens." On Rousseau's Saint-Domingue relation, see Desdunes 81.

people of color situate themselves in an in-between and express a lack of orientation, an instability between the worlds. And yet the colonial bond with the former mother country, France, remains the driving force. French colonialism is so strong that in spite of an experience of in-betweenness, its drawing power flourishes precisely within that weakness.

Rousseau's article also introduces Louisiana's white poets—Adrien Rouquette, Alexandre Latil, Oscar Dugué, and Tullius St. Céran—and describes the unique kind of Creole writing practiced by these poets. He also predicts the burden of a white Bovarysm that can stand in for all of nineteenth-century French-language Louisianan literature.

> Nevertheless, they remained themselves, and an indelible cachet of originality appears to be stamped upon their productions. Whether they are speaking of France or of their country, the idea of the fatherland never leaves them: it has always remained a background upon which they have embroidered their richest scenes. ... Children of the soil, exiled to France to work on the care of their education, they also sang of their cyprus trees, their bayous, their lakes and their pine trees; a thousand varied and precise descriptions of the savage wandering over his rambling pathways. (*L'Opinion Nationale*, October 25, 1862, cited in Duplantier 155–156)[18]

However, Rousseau also emphasizes the importance of *Les Cenelles*, an anthology of poetry by colored writers. The anthology did much more than just unite these poets, because describing the community was an existential act for them:

> After having watched several other volumes be published one after the other, following those by St. Céran, Rouquette, Latil, and Dugué, of whom we spoke earlier, these young men, full of a sincere and respectful admiration for everything that could contribute to the instruction of their race, decided to brave the hurricanes of publicity and launch their own volume of native poetry. They met and decided that each of them would contribute his own quota.
> In less than two weeks, seventeen of them had brought eighty-six poems, the fruit of their labor. Each of them gave his share for the printing, and a month later, a volume of poetry appeared ... composed of two hundred-some pages, entitled *Les Cenelles* (The Hollyberries). (*L'Union* 87, 1863, cited in Duplantier 157–158)[19]

---

18 "Ils sont restés eux quand même, et un cachet d'originalité indélébile semble sceller leurs productions. Soit qu'ils parlent de la France, soit qu'ils parlent de leur pays, l'idée de la patrie ne les abandonne jamais: Elle est toujours restée pour eux un fond sur lequel ils brodaient leurs plus riches tableau. ... Des enfants du sol, exilés en France pour travailler aux soins de leur éducation, chantèrent aussi leurs cyprières, leurs bayous, leurs lacs et leurs pinières; mille descriptions variées et précises du sauvage errant dans ses courses vagabondes."

19 "Après avoir vu se succéder plusieurs autres volumes de poésie qu'on publia après ceux de St. Céran, Rouquette, Latil et Dugué, dont nous avons déjà parlé plus haut, ces jeunes gens,

Following this announcement by Rousseau, let us now look more closely at this group, which seems to exemplify attempts to position oneself in the in-between.

VI.3 *Les Cenelles:* Writing in the In-Between

The critical gaze of the United States governmental agencies and of the public forced free people of color to pour their thoughts into forms that would escape the censorship of hegemonic society. In the eighteen-forties, free people of color in Louisiana were still engaging in an intensive intellectual exchange with the French-influenced Caribbean and with France, the cultural mother country. For the sons of wealthier families, travels to Paris and studies at one of France's famed universities were almost a requirement; for those with literary ambitions, this was even truer. It makes sense, therefore, that many of the free people of color who were engaged in literary activities in the eighteen-forties turned to French Romanticism. Möllers points out that Romanticism gave them a way to write poetry that followed European conventions—unlike forms of black literature such as the folktale and the slave narrative, which were also entering the market at that time—that would be regarded with less suspicion by the white southern public (Möllers 141).

The most important medium of publication for Creole poets of color was the *Album littéraire: Journal des jeunes gens, amateurs de littérature* (Literary album: The journal for young lovers of literature), first published in 1843. This literary magazine was officially published by the white Creole Jean-Louis Marciaq, but the short stories, essays, and poems that appeared in its pages were primarily written by Creoles of color. When this magazine disappeared, after appearing for a short period, a poetry anthology entitled *Les Cenelles* appeared in 1845. It included 86 poems by 17 Creole authors of color. The name of the collection refers to one of Louisiana's botanical rarities: the red berries of the hollyberry, a kind of hawthorn bush, only appear in isolated areas such as the swampy area around New Orleans (Möllers 142). They were made into jam because they were so delicious, and they commanded high prices in nineteenth-century

---

pleins d'une admiration sincère et respectueuse pour tout ce qui pouvait concourir à l'instruction de leur race, se sont décidés à braver les orages de la publicité, en lançant aussi leur volume de poésie indigènes. Ils se réunirent et décidèrent que chacun d'eux porterait son contingent à l'oeuvre proposée.

En moins de quinze jours, dix-sept d'entr'eux donnèrent 86 pièces de vers, fruit de leur labour. Chacun donna sa quote part pour l'impression et, un mois après, parut un volume de poésies, ... composé de 200 et tant de pages, intitulé: *Les Cenelles*."

Louisiana. Given this, Jerah Johnson has aptly interpreted the name of this unusual work: it "evoked the image of small, uniquely flavored and rare local delicacies that struggled for life in surroundings so hostile as to make the very gathering of them a dangerous travail, but one worth the risk because of the richness of the reward" (Jerah Johnson 410, cited in Möllers 142).

The authors of the poems, and in particular the author of the introduction, Armand Lanusse, made a point of foregrounding the uniqueness of their poetry collection. And this was not exaggerated, because it is in fact the first poetry anthology written by colored writers in North America. In terms of the book's reception, however, the startling nature of the slim volume remained hidden from the public, even though most of the poems were labeled with their author's name. But if a reader did not know any of the poets personally, they would not be able to deduce the ethnic identity of its writers from the collection's contents (Möllers 142). As a result, *Les Cenelles* was simply perceived as being yet another collection of Romantic poems in Louisiana's literary market. At first glance, in fact, most of the poems do look just like a copy of their French Romantic models (143).

In contrast with the exoticizing portrayals of the texts of inner-Caribbean Romanticism, there is almost no local color at all in *Les Cenelles*. Very few of the poems refer to the geographical specificity of New Orleans or Louisiana. Nor are there hardly any identifying characteristics that have to do with their writers' ethnic origins. With just a few exceptions (which are however very prominent), the protagonists of the poems are not ethnically marked. The titles refer to obvious signal words from French Romanticism like love, desire, passion, melancholy, and death. And yet, in spite of all of the imitative elements, it is difficult to deny the particular character of these representations and their commonality with the literary production of the French-speaking Antilles.

VI.3.1 The Imitation of French Romanticism

The *Les Cenelles* anthology is strongly modeled on Lamartine's *Méditations Poétiques*, as Lanusse's explicit reference to the French Romantic also makes clear: "In innocence one day / I playfully took up the pure and burning flame / Which Lamartine tends with such a sacred love" (Lanusse, "Besoin d'écrire"/"Compulsion to Write" 120–121).[20] In his introduction, the poet also

---

20 "Naïvement un jour, / Je pris pour un jouet la pure et vive flamme / Qu'entretient Lamartine avec un saint amour."

names other role models whom the young colored poets of *Les Cenelles* seek to emulate:

> But those who have most earned our sympathy are the young men whose imagination has been forcefully captured by everything that is great and beautiful in the careers so gloriously pursued by men such as Hugo and Dumas. Those whom we would wish to defend, with all the strength of our souls, against the indifference of some and the maliciousness of others are the youthful spirits, who, without ever deluding themselves into thinking that they could attain the heights achieved by those great masters of literature whom we just mentioned, are nevertheless beset by all of the troubles that those sublime geniuses experienced at the beginning of their literary lives. These same afflictions will no doubt follow them to the doors of their tombs if, indeed, they do not accompany them inside. (Lanusse, "Introduction" xxxvii)[21]

On closer inspection, the texts in the *Album littéraire* in particular, but also some of the poems in *Les Cenelles*, are more than just simple tracings of a template influenced by French Romanticism. They are, above all, also an indirect kind of positioning of identity within Louisiana's complex postcolonial sphere and its various ethnic, cultural, and social groups and influences. Thus Henry Louis Gates, Jr., for instance, extols the literature of the free people of color mainly because, by perfectly fulfilling the requirements of a Western aesthetic tradition, it pulls the rug out from under the prejudice that the black "race" and culture are inferior (Haddox 758, cited in Möllers 155). And Michel Fabre emphasizes that the Creoles of color had as their primary goal not social reform but the cultivation of French-influenced literature in Louisiana (Fabre, "The New Orleans Press" 33).

As I mentioned above, the free people of color did not take the African-American genres that were emerging in the mid-nineteenth century, such as the folktale and the slave narrative, as a model. Their decision to work with the French of high culture and with Romantic themes instead of the realistic rendition of African-American dialects highlighted the differences between them and non-Creole people of color (Möllers 155). In the eighteen-forties and eighteen-fifties, Creoles

---

21 "Mais ceux pour qui nous éprouvons le plus de sympathie, ce sont ces jeunes hommes dont l'imagination s'est fortement éprise de tout ce qu'il y a de grand et de beau dans la carrière que suivent avec tant de gloire les Hugo et les Dumas; ceux que nous voudrions défendre de toutes les forces de notre âme contre l'indifférence des uns et la méchanceté des autres, ce sont ces jeunes esprits qui, sans avoir la folle prétention d'atteindre jamais à la hauteur où sont arrivés les grands maîtres en littérature dont nous venons de parler, sont pourtant en butte à toutes les tracasseries que ces génies transcendants éprouvèrent au commencement de leur vie littéraire; tracasseries qui les poursuivront sans doute jusqu'aux portes de leurs tombeaux, si elles n'en franchissent pas les seuils" (Lanusse, "Introduction" xxxvi).

of color, who were being increasingly marginalized, wanted to prove in their literature how much they were similar and belonged to white Creole society. By inscribing themselves into the French Romantic literary tradition and thereby also evoking shared points of identity such as Catholicism, they also created a counterbalance to the developing Protestant Anglo-American identity (156).

The important point here is that the *Les Cenelles* poetry anthology stood in clear opposition to the emerging tradition of genuinely African-American literature that could otherwise have connected the free people of color with the slaves and with free Protestant colored people of other southern states.

VI.3.2 In-Between: Inner Conflict and Productivity

The poems written by the free people of color often point to their inner conflicts, on both the individual and the societal level. To begin with, free people of color were largely the product of interethnic relationships, unofficial alliances that were a widespread phenomenon and around which a system called *plaçage* had developed, an institutionalized recognition of what could never be a fully legal marriage. Given this, any criticism of the *plaçage* system would have been difficult for free people of color to make, and the writers shied away from clearly and unambiguously expressing their displeasure with it. In a way that paralleled the exoticism of travel literature, the quadroon as a sexual object was emblematic of the imbalance in power between free people of color and the white upper class (Möller 156). But the main focus of the critique of the *plaçage* system was not the sexual exploitation of women but rather the immoral aspect of *plaçage* that made a functioning family life impossible and inhibited the idea of a kind of collective identity. Nevertheless, people did try to consolidate the community from the inside in order to uphold their social and economic position within Louisiana.

The unresolvable contradiction with which Afro-Creoles were faced in their literary production was that they were critizing a system to which, in large part, they owed their existence and their particular social position (ibid.). Given this quandary, it is not surprising that the style and expression these authors chose reflected their precarious position. The use of novel literary elements like those that were used in the emerging African-American literary trends would have gained greater attention for the Creole writers of color, and maybe they would have been more successful at articulating their protest against hegemonic society. But embedded as they were in their French-Creole heritage, which clearly placed them culturally closer to white Creole society than to the Protestant Anglo-Americans, their goal was not just to participate in the ruling society but also to continue to exclude other influences from the African-American culture that was positioned below them. These are, therefore, the indirect consequences of the French model of integration, still at work decades after the society was politically detached from the mother country.

The poems are marked by the experience of being in-between that the Creoles of color lived and by the contradictions of the demands posed by that experience: on the one hand, they resisted the caste system of white society that denied them an equal place in that society, while on the other hand they furthered and contributed to that very society in their attempts to continue to distinguish themselves, both socially and in terms of identity, from the slaves (157). In their preface to the bilingual edition of *Les Cenelles* that was published in Boston in 1979, Régine Latortue and Gleason Adams emphasize this aspect of uncertain affiliation:

> The legacy of Rousseau, of the French Revolution, of the Declaration of the Rights of Man and Citizen, and the foils of Classicism and Rationalism which gave substance to the musings of Lamartine and Hugo do not reverberate in the verses of their Louisiana imitators; these verses consequently have a somewhat hollow ring. Trapped between races, between classes, between cultures, the Louisiana Creole could not and would not confront the problems and conflicts that blacks, no matter how elevated, experienced; yet, no matter how much they tried, they could not succeed in completely immersing themselves in that culture which seemingly represented salvation. (Lanusse, *Les Cenelles* xiii)

This in-between writing by the *Les Cenelles* poets gains yet another dimension in its imitation not only of the French Romantics but also of the white poets of New Orleans, which also becomes clear from the introduction to the anthology:

> Therefore, we are publishing this collection to make known the works of several young lovers of poetry who doubtless do not envy the success achieved in the theater or in the literary world by poets of Louisiana who have had the good fortune to draw knowledge from the best sources in Europe. This latter group will always be for the former a subject of emulation but never an object of envy. (Lanusse, "Introduction" xxxix–xli)[22]

Louisiana's defining characteristic in the nineteenth century is its trans-area dimension, as the nodal point for multiple layers of transfer processes: politically motivated waves of refugees from Haiti to New Orleans and from New Orleans

---

[22] "Nous publions donc ce recueil dans le but de faire connaître les productions de quelques jeunes amans de la poésie qui ne jalousent point sans doute les beaux succès obtenus sur la scène ou dans le monde littéraire par des poètes louisianais qui ont eu le bonheur de puiser le savoir aux meilleures sources de l'Europe, car ces derniers seront toujours pour les premiers un sujet d'émulation, mais jamais un objet d'envie" (Lanusse, "Introduction" xxxviii–xi).

back to the Caribbean and to France; shifting colonial affiliations and multiple systems of cultural reference with varying degrees of influence; and the literary orientation of the Creole poets towards French Romanticism, both as the white high culture and as a symbol of their own precarious social situation and conflict. These multifaced relationalities are reflected in the dynamic constructions of identity which, among the free people of color, range from an early pan-Africanism all the way to a frenetic imitation of whites.

VII Excursus: Paradigm Change within Historical Caribbean Research and Its Narrative Representation

In this chapter, I would like to jump from the nineteenth century to the present, using two Caribbean writers as contemporary reference points, namely Raphaël Confiant and Maryse Condé. While my aim with Confiant is to look at a narrative representation of the nineteenth century and to show how theory production in the contemporary Caribbean cannot manage without reference to the nineteenth century, a parallel reading of Condé and of Gómez de Avellaneda shows the extent to which looking backwards from contemporary literary texts can enrich the reading of a nineteenth-century literary text in key ways. With his theory of coolitude, Khal Torabully, a cultural theoretician, film director, and writer from Mauritius, brings the Indian dimension into play, a dimension that goes beyond essentialism and broadens the formation of the Caribbean paradigm and that also refers back to the nineteenth century and the experience of the ship crossing. And finally, by bringing in the contemporary writers J.-M.G. Le Clézio, Édouard Glissant, and Epeli Hau'Ofa, I open up a transoceanic perspective among the Indian, Atlantic, and Pacific Oceans and bring up the question of an archipelagic or transoceanic avant-garde.

VII.1 Reading Gómez de Avellaneda with Maryse Condé

I want to look here at two novels by Caribbean women writers: *Sab*, by Gertrudis Gómez de Avellaneda (1841), and *Traversée de la Mangrove* (Crossing the Mangrove, by Maryse Condé (1989) (see also Müller, "Transkoloniale Dimensionen"; Müller, "Variantes de miradas"). What can this juxtaposition tell us? What, besides geographical space and the gender of the writers, connects these two novels, which are separated in time by almost a hundred and fifty years?

In both of these novels the authors are dealing with their islands of origin, which are isolated enclaves with the status, then as now, of colonies or overseas departments, surrounded by other islands that are already politically independent; in addition, the writers are also trying to connect their islands of origin more firmly (again) into their regional contexts, given the loosening of cultural ties to the center. Both of these writers dramatically embody the problematics of the in-between: after leaving their countries of origin at a very early age (Avellaneda around 1837 and Condé around 1953), they devote their literary labors (or at least a part of them) to their homeland, or rather what they call their homeland, not least because of a latent experience of foreignness in their host and mother countries of Spain and France.

Both of them argue, in the context of writing from the outside—that is to say, from the distance of a so-called center—for a stronger emphasis on what is specifically Cuban or, respectively, Guadeloupean; both of them experience a sense of alienation[1] on their return to their island of origin, among other things because they are perceived as strangers. This experience, which is symptomatic and traumatizing for many intellectuals from colonies or former colonies, reflects an issue that lies even deeper and that both of these writers anticipate and reflect on, in similar ways: as we have already seen for Gómez de Avellaneda, the attempt to make the metropolis's categories of identity serviceable for the description of what is proper to the non-European leads to an in-between, in other words to a tension that can usually not be resolved through a dialectial synthesis. Both of these writers show themselves to be extraordinarily sensitive to this tension in their writing about the in-between. In both of them, this sensitivity is expressed in a similarly ambivalent way of dealing with the question of their own authorship, a theme that then becomes a nodal point for a whole series of subtle crossings of borders that call existing gender and ethnic hierarchies into question; in both cases of literary representation, issues around the construction of personal and collective identity are presented as tightly interconnected with each other.

To be more concrete, both Gómez de Avellaneda and Condé take back their authorship, in a certain way, when they integrate their writing process itself into the novel and attribute it to their protagonist—in both cases a man. In Avellaneda's novel, the entire story turns out at the end to have been a farewell letter from the slave and title character, Sab; in Condé, the dead main character, Francis, around whose nighttime funeral the many stories wind, turns out to be a novelist who had been working on a novel entitled "Crossing the Mangrove."[2]

VII.1.1 Mangroves and the Staging of a Relational Identity

While all of the plotlines in Avellaneda's novel lead to Sab, who then finally, as the narrator as well as the main character, moves into the indispensable integra-

---

[1] On the description of Condé's feeling of foreignness and alienation, see Ette, *Literature on the Move* 274f.
[2] On *Crossing the Mangrove*, see Ette's essential interpretation in "Crossing the Mangrove." On strategies of authorship in Condé, see Gewecke, "Der Titel als Chiffre einer Subversion" 171.

tive center of the construction of identity there, in Maryse Condé's *Crossing the Mangrove*, the conceptions of identity are more fragmented and decentralized, even though many of the basic formal and substantive constellations are totally comparable to those in *Sab*. Like Avellaneda, Maryse Condé relinquishes her authorship, at least in part, to her protagonist, Francis Sancher alias Francisco Alvarez Sanchez. Thus, for example, his former lover Vilma tells of their first meeting in his house, where she saw him working on a manuscript. When she asked what he was writing, he answered:

> "You see, I'm writing. Don't ask me what's the point of it. Besides, I'll never finish this book because before I've even written the first line and known what I'm going to put in the way of blood, laughter, tears, fears, and hope, well, everything that makes a book a book, ... I've already found the title: 'Crossing the Mangrove.'"
> I shrugged my shoulders.
> "You don't cross a mangrove. You'd spike yourself on the roots of the mangrove trees. You'd be sucked down and suffocated by the brackish mud."
> "Yes, that's it, that's precisely it." (Condé, *Crossing the Mangrove* 158)[3]

Thus, the project of identity is doomed to failure from the beginning. We can read the doubled authorial structure as an indication that it took the female writer Condé to complete the project of a "rhizomatic" identity (as defined by Deleuze and Guattari; cf. Ette, *Literature on the Move* 284 ff.) and to make it possible to navigate the mangrove roots—roots that are not primarily anchored in the depths of the earth (read history), as with Western trees, but that find their rootedness on the surface instead, horizontally, intertwined with each other like branches and so that the individual plants support each other. This is an argument for a relational identity, as opposed to a root-identity (to use Édouard Glissant's terms; cf. Ette, *Literature on the Move* 274). And yet it nevertheless becomes clear that the question of the representation of authorship is not insignificant here, because the structure of the novel actually answers this question quite

---

[3] —Tu vois, j'écris. Ne me demande pas à quoi ça sert. D'ailleurs, je ne finirai jamais ce livre puisque, avant d'en avoir tracé la première ligne et de savoir ce que je vais y mettre de sang, de rires, de larmes, de peur, d'espoir, enfin de tout ce qui fait qu'un livre est un livre et non pas une dissertation de raseur, la tête à demi fêlée, j'en ai déjà trouvé le titre: "Traversée de la Mangrove".
J'ai haussé les épaules.
—On ne traverse pas la mangrove. On s'empale sur les racines des palétuviers. On s'enterre et on étouffe dans la boue saumâtre.
—C'est ça, c'est justement ça (*Traversée de la Mangrove* 202–203). Cf. Ette, *Literature on the Move* 264).

clearly. The novel has twenty chapters, and every chapter is a story told by a different narrator. The narrators are the participants in a wake for Francis.

Much like in García Márquez's *Hundred Years of Solitude*, the plot of *Crossing the Mangrove* takes place in the closed microcosm of a village, in this case the godforsaken Guadeloupean village of Rivière au Sel, where so far the inhabitants have apparently lived alongside each other in a very isolated and uncommunicative way. But what creates a feeling of belonging among them is not the eternal succession of generations within a shared mythical, magical world of imagination but rather the numerous interwoven connections among the individual villagers. Where in García Márquez's origin story we find the circular and almost metabolic diachronicity of never-changing sameness, the narrated time presented in Condé is extraordinarily compact and concise, which reinforces the impression of the synchronicity of the varied interpersonal connections. Thus, it takes Sancher's (mysterious) death to not only bring the villagers together at his burial but also to make them aware of the dynamic of their network of relationships, a dynamic that is only created in the first place through the verbal interaction of the villagers telling each other their stories. As an attempt at constructing identity, therefore, Sancher's novel must fail, because relational identity can no longer even be described by one single author (Malena 69); it requires, instead, the dissolution of authorial control in favor of a multiplicity of narrators, who only even constitute identity in the first place—which in this case means dynamic connection—through the overlapping and interweaving of their stories. The juxtaposition of their stories without the benefit of any single stage direction, autonomously fitting together into the mosaic of a microcosm, shows that their cohesion and their equality are based not on any overarching general principle—for instance, something symbolized in an overlaid narrative—but instead only on the shared, interactive initiative that they themselves take in speaking up.

While in *Sab*, an oppressed subject takes authorial initiative and finds his way to his own literary voice, which then becomes the mouthpiece and the center for colonial subjects trapped and entangled in a great variety of relationships of dependence and power, in Condé in many ways the protagonist—as the center around which the various polyphonic voices circle, as though in a centrifuge—constitutes a void or is, in a peculiar way, set aside.

On the one hand, no one really knows anything concrete about Sancher's past: at some point, he came to the village from somewhere else, and he has two names, the French name Francis Sancher and a Spanish equivalent, Francisco Alvarez Sanchez, which does not resolve the question of whether he is now Guadeloupean, or maybe Colombian—but all conjectures remain within the Caribbean region. When he moved into an old, abandoned house, the locals looked at him suspiciously for a long time and always considered him a stranger, until the stories they tell at the wake reveal that each of them has a particular relationship to him. On the other hand, Sancher—who worked on the manuscript of "Crossing the Mangrove" and came to the realization that in so doing he had devoted himself to a hopeless undertaking—is the only one who does not have a chance to tell any stories. His death, and with it the renunciation of any initiative, is in this case the prerequisite for initiative on the part of the many. Barthes's saying about the death of the author plays out very literally here, except that the author's authority does not give way to some self-referentiality, in whatever form, of an anonymous, subject-less text, but rather to multiple voices and to an interactive referentiality.

The openness of the text is key for this interactivity and intersubjectivity, and the fact that these narratives are oral narratives is crucial for the text (see Ette, *Literature on the Move* 265). Their juxtaposition in the context of oral communication puts them at the intersection of, on the one hand, an unchangeable past, and, on the other, a dynamic present that points the way towards an open future and that is under the control of the actors themselves. In diachronic perspective, as a completed narrative, each story points backwards into a past that also reveals the Guadeloupe of that time to be full of stereotypes and essentialist attributions of identity. As in Avellaneda's novel, skin color and gender are still the most important factors here, even though several of the speakers indicate that education had recently become an important factor in social identity, only to then be pushed aside by what is then, most recently of all, the only valid social measure: the bank balance—a criterion that in *Sab* only means something to the illegitimate Otways. From this perspective, Guadeloupe is finally still a heterogeneous patchwork, a society without cohesion, divided and seamed in many ways.

From a synchronic perspective, however, as open communication, the stories within these narratives become the basis of encounter and a pluralist exchange. It is the individual background of each person and the story told by that person—not the sameness of them all—that allows each of them to have their own perspective on what they do all share: in this story, concretely, their memory of the dead man and through that of their shared village, which stands as a microcosm for the entire island. It is these different standpoints that make communication meaningful in the first place, and it is only in their communicative exchange, in the dynamic of narrating, listening, and answering, that the villagers can recognize themselves and each other as equal, in the sense of having equal rights, on the basis of their very difference. Through their shared center, the "dead author," they speak not against each other, but with each other.

Both of these novels portray the Caribbean as an extraordinarily productive and, above all, self-sufficient cultural and literary space that produces an unheard-of conceptual depth out of the very dilemma of identity posed by its heterogeneity. To put it another way, it is precisely the gap between Europe and their island of origin—even though, because of their divided biographies, their intellectual sense of belonging does not accord with their emotional one—that challenges these writers to their productive engagement with contemporary European discourses, discourses that both of these writers, in different ways (and of course in the context of their respective times), definitely understand in the dialectical tension between liberation and dominance, even though the recognition of this ambivalence does not therefore protect them from the doubled experience of alienation.

In the attempt to overcome the essentialist model of identity—an attempt that is, in my opinion, constitutive of both novels, each in its own way—Condé's novel, unsurprisingly, offers a more convincing alternative than Avellaneda's *Sab* was able to do in the first half of the nineteenth century. Although it is oriented towards the relational identity of the poststructuralists, this model is marked by its own very particular nuance. The perspective it provides based on multiple voices and an interactive dynamic is certainly more consistent than that of Sab, who is a figure of integration, consisting precisely of the utopia (which has a Christian character) of his own self-sacrifice. Nevertheless, it may still be that, even given all of the mangrove's conceptual persuasiveness, Sab, with his emotional appeal and the shock that his self-sacrifice produces in the reader, makes a greater historical impact. It is the very interplay between these two ways of reading that reveals the universal dimension of Caribbean literatures.

VII.2 Raphaël Confiant

The contemporary literary production of the French-speaking Caribbean finds itself in an exceedingly complicated cultural and political situation. Its orientation towards both the Parisian literary industry and the mainland French academic world, on the one hand, and its Caribbean and Latin American neighbors, on the other, only intensifies the question of where, exactly, the literary field of today's French Antilles is located. In France, the literary industry and the academy are closely connected, and so it is no coincidence that most of the well-known writers of the French Antilles are also professors of literary studies. This intersection of literary production and cultural-theoretical reflection is particularly salient in the case of Raphaël Confiant (see also Müller, "Raphaël Confiant"; Müller, "Modelos caribeños").

Raphaël Confiant was born in 1951 and has taught English language and literature at the University of the French West Indies and Guiana, in Martinique, since 1979. He first wrote in Creole; in 1988 he wrote his first novel in French, *Le Nègre et l'Amiral* (The Negro and the admiral). In 1993, he received the Casa de las Américas prize and the Jet Tours prize for his novel *Ravines du devantjour* (Ravines of early morning). He and Patrick Chamoiseau were the co-creators of *Créolité*, which builds on earlier movements such as négritude and *Antillanité* and strives to develop a new, multi-voiced concept of identity which, unlike the ideas of their peer, Édouard Glissant, exhibits a concrete connection to Antillean societies and is thus exposed to the critique that it has developed a new essentialism.

The following discussion is intended to serve as an examination of the relevance of research on the nineteenth-century Caribbean to present-day narrative representations of the Caribbean. In looking at contemporary literature, given that literary scholarship very often considers Latin America and the Caribbean together, the question arises of the degree to which the writing in France's overseas departments can be differentiated from current Latin American productions. This question consciously goes against the grain of the tendency to do away with regional categorizations altogether (as in the Crack Manifesto[4]). On the other hand, the connection between Caribbean theoretical production—which has made a name for itself in literature and philosophy, especially in the canonized texts of Derek Walcott, Édouard Glissant, and Benítez Rojo—and literary forms of expression is of particular interest. I focus on how the paradigm of identity is dealt with, although among all of the variation in how the most recent Latin American and Caribbean literatures express themselves, one thing they share is surely their general renunciation of this paradigm. It is no surprise, given his commitment to *Créolité*, that Raphaël Confiant is one of the main actors here. His 2005 novel *Adèle et la pacotilleuse* is set in the second half of the nineteenth century in the Caribbean, its diaspora (with a center in Halifax, Canada), and in France. The most immediate question that arises here is whether that novel is a new historical novel, along the lines of García Márquez's Bolívar novel, *El general en su laberinto* (The General in His Labyrinth) or Carlos Fuentes's *La campaña* (The Campaign).

---

4 Crack is the name of a group of Mexican writers, all born around 1968, whose 1998 Crack Manifesto (*Manifiesto Crack*) calls for a conscious departure from magical realism, which was all too dominant in Latin America. Its most important representatives are Jorge Volpi and Ignacio Oadilla. See Müller, *Die Boom-Autoren heute* 280–281.

VII.2.1 *Adèle et la pacotilleuse* (Adèle and the Tinkerwoman)

Driven by her unhappy love affair with Albert Pinson, a British officer, Adèle Hugo (the daughter of the great French poet) goes to North America in search of him. After several years in Canada, during which Pinson apparently fails to reciprocate her love, she follows him to Barbados, where she learns that he is actually in Burma. A tinkerwoman named Céline Alvarez Bàà—a *pacotilleuse*, peddling small goods among the Caribbean islands—finds her in this situation, deeply unhappy, in mental distress, caught between two black men who are fighting over her. Céline, of African, Andalusian, and Caribbean descent, develops a maternal relationship towards the white Frenchwoman, taking care of Adèle from that point on with selfless solicitude and doing everything in her power to help the disturbed young woman reach her father. She takes the young lady to St. Pierre, in Martinique, where through great difficulties, and with the help of Verdet, a wealthy admirer of Hugo's, she succeeds in making contact with the poet in France. In the meantime, Adèle is put into a sanitarium, but Céline is able to get her out again and, with Verdet's help, to make the trip to Paris in April of 1872.

After a short-term recovery, however, it becomes clear that Adèle's mental disorder cannot be reversed. Céline, who has become Hugo's mistress, returns to the Caribbean and asks Hugo to let Adèle go with her because she does better in the Antilles, but he refuses. When Céline is back in the Caribbean, however, she receives a letter from Hugo asking her to return to Paris, since he has noticed that Céline is the only person who can calm his daughter. She makes a second trip in the fall of 1872, and for the first time Hugo treats Céline as an adult. He asks her to stay with his daughter, because he is about to die, but she refuses and returns to the Caribbean for good. Although Céline asks Hugo not to put Adèle into an institution, he does it anyway for fear that his heirs might otherwise put his daughter out onto the street after his death.

Confiant divides his novel into seven chapters, using a polyphonic narrative style in which a narrator and the protagonists take turns speaking. This allows for a variety of perspectives and also involves the frequent use of fragments of several Caribbean languages. Because Confiant does without any linear description of time or place, the whole picture of an event sometimes does not become clear until it has been mentioned the second or third time. This leads to an unusual reading experience. Although the novel is written in French, we learn that this is nothing more than an official language for many. When Céline arrives in Bordeaux, her linguistic world is described as existing somewhere between French and Spanish, and it turns out that her French is actually not very strong, because everywhere where French had been spoken, Creole was spoken as well.

Céline also prays only in Spanish or English, but not in French. In terms of the variety of languages, the key scene is the moment when Céline learns that her mother is on her deathbed in Haiti. She visits Chrisopompe to have him write a farewell letter for her, and she cannot decide on a language. She finally chooses Creole, and Chrisopompe turns out to be a true master in writing this language, which does not actually have a written form. He is inspired by François Marbot, who had written "Fables de la Fontaine travesties en créole par un vieux commandeur" (La Fontaine's fables distorted into Creole by an old commander) in around 1850. Another fascinating and very inventive passage describes a seance held by Céline, Adele, and Victor Hugo to summon spirits on the evening of April 22, 1872, at ten thirty in the evening. The first question that they ask the spirit is what language they should speak.

VII.2.2 From Insularity to an Archipelagic Model

The two women, Adèle and Céline, could not be more different from each other. One of them embodies Europe and the other the Caribbean, in its entire diversity, a diversity that is seen more as a treasure than as a handicap. This diversity can be divided up in many ways but also unified in one place or person, as with the character of Céline and the other tinkerwomen. They are the ones who speak the languages of this world, they connect the islands, and they are also the ones who, with their wares, allow their buyers to experience other worlds. The Caribbean functions as a mirror and a miniature model of the entire world, with influences from Europe, the Levant, and the Orient, through India, and all the way to China (Confiant, *Adèle* 69–72). As Confiant puts it: "Each island, mysteriously, has its own favorite product, a commodity, a plant, a tool, special potions and ointments, fabrics that are scorned elsewhere. But much of this does not even come from the archipelago. The entire planet seems to be pouring out its dreams there" (69).[5] Every island on which the tinkerwomen buy their wares has its own specialty. In Cuba it is mirrors and combs made of Chinese tortoiseshell; in Trinidad, where the indigenous population is still relatively large, there are spices from India. In St. Pierre, in Martinique, there is silk from Syria, Palestine, and Lebanon—it is the Little Paris of the Antilles. Céline buys her wares from Abdelwahab El Fandour and sells her silk in St. Vincent and Granada. The imports

---

5 "Chaque île, mystérieusement affectionne un produit, une marchandise, une plante, un outil, des philtres et des onguents particuliers, des tissus dédaignés ailleurs. Pourtant, beaucoup de tout cela ne provient pas de l'Archipel. Toute la planète semble y déverser ses rêves."

from industrialized Europe include encyclopedias, pocket watches, binoculars, pens and inkwells, saws and hammers, compasses and rulers. Sometimes the tinkerwoman comes upon a one-of-a-kind piece, like the old Chinese merchant's crystal hourglass that Céline has been dreaming of and that he has promised her after his death. Every time that she leaves Jamaica, she is afraid that she will never see the piece again, fearing that his hut will be plundered before she returns. Five years later he dies of the flu, cared for by Céline, who receives the hourglass, filled with sand from the Gobi Desert. She keeps it for two years, but then she sells it to a plantation owner for a couple of pieces of gold, which she will regret for the rest of her life. Granada has the best nutmeg and the rum from Martinique is the "emperor of rums" (*l'empereur des rhums*). And the coffee from Guadeloupe and the tobacco from Cuba are preferred to all others (78–82).

When Adèle meets Céline, the older woman is 42 years old. Born on the sea, she is the "daughter of no land, of none of those islands that the Spaniards, English, French, Dutch, Danish, Swedish, and Americans have been fighting over for centuries" (61–62).[6] She talks about the tinkerwomen, the vagabonds of the Caribbean Sea who have no homeland and who make the sea their home, as:

> we, the tinkerwomen, women of ocean wanderings, more so, anyway, than those who languish on the islands, glued to lands that do not properly belong to them. That will never belong to them. Every island, in fact, has kept its Carib name, and that is why they continue to belong to the first peoples who lived there, even if those peoples have been massacred to the very last one of them. We will be eternal tenants there, which explains why we can feel at ease, like Blaise, in any part of the vast world. Without any home countries of our own, the universe has become ours. (303)[7]

The tinkerwomen represent a particular geopolitical solidarity with the peoples of the Caribbean and an anthropological (or perhaps Creole) solidarity with the non-Caribbean societies that have been subjected to similar processes of colonization and/or Creolization. Because of them, the Antilles no longer seem like a

---

[6] "fille d'aucune terre, d'aucune de ces îles que se disputent depuis des siècles Espagnols, Anglais, Français, Hollandais, Danois, Suédois, Américains."

[7] "nous les pacotilleuses, femmes de vagabondages marin, bien plus en tout cas que ceux qui croupissent dans les îles, rivés à des terres qui ne leur appartiennent pas en propre. Qui ne leur appartiendront jamais. Chaque île, en effet, a conservé son nom caraïbe et c'est pourquoi elle continue d'appartenir au premier peuple qui l'a habitée quand bien même il a été massacré jusqu'au dernier. Nous y demeurons d'éternels locataires, ce qui explique pourquoi nous pouvons nous sentir à l'aise comme Blaise dans n'importe quelle partie du vaste monde. Privés de nos patries d'origines, l'univers est devenu le nôtre."

site of dispersal but, instead, like a place where in future that which was dispersed can be brought together and connected (Ette, *Literature on the Move* 256).

While the function of the island in the nineteenth century was primarily based on isolation and exoticism, archipelagic thinking was consistently relational (König, "Édouard Glissants *pensée archipélique*"). Thus, Martinique, which is at the center of the novel, is part of an alliance of islands that derives its coherence from particular linguistic and cultural communicative "trans-processes." In the novel, the creation of the archipelagic system becomes a model of boundary-lessness, a metaphor for the overcoming of closed national boundaries (Ludwig and Röseberg 9).[8] In his *Traité du Tout-monde* (Whole-world treatise), on the other hand, Édouard Glissant defines "archipelagic thinking":

> Archipelagic thinking suits the pace of our worlds. It borrows their ambiguity, fragility, derivativeness. ... It means fitting in with that part of the world that has, precisely, disseminated itself into archipelagoes, these kinds of diversities within the vastness, which nevertheless reunite riverbanks and marry horizons. We see what was continental and thick and weighed on us, in those sumptuous systematic thoughts that have ruled the history of the humanities to this day and which are no longer adequate to our explosions, to our stories, nor to our no-less-sumptuous wanderings. (31)[9]

As Torsten König points out, given the diversity in which today's worlds present themselves and the varying courses taken by their histories, we must abandon the homogenizing discourses that have so far determined our view of world his-

---

8 Glissant himself describes the growing process by which the archipelagic system is created as follows: "What I see today is that the continents are increasingly turning into archipelagoes, at least as seen from the outside. The Americas are turning into archipelagoes, forming themselves into regions that transcend national frontiers. And I think that that is a term that needs to be restored to dignity, the term 'region.' Europe is turning into archipelagoes. The linguistic regions, the cultural regions, which go beyond national barriers, are islands, but open islands, that is the main condition of their survival." ("Ce que je vois aujourd'hui, c'est que les continents 's'archipélisent,' du moins du point de vue d'un regard extérieur. Les Amériques s'archipélisent, elles se constituent en régions par-dessus les frontières nationales. Et je crois que c'est un terme qu'il faut rétablir dans sa dignité, le terme de région. L'Europe s'archipélise. Les régions linguistiques, les régions culturelles, par-delà les barrières des nations, sont des îles, mais des îles ouvertes, c'est leur principale condition de survie.") (Glissant, *Introduction à une poétique* 44).
9 "La pensée archipélique convient à l'allure de nos mondes. Elle en emprunte l'ambigu, le fragile, le dérivé. ... C'est s'accorder à ce qui du monde s'est diffusé en archipels précisément, ces sortes de diversités dans l'étendue, qui pourtant rallient des rives et marient des horizons. Nous nous apercevons de ce qu'il y avait de continental, d'épais et qui pesait sur nous, dans les somptueuses pensées de système qui jusqu'à ce jour ont régi l'Histoire des humanités, et qui ne sont plus adéquates à nos éclatements, à nos histoires ni à nos non moins somptueuses errances."

tory, which Glissant calls "continental." This is why the Martinican scholar calls the kind of thinking that is appropriate to today's world "archipelagic" thinking. He closes his *Traité* with an emphatic reference to "the thinking of the archipelago, of the archipelagoes" (*la pensée de l'archipel, des archipels*), conjuring up the overcoming of the old order (cf. König, "Édouard Glissants *pensée archipélique*" 117–118).

VII.2.3 From the Static Concept of Exile, passing by the Black Atlantic to the In-Between

A large part of the novel takes place in St. Pierre, in Martinique. Another important scene of action is Victor Hugo's residence in Paris. Almost the entire story takes place between Paris and Little Paris, where colonial society is depicted with its racial teachings and segregation, with its prejudices but also its zest for life, through carnival, sex, and poetry. It is also noteworthy that Halifax is often described as being the link between Europe and (French) America, because Adèle spends several years there. This positioning in the in-between seems to be symptomatic of the nineteenth-century Caribbean Creole upper classes. That inbetween, which is often referred to in postcolonial theory, finds its strongest expression in the sea as the central scene of action, the true connection between Europe, the Caribbean, and Africa. Céline says that she only feels comfortable when she is traveling, in other words on board ship. Here, the ship represents a kind of threshold: it can be seen as a vehicle that crosses the boundaries of time, transports the protagonist from one level to another, and thus makes possible an oscillation between regions defined by time and by space. Exile also plays an important role, as Céline notes: "The thing is that exile is our condition, for us Amerindian-Negro-White-Mulatto-Chabin-Indian-Chinese-Syrians of the archipelago. Exile created us" (Confiant, *Adèle* 59).[10]

Adèle's diary is also called "a journal of exile" (*journal d'exil*). Characteristically, however, there is also a critical engagement with the concept of exile: "Exile does not mean the same thing to Adèle as it does to me" (*Le mot exil n'a pas le même sens pour Adèle et pour moi*; 67–68). To Céline, exile is the condition of the native population. They do not necessarily like the sea itself, unless they are sailors or tinkerwomen. Céline's father hates the sea, because it swallows up souls. "The Atlantic is the world's largest cemetery" (*L'Atlantique est*

---

10 "C'est que l'exil est notre condition, à nous les Amérindiens-Nègres-Blancs-Mulâtres-Chabins-Indiens-Chinois-Syriens de L'Archipel. L'exil nous a créé."

le plus grand cimetière du monde; 60; cf. Gilroy, *Black Atlantic*). He was a former slave who had stayed with his master after slavery was abolished. For Adèle, exile is a test, a crucial ordeal. In Adèle's diary, which Céline reads while Adèle is asleep, she talks about her father's exile on Jersey and Guernsey.

"Exile," as a conventional concept having to do with migration, is critically examined, in its function as a stabilizer, per se, of a binary opposition between the center and the periphery. Confiant plays with the balance of power between colonial Europe and the colonized Caribbean. In the form of the relationship between Adèle and Céline, the Caribbean plays the role of the mother while Europe is the helpless and needy daughter. One can also see the whole as mutual affection. Céline desperately wants to have a daughter (and also calls Adèle "my daughter" [*ma fille*]), while Adèle sees a mother in Céline and soon confides in her:

> And, you Negress, you have almost become a mother to me. You are the first person who has listened to me without judging me. You do not treat me like a madwoman, when I tell you about the love I feel for Albert Pinson. You understand me, you who have never eaten from a porcelain plate nor danced the minuet. You, Céline Alvarez Bàà! And like Bug Jargal making the sublime request to D'Auverney, the white colonist: "may I call you brother?" I claim you as my mother from now on. Yes ... (Confiant, *Adèle* 53)[11]

On Céline's first visit to Paris, it becomes clear that Hugo, as the master of the house, repeatedly and as a matter of course commands the services, including sexual services, of the women working in his house, and that that now includes Céline as well. He literally overpowers her. The following quotation, which can almost be read as a mockery of island theories, shows that Céline does not consider this rape and to a certain degree also enjoys it:

> As soon as calm had returned, Hugo regained his usual energy, an amazing energy for a man on the threshold of old age. We went up to the attic, by a sort of tacit agreement, and he threw himself on my person and plowed my flesh, his eyes curiously closed. I let it happen, although I seldom felt pleasure. On the other hand, the sensation of being caught up by an unleashed wave, of being lifted up, rolled over, manipulated as though

---

[11] "Et toi négresse, tu es devenue presque une mère pour moi. Tu es la première personne à m'écouter sans me juger. Tu ne me traites point de folle à lier lorsque je te parle de l'amour que j'éprouve pour Albert Pinson. Tu me comprends, toi qui n'as jamais mangé dans une assiette en porcelaine ni dansé le menuet. Toi, Céline Alvarez Bàà! Et comme Bug-Jargal adressant à D'Auverney, le colon blanc, cette requête sublime: 'puis-je t'appeler frère?,' je te réclame désormais pour mère. Oui ..."

I weighed no more than a piece of straw, was very agreeable to me. I became an island, a small tropical island, being covered by powerful Europe with its enormous wing. (271)[12]

Here we see a representation of Europe's superior strength. Hugo calls Céline a little dove and would like, for his part, to be seen as a lion. But here, too, first appearances are deceptive, because Céline makes it clear that Hugo actually sees her instead as a bird of prey, as an eagle. In Michel Audibert, a mulatto poet who is Céline's lover, we see a certain competitiveness. Audibert had resented that Hugo had neglected to mention the uprisings in Martinique with even a word, and criticized him as a Negrophobe. This stereotyped representation is then brought to a head when the mulatto Audibert is confronted with the fact that Céline has been with Hugo, whereupon he breaks off contact with her. The colonial power relationship is displaced onto a competition over who is the better poet.

VII.2.4 From Concepts of Identity to Questions of Conviviality

Confiant continually creates situations in which beliefs of that time about the different races are made clear. It makes sense that in the nineteenth century, given the colonial constellations, the question of the conviviality of ethnic groups would be dealt with in a particularly intense way (see section I.5): Alexandre Verdet reads Count Gobineau's *Essai sur l'inégalité des races humaines* (Essay on the inequality of the human races). He forbids Céline and Adèle to share a room. Adèle recounts how Hugo himself would frighten her and her brother, when they misbehaved, by threatening to send them both to Bug Jargal. But she also tells Céline that since she was in Canada, she has had very different experiences, most of them positive, with black people. The fact that they have biblical names is seen as an implicit sign of how civilized they are. And Hugo and Verdet both dismantle their prejudices. Hugo also says that if he had known more about blacks before he wrote *Bug-Jargal*, that story would not have been written (Confiant, *Adèle* 276).

---

[12] "Aussitôt le calme revenu, Hugo retrouvait son énergie habituelle, énergie étonnante pour un homme au seuil de la vieillesse. Nous montions au galetas, par une sorte d'accord tacite, et il se jetait sur ma personne, me labourait les chairs, les yeux curieusement clos. Je me laissais faire quoique j'éprouvai rarement du plaisir. La sensation d'être happée par une houle déchaînée, d'être soulevée, roulée, triturée comme si je ne pesais pas davantage qu'un fétu de paille, m'était par contre fort agréable. Je devenais une île, une petite île tropicale, que couvrait, de son aile immense, la puissante Europe."

Doctors Rufz and de Luppe, who work in the mental institution in Martinique, are openly racist: blacks cannot lose their mental facilities, because they have none to begin with (166). Henry de Montaigue makes an observation about the way that mulattos and blacks interact with each other in Martinique:

> The hatred between the two races, though they rubbed elbows with each other daily, had taken me aback. It is not that I felt any particular affection for people of color, but those in Martinique seemed to me to be so well-regulated, so well molded into French culture, that I forgot their origins. And by the way, no one mentioned Africa! (232)[13]

Adèle tells Céline about her father. He wrote his first book, *Bug-Jargal*, set in the West Indies, when he was sixteen. In it, he described the blacks, she says, as "strange creatures, having just barely left their animal state, bloodthirsty ... but endowed with a sense of cunning ... that was able to baffle European minds, too ensconced in cold reason, further magnified by Descartes" (60–61).[14] For Victor Hugo, she reports, the soul counts more than the intellect: "the sensations of the soul are a thousand times superior to the quibbles of the mind. ... There are invisible forces surrounding us—which we can approach by turning the tables."[15] Hugo believes that the blacks are the only race that does not close itself to these powers, and that that explains their victory over Napoleon's troops. Adèle was shocked to see a black man on the quay at Halifax who was able to speak perfect English (57–61).

While in earlier novels Confiant developed arguments for identity, such as the discourses of *Créolité*, which were never able to do without essentialist attributions, the nineteenth-century ethnic constellations shed light on historic connections that were never, not even then, reducible to pithy descriptions like "thoroughly racialized society." The historical representation of togetherness takes the place of an agenda. Thus, in his novel, Confiant completes the move away from a specific kind of concept of Caribbean identity to questions of conviviality. Unlike the other paradigm shifts staged within Caribbean research that I have presented here, such as the development of the archipelagic model, this

---

13 "La haine entre les deux races, qui pourtant se côtoyaient journellement, m'avait interloqués. Ce n'est pas que j'éprouvai une affection particulière pour les gens de couleur, mais ceux de la Martinique me paraissaient si policés, si bien moulés dans la culture française, que j'en oubliais leur origine. D'ailleurs, personne n'évoquait l'Afrique!"
14 "des créatures étranges, à peine sortis de l'animalité, sanguinaires ... mais dotés d'un sens de la ruse ... qui pouvait dérouter les esprits européens trop engoncés dans la froide raison magnifiée par Descartes."
15 "les sensations de l'âme sont mille fois supérieures aux arguties de l'esprit. ... Des forces invisibles nous entourent—que nous pouvons approcher en faisant tourner les tables."

one has less of a theoretical foundation, but nevertheless the latent presence of the theme of conviviality can be seen as a symptom that the knowledge of conviviality (Ette, *ZusammenLebensWissen*) will prevail as a theoretical paradigm; I discuss this further in section VIII.1.

VII.2.5 Themes within Caribbean Research, or from *Créolité* to the *Tout-monde*

In *Adèle*, Raphaël Confiant takes up the Caribbean research theme in which the Caribbean is interpreted as a "laboratory of modernity," which is not just the object of European theorization but has made an important name for itself globally with the production of cultural theories.

The novel certainly displays some similarities with the genre of the new historical novel: there is no longer any literary construction involving a cyclical chronology and mythical elements set up as an alternative to the linear chronology of the European understanding of history. The filters of subjectivity and a personal presentation are explicitly reflected by the narrator. Confiant illustrates that history can in fact only be subjective, that it is for a subject that receives and narrates it. In the course of this self-reflection, historical philosophical preconditions such as continuity, progression, and teleology are unmasked as constructions. In a way that is symptomatic of the shift towards the modern in literary studies and the humanities, many narrated stories, coexisting with no claim to absolute truth, take the place of one universal history. The focus on questions of the circulation of knowledge and different transfer processes distracts us from the question of history and memory. In contrast to the classic new historical novel, here the nineteenth century is revalued as a background to current debates, since it is not so much that the representational nature of history is being problematized on a metalevel as it is that the historiographically established relationalities are being transformed. The novel is inscribed into the long-established transnational turn.

Writing in the in-between; the tinkerwoman as an exemplary bearer of subversive knowledge; relationality; the archipelagic model: what these paradigms have in common is breaking free of the concentration on constructions of identity and opening up the Caribbean, as a case study of a "testing of conviviality" (cf. Ette, *ZusammenLebensWissen*), to universal dimensions. It is no longer a question of exposing constructions of identity as essentialist but of declaring questions of identity per se to be obsolete. In *Adèle et la pacotilleuse*, Raphaël Confiant offers us a reversion to an earlier phase of accelerated globalization in order to show that many of the phenomena that we consider to be characteristic of our present time began much earlier than we assume.

It is no surprise that he plays with the concepts so easily; after all, as a literary theorist, he has a particular kind of access to these topics. But this brings up the question of his audience's expectations and his own orientation towards that audience. While the discourses of Latin American literature's Boom movement and magic realism, which fulfilled a particular kind of expectation having to do with the exotic and with themes specific to Latin America, were rejected, at the very latest, by the Crack and McOndo movements and their manifestos, French-speaking Caribbean writers of the present and of this phase, on the other hand, are attuned to expectations having to do with the production of theory that originates in the Caribbean, with representatives such as Confiant and Glissant, but is open in a universal way. Thus, Confiant subjects his earlier *Éloge de la Créolité* (In Praise of Creoleness) to a critical retrospective review. But what is there to offer instead? Glissant calls his alternative model *Tout-monde* (the all-world). He takes as his guiding concept a view of the world that substitutes a positive understanding of chaos for the negative tendencies of globalization; this positive chaos model creates non-hierarchical relationships between the elements of its diversity in a network that is not fixed but consists of an ongoing process.

> The *Tout-monde* is the whirling movement by which cultures, peoples, individuals, notions, aesthetics, sensibilities, etc. are perpetually changing through their connections with each other. It is this whirlwind. ... Because when you say a conception of the world, it is an a priori that gives the world an axis and a goal. The *Tout-monde* is a conception of the world without an axis and without a goal, with nothing but the idea of the whirling, necessary, and irrepressible proliferation of all of these contacts, all of these changes, all of these exchanges. (Glissant, "À propos de Tout-Monde," cited in Ludwig and Röseberg 10)[16]

Adèle et la pacotilleuse provides a consistent implementation of the concept of creolization or of the *Tout-monde* that Glissant formulated. The literature is ahead of its own theory: on the theoretical level, Confiant continues to insist on the old concept of *Créolité*, albeit with modifications, but in his literary work he implements all of the theoretical paradigm shifts. The novel's first sentence provides a fitting conclusion:

---

16 "Le Tout-monde, c'est le mouvement tourbillant par lequel changent perpétuellement—en se mettant en rapport les uns avec les autres—les cultures, les peuples, les individus, les notions, les esthétiques, les sensibilités etc. C'est ce tourbillant. ... Parce que quand on dit une conception du monde, c'est un a priori qui donne au monde un axe et une visée. Le Tout-monde, c'est la conception du monde sans axe et sans visée, avec seulement l'idée de la prolifération tourbillante, nécessaire et irrépressible, de tous ces contacts, de tous ces changements, de tous ces échanges."

It is not true that all it takes to hear the rumors of the archipelago is to hold a pearly pink queen conch shell to your ear. All you will hear are indecipherable musics and unappeased sufferings. They spring from the all-world, from the African Guinea, forever lost, from Europe, the merciless lookout that never stops sneering with its great haughtiness. Other lands as well, whose names I have difficulty pronouncing and whose vastness I have difficulty imagining. (Confiant, *Adèle* 13; cf. also Ludwig and Röseberg)[17]

VII.3 Khal Torabully

One of the most important voices addressing cultural theory concepts from the Caribbean and engaged in developing them further is that of Khal Torabully, a poet, filmmaker, and cultural theoretician who was born in Port Louis, Mauritius, in 1956 and now lives mostly in France (cf. Bragard).[18] His concept of "coolitude" builds on Glissant's work but critiques the lack of any Indian perspective in that work; coolitude has a transoceanic orientation. Whether in the islands of the Indian Ocean or those of the Caribbean, the importation of Indian contract workers as an alternative to slavery created a worldwide Indian diaspora, starting in 1830, that revealed its own mechanisms of acculturation and transculturation, because this "population with an ancient culture" refers to people who are both "Creoles *and* Indians" (Glissant, *Kultur und Identität* 41; emphasis in the original; see also Müller and Ueckmann, "Einleitung" 16). Torabully started developing his coolitude project in the 1980s. It is a poetic and poetological attempt to develop a vision and a revision of historical and current globalization processes based on the inclusion of what history has excluded, trying to give voice, as living subjects, to all of those who were forced to hire themselves out as wage and contract workers, usually under miserable circumstances, the world over (cf. Ette, *TransArea* 291).

The coolitude project not only created a literary monument and a memorial site for the coolies—who were primarily from India but also from China and other countries—but also developed a poetics of global migration, as expressed in Torabully's *Cale d'étoiles, Coolitude* (Stardock, Coolitude), published in 1992:

---

17 "Il n'est pas vrai qu'il suffit de porter à l'oreille une conque de lambi au rose nacré pour entendre les rumeurs de l'Archipel. On n'y perçoit que musiques indéchiffrables et douleurs inapaisées. Celles-ci jaillissent du Tout-Monde, de l'Afrique-Guinée à jamais perdue, de l'Europe, implacable vigie qui n'a de cesse de ricaner avec tant et tellement de hautaineté. D'autres terres aussi dont j'ai peine à prononcer les noms et à imaginer l'étendue."
18 Except for some small changes, the following observations are taken from Abel and Müller, "Cultural Forms of Representation of 'Coolies'"; Abel and Müller, "Korallen: Migration und Transozeanität."

> Coolitude to lay the first stone of my memory of all memory, my language of all languages, my share of the uncharted that many bodies and many stories have often deposited in my genes and my islands. ... Here is my love song to the sea and to travel, the odyssey that my marine peoples have not yet written. ... My crew will be among the number of those who erase frontiers in order to enlarge the Country of Man. (Torabully, *Cale d'étoiles* 7)[19]

The crucial thing for Torabully is that he is not concerned just with the memory of certain forms of the most brutal exploitation, but also with a relationality that has become historical and that, in the process of intersecting migrational movements, creates a particular space:

> You from Goa, from Pondicherry, from Chandannager, from / Cocane, from Delhi, from Surat, from London, from Shanghai, / from Lorient, from Saint-Malo, peoples of all the boats / that brought me towards another me, my dock of stars / is my travel plan, my zone, my vision of / the ocean that we all cross, even though we do not / see the stars from the same angle. // When I say coolie, I also say navigator without any / logbook; I say every man who has set off towards the horizon / of his dream, whatever boat he docked or / was supposed to dock. Because when you cross the ocean to be born / elsewhere, the sailor of a voyage with no return likes to plunge back / into his stories, his legends, and his dreams. For the time of an absence of memory. (Torabully, *Cale d'étoiles* 89, cited in Ette, *TransArea* 292)[20]

Significantly, Torabully makes a point never to think of the concept of the coolie in an exclusionary way. Instead, it is used figuratively, to illuminate specific phenomena of a globalization "from below," a globalization of the migrants who cross oceans in search of work. In a lyrical compression, this becomes a worldwide network of all those "travelers" who, as the objects of extreme exploitation, bind together the islands and cities of India, China, and Oceania with Europe's colonial ports (cf. Ette, *TransArea* 293).

---

19 "Coolitude pour poser la première pierre de ma mémoire de toute mémoire, ma langue de toutes les langues, ma part d'inconnu que de nombreux corps et de nombreuses histoires ont souvent déposée dans mes gènes et mes îles. ... Voici mon chant d'amour à la mer et au voyage, l'odyssée que mes peuples marins n'ont pas encore écrite. ... Mon équipage sera au nombre de ceux qui effacent les frontières pour agrandir le Pays de l'Homme."
20 "Vous de Goa, de Pondicheri, de Chandernagor, de / Cocane, de Delhi, de Surat, de Londres, de Shangai, / de Lorient, de Saint-Malo, peuples de tous les bateaux / qui m'emmenèrent vers un autre moi, ma cale d'étoiles / est mon plan de voyage, mon aire, ma vision de / l'océan que nous traversons tous, bien que nous ne / vissions pas les étoiles du même angle. // En disant coolie, je dis aussi tout navigateur sans / registre de bord; je dis tout homme parti vers l'horizon / de son rêve, quel que soit le bateau qu'il accosta ou / dût accoster. Car quand on franchit l'océan pour naître / ailleurs, le marin d'un voyage sans retour aime replonger / dans ses histoires, ses légendes, et ses rêves. Le temps d'une absence de mémoire."

VII.3.1 Coolitude: Migration and Transoceanism

Torabully's inclusion of the ethnic complexity of post-abolitionist societies in the Caribbean and the Indian Ocean makes it possible to conceive of the process of creolization in a less essentialist way. With his coolitude concept, he extends such French-Caribbean-marked models of archipelagic creolism as négritude, *Créolité, Antillanité*, and creolization, as well as Indianism and Indianoceanism (cf. Carter and Torabully 5–7, 16). Coolitude does not derive from geographical belonging or ethnic origin but rather from the economic and legal situation of the coolies, contract workers who came from India, China, Europe, and Africa to work in various archipelagic regions such as the Caribbean, the Indian Ocean, and the Pacific. In his mosaic model of composite identities, Torabully introduces social status as the theoretically decisive factor in creolization (see Abel, "Orientalische Dopplungen").

In his foundational poetic texts *Cale d'étoiles, Coolitude* (Stardock, Coolitude, 1992) and *Chair corail: fragments coolies* (Coral flesh, coolie fragments, 1999), Torabully established the theoretical premises of coolitude. But coolitude first attained an international reception and dissemination through the volume that Torabully put together with the historian Marina Carter: *Coolitude: An Anthology of the Indian Labour Diaspora* (2002). This volume is a collection in multiple ways. It unites Khal Torabully's own poetry on worldwide Indian labor migration with a literary-historical anthology of the poetry and prose of Indian diaspora writers, going back to the mid-nineteenth century, especially in the Indian Ocean—Mauritius (beginning in 1843), Fiji, Java, Goa (1860–1870)—but also in the Americas—Trinidad, Guiana, Suriname, Guadeloupe, and Martinique, starting in 1846. In addition, it represents a monograph on the theory and poetics of coolitude. Formally, it is a mixture of a historical anthology in the narrower sense, a workbook including short definitions, and a theoretical positioning of coolitude in the form of interviews by the authors. Through the hybridity of its textual format, *Coolitude* offers both an academic interpretation of and artistic access to the world of the Indian diaspora by recounting "the essence, or the essences" (Carter and Torabully 148) of the colonial Indian diaspora and deconstructing traditional conceptions from the British empire, using previously unpublished texts including poems and dramatic pieces.

There follows a situating of the theoretical genesis of the concept among a series of theoreticians of creolization and relationality, including Glissant, Deleuze and Guattari, Confiant, Bernabé and Chamoiseau, and Benoist; then, the development of one of the key themes of coolitude, namely the coolie odyssey, the taboo ocean crossing from the Indian subcontinent, is traced. After that, there is a look at the cultural-theoretical aspects of the perception of the

Other, such as the tripled stigmatization of coolies and the experience of contract work. The three models that Torabully and Carter have identified as marking coolies as Other and trapping them in their role as victims are, first, the mystery of the Orient; second, the barbarian invader; and third, the "ambassador of exoticism and sensuality" (187–188). The closing reflections are dedicated to the coolie legacy and consider the memorial politics of the Indian diaspora in the nineteenth and twentieth centuries. Before the anthology ends, with a conclusion called "Revoicing the Coolie" and a collection of Torabully's own prose and poetry, it incorporates a long theoretical section that explains important "Theoretical Premises of Coolitude" in the form of a conversation. The first part addresses the relationships among "Césaire, Négritude and Coolitude" (143–159). The second part stakes out "Elements of the Coolie's Memory" (160–165). In the third part of the interview, aesthetics and literature come into play (165–189), while the fourth section deals with "Tradition, Society and Indianness" (190–194). The fifth section, which is concretely poetological, tries to define "Some Literary Characteristics of Coolitude" (195–213).

The Belgian theorist Véronique Bragard, who continued the theoretical reception of coolitude with her *Transoceanic Dialogues. Coolitude in Caribbean and Indian Ocean Literatures* (2008), pointed out, as an important poetological characteristic, that what was at the center of coolitude was not the coolie per se but rather the nightmarish transoceanic voyage, both as a historical migration and as a metonym for cultural encounters (Carter und Torabully 15). The literary focus therefore always returns to the sea voyage, as an element that destroys and continually reconstructs identity. The voyage thus becomes an incision, displacing the loss of the homeland from the center of diasporic identities. On a more abstract level, the voyage thereby connects with a suppressed meta-memory of diasporic island identities in general, building human bridges, or so-called *hommes-ponts*, who in turn become the interpreters of the world's cultures within their respective island microcosms (Turcotte und Brabant 1983, cited in Carter und Torabully 216).

Torabully's particular contribution to the figure of the transoceanic journey now refers to a poetics of the "Indian Element" (148). The trauma of the ocean crossing takes on a special status in the Indian context, because of the Kala Pani taboo, the taboo against the evil black waters, referring to the leveling of caste differences in the threshold situation that the ship represents. These psychosocial aspects of the ocean trauma are picked up linguistically in coolitude and characterize its particular aesthetic.

VII.3.2 The Maritime Symbolism of the Coral

A further aesthetic circumstance, arising from the focus on the ocean voyage, is the search for maritime symbols. The central image of coolitude is therefore the metaphor of coral flesh (*chair corail*), which stands for hybrid relationalities in the island cultures: "No longer the Hindu man of Calcutta // But coral flesh of the Antilles" (Torabully, *Chair corail* 108).[21]

The coral metaphor is not unlike the mangrove and rhizome images of *Créolité*, but formulated transoceanically. As a symbol for the fluidity of relationships and influences, it uses the coral's properties as an intermediate entity, a creature between stone and animal, that only appears in the sea, and mostly in the tropical belt. Thus, the coral represents archipelagic thinking, in the sense of Glissant's ambiguous thinking (*pensée de l'ambigu*), as well as the porousness of various currents. The coral's characteristic spiral shapes, its circumvolutions, are connected to visualizations of the fractal logics in processes of creolization. Thus, coolitude turns out to be related not just theoretically but also aesthetically to Glissant and the *Créolité* writers, who also consider diasporic identities to be not static and fixed but rather subjected to the ongoing interplay of history, culture, and power (Carter und Torabully 11).

Unlike the rhizome, however, which lives under the earth, the coral can be observed in its living habitat. In addition, it allows for an agglutinating connectedness which is built out of layering, consolidation, and sedimentation, like a palimpsest; this is not just an erratic connectedness but it maintains the egalitarian aspect of connection because it is open to all currents. The very nature of the coral is hybrid, because it is born out of the symbiosis of phytoplankton and zooplankton. For a metaphor of diversity, nothing could be better. The coral is root, polyp, and flattening; it is a form that changes on its own, pliable and hard, dead and alive, and even varied in color. Although it is rooted, it releases the world's largest migration, that of plankton, which can be seen from the moon, like the Great Barrier Reef, a coral archipelago that was named to UNESCO's World Heritage list and is simply the most broadly spread out living sculpture on earth (Torabully, "Quand les Indes" 70; cf. Ette, *TransArea* 295).

In addition to coolitude's "maritime spirit" (Carter and Torabully 158), however, it also has more static visualization components that rely not on dynamic three-dimensional models but on structures of two-dimensional composition, such as the mosaic, in which Creole Indian tiles complete the overall picture of creolization, but it is not the idea of the melting pot that is central. Torabully

---

[21] "Non plus l'homme hindou de Calcutta // Mais chairs corail des Antilles."

sometimes also translates the composite pieces of the mosaic into three-dimensionality in the form of individual roots of the rhizome (Carter and Torabully 152). Even in the coral metaphor, however, the idea of the stone, of that which is solid, does not disappear, and it always leads back to the Césaire-related founding moment of coolitude. Torabully's appeal to négritude and to *Antillanité*, which is understood as négritude's direct heir, are therefore indispensable for an understanding of the theoretical positioning of coolitude. A deep empathy with Aimé Césaire, the founder of the Franco-Caribbean négritude movement, and a 1997 conversation with him in Fort-de-France, Martinique, about the legacy of négritude and its continuation in coolitude, are part of the founding myth of this concept of creolization.

The connection between the two theories involves two ideas: the reconciliation of the "descendants of the oppressed" (Carter und Torabully 172), which understands itself as contributing to the processing of the historical tensions between the legacy of Atlantic slavery and the legacy of the coolies in Creole societies; and the idea of a conceptual bridging or redefinition. The theoretical limits of négritude, which, because of its demand for and recognition of a "black" identity, is seen as being inadequate to the ethnic complexity of post-slavery creolized societies, are thus transcended by the coolitude model. In several places, Carter and Torabully argue that coolitude is not just an Indian version of négritude. First of all, it is not an ethnic or essentialist category (150, 153), and secondly, its focus on the crossing means that neither a mythical origin nor exile itself is thematized but identity is instead dissolved in permeability. Négritude and coolitude share a discursive reclassification of stigmatized colonial alterities; they part ways over the issue of the recognition of the cultural influence that contract migration from India had on some modern societies around the world, societies that it either decisively shaped, such as Mauritius, Trinidad, Guiana, and Fiji, or on which it at least left a mark, such as Guadeloupe, Martinique, and eastern and southern Africa.

Coolitude represents a spatial understanding that not only emphasizes an internal archipelagic relationality in the manifold communications between islands and archipelagoes but also draws attention to the dynamics of an external relationality (Ette, *TransArea* 40). Coolitude thus becomes the model of a spatial history, which is always a history of movement: the forced deportations of enslaved peoples as well as Indian contract workers show that internal and external relationalities must be connected in order to comprehend spaces in a complete and holistic way.

VII.4 J.-M.G. Le Clézio, Édouard Glissant, and Epeli Hau'Ofa: Avant-Gardes in Oceania

The previous reflections on paradigm shifts in Caribbean research and in narrative stagings of the same bring up the question: is there such a thing as a Creole, archipelagic, or transoceanic avant-garde?[22] In fact, a group of writers has recently spoken up, including the three writers J.-M.G. Le Clézio, Édouard Glissant, and Epeli Hau'Ofa. For these authors, Oceania is a crucially significant cultural space, and in their work they take up, in an innovative way, concepts that are important for Caribbean theorization. In his poetological treatise *La cohée du Lamentin* (2005), Édouard Glissant writes:

> In truth, what [Wilfredo Lam] confirms, whether with Picasso, the Surrealists, or Césaire, is the organic and historic convergence of these revolutions in sensibility. It is "modern" with Picasso and "African" with Césaire, because the poetics of their universes address the same archipelagoes of excess, of revolt, and of convulsive beauty that André Breton and his friends, for other reasons, sensible or foolish, also frequent. (182)[23]

These words illustrate on the one hand what a central point of reference the avant-gardes represented for Caribbean intellectuals talking about cultural theory and, on the other, that in their reception there has always been a tension between the European and the non-European.

In fact, the avant-gardes, and especially their second phase, that is to say from the nineteen-fifties to the early nineteen-seventies, did constitute a key reference point for many intellectuals from postcolonial constellations. Given the per se non-European dimension of the historical Breton-centered avant-garde, their attraction for precisely non-European writers, which also always involves a provocation, makes sense. Thus, it is not surprising that Glissant feels it necessary to process his intellectual father, Aimé Césaire, who as the representative of négritude was in close contact with André Breton. But what are the dynamics that determine the specifically non-European avant-gardes? With reference to Hal Foster, Geeta Kapur writes, "if the avant-garde is a historically conditioned phenomenon and emerges only in a moment of real political disjuncture, it will appear in various forms in different parts of the world at different times"

---

[22] With regard to the following remarks, see Müller, "J.-M.G. Le Clézio."
[23] "En réalité, ce que [Wilfredo Lam] vérifie avec Picasso comme avec les Surréalistes ou avec Césaire, c'est la convergence organique autant qu'historique de ces révolutions de la sensibilité. Il est 'moderne' avec Picasso et 'africain' avec Césaire, parce que les poétiques de leurs univers abordent aux mêmes archipels de la démesure, de la révolte et de la beauté convulsive que fréquentent, pour d'autres raisons ou déraisons, André Breton et ses amis."

(Kapur 374). The Nigerian writer and curator Okwui Enwezor expressed himself in a similarly provocative way in a contribution to the Documenta 11 catalogue:

> What, then, is the fate of the avant-garde in this climate of incessant assault upon its former conclusions? ... While strong revolutionary claims have been made for the avant-garde within Westernism, its vision of modernity remains surprisingly conservative and formal. ... The propagators of the avant-garde have done little to constitute a space of self-reflexivity that can understand new relations of artistic modernity not founded on Westernism. (Enwezor 46)

I would now like to look at two representatives of French-speaking constellations, namely Édouard Glissant and Jean-Marie Gustave Le Clézio. Glissant was from Martinique and lived for a long time in France and in the United States; Le Clezió, though he was born in Nice, had family roots in Mauritius and indeed grew up there. Both of them, in terms of their biographies as well as in the way they publicly positioned themselves as writers, belonged to the second phase of the historical avant-garde project[24]; they went through various stages of boundary drawing and in 2006, in a common project that I call the "oceanic turn," they chose new emphases that, although they were not explicitly called avant-garde, nevertheless implicitly corresponded to two established criteria for the avant-garde: first, the dissolution of the line separating art and life, and secondly, the group character of the avant-garde project. My thesis is that non-European, and at the moment, specifically, oceanic positionings have the particular potential to produce alternative avant-garde projects still today, because the tension that is inherent to their writing, with respect to colonial dimensions at the time of the historical avant-gardes, creates a productive dialectic, over the long term, at different phases of differentiation.

After we take a quick look at the first phase of Le Clézio's and Glissant's avant-gardist positions, I want to then look briefly at a Creole current in which Le Clézio and Glissant are not the main players but with which they are nevertheless closely connected and which is key to understanding their later development: the *Créolité* discourses of the Martinican novelists and cultural theorists Raphaël Confiant, Jean Bernabé, and Patrick Chamoiseau, who can be counted as the intellectual sons of their mentor Glissant. At the end of the nineteen-eighties, these three writers produced a manifesto that not only offered an answer to the urgent question of a Caribbean aesthetics but was also clearly avant-gardist. This current is then in turn followed by a reaction from Glissant and Le Clézio, the erstwhile mentors of the advocates of *Créolité*; Glissant and Le Clézio issue a

---

24 On the project character of the avant-garde, see Asholt.

plea for a transoceanic identity. With respect to this third phase, finally, extracts from the work of the Fijian essayist Epeli Hau'Ofa will show that the networked character of the avant-garde project is particularly significant for a transoceanic continuation. The writers I highlight here also represent three different oceans: Hau'Ofa the Pacific, Le Clezió the Indian Ocean, and Glissant the Atlantic.

VII.4.1 Le Clézio und His Relationship to the Classic Avant-Gardes of the Nineteen-Fifties

> Too often, as well, this notion of culture is reduced to just the arts. Why should that be where culture is? In this life, everything is important. Rather than saying of a man that he is cultivated, I would rather that I were told: he is a man. (Le Clézio, *L'extase matérielle* 17)[25]

This is what Le Clézio writes in *L'extase matérielle* (Material ecstasy, 1959), the author's early theoretical manifesto in which he develops fundamental poetological ideas. Material ecstasy can be described as a form of a different condition (Rimpau 20). What is meant is a kind of pattern of religious experience in which, as in mysticism, the borders between spirit and matter and between self and world become fluid. It is about the attempt to relate the visible with the invisible and, ideally, to experience the transcendent through the world (21).

In her study of J.-M.G. Le Clézio, Laetitia Rimpau points out that the central theme in *L'extase* is the suffering of consciousness and the search for ways to avoid this suffering. Material ecstasy can be seen as a redemption myth: a form of metamorphosis—both punishing and liberating at the same time—in which a spiritual connection with basic forms of nonhuman existence is sought through a mimetic immersion. This is expressed, programmatically, as "one requires metamorphoses" (*on oblige aux métamorphoses*; Le Clézio, *L'extase matérielle* 246). With respect to this particular aspect, Rimpau aptly works out that this is about a voyage into the material world, which is both resistant and at the same time challenging. Materiality represents the experimental field that thinking is able to process and through which it can change itself (Rimpau 20). This aspiration of Le Clézio's to dissolve the boundary between art and life, along with his connection to the Tel Quel group, ties him very closely to the avant-gardes, although he makes no radical confession in that direction. His at-

---

25 "Trop souvent aussi, on réduit cette notion de culture au seul fait des arts. Pourquoi serait-ce là la culture? Dans cette vie, tout est important. Plutôt que de dire d'un homme qu'il est cultivé, je voudrais qu'on me dise: c'est un homme."

titude is thus ambivalent; he only partially incorporates avant-gardist tendencies. This is particularly clear in the following passage:

> In order to say of a man that he is civilized, we often use the word "cultivated." Why? What is this culture? Often, too often, it means that this man knows Greek or Latin, that he is able to recite poetry by heart, that he knows the names of Dutch painters and German musicians. In that case, culture is a way to shine in a world where futility is in order. This culture is nothing but the flip side of ignorance. Cultivated for this person, uneducated for that one. Being relative, culture is an infinite phenomenon; it can never be completed. What is he then, this cultivated man that they want to give us as a model? (Le Clézio, *L'extase matérielle* 22)[26]

VII.4.2 Glissant and Surrealism

A dialectical relationship between independence, on the one hand, and influence from the European avant-garde project, on the other, appears to be constitutive of Glissant's integration into the second phase of the avant-gardes. In the late nineteen-fifties, Glissant follows Césaire quite closely and, after a certain period of conflict, reproaches him for only emulating the European avant-gardists, who, Glissant says, are not creating any literature but are only giving a new look to things that already exist.

Starting in the nineteen-forties, négritude slowly became a broader movement. From 1941 to 1945, Césaire published the journal *Tropiques* in Martinique. This journal made a point of presenting surrealism as a way for the Antillean, in particular, to be able to find a way back to his unconscious, buried, actual personality; in this, Césaire goes against the established order.[27] Glissant, who as a student at the Lycée Schoelcher in Fort-de-France was under Césaire's influence and who was later one of his most dedicated critics, affirms the tremendous significance and richness of *Tropiques* for Martinique's later literary development. On the one hand, the articles about modern French poetry are formative for Glissant (Ludwig 146). On the other hand, Chamoiseau has aptly summarized Glis-

---

26 "Pour dire d'un homme qu'il est civilisé, on dit souvent 'cultivé.' Pourquoi? Qu'est-ce que c'est que cette culture? Souvent, trop souvent, cela veut dire que cet homme sait le grec ou le latin, qu'il est capable de réciter des vers par cœur, qu'il connaît les noms des peintres hollandais et des musiciens allemands. La culture sert alors à briller dans un monde où la futilité est de mise. Cette culture n'est que l'envers d'une ignorance. Cultivé pour celui-ci, inculte pour celui-là. Étant relative, la culture est un phénomène infini; elle ne peut jamais être accomplie. Qu'est-il donc, cet homme cultivé que l'on veut nous donner pour modèle?"
27 Ralph Ludwig's research laid an important foundation for my observations on *Créolité* in the following. See Ludwig 106.

sant's role as the antithesis in literary development, as the conqueror of négritude.

Between 1950 and 1970, Glissant and Le Clézio both engaged vigorously with prominent representatives of the avant-garde, including the Tel Quel group and Aimé Césaire. Both of them participated in the avant-garde movement to some degree, but not consistently. They are paradigmatic of Luhmann's oft-cited dictum that the avant-garde only articulated the problem and shaped it. But now we have to observe how the art world deals with this problem that it has set for itself (see Magerski 99). In Le Clézio's case, this occurs in a question about art and life, and in Glissant's case through the attempt to stage an otherness without falling back into essentialisms.

VII.4.3 Creolization as an Avant-Garde

> We are no longer afraid ... to inhabit the French language in a Creole way; we are not talking about decorating it with little Creole words to create a kind of folkloristic and regionalist French, that is not at all what we mean. What we are talking about is recuperating all of the rhetoric of the Creole language and trying to graft it through French linguistic material. (Chamoiseau and Confiant, "En guise d'introduction" 14; cf. Ludwig 146)[28]

This is the Martinican writer Raphaël Confiant, in an interview with Ralph Ludwig and Ottmar Ette. In his analysis, Ralph Ludwig makes it clear that Confiant's statement means that the act of resisting the cultural assimilation of the Antilles —an act that represents an important stimulant for Antillean literary debate—is connected not to the semantic but rather to the aesthetic plane. On the linguistic level, it is clear that the success of the literary language that is thus described may well have consequences for standard French. As the great literary prizes go to literary texts written in a French that is shot through with oral Creole, thus introducing them into a newly contoured canon whose traditional form was always the basis of proper written French (the *bon usage*), this orally influenced French-language literature is also shaking up the conventional standard for prestige (Ludwig 146).

In the same interview, Patrick Chamoiseau says:

---

28 "Nous n'avons plus peur ... d'habiter la langue française de manière créole; non pas de la décorer avec des petits mots créoles pour créer une espèce de français folklorique et régionaliste, il ne s'agit pas du tout de cela. Il s'agit de récupérer toute la rhétorique de la langue créole et d'essayer de la greffer à travers un matériau linguistique français." Concerning the following remarks see also Müller and Ueckmann, "Einleitung" 18 ff.

> We have a Creole imaginary that is our own, but which has been suppressed, and without which we cannot exist. This work of recuperating Creole culture is done, among other places, in the novel. This recuperation of Creole culture has a necessarily historical coloring, and that is why many of our novels are also historical explorations, because we cannot try to reinvest the times and the cultural moments of our vision of the world if we do not include themes that have a profound resonance in our substance, in our imaginary. (Chamoiseau and Confiant, "En guise d'introduction" 14)[29]

In his novel *Le Nègre et l'Amiral* (The Negro and the admiral, 1988), Confiant deals with the period from 1939 to 1945, when Martinique was cut off from the outside world. In it, the avant-garde project experiences a mise-en-abîme, with the appearance of Claude-Lévi Strauss, the Russian revolutionary Victor Serge, und André Breton. With his own particular brand of irony, Confiant shows Breton discovering the journal *Tropiques* (Confiant, *Le Nègre et l'Amiral* 98–99; cf. Ludwig 147).

In their *Éloge de la créolité* (1989), Chamoiseau and Confiant, along with the linguist Jean Bernabé, define their fundamental theoretical positions (cf. Ludwig 148). *Créolité* is based on the historical reality that established Antillean society: the forced contact between cultures. In this respect, the Antilles went through a process that is now increasingly shaping the world: "The world is entering a state of *Créolité*" (*Le monde va en état de créolité*; Bernabé, Chamoiseau, and Confiant 52; cf. Ludwig 148). Ludwig points out that to begin with, *Créolité* has exemplary anthropological value because the kind of patchwork identity that ends in *Créolité* is the appropriate way towards (post-)modern self-discovery (Ludwig 148). But the primary goal of *Créolité* has to do with the Creole societies of the Antilles themselves and includes the appreciation and preservation of the collective oral memory. This act is not an exclusively semantic one but extends into the macro- and microstructure of literary texts; this is the only way to achieve what Confiant and Chamoiseau call a Creole rhetoric (Ludwig 149).

Compared to Le Clézio's and Glissant's early forms of expression, the avant-gardist *Créolité* project of *Éloge de la créolité* has a consistent agenda: the group expresses itself as a vanguard in the classical sense and leaves no doubt about its ambiguity. There is a very obvious imbalance that appears here: while the Eu-

---

[29] "Nous avons un imaginaire créole qui nous appartient, mais qui a été refoulé, et sans lequel nous ne pouvons pas exister. Ce travail de récupération de la culture créole se fait, entre autres, dans le roman. Cette récupération de la culture créole a nécessairement une coloration historique, et c'est pourquoi beaucoup de nos romans sont aussi des explorations historiques, parce qu'on ne peut pas tenter de réinvestir des temps, des moments culturels de notre vision du monde si on n'inclue pas des thématiques ayant des résonances profondes dans notre fond sensible, dans notre imaginaire."

ropean avant-gardes incorporate non-European cultures, the non-European and anticolonial avant-gardes appropriate European culture, but with a critical stance. The ever-present asymmetry of the avant-garde, which the Creole writers note and critique so strongly, leads to the question of whether an avant-garde position is in fact only possible in the first place from the point of view of an imperial understanding.

VII.4.4 Transoceanism as an Avant-Garde

Critics have claimed that the representatives of *Créolité* failed, in the end, to capture ethnic difference without falling back into essentialisms (Mignolo, *Local Histories/Global Designs* 241–242). As a result, there has been some discussion about basic principles and some further development: as already mentioned in this volume, since the turn of the millennium, new positions have been established, among which Glissant's *Introduction à une poétique du divers* (Introduction to a poetics of variety) has met with a particularly strong resonance. In it, Glissant drafts the alternative model of "archipelization" and describes the whole world as being in a process of creolization and archipelization. The last and most comprehensive step in Glissant's thinking is then the *Tout-monde*, the all-world (cf. Ludwig and Röseberg 9)[30] that we have already discussed, in which non-hierarchical relationships among the elements of variety are recognized in an ongoing process. Put more abstractly, and expanded into a societal model, the *Tout-monde* implies a rejection of one-dimensionality, of a hierarchically structured understanding of culture, of a closed and inflexible social order (9, 10). A consistent understanding of the *Tout-monde* also implies that the various "media implementations" of communicative and aesthetic expression, such as literature, poetry, music, and the visual arts, cannot be separated from each other (10). Although the *Tout-monde* has the potential to function as an avant-garde, it nevertheless requires an additional concretization of art: a few years before his death in 2011, Glissant began a radical project using life itself, called *Les peuples de l'eau* (The water peoples). Here, for the first time, art and life are united in an innovative way, giving the project an avant-garde character:

> On July 27, 2004, under the auspices of UNESCO, the ship *La Boudeuse* set off from Bastia, in Corsica, under the command of Captain Patrice Franceschi, with twenty-four scientists

---

30 Ludwig and Röseberg refer to Beate Thill's translation and commentary in Glissant, *Kultur und Identität* 73.

on board. After 1063 days and having traveled sixty thousand kilometers, the ship returned to Bastia on June 25, 2007.

There were twelve expeditions planned to visit eight populations that are only reachable by water because they live on secluded islands, river banks, or coasts: in other words, "peoples on the water." The expeditions took the team to the Yuhup in the Amazon; to Easter Island (aka Rapa Nui); to Fatu Hiva, the most remote of the Marquesas Islands; to Raga Island (Vanuatu), in Oceania; to the Buginese people on Sulawesi in Indonesia; and to the Badjao people who live between the Philippines and Indonesia. Twelve writers and journalists, chosen by Édouard Glissant, each took part in one of the expeditions; [these included] Alain Borer, Gérard Chaliand, Régis Debray, Patrick Chamoiseau, Jean-Claude Guillebaud, J.-M.G. Le Clézio, Federica Matta, Edwy Plenel, Antonio Tabucchi, and André Velter.[31]

VII.4.5 Transoceanic Representations. Le Clézio, *Raga*; and Hau'Ofa, *We Are the Ocean*

While Le Clézio advocated an inner voyage in his 1959 book *L'extase matérielle*, with his fictional travel journal *Raga* he staged a very concrete voyage: in a total of nine chapters, the Nobel Prize winner interwove several stories with historical, anthropological, and documentary references to Raga Island (in what was once the New Hebrides, now the Republic of Vanuatu). He begins with a short exposition on the early European expeditions to the Pacific, in search of the Australian continent, with its fabled treasures. He calls Oceania, with its many islands, an invisible continent that the Europeans neither could nor wanted to see. Raga is a part of the European colonization. After the historical excursus there follows a fictional story about the long trip that one family took in a boat across the sea, and about the family's arrival on Raga. The story combines some of the myths and legends of the Vanuatans. The author also reports on his own trip to

---

31 "Unter der Schirmherrschaft der UNESCO brach am 27. Juli 2004 das ... Segelschiff *La Boudeuse* unter dem Kapitän Patrice Franceschi mit 24 Wissenschaftlern an Bord von Bastia (Korsika) zu einer Weltumsegelung auf. Nach 1063 Tagen und 60.000 zurückgelegten Kilometern kehrte das Schiff am 25. Juni 2007 nach Bastia zurück.
Geplant waren zunächst zwölf Expeditionen zu acht Völkern, die nur vom Wasser aus erreichbar sind, da sie auf abgeschiedenen Inseln, an Flussufern oder an Küsten leben, also 'Völker am Wasser.' Die Expeditionen brachte die Mannschaft dann zu den Yuhup/Amazonas; zu den Osterinseln der Rapa Nui; nach Fata Hiva, der abgeschiedensten Marquesasinsel; auf die Insel Raga/Vanuatu in Ozeanien; zu den Bugis der Celebes Inseln (Indonesien) und zum Jaranga-Archipel, wo die Badjaos zwischen den Philippinen und Indonesien leben. Zwölf Schriftsteller und Journalisten, ausgewählt von Édouard Glissant, nahmen jeweils an einer der Expeditionen teil[, darunter]: Alain Borer, Gérard Chaliand, Régis Debray, Patrick Chamoiseau, Jean-Claude Guillebaud, J.-M.G. Le Clézio, Federica Matta, Edwy Plenel, Antonio Tabucchi und André Velter." See the Wunderhorn Verlag's publishing program ("Völker am Wasser").

Raga, made on the invitation of Édouard Glissant, on board the three-masted ship *La Boudeuse* (described above). He tells of his encounters with the people there and of their stories, which deal with life, customs, and their confrontations with the Europeans. Le Clézio notices the traces of colonization, which can still be felt today: the islands have been drastically depopulated through imported diseases, slavery, and the caprice of the colonial powers. He mentions that after colonization ended, the people returned to their natural gardens, where the spirits lived, and that they stopped tending to the Europeans' plantations, which relied on clearing and monoculture, instead allowing them to become overgrown. Finally, he shows the many various forms of the island peoples' resistance to colonization, along with their consequences. That resistance expresses itself in the Creole language and, most of all, in music.

Le Clézio then leaves Raga, taking with him the stories and the impressions that the island and its people made on him. He hopes that all of Oceania, that "invisible continent," will some day have its freedom finally returned to it, and he analyzes the degree to which the recent history of Vanuatu has become a caricature. It is said that Bislama, the official language, is a *patois*, a dialect. By the time the West had taken hold of the archipelagoes of this ocean, it was already too late. The drums of Ambrym, of Efate, the conch shells of Tahiti were not enough to keep the intruders away who came in steel ships nor to ward off the motley crowds of people who followed them: settlers, tourists, pedophiles—fourteen-year-olds were married off to Gauguin and Fletcher—and, on top of those, missionaries, who wanted to root out the demons and clothe the inhabitants' nakedness (Le Clézio, *Raga* 92–93). The "paradise islands" became a hell for prisoners and prostitutes. Later, the Pacific became the battleground for a merciless war and then an open testing ground for nuclear weapons. Le Clézio asks, provocatively: Is this embarrassing for the French? Have these far-off archipelagoes not been a no-man's-land ever since they were first conquered? Did we not have every right to do whatever we wanted with them and with their inhabitants, shamelessly? Disunited, chopped into pieces, divided up among the colonial powers, the Pacific continent became invisible. A non-place, inhabited by "savages," by former cannibals. Or, what amounts to the same thing, a Garden of Eden where everything existed in excess: flowers, fruits, women.

Given the critique of colonialism on the one hand and the emphasis on the relational dimension of transcolonial thinking, paired with fictional elements, on the other, Le Clézio's staging of Raga Island proves to be trans-archipelagic and represents a worldwide cultural model: a crossing and interpenetration of relationships among various archipelagoes that have entered into a reciprocal process of transformation. Epeli Hau'Ofa, from Fiji, also records this transoceanic dimension (see Müller and Ueckmann, "Einleitung" 28 f.):

> There is a world of difference between viewing the Pacific as "islands in a far sea" and as "a sea of islands." The first emphasizes dry surfaces in a vast ocean far from the centres of power. Focussing in this way stresses the smallness and remoteness of the islands. The second is a more holistic perspective in which things are seen in the totality of their relationships. (Hau'Ofa, *We Are the Ocean* 22)

Hau'Ofa takes up Glissant's and Le Clézio's ideas and advocates a paradigm shift in how we see the Pacific by thinking of it through the relational dimension of a transoceanic space. The element of relationality has an existential character for every interpretation of Oceania, expressed as the paradigm of a "sea of islands" in contrast to the vision of many "islands in a far sea":

> Continental men, namely Europeans, on entering the Pacific after crossing huge expanses of ocean, introduced the view of "islands in a far sea." From this perspective the islands are tiny, isolated doors in a vast ocean. Later on, continental men—Europeans and Americans—drew imaginary lines across the sea, making the colonial boundaries that confined ocean peoples to tiny spaces for the first time. These boundaries today define the island states and territories of the Pacific. (ibid.)

Hau'Ofa implements Derek Walcott's dictum that "The sea is history." In Hau'Ofa's manifesto *We Are the Ocean*, he argues for reclaiming the ocean as a significant cultural space. Like Le Clézio, he, too, refers to Glissant and the *Peuples de l'eau* project. Thus, a worldwide network of oceanic connections is created, connections that position themselves as avant-garde in that the outmoded idea of a manifesto is replaced with the radical staging of art as life: the sea voyage becomes text. This radicalism can only arise because Glissant and Le Clézio, its main proponents, displayed a certain ambivalence in their integration into the historical avant-gardes. The dialectical tension experiences a productive dissolution in a new avant-garde tension. The relational connection across the oceans becomes a constitutive element. What functions as a network on the spatial level can be understood as a project on the level of time (Asholt 97–120; Berg and Fähnders 14). The concept of the network is of course a product of the late twentieth century, the World Wide Web, and computer networks. But it is no coincidence that understanding the avant-garde as a network was and is not strange to the avant-garde itself (Berg and Fähnders 12).

In summary, we can say that the writers discussed here are representative of two epistemological turns: first, a trans-essentialist one, and second, a transterritorial one. The step of aggregating the two paradigm shifts is then crossed with the different respective roles as avant-garde movements. We have seen three different variations of the avant-gardist dimension: 1. ambivalent, in the early writings of Glissant and Le Clézio; 2. radical, that is to say consistently avant-garde, in the *Créolité* writers; and 3. truly avant-garde, in the late work of Glissant and Le Clézio. To put it concretely, both Glissant and Le Clézio developed their positions over the period from 1950 to 1970 through intensive engagement with prominent representatives of the avant-garde such as the Tel Quel group and Aimé Césaire. Both of them participated to a certain degree, but they were not able to implement the consistent radicalism of the following generations: with a manifesto and all of the characteristics that can be classified as avant-garde, the representatives of *Créolité*—the "sons"—put their faith in a paradigm shift. It is not until forty years later that a new (avant-gardist) paradigm is successfully formulated, which, though it does not explicitly call itself avant-garde, for that very reason in fact contains in itself a latent avant-garde dimension.

VIII Knowledge about Conviviality, or on the Relevance of Research into the Nineteenth-Century Caribbean

VIII.1 Norms of Knowledge about Conviviality: Utopias of Caribbeanness

Following from the third thesis that began this study, about the current relevance of nineteenth-century Caribbean research, I now propose, after the excursus into contemporary literature, to submit the texts we have already discussed to a new interpretive paradigm. This is a reading that connects to the question of conviviality that I raised in the introduction. To what extent is the theoretical apparatus that has been developed by present-day theorists such as Gilroy, Appadurai, Mignolo, and above all Ette useful for nineteenth-century texts? To address the question of the extent to which norms of knowledge about conviviality are represented in literary texts, I want to juxtapose pre-1848 textual examples with post-1848 examples that make the explicit expression of an agenda of good or ideal conviviality legible. This approach proves to be particularly useful for pointing out the potential of the texts' normative content. For the pre-1848 texts, this involves utopias of slaveowning societies, on the one hand, and of a united, mixed-race society, on the other. For post-1848 texts, mostly characteristic of the Spanish-speaking Caribbean of the second half of the nineteenth century, it is utopias of *Caribeanidad* (Caribbeanness).

Outre-mer, the 1835 novel by the *Béké* writer Maynard de Queilhe, from the French colony of Martinique, draws a utopia of a peaceful slave society. As I have shown, this literary example represents the model of an ideal conviviality on the basis of a social order in which everyone has their place and where the slaves are treated very well. While the pro-slavery stance of someone like Maynard de Queilhe is symptomatic of French Antillean writers from the plantation owner class, there are also definitely utopian future-oriented projects that see the mixing of the "races" as a positive thing. It is not a coincidence that such ideas often arise in the colonial centers. Thus, one year after the publication of *Outre-mer*, it was possible to read about the utopia of a new, mixed race in the anti-slavery *Revue des Colonies*:

> From these whites, from these blacks, from these reds, a mixed race will be founded of Europeans, Africans, and Americans who, in a few generations and through diverse intersections, will arrive at the brown, the caramel, the plum—sir, the orangeish, to a pale yellow, lightly coppered. All of these singularities, all of these marvels of civilization that raise and

interest our hearts and our minds are more or less near. (*Revue des Colonies* July 1836, 20–21)[1]

Thanks to this imminent intermixing, which will lead to unpredictable results, there are miracles of civilization to be expected—a norm of knowledge about conviviality being communicated in this quotation that is very unusual for its time.

Starting in 1860, there was a new group that entered the scene in the Spanish Caribbean: the Puerto Rican intellectuals Ramón Emeterio Betances and Eugenio María de Hostos, as well as the Cuban Antonio Maceo, had realized that they shared the same history. Antonio Maceo was a dedicated anti-racist. He was against slavery, against the inequality of the races, and against every kind of oppression. His commitment to better humanitarian conditions was inextricably bound up with the struggle for independence from Spain, which for him implied a commitment to "the dignity of the black race" (Torres Cuevas 115, cited in Zacair 57). And this in turn led Maceo, exactly as it did for Betances, to an even stronger orientation towards Haiti. Haiti, too, was supposed to be a part of the new Caribbean federation. Maceo merged anti-racist and pro-Caribbean attitudes into an agenda called *Caribeanidad*.

Betances himself also had both European and African ancestors. He spent his entire life fighting for the independence of Puerto Rico and of Cuba and working towards a Caribbean confederation, as in this speech that he gave in Port-au-Prince in 1870:

> Thus, my brothers and sisters, our past is so intertwined that I cannot sketch a history of Cuba without encountering other features that are already inscribed into Haiti's history. We may no longer separate our respective lives. I repeat: from one point to another on the largest island in the Caribbean Sea, every mind is stirred by the same question: the future of the Antilles. Who could be so blind as not to see it? We are carrying the same struggle forward; we are fighting for the same cause, and therefore we must live the same life. ... United, we will form a chain of forces that will dominate our enemies, the only net that is able to save us. ... Spain's efforts to crush the insurrection, to sell Cuba to the United States, and to open the way for all of the Antilles to be absorbed into the Anglo-Saxon race, will be in vain. Let

---

[1] "De ces blancs, de ces noirs, de ces rouges, il se fondera une race mélangée d'Européens, d'Africains et d'Américains, qui en quelques générations et au travers des croisements divers, arrivera, par le brun, le carmélite, le prune—monsieur, l'orangé, à un jaune pâle, légèrement cuivré. Toutes ces singularités, toutes ces merveilles de civilisation qui élèvent et intéressent notre cœur et notre esprit, sont plus ou moins prochaines."

us unite, let us love one another, and let us form one single people. (Bonafoux 114–115, cited in Zacair 51)[2]

For Eugenio María de Hostos, the Antilles were an abstraction, a place where he first set foot after having lived many years in Spain and visiting both North and South America. His ideas changed significantly between the publications of *Bayoán*, in 1863, and *Liga de los Independientes* (League of the independents), in 1876.

La peregrinación de Bayoán (The pilgrimage of Bayoán) differs in many ways from other works in Latin America's canon of founding fiction, and it does not correspond to the interpretation developed by Doris Sommer for a foundational fiction. The innovation of *Bayoán* lies in the way in which it distances itself from an organic model of the nation and in its argument for a supranational model. The novel was first published in Spain, in 1863, with the intention of reaching the liberal circles of Spanish society. However, it met with a very scant reception, with the well-known exception of Giner de los Ríos. This made it all the more surprising that the novel was then banned in Puerto Rico itself. According to Richard Rosa, the political function of the novel lay precisely in the fact that it was specifically directed at Spanish liberals:

> The novel thus has a political character that is explicitly addressed to Spanish liberals—many of whom were Hostos's friends and companions—so that they would include, in their political platform, an administrative and economic reform of relationships with the Antilles, which would manifest itself in a new friendly union. Hostos believed that if they read the novel, they would be convinced that it was not just convenient but also necessary to include, in their politics, a colonial reform that could include the idea of the federation. (Rosa 46)[3]

---

2 "De ese modo, hermanos míos, nuestro pasado está tan entretejido que no puedo trazar un boceto histórico de Cuba sin encontrar otros rasgos que ya están inscritos en la historia de Haití. Ya no nos está permitido separar nuestras vidas respectivas. Lo repito: desde un punto al otro de la mayor isla del mar Caribe, cada mente está agitada por la misma cuestión: el futuro de las Antillas. ¿Quién puede ser tan ciego como para no verlo? Llevamos adelante la misma lucha; luchamos por la misma causa, por eso tenemos que vivir una misma vida. ... Unidos formaremos esa cadena de fuerzas que dominará a nuestros enemigos, la única red capaz de salvarnos. ... Vano será que España intente aplastar la insurrección, venderles más tarde Cuba a los Estados Unidos y abrir el camino para la absorción de todas las Antillas por parte de la raza anglosajona. Unámonos, amémonos los unos a los otros, formemos un solo pueblo."
3 "La novela en ese sentido tiene un carácter político explícitamente dirigido a los liberales españoles—muchos de los cuales eran amigos y compañeros de Hostos—para que incluyan dentro de su agenda política la reforma administrativa y económica de las relaciones con las Antillas, que se manifiesta en una nueva reunión familiar. Hostos pensaba que al leer la novela éstos

Hostos's aim was a revolution in Spanish society. Only when that had been successfully carried out would it be possible to turn one's gaze towards the Antilles in a productive way.

> What he had implied was not merely a kind of pro-colonial, or conciliatory, project, but rather an attempt to completely transform Spain's political, and even cultural, system and to carry out a complete decentralization of that system, which he hoped to see when the democrats and federalists of the peninsula came to power. (45)[4]

The Antilles themselves, however, were unknown territory for Hostos, which led him to idealize them to a certain degree. His 1868 speech at the *Ateneo de Madrid* shows his clear break with Spain's liberals. For him, the federation is the "absolute republic" and the "liberal alliance of all national biases."

> I am an American: I have the honor of being Puerto Rican and I must be a federalist. I am a colonist and a product of colonial despotism. ... and I took revenge on it, imagining a definitive form of liberty, and I conceived a confederation of ideas, since a political federation was impossible for me. Because I am American, because I am a colonist, because I am Puerto Rican, because I am a federalist. From my island I can see Santo Domingo, I can see Cuba, I can see Jamaica, and I think about the confederation: I look to the north and I can feel the confederation, I follow the semicircle of islands that geographically link and "federate" Puerto Rico with Latin America, and I prophesy a providential confederation. (Hostos, "¿Cuál de las dos formas?" 97–98, cited in Gaztambide Géigel 47)[5]

Hostos takes a decidedly political stance: his declared goal is the independence of Cuba and of Puerto Rico. His Latin Americanism did not just develop after his trip to the Latin American mainland (to Peru); it was already expressed earlier, for example in a text he wrote in Panama in 1870, "En el Istmo" (On the isthmus),

---

quedarían convencidos de que es no sólo conveniente sino necesario incluir en su política una reforma colonial que podía hasta incluir la idea de la federación."
4 "Lo que había implícito no era meramente un tipo de proyecto pro-colonial o conciliatorio sino una tentativa de transformar por completo el sistema político y hasta cultural de España, operar una descentralización completa de este que esperaba ver con el acceso al poder de los demócratas y federalistas peninsulares."
5 "Yo soy americano: yo tengo la honra de ser puertorriqueño y tengo que ser federalista. Colono, producto del despotismo colonial ... me vengué de él imaginando una forma definitiva de libertad y concebí una confederación de ideas, ya que me era imposible una confederación política. Porque soy americano, porque soy colono, porque soy puertorriqueño, por eso soy federalista. Desde mi isla veo a Santo Domingo, veo a Cuba, veo a Jamaica, y pienso en la confederación: miro hacia el norte y palpo la confederación, recorro el semicírculo de islas que ligan y 'federan' geográficamente a Puerto Rico con la América Latina, y me profetizo una confederación providencial."

shortly before his voyage to Peru on board ship. His view is also expressed very clearly in an 1876 article:

> Now an even more extensive horizon, Bolívar's culminating design—the Latin American union—takes an accessible form in our time. That form is the diplomatic league of all of the governments of this America, in an international entity. Without this entity, our Latin America lacks strength with respect to the rest of the world. Of all the obstacles that get in the way of the establishment of this international entity, the lack of a common interest is the greatest. Neither governments, nor peoples, there is no one among the Latin American peoples who does not know, who does not sense, that the independence of the Antilles is their common interest. (Hostos, "Lo que intentó Bolívar," cited in Gaztambide Géigel 49)[6]

Hostos combines *Puertorriqueñismo*, *Antillanismo*, *Latinoamericanismo*, and *Americanismo*. What all of his conceptions share is that they do not refer to a purely geographical territory. A key difference between Betances and Hostos is that Betances always includes Haiti in his considerations, while for Hostos, Haiti plays no role. During his stay in New York, Hostos provides a clear geopolitical definition of his efforts:

> I think it is necessary for the Americas to complete their process of civilization by serving two ideas: the unification of freedom through the federation of nations, and the unification of the races through the fusion of all of them. All the members of the continent—mainlands and islands—should take part in this work. The mainlands have begun their fusion ... the Antilles are outside this American sphere of action and attempting to enter it. What are the Antilles? They are the bond, the connection between the fusion of European standards and ideas in North America and the fusion of races and disparate natures which is being painfully carried out in Latin America. They are the natural geographic median between both parts of the continent as well as the producers of a transcendental fusion of races; politically, the Antilles are the pivot of the scales, the true federal bond of the giant federation of the future; socially, humanly, they are the natural center of fusions, the definitive crucible of races. (Hostos, "Pages from the Hostos Diary" March 28, 1870)[7]

---

6 "Horizonte más extenso todavía, el designio culminante de Bolívar—la unión latinoamericana —, tiene una forma accesible en nuestro tiempo. Esta forma es la liga diplomática de todos los gobiernos de esta América, en una personalidad internacional. Por falta de esa personalidad carece de fuerza ante el mundo nuestra América Latina. De todos los obstáculos que dificultan la institución de esa personalidad internacional, la falta de un interés común es la mayor. Ni gobiernos, ni pueblos, nadie hay en los pueblos latinoamericanos que no sepa, que no presienta que es interés común de todos ellos la independencia de las Antillas."

7 "Pienso que es necesario que América complete la civilización, sirviendo a estas dos ideas: unidad de la libertad por la federación de las naciones; unidad de las razas por la fusión de todas ellas. A este trabajo han de concurrir todos los miembros del Continente; tierra firme e islas: la tierra firme ha entrado en fusión ... fuera de la esfera de acción americana, intentando entrar en ella, las Antillas ¿qué son las Antillas? El lazo, el medio de unión entre la fusión de

The idea of a conviviality of the races has both a political and a cultural side in Hostos; the combination of the two serves not just the union of the nations but also, and equally, the higher idea of unity. Hostos proclaims "the confederation of all the Antilles and, as a future goal, a league of the Latin race in the new continent and in the archipelago of the Caribbean Sea" (Letter to J.M. Mestre dated November 7, 1870, cited in Gaztambide Géigel 50).[8] The two ideas of a merging of the races and of an Antillean confederation are directly linked in the program of the *Liga de los Independientes:*

> In the Antilles, nationality is an organizing principle in nature; because it completes a spontaneous force of civilization, because it can only be based on a rational covenant, and because it contributes to one of the positive goals of Antillean societies and to the historical aim of the Latin American race. The natural organizing principle to which nationality corresponds in the Antilles is the principle of unity in variety. The spontaneous force of civilization that it will complete is peace. The rational covenant that is the only one on which it can be founded is the confederation. The positive goal to which it will contribute is the commercial progress of the three islands. And the historical aim of the race that it will help to achieve is the moral and intellectual union of the Latin race on the New Continent. ("Programa [de la Liga] de los Independientes," *La Voz de la Patria* October 18 to November 24, 1876, cited in Gaztambide Géigel 51)[9]

Hostos touts the geopolitically strategic position of the Caribbean archipelago as the "center of the civilized world, path of universal commerce, objective of the

---

tipos y de ideas europeas de Norte América y la fusión de razas y caracteres dispares que penosamente realiza Colombia (la América Latina): medio geográfico natural entre una y otra parte del Continente, elaborador también de una fusión trascendental de razas, las Antillas, son, políticamente, el fiel de la balanza, el verdadero lazo federal de la gigantesca federación del porvenir; social, *humanamente,* el centro natural de las fusiones, el crisol definitivo de las razas" (Hostos, *Diario,* entry of March 28, 1870, cited in Gaztambide Géigel 48).
8 "La confederación de todas las Antillas y, como fin por venir, la liga de la raza latina en el nuevo continente y en el archipiélago del Mar Caribe."
9 "En las Antillas, la nacionalidad es un principio de organización en la naturaleza; porque completa una fuerza espontánea de la civilización, porque sólo en un pacto de razón puede fundarse, y porque coadyuva a uno de los fines positivos de sociedades antillanas, y al fin histórico de la raza latinoamericana. El principio de organización natural a que convendrá la nacionalidad en las Antillas, es el principio de unidad en la variedad. La fuerza espontánea de civilización que completará, es la paz. El pacto de razón en que exclusivamente puede fundarse, es la confederación. El fin positivo al que coadyuvará, es el progreso comercial de las tres islas. El fin histórico de raza que contribuirá a realizar, es la unión moral e intelectual de la raza latina en el Nuevo Continente."

industry of both worlds, and faithful to a balance that will one day weigh the fates of cosmopolitan civilization" (ibid.).[10]

For Hostos, as for his colleagues, the concept of race has not been developed in a nuanced way and is very internally contradictory. For him, too, the essentialist dimension remains the basis of conviviality. On the one hand, he identifies a "true Antillean race" (*verdadera raza de las Antillas*) as a fusion of African, Latino, and American elements. But on the other hand, his talk of the "white race" (*raza blanca*) and "inferior races" (*subrazas*) incorporates Europe's racist discourses.

And yet, while discourses of difference characterize the thinking of Hostos, Betances, and Maceo, they are nevertheless implemented productively, unlike in earlier texts. Maceo's *Caribeanidad* wants to dissolve difference. The fact that, in Hostos's thinking, this utopian idea reaches beyond the Caribbean archipelago is a testimony to its universal dimension.

VIII.2 Forms of Knowledge about Conviviality. An Ethnographic Quest, or the Question of Distance and Separation from the Other

Let us now turn our attention away from normative attempts to project conviviality and concentrate instead on forms of knowledge (cf. Ette, "Literaturwissenschaft" 28). These forms manifest themselves in the attempt to position oneself or the Other, either in an explicitly descriptive way or as an implicit quest. Thus, in *Les créoles ou la Vie aux Antilles* (1835), J. Levilloux takes a definitely critical look at the ethnic caste system.

> The whites heap contempt on the mulattos. The mulattos in turn give to their fathers the hatred of envy and seek revenge on the blacks for the degrading nuance of the epidermis to which they are heir. On their side, the Negroes recognize the superiority of the whites, rejecting the pretensions of the class of people of color, and conspire against the former because they are the masters and hate the latter because they would like to become masters. (Levilloux 9–10)[11]

---

[10] "centro del mundo civilizado, camino del comercio universal, objetivo de la industria de ambos mundos, fiel de una balanza que ha de pesar algún día los destinos de la civilización cosmopolita."

[11] "Les blancs laissent tomber le mépris sur les mulâtres. Ceux-ci laissent à leurs pères la haine de l'envie et se vengent sur les noirs de la nuance dégradante d'épiderme dont ils sont héritiers. De leur côté, les nègres reconnaissant la supériorité des blancs, repoussant les prétentions de la

Here it becomes clear that the ethnic caste system, which is often proclaimed as normative, is in fact constantly being called into question by all the groups involved. From every side, people are trying to break through the barriers. Levilloux's portrayal of the whites is also revealing: "the Creoles, descendants of the European colonists: lightweight intellects, generally uncultivated, but lively, penetrating, enthusiastic about marvels and disdainful of Europe's philosophical knowledge" (19).[12] The matter-of-factness of the definitional precision of the actual situation is relativized by the astonishing self-critique of a white writer from Martinique, proclaiming a lack of intelligence. We see here that not all whites are equally white. Who are the Creoles? Which whites are writing for which whites?

At one point in Levilloux, it becomes clear to what extent the uncertainty of whiteness is directly linked with a fear that the Creole upper class has, usually a fear of losing the privileges of the good old times: "Men felt the old world falling apart under their feet and were already throwing themselves towards that future, so near, in which a new society was to be rebuilt" (21).[13] The good old times are the prerevolutionary times, and on the eve of the abolition of slavery in the French colonial empire, people are reminded of the trauma of the French Revolution. They are afraid that in the future, new forms of conviviality will develop. The unpredictable is frightening.

Nell Irvin Painter has convincingly shown the connection between fear and racial discourses, explaining how racial discourses always have social, political, and economic dimensions. Thus, on the subject of 1840s European racial discourses, she argues:

> In truth, the era's sociopolitical context had created much anxiety. The Western world was being buffeted by an extraordinary set of crises in the mid-1840s. In France, Germany, Italy and central Europe, political unrest spurred by widespread unemployment and poverty culminated in revolution in 1848. Such uprisings crystallized the thinking of writers eager to interpret class conflict as race war. In France, Arthur de Gobineau wrote his *Essay on the Inequality of Races*, published in the mid-1850s. Robert Knox in London published his mean-spirited lectures on race in 1850 as *Races of Men: A Fragment*. (Painter 137)

---

classe de couleur, conspirent contre les uns parce qu'ils sont maîtres, et haïssent les autres parce qu'ils aspirent à le devenir."
12 "Les créoles, descendants des colons européens: intelligences légères, en général incultes, mais vives, pénétrantes, enthousiastes du merveilleux, dédaigneuses des connaissances philosophiques de l'Europe."
13 "Les hommes sentaient le vieux monde s'abîmer sous leur pieds et se jetaient déjà vers cet avenir si prochain où devait se reconstruire une nouvelle société."

The very attempt to grasp the indefinable in-betweenness of the mulattos' social position and their positioning of their own identity reveals the strenuousness of the whites' efforts to be white. Thus the already mentioned ambiguous and racism-tinged positioning of the mulattos in a paradoxical in-between space.

> This mulatto, it must not be forgotten, was not a man like any other. He was an image of those strong natures where precipices, venomous plants, and malicious animals abound, but where nevertheless one has to go in order to find the most treasured wonders of this universe. (Maynard de Queilhe II:16)[14]

Even from the blacks' point of view, the mulattos are pitied, and their situation in the in-between is perceived as miserable: the herbalist Iviane in *Les créoles ou la Vie aux Antilles* shows compassion for the protagonist, Estève, which Levilloux stages through a deliberately flawed French, thus relativizing the position of standard French as the single normative authority. It is interesting to note that the concept of the nation plays a role here as well. "'Me possessed of God alone,' the old woman replied. 'You mulatto, me Negress. My nation large in a large country. You not have a nation, you'" (Levilloux 104).[15] The *Revue des Colonies*, likewise on a quest for an appropriate description of the mulatto, comes to similar conclusions:

> The Negro stems from pure blood; the mulatto, on the contrary, comes from mixed blood; he is a composite of the black and the white, a bastardized species. From this truth it is as obvious that the Negro is above the mulatto as it is that pure gold is above mixed, impure gold. (*Revue des Colonies* November 1838, 277)[16]

A strained requirement of purity has to do the job of drawing a barrier between blacks and mulattos by way of "blood."

The topic of impossible transfers of ideas between the metropolis and the colony (see sections I.3.3 and II.2.2) from the pro-slavery quotation from Maynard de Queilhe, which has already been introduced as a norm of knowledge about

---

14 "Ce mulâtre, il ne faut pas l'oublier, ce n'était pas un homme comme un autre. C'était une image de ces fortes natures où les précipices, les plantes vénéneuses et les animaux malfaisants abondent, mais où néanmoins on doit aller chercher les merveilles les plus estimées de cet univers."
15 "'Moi possédée de Dieu seul, répliqua la vieille. Vous mulâtre, moi negresse. Nation à moi est grande dans un grand pays. Vous pas avoir une nation, vous.'"
16 "Le nègre est issu d'un sang pur; le mulâtre est au contraire issu d'un sang mélangé; c'est un composé du noir et du blanc, c'est une espèce abâtardie. D'après cette vérité, il est aussi évident que le nègre est au-dessus du mulâtre, qu'il l'est que l'or pur est au-dessus de l'or mélangé."

conviviality, takes on a new aspect as a *form* of knowledge about conviviality in *Les créoles ou la Vie aux Antilles*. In a letter to his son, the father issues a warning about the ideas of the French Revolution. In the colonies, there can be no equality:

> It is important, my son, to guard against the maxims and the theories that now invade all minds and to which the candor of your age makes you more vulnerable. Remember that you will soon have to return to Guadeloupe, where you will find a society that, although it allows one to feed oneself speculatively on these ideas of equality, forbids one to openly scorn conservative prejudices. I think I have seen, in your letters, a marked tendency to praise yourself for subscribing to those dogmas that you call regenerative, but which can only be that after they have killed us. This is now the time for me to say a word to you about connections that chance might cause you to form with young people of color that whites send to Europe. Do not stop at outward signs; they are often misleading. Sound out and question all of the Creoles, your comrades. The number of them must not be too large, and thus it will be easy to discover their origins and to escape from dangerous friendships which would become a source of regrets and vexations in the future, because you would not be able to enjoy a complete liberty in your connections when you return to the colonies. However great the energy of your will in this respect, you will not be able to fight against society, which will lay all of the weight of its customs and of its embodied ideas upon you. Remember that, my son, and while granting your benevolence, be careful not to match yourself, by bonds of friendship, with compatriots of color. I will not say more; may your reason light your way. (Levilloux 23)[17]

The knowledge of a conviviality of ethnic groups, but also of the conviviality of white philanthropists in Paris and white Creoles from the colonies, is represented as a balancing act between norms and forms of knowledge about conviviality.

---

17 "Il est important, mon fils, de te prémunir contre les maximes et les théories qui envahissent maintenant tous les esprits, et auxquelles la candeur de ton âge te rend plus accessible. Songe que tu dois retourner bientôt à la Guadeloupe, où tu trouveras une société, qui, tout en permettant de se nourrir spéculativement de ces idées d'égalité, défend de mépriser ouvertement des préjugés conservateurs. J'ai cru deviner, par tes lettres, une tendance marquée à t'exalter pour ces dogmes que tu nommes régénérateurs, mais qui ne peuvent l'être qu'après nous avoir tués. C'est ici le moment de te dire un mot des liaisons que le hasard pourrait te faire contracter avec des jeunes gens de couleur que des blancs envoient en Europe. Ne t'arrête pas aux signes extérieurs, ils sont souvent trompeurs. Sonde, questionne tous les créoles, tes camarades. Le nombre ne doit pas être grand ainsi sera-t-il plus facile de découvrir les origines et d'échapper à des dangereuses amitiés qui deviendraient une source de regrets et de contrariétés à venir, ne pouvant jouir d'une entière liberté dans vos rapports à votre retour dans les colonies. Quelle que soit l'énergie de ta volonté à cet égard, tu ne pourras lutter contre la société qui pèsera sur toi de tout le poids de ses usages et de ses idées incarnées. Songes-y, mon fils, et tout en accordant ta bienveillance, garde-toi de t'égaler par des liens d'amitié à des compatriotes de couleur. Je n'en dis pas d'avantages; que ta raison t'éclaire."

Only in death can the philanthropic ideas that are called dogmas here be reconciled with the conditions of life in the colony. The clarity of the vision representing the opposite of conviviality can be experienced as a definitional predictability in the act of reading.

Let us turn again to the Spanish Caribbean, or to be more exact, to Eugenio María de Hostos, whose work communicates, more than any other texts of the time, the degree to which the Caribbean can be a privileged space for testing conviviality. In the novel *La peregrinación de Bayoán,* just as in the speeches I have already quoted, the idea of a pan-Antillean confederation is fundamental. This idea is staged through a quest and odyssey that remains open to the end and is never clearly resolved. Thus, the protagonist sees himself as a constantly searching pilgrim in an in-between space: "I am a man wandering in a desert, and you are my only oasis [he is speaking to his home island]. I am a pilgrim. ... Must I go on this pilgrimage? All right then, onward!" (Hostos, *Peregrinación* 18).[18] The pilgrimage here is a multidimensional quest; an expression of openness, but also of alienation; it is goal-directedness but also makes the journey into the goal; a circular structure that is broken in many places. Bayoán writes some of his journal entries on board ship, which is why it is called *Diario de a bordo* (logbook), with a reference to Columbus. Thus, the ship represents a sort of threshold space. It can also be seen as a vehicle that crosses temporal boundaries and transports the protagonist from one level to another—so that he is almost commuting between regions of time and of space: "The wind pushed the frigate, and the frigate moved the way that I move, pushed by a wind about which I still do not know whether it leads to port" (192).[19] The representation of the waves as oscillations between open spaces relativizes the determinacy of a discourse of *Caribeanidad*.

VIII.3 The Rejection of Essentialist Models of Identity

In an era in which it is first necessary to discuss who may even call themselves human beings in the first place, a conscious affirmation of the unpredictable potential inherent in every conviviality would be impossible. And yet, against the background of today's discussions of conviviality, new ways of reading historical texts become possible. The examples have shown that cultural forms of represen-

---

18 "Yo soy un hombre errante en un desierto, y mi único oasis eres tú [se está dirigiendo a su patria]. Yo soy un peregrino... ¿Necesito peregrinar? Pues, ¡adelante!"
19 "El viento empujaba a la fragata, y la fragata andaba como ando yo, empujado por un viento que aún no sé si lleva a puerto."

tation of the nineteenth-century Caribbean offer an entire arsenal of norms of knowledge about conviviality: for example, Maynard de Queilhe's utopian model of a slave society or the outline of a mixed-race society in the *Revue des Colonies*. Our focus on these constellations of conviviality has brought out a new productive dimension: the kinds of strenuous efforts that whites found it necessary to undertake in order to defend their whiteness.

Whereas ethnic differences before 1848 primarily reproduce binary structures—whether as a system of slavery that works very well for everyone involved, or as an early utopia of a melting pot—after 1848, the normative models change: especially in the Spanish-speaking Caribbean, visions of a future pan-Caribbean confederation are developed. For all normative projections of conviviality, what remains crucial is that in spite of utopian constellations of relationality, the defining constructions of identity are essentialist.

But what about the various forms of knowledge about conviviality? They can be found more often in literary texts than in other genres. Conviviality often takes the shape of an uncertain testing ground (Ette, "Literaturwissenschaft" 27), of an exploration of boundaries, of an in-between that is much less capable of being clearly defined than in normative forms of cultural representation. Thus, it is no coincidence that in the context of an ideal of whiteness that only appears to be susceptible to a clear articulation, there is often a struggle over the definition of the mulatto: the indeterminability of the Other provokes fear. In addition, there is an expression of uncertainty and fear of losing the old privileges.

If we take a closer look at the topic of the "impossibility of the transfer of ideas," it becomes clear how necessarily connected the norms and the forms of knowledge are to each other. This can be seen most clearly in Hostos, who formulates a pan-Antillean confederation as a normative ideal but in his novel, which appeared at the same time, depicts a quest for *Caribeanidad* whose end is much more vaguely expressed than in his speeches. Even though nineteenth-century programmatic texts are unimaginable without the essentialisms they contain, the established frame of reference, including race and nation, is nevertheless relativized through the focus on forms of knowledge. Significantly, it is in the literary texts that a clear division between norms and forms of knowledge about conviviality is not always possible. Literature lives up to its role as an interactive storage medium for knowledge about conviviality (Ette, "Literaturwissenschaft" 31). It is therefore not surprising that Hostos so clearly demonstrates this interwovenness of norms and of forms of knowledge about conviviality, given that he wrote so explicitly, in *Moral social:*

> The novel, a genre that still has life in it because it still contains contrasts between what human society is and what it should be, can contribute to the completion of art, being

true and being good. Then it will be an element of social morality. If it fulfills its responsibility, it will be. In the meantime, however, it is not, for this ultimate reason: because it is not fulfilling its responsibility. (Hostos, *Moral social* 248)[20]

Just as this quotation does a very good job of indicating the degree to which literary studies have always borne up as privileged knowledge about life, including in the nineteenth century, which was so strongly determined by scientific debates, the preceding exposition has shown that the discourses of *Caribeanidad* can be understood as the precursors to today's conceptual debates over conviviality. Even though valuable approaches to thinking about knowledge about conviviality have come from the Caribbean, the concept has so far not been used in a defined way in current debates. It is interesting to note, however, that in January of 2009, during the agricultural crisis in Guadeloupe, an organization was founded with the Creole name *Lyannaj kont pwofitasyon* (LKP). *Lyannaj* means "conviviality."[21] It is characteristic of late Glissant that three years before his death, he took this concept as an occasion to think about *vivre-ensemble* (conviviality): "Let us project our imaginaries into these high necessities until the strength of *Lyannaj*, or of conviviality, is no longer a 'housewives' basket' but, instead, the plentifully amplified concern with the idea of the human" (*Manifeste pour les "produits" de haute nécessité*).[22]

---

20 "La novela, género que aún dispone de vida, porque aún dispone de contrastes entre lo que es y lo que debe ser la sociedad humana, puede contribuir a que el arte, siendo verdadero y siendo bueno, sea completo. Entonces será un elemento de moral social. Cumpla con su deber, y lo será. Mientras tanto, no lo es, entre otros, por ese motivo final: porque no cumple con su deber."
21 The general strike in Guadeloupe was carried out by a coalition of fifty organizations and movements; *Lyannaj kont pwofitasyon* (LKP) was the name of the strikers' league. See *Manifeste pour les "produits" de haute nécessité*.
22 "Projetons nos imaginaires dans ces hautes nécessités jusqu'à ce que la force du Lyannaj ou bien du vivre-ensemble, ne soit plus un 'panier de ménagère', mais le souci démultiplié d'une plénitude de l'idée de l'humain."

IX Conclusion

What follows, then, from the insight that we might be able to look at relationalities in colonial literatures from a new perspective? What can we learn from the findings of a comparative viewpoint, in connection with research on transfer processes, and to what extent can these findings, which relate to a specific region in a particular period of time, be connected with today's theoretical debates?

My research has centered on processes of transfer. What I have looked at were not static conditions but developments, changes, and interconnections. The supporting characters were writers, ethnologists, editors, but also itinerant tinkerwomen. We could add many, many more. Transfers in conceptions of society[1] brought up the question of how to deal, on the one hand, with experiences of revolution—especially the Haitian Revolution—and, on the other, with the gradual process of abolition, in this case British abolition: what was transferred, and from where and to where? I was concerned not with defining a national identity nor emphasizing a transnational dimension in the sense of competing cultures, but rather with the ways in which the actors in a variety of situations deal with and reshape more or less hegemonic cultural models. I was not interested in starting from predetermined entities or categories but wanted, instead, to begin with problems and questions that would arise from the analytical process itself, because they were themselves understood as part of an ongoing dynamic transformation. I tried to avoid prescribed models or globally defined constructions of nation, society, culture, or religion: these would have been inadequate to the colonial context. In addition, I was able to address the question of theoretical transfer: at the beginning of the twenty-first century, the Caribbean has become a privileged site for the production of a Latin American and Caribbean cultural theory. And it has become increasingly clear that even theories that are oriented towards the present have a focus, if not in fact their central focus, in the nineteenth century. Benítez Rojo, for instance, already vividly pointed out the connection between creolization and the plantation: "Well then, what relationships do I see between the plantations and creolization? Naturally, first, a relationship of cause and effect; without one we would not have the other. But I also see other relationships" (*La isla* 396; not present in English translation).[2]

---

[1] On this complex topic, on a more general level, compare the insights on political, economic, and sociocultural cultural transfers in Lüsebrink, *Interkulturelle Kommunikation* 152–153.
[2] "Bien, entonces, ¿qué relaciones veo entre plantación y criollización? Naturalemente, en primer término, una relación de causa y efecto; sin una no tendríamos la otra. Pero también veo otras relaciones."

This existential reference backwards towards the colonial experiences of the nineteenth century can be traced all the way through to Khal Torabully and the theory of coolitude, which transcends the essentialisms of earlier discourses of *Créolité*.

The point of combining a comparatist approach with the research on transfers was to direct the focus to the interdependency and mutual conditionality of the planes of investigation. While it was the Caribbean islands that formed the point of intersection, the impression of symmetry that was produced, at first glance, by the intersection of viewpoints turned out to be mostly illusory. The closer up the view on the historical contexts, the clearer the asymmetries appeared. And yet that is precisely where we find the power of the intersectional approach.

In comparing the texts of the French-speaking Caribbean with those of the Spanish-speaking Caribbean, two different constellations can be seen: a bipolar axis, with the colony and the mother country at either end; and a multilateral web of relationships with multiple axes, especially colony to center and colony to other (ex-)colonies. The tight interlacing of literature and scholarly discourses about the colonial Other, which appeared especially in the French sphere of influence, is connected to the fact that the nineteenth-century Caribbean literary class were important figures in the knowledge production of the mother country. Just as the multirelational interconnectedness of the Spanish-speaking Caribbean intellectual world formed the basis for a trans-area literature, so too was the accompanying cultural emancipation from the mother country a precondition for political disentanglement.

The first central question had to do with the positioning of the colonial status quo: how the writers appropriated European discourses, and which ones they chose, how they asserted the cultural identity of their own islands of origin, and in what way they thereby reflected the potential contradiction between emancipation and intellectual obligation. The political positions taken in literature proved to be quite unambiguous. In the Spanish-speaking Caribbean, with a few exceptions such as that of the Countess of Merlin, they went in a clear direction: people were for abolition and independence. In the French-speaking Caribbean, it was different. There were contrary positions that could be determined with respect to the question of abolition. On the one hand, there were the abolitionists: Levilloux, Chapus, Bonneville, and Agricole; on the other, there were the advocates of slavery: the white *Békés* Prévost de Sansac, Eyma, Maynard de Queilhe, and Rosemond. And yet, while the question of abolition caused differences of opinion before 1848, the writers were nevertheless all united in staying closely connected to France.

Novels from the French Antilles are frequently highly political in their subject matter: philanthropists need to be convinced to give up on any form of abolition; the existing colonial discourses are reaffirmed. In the Spanish texts, on the other hand, there are anti-colonial attitudes to be found, attitudes that could also be considered to fall into the category of epistemological postcolonialism. It is true that here and there—for instance in Galván's novel *Enriquillo*—a latent sympathy can be observed toward Spain, the world power, with its great minds Columbus and Las Casas. But unlike with the literary examples from the French Caribbean, this does not stop the protagonists from rebelling, which must be seen as an anticipation of the freedom struggles and wars of independence against the colonial power of Spain.

What the literary production of the Spanish and French Antilles share is that the Haitian paradigm takes up surprisingly little space. In spite of a few differences between the two colonial spheres, both of the colonial literary fields contribute to a cementing of Western discourses of modernity. The often complex structure of space and movement in texts about, and especially from, Haiti (for example d'Alaux's articles, but also a novel such as Bergeaud's *Stella*), indicates that the multirelationality of the new Haitian society has far-reaching spatial implications. The texts represent colonial independence insofar as they illustrate how the young country of Haiti consolidates the connection between external and internal relationality. At the same time, individual spaces often turn out to be very immobile. This may have to do with Haiti's problematic self-understanding, which vehemently defends its political independence while at the same time proclaiming its cultural dependence on the former mother country, a combination that is made particularly clear in Massillon Coicou's poems. While Haiti is an exception in every way, not only in the Caribbean but in the entire Western hemisphere, representative novels of the French- and Spanish-speaking colonial spheres communicate other stagings of space or in some cases perspectives on movement—this can already be seen from the titles of the novels. They often reflect the view from the metropolis, as for instance in the *Description de l'île de Martinique* (Description of the island of Martinique): an affirmation of the colonial status quo echoes the one-dimensional colonial gaze. In contrast, in *La peregrinación de Bayoán*, the focus is on the moment of movement.

The antithesis between nature and culture is more clearly polarized in the literatures of the French Caribbean than in the Spanish texts. This corresponds to the different functions that the island topos takes on in the two colonial literatures: in the French Antilles, the island is often identified with exile and isolation (regardless of the fact that the literary class, the plantation-owning oligarchy, voluntarily chose to settle there), while in the Spanish Caribbean this identification barely appears. Because the individual islands are usually only "tolerated," as way stations, in the French Antilles, they are also part of an in-between that is symptomatic of writing in and about the nineteenth-century Caribbean.

In spite of the many differences between French and Spanish colonialism, however, there are also revealing commonalities to be found. The literary class of France's (former) Caribbean colonies and the writers in the Spanish colonies both orient themselves mainly towards French Romanticism. Certain texts caught on in particular, including those of Hugo, Lamartine, and Chateaubriand. Even though it would be far wide of the mark to reduce the Caribbean's rich literary tradition to this interpretation, it still must be mentioned that the imitation of models and ideas from the colonies' mother country, often in the form of plagiarism, can never be identical to the so-called original. The process of translation —the repetition within a different context—necessarily creates a gap in what is assumed to be the original, often at the expense of aesthetic believability.

The literary production of the colonies, therefore, is not necessarily oriented towards their respective mother countries. French colonialism's political and cultural gravitational force was far more formative and effective than was the Spanish model, which can also be seen in the transoceanic comparison of the paradigms of conviviality and relationality in Victor Hugo's Atlantic texts and Pierre Loti's Pacific texts. With the exception of Haiti, there is a clear connection between cultural and political dependence on France as the mother country. Accordingly, in some of the novels of the French-speaking Caribbean, the literary staging of a binary opposition between metropolis and colony is extremely effective. The literary efforts anticipate the political events, namely a rather marginal independence movement that is ultimately unsuccessful. Even though, given the special situation of the Creole upper class in Latin America and the Caribbean in the nineteenth century, postcolonial theorization[3] can only be of limited use, one could say, broadly, that in the case of the French-speaking Caribbean, the intensive reception of literature from the mother country creates a "consensus" between the colonizer and the colonized that then cements French cultural hegemony. This nexus of culture and politics has the opposite effect on the colonial relationship of the Spanish Caribbean—which explains the rather violent detachment of the Spanish colonies from the mother country.[4] For the Spanish colonies,

---

[3] On this topic, see Lüsebrink's extremely constructive discussion and productive critique of some postcolonial studies that have fallen into the trap of looking at "hybrid writing styles" from "all-too abstract and trendily theoretical perspectives" (*Interkulturelle Kommunikation* 175).
[4] This is assuming a cultural theory that grants cultural hegemony the decisive role in legitimizing the relations of power.

the intensive reception of French literature already means a cultural emancipation, whereas for the French colonies, it only perpetuates their relationship of dependence: the cultural acceptance of the mother country and the dependence on their own mother country legitimizes the continuation of their political subordination.

Creole writing was the expression of a perpetual in-betweenness, an inner conflict, which on the one hand led to a creative stasis, limited by conservative structures of thought, but on the other hand could also be highly productive. Tellingly, the literary texts of the French and Spanish Caribbean share the characteristic that attributions of nation, *patrie*, and exile are often ambiguous. These denominations do not follow clear criteria but change to fit various situations. The nation as a reference point becomes exceedingly problematic. It is not so much the nation that is staged in literature but in fact its fragility that becomes the crux of the writing, and here, in fact, we find one of the central motifs in the colonial reshaping of discourses and models from the mother country. This kind of literary representation seems particularly surprising for the nineteenth century. At any rate, it certainly calls Doris Sommer's thesis of foundational fictions into question: there can be no question here of a clear articulation of the national through allegorical procedures that could be seen as analogous to the phenomena of the contemporary European national movements. And thus, it is no coincidence that the toolkit of the *histoire croisée*, which was developed in the social sciences, is existentially enriched by this intensive consideration of literary texts. Literature can allow that specific situation of the in-between to be shown and experienced in a way that cannot happen anywhere else. And thus, literature is the privileged site of knowledge circulation: one could never do justice to the complexity of the texts if they were forced into identity-based categories; it is only the dazzling dimensions of the in-between that are capable of grasping this multilayer intricacy. They are supplemented by the paratextual material—thus, long forewords, as well as letters and newspaper articles, were particularly popular ways for nineteenth-century Caribbean writers to position themselves.

Skin color is an omnipresent theme. Whiteness is the necessary precondition for superiority and power; in fact, it is often even the criterion for belonging to the human race. Sugar and (non-white) skin color can be seen as the two basic pillars of (anti-)slavery debates between the metropolis and the colonial projection, and become part of a discourse about strategies for appropriating "foreign things." Nothing can sound more essentialist than such attributions. Where is there room, here, for ambiguities or even transfers? And yet it is in the very determination of skin color that the greatest uncertainties are expressed. After all, the attribution of whiteness is anything but clear-cut, and this is a constant theme in the literary texts. Thus, for instance, one topic is the difficulty of how to treat the freed slaves and mulattos after the Haitian Revolution. There is no longer any consensus about what to call them. They are no longer black, but they are also not white. In a play, even important representatives of the upper classes, who would otherwise be accorded interpretive sovereignty, can only react in stutters. The clear attributions of skin color that no one would even have dreamed of questioning in prerevolutionary times seem not to work anymore, in the very context in which skin color continues to be given legal meaning, possibly even the decisive legal meaning. It becomes clearer here than almost anywhere else that what used to be fixed points have now become movable. The core essentialist domain becomes one of the most important fields for fluctuations and the changing dynamics of discursive power.

If we widen our focus from the world of the Caribbean islands to the Caribbean periphery, and consider the "black" French-speaking center that is New Orleans, we find another intersection point for the most diverse transfer processes, for instance when Joseph Colastin Rousseau clearly demonstrates how the bands of the Creole layer are constituted through a hybrid or relational experience (Duplantier 155). Like the Creole upper class in Martinique and Guadeloupe, New Orleans's free people of color position themselves in the in-between: they express disorientation and a deep-seated uncertainty about their position between worlds. And in this context, the colonial connection to the (former) mother country, France, remains the most important force, even after decades of disentanglement. French colonialism is so strong that it develops a great attraction even in spite of (or in fact because of) the experience of the in-between and the accompanying feeling of weakness.

In general, the nineteenth century's geographic and ethnological societies are seen as important lobbyists for French imperialism. Insofar as we can even speak of a division into disciplines in the first half of the nineteenth century, we can say that the ethnologically oriented institutions, in particular, are highly complex and multifaceted. The *Revues des Colonies* occupies a singular position. This journal, edited by men of color, cultivates a language that is already demystifying attributions of identity in the nineteenth century. Nothing can make the questionable nature of a politics of identity clearer than the paradox of the literature of those men of color in 1834. The in-betweenness of a man of color who, like the mulatto writer Cyrille Bissette, takes on that position "officially" is nothing more than a product of colonialism and reaches ahead into our present-day world of global and transcultural enmeshments.

The expression "setting into relationship (and into motion) through comparison" (*durch Vergleich in Beziehung [und in Bewegung] setzen*; Ette, *Alexander von*

Humboldt 152),⁵ which has been cited several times in this study, has shown the productivity of its interpretive power on several levels. The comparative approach, paying particular attention to transfer processes, provides new understandings about the connection between culture and imperialism, and—and this is the decisive factor—sensitizes us to the category of the in-between, which literature is singularly able to communicate. But this in-between is not simply a (problematic) spatial location that weakens the actors in their social, cultural, and political positioning, but it can also release productive forces. From 1860 on, utterances on this topic can be heard in the Spanish Caribbean: while even earlier, the thinking of Hostos, Betances, and Maceo was characterized by discourses of difference, now, however, unlike in earlier texts, they are productively implemented. Maceo's *Caribeanidad* is intended to dissolve difference. It is significant that this idea, as a utopia very much in line with Hostos's thinking, extends beyond the Caribbean archipelago. Hostos's emphasis on the geostrategic position of the Caribbean archipelago anticipates hemispheric constructions of America. It is not for nothing that some of the places where this writing happens are also in Central America: Hostos writes from Panama, "in the isthmus," and Maceo from Guaynava, the "first Cuban colony" in what is now Costa Rica. Further pleas follow from both of them, from New York. This transterritorial dimension, for which I could give countless more examples, is admittedly (given the times) not free of racist elements, but it projects a new "testing ground for conviviality" (*Erprobungsraum von Zusammenleben*; Ette, "Literaturwissenschaft" 27) that has a prospective dimension to it. Gaztambide Géigel pointed out, correctly, in the particular context of the intellectuals mentioned here, that starting in 1860, with the emergence of the discourse of *Caribeanidad* and the project of a Caribbean confederation, it was no longer the postulations of identity that were in the foreground but rather a movement toward solidarity. I do not want to go into the evaluative character of Géigel's concept of solidarity, but putting that aside, in his research on the Caribbean, we can see the shift from identity to a focus on what can be neutrally formulated as conviviality. The ideas of such people as Hostos and Betances, which are then also substantially enriched by the Haitian Atenor Firmin, are ahead of their times, both spatially—in trans-area dimensions, by substituting a history of movement for the history of space—and on the level of ethnological constellations, which provide an argument for the focus on conviviality and thus declare clear classifications of skin color to be obsolete.

---

5 See also the connection between "comparing and understanding" (*Vergleichen und Verstehen*; Lüsebrink, *Interkulturelle Kommunikation* 33).

The recognition that it is precisely the category of the in-between that is of central significance for the understanding of nineteenth-century Caribbean literatures would not have been possible using the analytical toolkit of the concept of identity. An inductive approach, focusing on transfers of various dimensions—which is why, in the preface to the chapter on the in-between, I added the note that I had consciously avoided any typologizing—revealed in retrospect that the issue is always a negotiation of conviviality, which is central to the most varying forms of cultural representation. While this is mostly expressed in a programmatic way in the ethnological journals, in the sense of new norms of knowledge about conviviality, the potential in literary texts expresses itself on the level of an interplay between the representations of both forms and norms of knowledge about conviviality.

This way of reading these texts was based on Ottmar Ette's paradigmatic works on knowledge about conviviality (*ZusammenLebensWissen*). The present-day context for these is the international debates over alternatives to concepts based on identity. Thus Paul Gilroy, for instance, in 2004, talks about conviviality as a programmatic concept. Arjun Appadurai, building on that in a lecture in Berlin in 2009 in which he asks about a politics of dialogue, points out three kinds of so-called risk dialogues. Insofar as dialogue represents an important tool for questions of conviviality, there are three related risks to consider: first, the risk of not understanding each other; second, the risk of understanding too much; and third, the risk of exposing too much or too little about existing internal differences that might exist inside each of the two sides, partners, or groups involved in the dialogue. In order to be effective, a dialogue cannot address everything. Agreement is always limited, and the risk of an inflated understanding is always present. Because complete understanding always remains an illusion, there is a serious danger in the elimination of fundamental difference and the creation of false universalisms—of an excess of understanding. In every dialogue, all of the participants bring their own tensions and contradictions to the table. There can be no productive negotiation with the "Other" if there are not also negotiations with the "self." This brings up the question of representation.

Within his concept of creolization, Glissant (as I stated in the introduction) emphasizes the affirmation of the unpredictability that is inherent to any process of creolization. Are these not exactly the questions that are explicitly discussed in the Caribbean in the nineteenth century? While the literary texts of such writers as Eyma and Maynard de Queilhe primarily address forms of knowledge about conviviality, and the dialogues of their protagonists are often destined to fail because they usually succumb to the danger of understanding too well who is even allowed to call themselves human, the texts of someone like Bissette in the *Revue des Colonies* show how an affirmation of the unpredictable can take on programmatic forms of a conviviality in a global French-speaking diaspora. Discussions of racism have always been characteristic of the nineteenth century. Without including Caribbean literatures, which have always also been "literatures-without-a-fixed-abode" (cf. Ette, "Literaturen ohne festen Wohnsitz"; Ette, *Writing-between-Worlds*), significant dimensions of an experientially tested conviviality would be missing.

The paradigms of Caribbean research in literary and cultural theory in the late twentieth and early twenty-first centuries had crucial precursors in the nineteenth century. Thus the texts of Hostos, Maceo, and Betances, with their conceptions of the Caribbean, for example, anticipate Édouard Glissant's universal ideas (Glissant, *Tout-monde*; see also Gewecke, "Les Antilles"). To close with the words of that Martinican writer and theorist, it is a matter of a "prophetic vision of the past."

X Works Cited

X.1 Primary Sources

Arenas, Reinaldo. *La loma del Angel*. Malaga: Dador, Traición, 1986.

Bentzon, Thérèse. *Yette. Histoire d'une jeune Créole*. [Reprint of Paris: J. Hetzel, 1880 edition.] In one volume with J. Levilloux, *Les créoles ou la Vie aux Antilles*. Morne-Rouge: Éd. des Horizons Caraïbes, 1977, pp. 273–409.

Bergeaud, Émeric. *Stella*, translated by Adriana Umana Hossman. N.p.: Markus Wiener, 2014. (*Stella*, edited by Beaubrun Ardouin. Paris: E. Dentu, 1859.)

Catineau-La-Roche, Pierre-Marie. *Notice sur la Guyane française, suivie des motifs qui font désirer que la colonisation projetée sur la Mana soit dirigée par une association en concurrence avec le gouvernement*. Paris: Imprimerie de Fain, 1822. Available online at http://gallica.bnf.fr/ark:/12148/bpt6k5460709r.r=Catineau-La-Roche.langEN. Accessed 23 June 2016.

Chapus, Eugène, Victor Charlier: *Titime? Histoires de l'autre-monde*. Paris: E. Renduel, 1833.

Chateaubriand, François-René de. *Atala; René*, translated by Rayner Heppenstall. Richmond: Oneworld Classics, 2010.

Chateaubriand, François-René de. *Memoirs from beyond the Tomb*, translated by Robert Baldick. London: Penguin Classics, 2014. (*Mémoires d'outre-tombe* [1848], edited by Maurice Levaillant. Paris: Gallimard, 1958.)

Chenêt, Jean-Baptiste. *Études poétiques ou chants du barde glanés chez les muses*. Paris: Imprimerie administrative de Paul Dupont, 1846.

Coicou, Massillon. *Poésies nationales*. Paris: Goupy et Jourdan, 1892.

Condé, Maryse. *Crossing the Mangrove*, translated by Richard Philcox. New York: Anchor Books, 1995. (*Traversée de la Mangrove*. Paris: Mercure de France, 1989.)

Condesa de Merlín, Maria de las Mercedes Santa Cruz y Montalvo. *La Havane*. 3 vols. Paris: Amyot, 1844.

Condesa de Merlín, María de las Mercedes Santa Cruz y Montalvo. "Les esclaves dans les colonies espagnoles." *Revue des deux mondes*, initial period, series 4, no. 26, 1841, pp. 734–769.

Confiant, Raphaël. *Adèle ou la pacotilleuse*. Paris: Mercure de France, 2005.

Confiant, Raphaël. *Le Nègre et l'Amiral*. Paris: Grasset, 1988.

Constant, Benjamin. "Écrits d'un humaniste." *Revue encyclopédique*, 1825, p. 59.

Copans, Jean, and Jean Jamin, editors. *Aux origines de l'anthropologie française. Les mémoires de la Soc. des Observateurs de l'Homme en l'An VIII*, with a preface by Jean-Paul Faivre. Paris: Le Sycomore, 1978.

Coussin, J.H.J. *Eugène de Cerceil ou les Caraïbes*. 3 vols. Paris: Igonette, 1824.

D'Alaux, Gustave. "La littérature jaune." *Revue des deux mondes*, new period, series 1. Part I: vol. XV, 1852, pp. 938–967; Part II: vol. XVI, 1852, pp. 1048–1085.

D'Alaux, Gustave. "Les mœurs et la littérature nègres." *Revue des deux mondes*, new period, series 1, vol. XIV, 1852, pp. 762–794.

del Monte, Domingo. "Letter of August 12, 1826." *Centón epistolario de Domingo del Monte*. Vol. 1. Havana, 1929.

Eyma, Louis-Xavier. "Les Borgias Noirs." *Les Peaux Noires*. Paris: M. Lévy, 1857, pp. 109–132.

Eyma, Louis-Xavier. *Le roi des Tropiques*. Paris: Michel Lévy Frères, 1860.

Eyma, Louis-Xavier. *La Vie aux Etats-Unis. Notes de voyage.* Paris: Plon, 1876.
Galván, Manuel de Jesús. *Enriquillo. Leyenda histórica dominicana (1503–1533)* [1879]. Mexiko: Porrúa, 1976.
Galván, Manuel de Jesús. *Enriquillo. Leyenda histórica dominicana (1503–1533)* [1879]. Notas del autor. Santo Domingo: Corripio, 1990.
Glissant, Édouard. "À propos de Tout-Monde. Ein Gespräch mit Ralph Ludwig." (Conversation with Ralph Ludwig.) Marie Galante, August 17, 1994.
Glissant, Édouard, and Patrick Chamoiseau. "De loin." (Protest letter written in January 2005 by Édouard Glissant and Patrick Chamoiseau to then French minister of the interior Nicolas Sarkozy.) *Potomitan.* 18 May 2016. Available online at: http://www.potomitan.info/articles/deloin.php. Accessed 23 June 2016.
Gómez de Avellaneda, Gertrudis. *Sab* [1841], edited by José Servera. Madrid: Cátedra, 1997.
Gómez de Avellaneda, Gertrudis. *Sab* [1841], edited by Mary Cruz. La Habana: Ed. Arte y Literatura, 1976.
Gómez de Avellaneda, Gertrudis. *Cartas inéditas y documentos. 1859 a 1864*, illustrated collection edited by José Augusto Escoto. Matanzas: Imprenta La Pluma de Oro, 1912.
Granier de Cassagnac, Adolphe. *Voyage aux Antilles françaises, anglaises, danoises, espagnoles, à St-Domingue et aux Etats-Unis d'Amérique.* 2 vols. Paris: Dauvin et Fontaine, 1842–1844.
Grégoire, Henri. *De la noblesse de la peau ou du préjugé des blancs contre la couleur des Africains et celle de leurs descendants noirs et sang-mêlés.* Grenoble: Million (1826) 1996, 2002.
Hänni, Eugène. *Trois ans chez les Canaques. Odyssée d'un Neuchâtelois autour du monde.* Lausanne: Payot, 1908.
Heredia, José María. *Niagara y otros textos. Poesia y prosa selectas*, edited by Ángel Augier. Caracas: Biblioteca Ayacucho, 1990.
Heredia, José María. *Obra poética*, edited by Ángel Augier. Havana: Letras Cubanas, 2003.
Heredia, José María. *Prosas*, edited by Romualdo Santos. Havana: Letras Cubanas, 1980.
Hostos, Eugenio María de. *La peregrinación de Bayoán* [1863]. Complete works. Vol. 1: Literature, edited by Julio César López. [Rio Piedras]: Editorial de la Universidad de Puerto Rico, 1988.
Hostos, Eugenio María de. "Pages from the Hostos Diary."*The Hostos Archives.* Bronx, NY: Hostos Community College website. http://commons.hostos.cuny.edu/archives/works-by-hostos/pages-from-the-hostos-diary/. Accessed 16 November 2016.
Hostos, Eugenio María de. "¿Cuál de las dos formas de gobierno, monarquía o república, realiza mejor el ideal del derecho?" *Obras completas.* 20 vols. San Juan: Instituto de Cultura Puertorriqueña, 1969 (Facsimile of edition of La Habana: Cultural S.A., 1939). Vol. 1.
Hostos, Eugenio María de. "Lo que intentó Bolívar." *La Opinión Nacional,* 21 December 1876.
Hostos, Eugenio María de. *Moral social. Sociología.* Caracas: Biblioteca Ayacucho, 1982.
Hugo, Victor. *Bug-Jargal ou la Révolution haitienne.* Les deux versions du roman 1818 et 1826 [1818 and 1826 versions of the novel], edited by Roger Toumson, Fort-de-France: Désormeaux, 1979.
Hugo, Victor. *The Letters of Victor Hugo: From Exile, and after the Fall of the Empire*, edited by Paul Meurice. Boston: Houghton, Mifflin, 1898.

Hugo, Victor. "La Mer et le vent." *"Cet immense rêve de l'océan ...". Paysages de mer et autres sujets marins par Victor Hugo* (Exhibition catalogue, Maison de Victor Hugo, December 2nd, 2005 to March 5th, 2006), edited by Pierre Georgel. Paris: Les Musées de la Ville de Paris, 2005.

Hugo, Victor. "Preface to Cromwell." *Prefaces and Prologues*, vol. 39, edited by Charles W. Eliot, The Harvard Classics. New York: P.F. Collier & Son, 1909–1914; available online at http://www.bartleby.com/39/40.html. Accessed 6 November 2016. ("Préface de Cromwell," cited in Chantal Maignan-Claverie. *Le métissage dans la littérature des Antilles françaises. Le complexe d'Ariel*. Paris: Karthala, 2005.)

Hugo, Victor. *The Toilers of the Sea*, translated by Mary Artois. Chicago: W. Irving Way, 1892. (*Les travailleurs de la mer* [1866]. 3 vols. Paris: Émile Testard, 1891–1892.)

Hurlbert, William Henry (writing as William Henry Hurlbut). "The Exile's Hymn." (Translation of "Himno del desterrado" by José María Heredia.) *Poems of Places:* An Anthology in 31 Volumes, edited by Henry Wadsworth Longfellow. Boston: James R. Osgood & Co., 1876–79; available online at http://www.bartleby.com/270/14/112.html. Accessed 14 November 2016.

Hurlbert, William Henry. "The Poetry of Spanish America." *The North American Review* 68, 1849, 129–159.

Isaacs, Jorge. *María* [1867], edited by Donald MacGrady. Madrid: Cátedra, 2007.

Jomard, Edme François. *Études géographiques et historiques sur l'Arabie*. Paris: Firmin Didot Frères, 1839.

Labat, Jean-Baptiste. *Nouveau voyage aux isles de l'Amérique*. 6 vols. Paris: Chez Guillaume Cavelier, 1722.

Labat, Jean-Baptiste. *Nouveau voyage aux isles de l'Amérique*. 8 vols. Paris: Chez J.B. Delespine, 1742.

Lanusse, Armand, editor. *Les Cenelles. A Collection of Poems* [1845]. Bilingual edition. Translated and with a preface by Regine Latortue and Gleason Rex W. Adams. Boston: Hall, 1979.

Lanusse, Armand. "Besoin d'écrire"/"Compulsion to Write." *Les Cenelles. A Collection of Poems* [1845], edited by Armand Lanusse. Bilingual edition. Translated and with a preface by Regine Latortue and Gleason Rex W. Adams. Boston: Hall, 1979, 120–123.

Lanusse, Armand. "Introduction." *Les Cenelles. A Collection of Poems* [1845], edited by Armand Lanusse. Bilingual edition. Translated and with a preface by Regine Latortue and Gleason Rex W. Adams. Boston: Hall, 1979, xxxvi–xli.

Laslo, Pablo, editor. *Breve antología de la poesía filipina. Poetas habla española*, with a preface by Luis G. Miranda. Mexico City: B. Costa-Amic, 1966.

Le Clézio, Jean-Marie Gustave. *L'extase matérielle*. Paris: Gallimard, 1967.

Le Clézio, Jean-Marie Gustave. *Raga*. Paris: Seuil, 2007.

Lerminier, [Eugène]. "Des rapports de la France avec le monde." *Revue des deux mondes*, initial period, series 4, no. 8, 1836, pp. 326–343.

Lespinasse, Beauvais. "Le Chevalier de Mauduit." Part 1, "30 octobre 1790—Le comité de l'ouest." *Revue des Colonies*, October 1836, pp. 166–170; Part 2, "Madame Martin et Schelec." *Revue des Colonies*, November 1836, pp. 206–211; Part 3, "4 mars 1791." *Revue des Colonies*, December 1836, pp. 245–248.

Levilloux, J. *Les créoles ou La vie aux Antilles* (1835), followed by Thérèse Bentzon, *Yette*. Morne-Rouge: Éditions des Horizons Caraïbes, 1977.

Loti, Pierre. *L'île de Pâques. Journal d'un aspirant de la Flore* [1899]. Saint-Cyr-sur-Loire: C. Pirot, 2006.
Loti, Pierre. *The Marriage of Loti*, translated by Clara Bell. London: T. Werner Laurie, 1915. (*Le mariage de Loti* [1880]. Paris: Flammarion, 1991.)
Louandre, Charles. "De l'association littéraire et scientifique en France." *Revue des deux mondes*, initial period, series 4, no. 16, 1846, pp. 512–537.
Manifeste pour les "produits" de haute nécessité, Martinique-Guadeloupe-Guyane-Réunion. Signataires: Ernest Breleur, Patrick Chamoiseau, Serge Domi, Gérard Delver, Édouard Glissant, Guillaume Pigeard de Gurbert, Olivier Portecop, Olivier Pulvar, Jean-Claude William. Paris: Éditions Galaade, co-published with l'Institut du Tout-Monde, 2009. Available online at: http://www.tlaxcala.es/detail_artistes.asp?lg=fr&reference=300. Accessed 23 June 2016.
Manzano, Francisco. *Autobiografía del esclavo poeta y otros escritos* [1835], edited by William Luis. Frankfurt am Main, Madrid: Vervuert, Iberoamericana, 1997.
Martínez, Melchor. *Memoria histórica sobre la Revolución de Chile. Desde el cautiverio de Fernando VII hasta 1814*, edited by Guillermo Feliú Cruz. 2 vols. Santiago de Chile: Biblioteca Nacional, 1964.
Maynard de Queilhe, Louis de. *Outre-mer*. 2 volumes. Paris: Renduel, 1835.
Mazade, Charles de. "La société et la littérature à Cuba." *Revue des deux mondes*, new period, series 1, vol. XII, 1851, pp. 1017–1035.
Nau, Ignace. *Isalina ou Une scène créole* [1836]. Port-au-Prince: Choucoune, 2000.
Ortiz, Fernando: *Contrapunteo cubano del tabaco y el azúcar.* [Habana:] Dir. de publicaciones, Universidad central de Las Villas, 1963.
Picquenard, Jean-Baptiste. *Adonis suivi de Zoflora et de documents inédits*, edited by Chris Bongie. Paris: L'Harmattan, 2006.
Prévost de Sansac, Auguste. *Les amours de Zémédare et Carina et description de l'île de Martinique* [1806]. Followed by Louis-Xavier Eyma. *Emmanuel*, edited by Auguste Joyau. Morne-Rouge: Edition des Horizons Caraïbes, 1977.
Questy, Joanni. "Monsier Paul." *La Tribune de la Nouvelle-Orléans*, 25 October to 3 November 1867. Available online at http://www.centenary.edu/french/textes/paul.html. Accessed 23 June 2016.
Raynal, Guillaume-Thomas. *Histoire philosophique et politique des établissemens et du commerce des européens dans les deux Indes.* 10 vols. Geneva, 1781.
Raynal, Guillaume-Thomas. *Essai sur l'administration de St. Domingue.* [Publisher not identified.] 1785.
Raynal, Guillaume, and Denis Diderot. *Die Geschichte beider Indien.* Compiled, with illustrations and an afterword, by Hans-Jürgen Lüsebrink. Nördlingen: Greno, 1988.
Recueils de Reglemens, Edits, Declarations et Arretes, Concernant le Commerce, l'Administration de la Justice & la Police des Colonies Françaises de l'Amérique, & les Engagés. Avec le Code Noir et l'Addition audit Code. Paris: Chez les Libraires Associez 1745. Available online at: http://www.archive.org/stream/recueilsdereglem00fran#page/n3/mode/2up. Accessed 26 June 2016.
Rousseau, Jean-Jacques. *Emile: Or, On Education*, translated by Allan Bloom. New York: Basic, 1979. (*Émile. Éducation. Morale. Botanique.* Œuvres complètes, vol. IV, edited by Bernard Gagnebin and Marcel Raymond. Paris: Gallimard, 1999.)

Rousseau, Jean-Jacques. *On the Social Contract, with Geneva Manuscript and Political Economy*, edited by Roger D. Masters and Judith R. Masters. New York: St. Martin's Press, 1978. (*Du contrat social ou Essai sur la forme de la République*. Manuscrit de Genève. Book 1, Chapter 2 [n.d.]. Available online at: http://philo.record.pagesperso-orange.fr/contrat/geneve.htm. Accessed 10 May 2010.)

Rousseau, Jean-Jacques. *The Social Contract*, translated by Maurice Cranston. Harmondsworth, Middlesex, England: Penguin, 1968. (*Du contrat social. Écrits politiques*. Œuvres complètes. Vol. III, edited by Bernard Gagnebin und Marcel Raymond. Paris: Gallimard, 1996.)

Rousseau, Jean-Jacques. *Émile. Éducation. Morale. Botanique*. Complete works, vol. 4, edited by Bernard Gagnebin and Marcel Raymond. Paris: Gallimard, 1999.

Séjour, Victor. "The Mulatto," translated by Philip Barnard. *The Norton Anthology of African American Literature*, 2nd edition, edited by Henry Louis Gates, Jr. and Nellie Y. McKay. New York: Norton, 2004, pp. 78–82. ("Le mulâtre." *Revue des Colonies*, March 1837, pp. 376–392.)

Tapia y Rivera, Alejandro. La palma del cacique. Leyenda histórica de Puerto Rico y Poesías. La leyenda de los veinte años. A orillas del Rhin. Mexico: Orion, 1977.

Torabully, Khal. *Cale d'étoiles, Coolitude*. Sainte-Marie: Azalées, 1992.

Torabully, Khal. *Chair corail, fragments coolies*. Petit-Bourg (Guadeloupe): Ibis Rouge, 1999.

X.2 Ethnological Journals

Revue des Colonies, edited by Cyrille Bissette.

Revue des deux mondes.

Revue encyclopédique, ou analyse raisonnée des productions les plus remarquables dans la politique, les sciences, l'industrie et les beaux-arts, edited by Marc-Antoine Jullien. Paris: Bureau de la Revue Encyclopédique, 1 (1819) –61 (1835).

X.3 Secondary Literature

Abel, Johanna. "'Aunque la virgen sea blanca, píntame angelitos negros.' Paradoxien in den kolonialen Schönheitsdiskursen der hispano-karibischen Literatur des 19. Jahrhunderts." *Grenzgänge. Beiträge zu einer modernen Romanistik*, vol. 17, no. 33, 2010 (issue title: *Die Maskeraden der Schönheit*), pp. 15–32.

Abel, Johanna. "Entre Island Hopping e Islas con Alas. Autoras en el Caribe y sus figuraciones archipiélicas en relatos de viaje del siglo XIX." *Worldwide. Archipels de la mondialisation. Archipiélagos de la Globalización*, edited by Ottmar Ette and Gesine Müller. Frankfurt am Main, Madrid: Vervuert, Iberoamericana, 2012, pp. 231–249.

Abel, Johanna. "Orientalische Dopplungen in der Karibik: Coolitude als inklusives Kreolitätsmodell und seine dissoziativen Dimensionen." *Kreolisierung revisited. Debatten um ein weltweites Kulturkonzept*, edited by Gesine Müller and Natascha Ueckmann. Bielefeld: transcript, 2013, pp. 65–81.

Abel, Johanna. "Tagungsbericht zur Konferenz 'Koloniales Kaleidoskop Karibik. Eine Inselwelt im Fokus kultureller Transferprozesse im 19. Jahrhundert' (09.–11. Juli 2009 in Berlin)." *Romanistische Zeitschrift für Literaturgeschichte*, 2009, pp. 471–479.

Abel, Johanna. *Transatlantisches KörperDenken. Reisende Autorinnen in der spanischen Karibik des 19. Jahrhunderts*. Berlin: tranvía (Walter Frey), 2015.

Abel, Johanna. "Viajes corporales al Caribe. Autoras del siglo XIX y sus saberes corporizados sobre las culturas." *Relaciones caribeñas. Entrecruzamientos de dos siglos = Relations caribéennes*, edited by Liliana Gómez and Gesine Müller. Frankfurt am Main: Lang, 2011, pp. 61–68.

Abel, Johanna, and Gesine Müller. "Korallen: Migration und Transozeanität: Khal Torabully/Indian Diaspora." *Handbuch Literatur und Raum*, edited by Jörg Dünne and Andreas Mahler. Berlin: De Gruyter, 2015, pp. 505–514.

Abel, Johanna, and Gesine Müller. "Cultural Forms of Representation of 'Coolies': Khal Torabully and His Concept of Coolitude." *Bonded Labour. Global and Comparative Perspectives (18th–21st Century)*, edited by Sabine Damir-Geilsdorf, Ulrike Lindner, et al. Bielefeld: transcript, 2016, pp. 219–228.

Adams, Gerry. "Two Island Peoples in the Same Sea of Struggle." *Independent Digital News and Media Limited*, 20 December 2001. Available online at http://www.independent.co.uk/voices/commentators/gerry-adams-two-island-peoples-in-the-same-sea-of-struggle-5363195.html. Accessed 19 September 2016.

Antoine, Régis. *La littérature franco-antillaise*. Paris: Éd. Karthala, 1992.

Appadurai, Arjun. *Fear of Small Numbers: An Essay on the Geography of Anger*. Durham: Duke University Press, 2006.

Arnold, Albert James. "Corsaires, Aventuriers, Flibustier et Pirates. Identité Régionale à la Frontière de l'Empire Espagnol dans la Caraïbe." In *Caleidoscopios coloniales. Transferencias culturales en el Caribe del siglo XIX = Kaléidoscopes coloniaux. Transferts culturels dans les Caraïbes au XIXe siècle*, edited by Ottmar Ette and Gesine Müller. Madrid, Frankfurt am Main: Iberoamericana, Vervuert, 2010, pp. 213–227.

Arzalier, Francis. "Changes in Colonial Ideology in France before 1848. From Slavery to Abolitionism." *The Abolitions of Slavery. From Léger Félicité Sonthonax to Victor Schœlcher, 1793, 1794, 1848*, edited by Marcel Dorigny. Paris: UNESCO, 2003, pp. 261–271.

Ashcroft, Bill, Gareth Griffiths, and Helen Tiffin. *The Empire Writes Back: Theory and Practice in Post-Colonial Literatures*. London: Routledge, 1999.

Asholt, Wolfgang. "Projekt Avantgarde und avantgardistische Selbstkritik." *Der Blick vom Wolkenkratzer. Avantgarde—Avantgardekritik—Avantgardeforschung*, edited by Wolfgang Asholt and Wolfgang Fähnders. Amsterdam, Atlanta: Rodopi, 2000 (Avantgarde Critical Studies no. 14), pp. 97–120.

Astier Loutfi, Martine. *Littérature et colonialisme*. Paris: Mouton, 1971.

Bachmann-Medick, Doris. *Cultural Turns: New Orientations in the Study of Culture*, translated by Adam Blauhut. Boston: Walter De Gruyter, 2016.

Bader, Wolfgang. "Martinique, Guadeloupe, Guyane. Eine periphere Literaturgeschichte." *Französisch heute*, no. 17, 1986, pp. 182–201.

Bandau, Anja. "Configuraciones atlánticas y modalidades de la circulación de saberes sobre la rebelión de Saint-Domingue entre 1791 y 1810. El caso de 'Mon Odyssée.'" In *Caleidoscopios coloniales. Transferencias culturales en el Caribe del siglo XIX =*

Kaléidoscopes coloniaux. Transferts culturels dans les Caraïbes au XIXe siècle, edited by Ottmar Ette and Gesine Müller. Madrid, Frankfurt am Main: Iberoamericana, Vervuert, 2010, pp. 399–419.

Barbéris, Pierre. *Chateaubriand, une réaction au monde moderne*. Paris: Librairie Larousse, 1976.

Barnett, Marva A., editor. *Victor Hugo on Things That Matter*. New Haven, London: Yale University Press, 2010.

Benítez Rojo, Antonio. *The Repeating Island: The Caribbean and the Postmodern Perspective*, translated by James E. Maraniss, Durham, NC: Duke University Press, 1996. (*La isla que se repite*. Barcelona: Casiopea, 1998.)

Bénot, Yves. "Haïti et la 'Revue encyclopédique.'" *Haïti 1804. Lumières et ténèbres. Impact et résonances d'une révolution*, edited by Leon-François Hoffmann, Frauke Gewecke, et al. Madrid: Iberoamericana, 2008, pp. 99–112.

Berg, Hubert van den, and Walther Fähnders. "Avantgarde als Netzwerk und Projekt." *Metzler Lexikon Avantgarde*, edited by Hubert van den Berg and Walther Fähnders. Stuttgart: Metzler, 2009, pp. 11–12.

Bernabé, Jean, Patrick Chamoiseau, and Raphaël Confiant. *Éloge de la Créolité* [1989]. Paris: Gallimard, 2002.

Blum, Hester, editor. *Turns of Event: American Literary Studies in Motion*. Philadelphia: University of Pennsylvania Press, 2016.

Blumenberg, Hans. *Theorie der Lebenswelt*, edited by Manfred Sommer, Berlin: Suhrkamp, 2010.

Blümig, Gabriele. *Retour au paysage natal. Zur Natur im postkolonialen Roman der frankophonen Antillen*. Diss. Würzburg, 2004. Available online at: https://opus.bib liothek.uni-wuerzburg.de/frontdoor/index/index/docId/1500. Accessed 23 June 2016.

Bonafoux, Luis. *Betances*. San Juan de P.R.: Instituto de Cultura Puertorriqueña, 1970.

Bongie, Chris. "'C'est du papier ou de l'Histoire en Marche?' The Revolutionary Compromises of a Martiniquan Homme de Couleur, Cyrille-Charles-August Bissette." *Nineteenth Century Contexts* no. 23, 2002, pp. 439–473.

Bongie, Chris. *Friends and Enemies. The Scribal Politics of Post/Colonial Literature*. Liverpool: Liverpool University Press, 2008.

Bongie, Chris. *Islands and Exiles. The Creole Identities of Post/Colonial Literature*. Stanford: Stanford University Press, 1998.

Bongie, Chris. "Politique, Mémoire, Littérature. L'Universalité fractionniste' d'Haïti au XIXe siècle." In *Caleidoscopios coloniales. Transferencias culturales en el Caribe del siglo XIX = Kaléidoscopes coloniaux. Transferts culturels dans les Caraïbes au XIXe siècle*, edited by Ottmar Ette and Gesine Müller. Madrid, Frankfurt am Main: Iberoamericana, Vervuert, 2010, pp. 231–252.

Boren, Mark E. *Sugar, Slavery, Christianity and the Making of Race*. Pompano Beach, FL: Caribbean Studies Press, 2013.

Borrego Plá, María del Carmen. "La influencia de la Francia revolucionaria en México. El texto constitucional de Apatzingán." *América Latina ante la Revolución Francesa*, edited by María del Carmen Borrego Plá and Leopoldo Zea. México, D.F.: Univ. Nacional Autónoma de México, 1993, pp. 9–30.

Bragard, Véronique. *Transoceanic Dialogues: Coolitude in Caribbean and Indian Ocean Literatures*. Frankfurt am Main: Peter Lang, 2008.

Bremer, Thomas. "Haiti als Paradigma. Karibische Sklavenemanzipation und europäische Literatur." *Karibik. Wirtschaft, Gesellschaft und Geschichte*, edited by Hanns-Albert Steger and Jürgen Schneider. Munich: Fink, 1982, pp. 319–340.
Bremer, Thomas. "Juan Francisco Manzano y su *Autobiografía de un esclavo* (Cuba, 1835/1840). La repercusión en Europa." *Caleidoscopios coloniales. Transferencias culturales en el Caribe del siglo XIX = Kaléidoscopes coloniaux. Transferts culturels dans les Caraïbes au XIXe siècle*, edited by Ottmar Ette and Gesine Müller. Madrid, Frankfurt am Main: Iberoamericana, Vervuert, 2010, pp. 439–448.
Breña, Roberto. *El primer liberalismo español y los procesos de emancipación de América, 1808–1824. Una revisión historiográfica del liberalismo hispánico*. México, D.F.: El Colegio de México, 2006.
Brickhouse, Anna. *Transamerican Literary Relations and the Nineteenth-Century Public Sphere*. Cambridge: Cambridge University Press, 2004.
Brutus, Edner. *Instruction publique en Haïti: 1492–1945*. Port-au-Prince: Imprimerie de l'État, 1948.
Candlin, Kit, and Cassandra Pybus. *Enterprising Women: Gender, Race, and Power in the Revolutionary Atlantic*. Athens, Georgia: University of Georgia Press (Race in the Atlantic World, 1700–1900), 2014.
Carter, Marina, and Khal Torabully. *Coolitude. An Anthology of the Indian Labour Diaspora*. London: Anthem Press, 2002.
Castells, Irene. *La ciudadanía revolucionaria*, 2002. Available online at: http://www.casa taule.org/cast/docs/la_ciudadania_revolucionaria.doc. Accessed 10 May 2010.
Castro Varela, María do Mar, and Nikita Dhawan. *Postkoloniale Theorie. Eine kritische Einführung*. Bielefeld: transcript, 2005.
Chambers, Stephen M. *No God But Gain: The Untold Story of Cuban Slavery, the Monroe Doctrine, and the Making of the United States*. London, New York: Verso, 2015.
Chamoiseau, Patrick, and Raphaël Confiant. *Lettres créoles. Tracées antillaises et continentales de la littérature: Haïti, Guadeloupe, Martinique, Guyane; 1635–1975*. Paris: Hatier, 1991.
Chamoiseau, Patrick, and Raphaël Confiant. "En guise d'introduction: 'Points de vue sur l'évolution de la littérature antillaise.' Entretien avec les écrivains martiniquais Patrick Chamoiseau et Raphaël Confiant (mené par Ottmar Ette et Ralph Ludwig)." *Les littératures antillaises—une mosaïque culturelle*, edited by Ottmar Ette and Ralph Ludwig. Dossier in *Lendemains*, no. 67, 1992.
Champion, Jean-Marcel. "30 Floréal Year X. The Restoration of Slavery by Bonaparte." *The Abolitions of Slavery. From Léger Félicité Sonthonax to Victor Schœlcher, 1793, 1794, 1848*, edited by Marcel Dorigny. Paris: UNESCO, 2003, pp. 229–236.
Chappey, Jean-Luc. *La Société des Observateurs de l'Homme (1799–1804) des anthropologues au temps de Bonaparte*. Paris: Société des Études Robespierristes, 2002.
Chinea, Jorge L. *Raza y trabajo en el Caribe hispánico: los inmigrantes de las Indias occidentales en Puerto Rico durante el ciclo agro-exportador, 1800–1850*. Sevilla: Asociación Cultural la otra Andalucía, 2014.
Corzani, Jack. *La littérature des Antilles-Guyane Françaises*. 6 volumes. Fort-de-France: Desormeaux, 1987.

Daston, Lorraine. *Things that Talk: Object Lessons from Art and Science.* New York: Zone Books, 2004.
Deleuze, Gilles, and Félix Guattari. *Rhizome: Introduction.* Paris: Minuit, 1977.
Delle, James A. *The Colonial Caribbean: Landscapes of Power in the Plantation System.* New York: Cambridge University Press, 2014.
Démier, Francis. "Slavery, Colonial Economy and French Development Choices during the First Industrialization (1802–1840)." *The Abolitions of Slavery. From Léger Félicité Sonthonax to Victor Schœlcher, 1793, 1794, 1848,* edited by Marcel Dorigny. Paris: UNESCO, 2003, pp. 237–247.
Desdunes, Rodolphe Lucien. *Our People and Our History; A Tribute to the Creole People of Color in Memory of the Great Men They Have Given Us and of the Good Works They Have Accomplished.* Baton Rouge: Louisiana State University Press, 1973. (*Nos hommes et notre histoire. Notices biographiques accompagnées de réflexions et de souvenirs personnels, hommage à la population créole, en souvenir des grands hommes qu'elle a produits et des bonnes choses qu'elle a accomplies.* Montreal: Arbour & Dupont, 1911.)
Díaz, Roberto Ignacio. "Merlin's Foreign House. The Genres of La Havane." *Cuban Studies,* no. 24, 1994, pp. 57–82.
Downey, Arthur T. *The Creole Affair: The Slave Rebellion that Led the U.S. and Great Britain to the Brink of War.* Lanham: Rowman & Littlefield, 2014.
Drescher, Seymour. "British Way, French Way. Opinion Building and Revolution in the Second French Slave Emancipation." *From Slavery to Freedom. Comparative Studies in the Rise and Fall of Atlantic Slavery,* edited by Seymour Drescher, Basingstoke: Macmillan, 1999, pp. 158–195.
Drescher, Seymour. "Two Variants of Anti-Slavery. Religious Organization and Social Mobilization in Britain and France, 1780–1870." *From Slavery to Freedom. Comparative Studies in the Rise and Fall of Atlantic Slavery,* edited by Seymour Drescher. Basingstoke: Macmillan, 1999, pp. 35–56.
Duchet, Michèle. *Anthropologie et histoire au siècle des lumières. Buffon, Voltaire, Rousseau, Helvétius, Diderot.* Paris: Maspero, 1971.
Duchet, Michèle. *Le partage des savoirs. Discours historique et discours ethnologique.* Paris: Éditions la Découverte, 1985.
Duke Bryant, Kelly. "Black but not African. Francophone Black Diaspora and the *Revue des Colonies,* 1834–1842." *International Journal of African Historical Studies,* vol. 40, no. 2, 2007, pp. 251–282.
Duplantier, Jean-Marc Allard. *"Nos frères d'outre-golf." Spiritualism, Vodou and the Mimetic Literatures of Haiti and Louisiana.* Diss. Louisiana State University 2006. Available online at http://etd.lsu.edu/docs/available/etd-11152006–152550/unrestricted/Duplantier_dis.pdf. Accessed June 23 2016.
Ecker, Gisela, and Susanne Scholz, editors. *Umordnungen der Dinge.* Königstein (Taunus): Helmer, 2000.
Enwezor, Okwui. "The Black Box." *Documenta 11 Platform 5: Exhibition.* Kassel, 2002, pp. 42–55.
Ette, Ottmar. *Alexander von Humboldt und die Globalisierung.* Frankfurt am Main: Suhrkamp 2009.

Ette, Ottmar. "Cirilo Villaverde: *Cecilia Valdés o La Loma del Angel.*" *Der hispanoamerikanische Roman*, edited by Volker Roloff and Harald Wentzlaff-Eggebert. Darmstadt: Wissenschaftliche Buchgesellschaft, 1992, vol. 1, pp. 30–43; 313f.

Ette, Ottmar. "Crossing the Mangrove." *Literature on the Move*, translated by Katharina Vester. Amsterdam: Rodopi, 2003, pp. 255–294. ("Die Durchquerung der Mangroven." *Literatur in Bewegung. Raum und Dynamik grenzüberschreitenden Schreibens in Europa und Amerika*. Weilerswist: Velbrück Wissenschaft, 2001, pp. 461–538.)

Ette, Ottmar. "Diskurse der Tropen—Tropen der Diskurse: Transarealer Raum und literarische Bewegungen zwischen den Wendekreisen." *Raum und Bewegung in der Literatur. Die Literaturwissenschaften und der Spatial Turn*, edited by Wolfgang Hallet and Birgit Neumann. Bielefeld: transcript, 2009, pp. 139–165.

Ette, Ottmar. *La escritura de la memoria. Reinaldo Arenas: Textos, estudios y documentación.* Frankfurt am Main: Vervuert, 1992.

Ette, Ottmar. "Europäische Literatur(en) im globalen Kontext. Literaturen für Europa." *Wider den Kulturenzwang. Migration, Kulturalisierung und Weltliteratur*, edited by Özkan Ezli, Dorothee Kimmich, et al. Bielefeld: transcript, 2009, pp. 257–296.

Ette, Ottmar. "Figuren und Funktionen des Lesens in Guillaume-Thomas Raynals *Histoire des deux Indes.*" *Ex nobili philologorum officio. Festschrift für Heinrich Bihler zu seinem 80. Geburtstag*, edited by Dietrich Briesemeister and Axel Schönberger. Berlin: Domus Ed. Europaea, 1998, pp. 589–610.

Ette, Ottmar. *Konvivenz. Literatur und Leben nach dem Paradies*. Berlin: Kulturverlag Kadmos, 2012.

Ette, Ottmar. *Literature on the Move*, translated by Katharina Vester. Amsterdam: Rodopi, 2003. (*Literatur in Bewegung. Raum und Dynamik grenzüberschreitenden Schreibens in Europa und Amerika*. Weilerswist: Velbrück Wissenschaft, 2001.)

Ette, Ottmar. "Eine Literatur ohne festen Wohnsitz. Fiktionen und Friktionen der kubanischen Literatur im 20. Jahrhundert." *Romanistische Zeitschrift für Literaturgeschichte / Cahiers d'Histoire des Littératures Romanes* (Heidelberg), vol. 28, nos. 3–4, 2004, pp. 457–481.

Ette, Ottmar. "Literaturwissenschaft als Lebenswissenschaft." *Lendemains*, no. 125, 2007, pp. 7–32.

Ette, Ottmar. "Le monde transarchipélien de la Caraïbe coloniale." *Caleidoscopios coloniales. Transferencias culturales en el Caribe del siglo XIX = Kaléidoscopes coloniaux. Transferts culturels dans les Caraïbes au XIXe siècle*, edited by Ottmar Ette and Gesine Müller. Madrid, Frankfurt am Main: Iberoamericana, Vervuert, 2010, pp. 23–64.

Ette, Ottmar. "Réflexions européennes sur deux phases de mondialisation accélérée chez Cornelius de Pauw, Georg Forster, Guillaume-Thomas Raynal et Alexandre de Humboldt." *HiN. Alexander von Humboldt im Netz. Internationale Zeitschrift für Humboldt-Studien* (Potsdam – Berlin), vol. 11, no. 21, 2010, pp. 1–28. Available online at: http://www.hin-online.de/index.php/hin/article/view/143. Accessed 17 July 2016.

Ette, Ottmar. "'Traición, naturalmente.' Espacio literario, poetología implícita en 'La Loma del Angel,' de Reinaldo Arenas." *Reinaldo Arenas. Recuerdo y Presencia*, edited by Reinaldo Sánchez. Miami: Ediciones Universal, 1994, pp. 87–107.

Ette, Ottmar. *TransArea. Eine literarische Globalisierungsgeschichte*. Berlin, Boston: De Gruyter, 2012.

Ette, Ottmar. "Von Inseln, Grenzen und Vektoren. Versuch über die fraktale Inselwelt der Karibik." *Grenzen der Macht—Macht der Grenzen. Lateinamerika im globalen Kontext*, edited by Marianne Braig, Ottmar Ette, et al. Frankfurt am Main: Vervuert, 2005, pp. 135–180.

Ette, Ottmar. *Weltbewusstsein. Alexander von Humboldt und das unvollendete Projekt einer anderen Moderne*. Göttingen: Velbrück Wissenschaft, 2002.

Ette, Ottmar. *Writing-between-Worlds: Transarea Studies and the Literatures-without-a-Fixed-Abode*. Translated by Vera M. Kutzinski. Boston: De Gruyter, 2016. (*ZwischenWeltenSchreiben. Literaturen ohne festen Wohnsitz*. Berlin: Kulturverlag Kadmos, 2005.)

Ette, Ottmar. *ZusammenLebensWissen. List, Last und Lust literarischer Konvivenz im globalen Maßstab*. Berlin: Kadmos, 2010.

Ette, Ottmar, and Werner Mackenbach, et al., editors. *Trans(it)Areas. Convivencias en Centroamérica y el Caribe. Un simposio transareal*. Berlin: tranvía (Walter Frey), 2011.

Ette, Ottmar, and Gesine Müller, editors. *New Orleans and the Global South. Caribbean, Creolization, Carnival*. Hildesheim: Olms, 2017.

Fabre, Michel. *From Harlem to Paris. Black American Writers in France, 1840–1980*. Urbana: University of Illinois Press, 1991.

Fabre, Michel. "The New Orleans Press and French-Language Literatures by Creoles of Color." *Multilingual America. Transnationalism, Ethnicity, and the Languages of American Literature*, edited by Werner Sollers. New York: New York University Press, 1998, pp. 29–49.

Faessel, Sonia. *Visions des îles: Tahiti et l'imaginaire européen. Du mythe à son exploitation littéraire (XVIIIe – XXIe siècles)*. Paris: L'Harmattan, 2006.

Fink-Eitel, Hinrich. *Die Philosophie und die Wilden. Über die Bedeutung des Fremden für die europäische Geistesgeschichte*. Hamburg: Junius, 1994.

Fischer, Sibylle. *Modernity Disavowed. Haiti and the Cultures of Slavery in the Age of Revolution*. Durham, NC: Duke University Press, 2004.

Fleischmann, Ulrich. *Ideologie und Wirklichkeit in der Literatur Haitis*. Berlin: Colloquium-Verlag, 1969.

Flory, Céline. *De l'esclavage à la liberté forcée: histoire des travailleurs africains engagés dans la Caraïbe française au XIXe siècle*. Paris: Éditions Karthala, 2015.

Foucault, Michel. *The Order of Things: An Archaeology of the Human Sciences*. New York: Vintage, 1994.

Fradera, Josep. *Colonias para después de un Imperio*. Barcelona: Ed. Bellaterra, 2005.

Garber, Jörn, and Heinz Thoma. *Zwischen Empirisierung und Konstruktionsleistung. Anthropologie im 18. Jahrhundert*. Tübingen: Niemeyer, 2004.

Gazmuri Riveros, Cristián. "Libros e ideas políticas francesas en la gestación de la independencia de Chile." *América Latina ante la Revolución Francesa*, edited by María del Carmen Borrego Plá and Leopoldo Zea. México, D.F.: Univ. Nacional Autónoma de México, 1993, pp. 81–108.

Gaztambide Géigel, Antonio. "La geopolítica del antillanismo en el Caribe del siglo XIX. *Memorias. Revista Digital de Historia y Arqueología desde el Caribe* 4, 8, 2007, 41–74. Available online at: http://www.redalyc.org/articulo.oa?id=85540808. Accessed 23 June 2016.

Gewecke, Frauke. "Les Antilles face à la Révolution haïtienne. Césaire, Glissant, Maximin." *Haïti 1804. Lumières et ténèbres. Impact et résonances d'une révolution*, edited by

Leon-François Hoffmann, Frauke Gewecke, et al. Madrid: Iberoamericana, 2008, pp. 251–266.
Gewecke, Frauke. *Die Karibik. Zur Geschichte, Politik und Kultur einer Region*. Frankfurt am Main: Vervuert, 2007.
Gewecke, Frauke. "Saint-Domingue/Haití—Santo Domingo. Proyectos de una isla/nación *une et indivisible*." *Caleidoscopios coloniales. Transferencias culturales en el Caribe del siglo XIX = Kaléidoscopes coloniaux. Transferts culturels dans les Caraïbes au XIXe siècle*, edited by Ottmar Ette and Gesine Müller. Madrid, Frankfurt am Main: Iberoamericana, Vervuert, 2010, pp. 253–281.
Gewecke, Frauke. "Der Titel als Chiffre einer Subversion. 'Moi, Tituba, sorcière ... Noire de Salem' von Maryse Condé." *Titel—Text—Kontext. Randbezirke des Textes. Festschrift für Arnold Rothe zum 65. Geburtstag*, edited by Jochen Mecke and Arnold Rothe. Glienicke, Berlin: Galda + Wilch, 2000, pp. 159–177.
Gewecke, Frauke. *Der Wille zur Nation. Nationsbildung und Entwürfe nationaler Identität in der Dominikanischen Republik*. Frankfurt am Main: Vervuert, 1996.
Gilroy, Paul. *After Empire. Melancholia or Convivial Culture?* London: Routledge, 2004.
Gilroy, Paul. *Postcolonial Melancolia*. New York: Columbia Univ. Press, 2005.
Gilroy, Paul. *The Black Atlantic. Modernity and Double Consciousness*. Cambridge: Harvard University Press, 1993.
Gisler, Antoine. *L'esclavage aux Antilles françaises XVIIe-XIXe siècle*. Revised and corrected edition, reprint of 1965 Fribourg, Switzerland edition. Paris: Karthala, 1981.
Glissant, Édouard. *Caribbean Discourse: Selected Essays*. Translated and with an introduction by J. Michael Dash. Charlottesville: University Press of Virginia, 1989.
Glissant, Édouard. *La cohée du Lamentin. Poétique. V.* Paris: Gallimard, 2005.
Glissant, Édouard. *Le discours antillais*. Paris: Gallimard, 1997.
Glissant, Édouard. *Introduction à une poétique du divers*. Paris: Gallimard, 1996.
Glissant, Édouard. *Kultur und Identität. Ansätze zu einer Poetik der Vielheit*. Translated by Beate Thill. Heidelberg: Wunderhorn, 2005.
Glissant, Édouard. *Mémoires des esclavages. La fondation d'un centre national pour la mémoire des esclavages et de leurs abolitions*. Paris: Gallimard, 2007.
Glissant, Édouard. *Poetics of Relation*, translated by Betsy Wing. Ann Arbor: University of Michigan, 1997. (*Poétique de la relation*. Paris: Gallimard, 1990.)
Glissant, Édouard. *Tout-monde*. Paris: Gallimard, 2003.
Glissant, Édouard, and Patrick Chamoiseau. "De loin." *Potomitan. Site de promotion des cultures et des langues créoles*. http://www.potomitan.info/articles/deloin.php. Accessed June 23 2016.
Graham, Maryemma, and Wilfried Raussert. *Mobile and Entangled America(s)*. Burlington, VT: Ashbate Publishing Company, 2016.
Haddox, Thomas F. "The 'Nous' of Southern Catholic Quadroons. Racial, Ethnic, and Religious Identity in *Les Cenelles*." *American Literature*, vol. 73, no. 4, 2001, pp. 757–778.
Haesendonck, Kristian von, and Theo D'Haen. *Caribbeing. Comparing Caribbean Literatures and Cultures*. Amsterdam: Rodopi, 2014.
Hallward, Peter. *Absolutely Postcolonial. Writing Between the Singular and the Specific*. Manchester: Manchester University Press, 2001.

Hartog, François. *Regimes of Historicity: Presentism and Experiences of Time*, translated by Saskia Brown. New York: Columbia University Press, 2015. (*Régimes d'historicité. Présentisme et expériences du temps*. Paris: Seuil, 2003.)
Hassauer, Friederike. *Santiago. Schrift, Körper, Raum, Reise. Eine medienhistorische Rekonstruktion*. Munich: Fink, 1993.
Hau'Ofa, Epeli. *We Are the Ocean. Selected Works*. Honolulu: University of Hawaii Press, 2008.
Hernández Sánchez-Barba, Mario. "Las cortes españolas ante la abolición de la esclavitud en las Antillas. Opinión institucional ante un tema de política social." *Quinto Centenario*, no. 8, 1985, pp. 15–36.
Hoffmann, Léon-François. *Littérature d'Haïti*. Vanves: Edicef, 1995.
Hoffmann, Léon-François. *Le Nègre romantique. Personnage littéraire et obsession collective*. Paris: Payot, 1973.
Hölz, Karl. *Zigeuner, Wilde und Exoten. Fremdbilder in der französischen Literatur des 19. Jahrhunderts*. Berlin: Schmidt, 2002.
Ianes, Raúl. "La esfericidad del papel. Gertrudis Gómez de Avellaneda, la condesa de Merlín y la literatura de viajes." *Revista Iberoamericana*, vol. LXIII, no. 178–179, January to June 1997, pp. 209–218.
James, C.L.R. *The Black Jacobins: Toussaint L'Ouverture and the San Domingo Revolution*. London: Penguin, (1938) 2001.
Johnson, Jerah. "*Les Cenelles*. What's in a Name?" *Louisiana History*, vol. 31, no. 4, 1990, pp. 407–410.
Johnson, Sara Elizabeth. *The Fear of French Negroes: Transcolonial Collaboration in the Revolutionary Americas*. Berkeley: University of California Press, 2012.
Kapur, Geeta. *When Was Modernism: Essays on Contemporary Cultural Practice in India*. New Dehli: Tulika, 2000.
Kielstra, Paul Michael. *The Politics of Slave Trade Suppression in Britain and France, 1814–48. Diplomacy, Morality and Economics*. Basingstoke, Hampshire: Macmillan, 2000.
Kirsch, Fritz Peter. *Epochen des französischen Romans*. Vienna: WUV, 2000.
Klein, Martin A. *Historical Dictionary of Slavery and Abolition*. Lanham: Scarecrow Press, 2002.
König, Torsten. "Édouard Glissants *pensée archipélique*. Zwischen Metapher und poetischem Prinzip." *Raum—Bewegung—Passage. Postkoloniale frankophone Literaturen*, edited by Gesine Müller and Susanne Stemmler. Tübingen: Narr, 2009, pp. 113–130.
König, Torsten. "L'imaginaire géopolitique de la Polynésie dans la littérature française: de Bougainville à Chantal T. Spitz." *Worldwide. Archipels de la mondialisation. Archipiélagos de la globalización*, edited by Ottmar Ette and Gesine Müller. Madrid, Frankfurt am Main: Iberoamericana, Vervuert, 2012, pp. 129–148.
Korte, Barbara. *Der englische Reisebericht. Von der Pilgerfahrt bis zur Postmoderne*. Darmstadt: Wissenschaftliche Buchgesellschaft, 1996.
Küpper, Joachim. *Ästhetik der Wirklichkeitsdarstellung und Evolution des Romans von der französischen Spätaufklärung bis zu Robbe-Grillet. Ausgewählte Probleme zum Verhältnis von Poetologie und literarischer Praxis*. Stuttgart: Steiner, 1987.
Latour, Bruno. *Politics of Nature: How to Bring the Sciences into Democracy*, translated by Catherine Porter. Cambridge: Harvard University Press, 2009.

Lehnert, Gertrud. "Des 'robes à la turque' et autres orientalismes à la mode." *Paris Croisé, ou comment le monde extra-européen est venu dans la capitale française (1760–1800)*, edited by Anja Bandau, Marcel Dorigny, et al. Paris: Karthala, 2010, pp. 183–200.

Leonard, Adrian, and David Pretel, editors. *The Caribbean and the Atlantic World Economy: Circuits of Trade, Money and Knowledge, 1650-1914*. New York: Palgrave Macmillan (Cambridge Imperial and Post-Colonial Studies Series), 2015.

Lepenies, Wolf. *Das Ende der Naturgeschichte. Wandel kultureller Selbstverständlichkeiten in den Wissenschaften des 18. und 19. Jahrhunderts*. Munich: Hanser, 1976.

Llorens, Irma. *Nacionalismo y literatura. Constitución e institucionalización de la "República de las Letras Cubanas."* Lérida: Asociación Española de Estudios Literarios Hispanoamericanos, 1998.

Lowe, John Wharton. *Calypso Magnolia: The Crosscurrents of Caribbean and Southern Literature*. Chapel Hill: The University of North Carolina Press, 2016.

Ludwig, Ralph. *Frankokaribische Literatur. Eine Einführung*. Tübingen, 2008.

Ludwig, Ralph, and Dorothee Röseberg. "Einleitende Fragen." *Tout-Monde: Interkulturalität, Hybridisierung, Kreolisierung. Kommunikations- und gesellschaftstheoretische Modelle zwischen "alten" und "neuen" Räumen*, edited by Ralph Ludwig and Dorothee Röseberg. Frankfurt am Main: Lang, 2010, pp. 7–30.

Lüsebrink, Hans-Jürgen. "Aufklärerisches Erkenntnispotential versus institutionelle Erkenntnisschranken. Zur Geschichtsschreibung Henri Grégoires (1751–1831)." *Von der Aufklärung zum Historismus. Zum Strukturwandel des historischen Denkens*, edited by Horst-Walter Blanke and Jörn Rüsen. Paderborn: Schöningh, 1985, pp. 203–218.

Lüsebrink, Hans-Jürgen. *Das Europa der Aufklärung und die außereuropäische koloniale Welt*. Göttingen: Wallstein, 2006.

Lüsebrink, Hans-Jürgen. *Interkulturelle Kommunikation. Interaktion, Fremdwahrnehmung, Kulturtransfer*. Stuttgart: Metzler, 2008.

Lüsebrink, Hans-Jürgen. "Missionarische Fremdheitserfahrung und anthropologischer Diskurs. Zu den Nachrichten von der Amerikanischen Halbinsel Californien (1772) des elsässischen Jesuitenmissionars Johann Jakob Baegert." *Lateinamerika. Orte und Ordnungen des Wissens. Festschrift für Birgit Scharlau*, edited by Sabine Hofmann and Monika Wehrheim. Tübingen: Gunter Narr Verlag, 2004, pp. 69–82.

Lüsebrink, Hans-Jürgen. "'Negrophilie' und Paternalismus. Die Beziehungen Henri Grégoires zu Haiti (1790–1831)." *Der karibische Raum zwischen Selbst- und Fremdbestimmung. Zur karibischen Literatur, Kultur und Gesellschaft*, edited by Reinhard Sander. Frankfurt am Main: Peter Lang, 1984, pp. 99–108.

Lüsebrink, Hans-Jürgen. "Transfers culturels et légitimation postcoloniale du pouvoir. L'émergence de la presse et de la littérature haïtienne pendant le règne du Roi Christophe en Haïti." *Caleidoscopios coloniales. Transferencias culturales en el Caribe del siglo XIX = Kaléidoscopes coloniaux. Transferts culturels dans les Caraïbes au XIXe siècle*, edited by Ottmar Ette and Gesine Müller. Madrid, Frankfurt am Main: Iberoamericana, Vervuert, 2010, pp. 305–325.

Magerski, Christine. *Theorien Der Avantgarde: Gehlen—Bürger—Bourdieu—Luhmann*. Wiesbaden: VS Verlag für Sozialwissenschaften, 2011.

Maignan-Claverie, Chantal. *Le métissage dans la littérature des Antilles françaises. Le complexe d'Ariel*. Paris: Karthala, 2005.

Malena, Anne. *The Negotiated Self. The Dynamics of Identity in Francophone Caribbean Narrative*. New York: Lang, 1999.
Maluquer de Motes, Jordi. "Abolicionismo y resistencia a la abolición en la España del siglo XIX." *Anuario de Estudios Americanos*, no. 53, 1986, pp. 311–331.
Martínez-San Miguel, Yolanda, Ben Sifuentes-Jáuregui, and Marisa Belausteguigoitia, editors. *Critical Terms in Caribbean and Latin American Thought: Historical and Institutional Trajectories*. Houndmills, Basingstoke, Hampshire; New York, NY: Palgrave Macmillan, 2016.
Mateos, Ana. "Dialéctica para una voz propia en *Cecilia Valdés*." *Caleidoscopios coloniales. Transferencias culturales en el Caribe del siglo XIX = Kaléidoscopes coloniaux. Transferts culturels dans les Caraïbes au XIXe siècle*, edited by Ottmar Ette and Gesine Müller. Madrid, Frankfurt am Main: Iberoamericana, Vervuert, 2010, pp. 103–120.
Matzat, Wolfgang. *Diskursgeschichte der Leidenschaft. Zur Affektmodellierung im französischen Roman von Rousseau bis Balzac*. Tübingen: Narr, 1990.
McIntosh, Malachi. *Emigration and Caribbean Literature*. New York: Palgrave Macmillan, 2015.
Méndez Rodenas, Adriana. *Gender and Nationalism in Colonial Cuba. The Travels of Santa Cruz y Montalvo, Condesa de Merlin*. Nashville: Vanderbilt University Press, 1998.
Méndez Rodenas, Adriana. "A Journey to the (Literary) Source. The Invention of Origins in Merlin's Viaje a La Habana." *New Literary History*, vol. 21, no. 3, 1990, pp. 707–31.
Méndez Rodenas, Adriana. "Voyage to La Havane. The Countess of Merlín's Preview of National Identity." *Cuban Studies*, no. 16, 1986, pp. 71–99.
Mesnard, Éric. "Resistance Movements in the French Colonies. The Bissette Affair (1823–1827)." *The Abolitions of Slavery. From Léger Félicité Sonthonax to Victor Schœlcher, 1793, 1794, 1848*, edited by Marcel Dorigny. Paris: UNESCO, 2003, pp. 255–260.
Meyer-Krentler, Leonie. "El Bois-Caïman y la mitificación de la figura negra en *Les Créoles ou la Vie aux Antilles* de J. Levilloux." *Relaciones caribeñas. Entrecruzamientos de dos siglos = Relations caribéennes*, edited by Liliana Gómez and Gesine Müller. Frankfurt am Main: Lang, 2011, pp. 69–88.
Meyer-Krentler, Leonie. *Die Idee des Menschen in der Karibik. Mensch und Tier in französisch- und spanischsprachigen Erzähltexten des 19. Jahrhunderts*. Berlin: tranvía (Walter Frey), 2013.
Meyer-Krentler, Leonie. "Los perros ingleses y los perros esclavos. Exclusión, animalización y convivencia en *Cecila Valdés* de Cirilo Villaverde." *Worldwide. Archipels de la mondialisation. Archipiélagos de la globalización*, edited by Ottmar Ette and Gesine Müller. Frankfurt am Main, Madrid: Vervuert, Iberoamericana, 2012, pp. 194–210.
Middelanis, Carl Hermann: *Imperiale Gegenwelten. Haiti in den französischen Text- und Bildmedien 1848–1870*. Frankfurt am Main: Vervuert, 1996.
Mignolo, Walter D. *Local Histories/Global Designs. Coloniality, Subaltern Knowledges, and Border Thinking*. Princeton: Princeton University Press, 2012.
Mignolo, Walter D. "La razón postcolonial. Herencias coloniales y teorías postcoloniales." *Postmodernidad y postcolonialidad. Breves reflexiones sobre Latinoamérica*, edited by Alfonso de Toro. Madrid: Vervuert, Iberoamericana, 1997, pp. 51–70.
Misevich, Philip, and Kristin Mann. *The Rise and Demise of Slavery and the Slave Trade in the Atlantic World*. Rochester, NY: University of Rochester Press, 2016.

Möllers, Nina. *Kreolische Identität. Eine amerikanische "Rassengeschichte" zwischen Schwarz und Weiß. Die* Free People of Color *in New Orleans*. Bielefeld: transcript, 2008.
Molloy, Sylvia. *At Face Value. Autobiographical Writing in Spanish America*. Cambridge: Cambridge University Press, 1991.
Mouffe, Chantal. *On the Political*. London: Routledge, 2005.
Müller, Gesine. *Die* Boom-Autoren heute. *García Márquez, Fuentes, Vargas Llosa, Donoso und ihr Abschied von den "großen identitätsstiftenden Entwürfen."* Frankfurt am Main: Vervuert, 2004.
Müller, Gesine. "El Caribe como caleidoscopio de dinámicas coloniales (1789–1886)." *Relaciones caribeñas. Entrecruzamientos de dos siglos = Relations caribéennes*, edited by Liliana Gómez and Gesine Müller. Frankfurt am Main: Lang, 2011, pp. 13–36.
Müller, Gesine. "Chateaubriand und Hugo in der Karibik. Literarische Inszenierungen des Anderen oder die omnipräsente Rezeption der französischen Romantik." *Das Andere Schreiben. Diskursivierungen von Alterität in Texten der Romania (16.–19. Jahrhundert)*, edited by Susanne Greilich and Karen Struve. Würzburg: Königshausen & Neumann, 2013, pp. 213–224.
Müller, Gesine. "Chorégraphies des paysages coloniaux: Victor Hugo et Pierre Loti." *Chorégraphies du paysage littéraire*, edited by Ottmar Ette and Gesine Müller. Dossier in *Lendemains*, vol. 145, no. 37, 2012, pp. 88–101.
Müller, Gesine. "Entre la francofilia y las aspiraciones de autonomía: Una mirada desde el Caribe sobre las diferentes constelaciones postcoloniales." *Escribiendo la Independencia. Perspectivas postcoloniales sobre la literatura hispanoamericana del siglo XIX*, edited by Robert Folger and Stephan Leopold. Frankfurt am Main, Madrid: Vervuert, Iberoamericana, 2010, pp. 125–139.
Müller, Gesine. "J.-M.G. Le Clézio, Edouard Glissant, Epeli Hau'Ofa: Avantgarden in Ozeanien." *Avantgarde und Modernismus. Dezentrierung, Subversion und Transformation im literarisch-künstlerischen Feld*, edited by Wolfgang Asholt. Berlin: De Gruyter, 2014, pp. 169–180.
Müller, Gesine. "Koloniale Achsen und ihre literarischen Repräsentationen in der Karibik im 19. Jahrhundert: Utopien vom Zusammenleben in transkolonialen Dimensionen." *Literarische Stadtutopien zwischen totalitärer Gewalt und Ästhetisierung*, edited by Barbara Ventarola. München: Meidenbauer, 2011, pp. 321–338.
Müller, Gesine. "Konvivenz und Relationalität im französischen Kolonialreich. Atlantische und pazifische Meerlandschaften im Vergleich." *Brücken bauen – Kulturwissenschaft aus interkultureller und multidisziplinärer Perspektive. Festschrift für Dorothee Röseberg zum 65. Geburtstag*, edited by Marie-Therese Mäder, Chantal Metzger, et al. Bielefeld: transcript, 2016, pp. 257–272.
Müller, Gesine. "*La littérature jaune*. Gustave d'Alaux und frühe Zeugnisse haitianischer Literaturgeschichtsschreibung." *Wort – Macht – Stamm*, edited by Markus Messling and Ottmar Ette. München: Fink, 2013, pp. 239–252.
Müller, Gesine. "La *Revue des colonies* comme média de transfert au sein d'une diaspora francophone transatlantique." *L'Atlantique littéraire: Perspectives théoriques sur la constitution d'un espace translinguistique*, edited by Jean Marc Moura and Véronique Porra. Hildesheim: Olms, 2015, pp. 125–142.

Müller, Gesine. "Las letras: el Caribe francófono e hispanófono en el siglo XIX." *Historia comparada de las Antillas*, edited by José Antonio Piqueras Arenas. Aranjuez: Ediciones Doce Calles, 2014, pp. 673–706.

Müller, Gesine. "Modelos caribeños de producción teórica: desde la Martinica al Tout-Monde." *El caribe como paradigma. Convivencias y coincidencias históricas, culturales y estéticas. Un simposio transareal*, edited by Ottmar Ette, Anne Kraume et al. Berlin: tranvía, 2012, pp. 43–57.

Müller, Gesine. "Processes of cultural transfer in 19th-century literature: The Caribbean within the context of the cultural radiance of Europe, exemplified by France and Spain (1789–1886)." *Transatlantic Caribbean*, edited by Ingrid Kummels, Claudia Rauhut, et al. Bielefeld: transcript, 2014, pp. 239–252.

Müller, Gesine. "Raphaël Confiant: *Adèle et la pacotilleuse* als Modell karibischer Theorieproduktion." *Sondierungen: Lateinamerikanische Literaturen im 21. Jahrhundert*, edited by Rike Bolte and Susanne Klengel. Frankfurt am Main, Madrid: Vervuert, Iberoamericana (Series: Biblioteca Ibero-Americana), 2013, pp. 209–221.

Müller, Gesine. "Transkoloniale Dimensionen zwischen Guadeloupe und Kuba: Maryse Condé und Gertrudis Gómez de Avellaneda." *Literatur leben. Festschrift für Ottmar Ette*, edited by Albrecht Buschmann, Julian Drews, et al. Madrid: Vervuert, Iberoamericana, 2016, pp. 137–145.

Müller, Gesine. "'Une misérable petite île! moins qu'une île. ...' Raumdynamiken und koloniale Positionierung in der Literatur der spanischen und französischen Karibik im 19. Jahrhundert." *Raum—Bewegung—Passage. Postkoloniale frankophone Literaturen*, edited by Gesine Müller and Susanne Stemmler. Tübingen: Narr, 2009, pp. 87–100.

Müller, Gesine. "Variantes de miradas caribeñas hacia constelaciones (pos-)coloniales: Gertrudis Gómez de Avellaneda y Maryse Condé." *Diferencia minoritaria en Latinoamérica / Diferença minoritária na America Latina*, edited by Cornelia Sieber, Eduardo Guerreiro Brito Losso, et al. Hildesheim, Zürich, et al.: Olms, 2008, pp. 43–50.

Müller, Gesine. "Victor Hugo y Pierre Loti: los océanos como paradigmas culturales." *TransPacífico. Conexiones y convivencias en AsiAméricas. Un simposio transareal*, edited by Ottmar Ette, Werner Mackenbach, et al. Berlin: tranvía (Walter Frey), 2013, pp. 159–178.

Müller, Gesine. "Vom 'Genuß der Dinge, die wir so weit herholen ...': Hautfarbe und Zucker bei J. B. Labat und G. Th. Raynal." *Präsenz und Evidenz fremder Dinge im 18. Jahrhundert*, edited by Birgit Neumann. Göttingen: Wallstein (Series: 18. Jahrhundert), 2015, pp. 356–372.

Müller, Gesine. "Writing In-Between: Transcultural Positionings of the Free People of Color in Nineteenth-Century Louisiana." *New Orleans and the Global South. Caribbean, Creolization, Carnival*, edited by Ottmar Ette and Gesine Müller. Hildesheim: Olms, 2017, pp. 115–133.

Müller, Gesine, and Natascha Ueckmann, editors. *Kreolisierung revisited. Debatten um ein weltweites Kulturkonzept*. Bielefeld: transcript, 2013.

Müller, Gesine, and Natascha Ueckmann. "Einleitung: Kreolisierung als weltweites Kulturmodell?" *Kreolisierung revisited. Debatten um ein weltweites Kulturmodell*, edited by Gesine Müller and Natascha Ueckmann. Bielefeld: transcript, 2013, pp. 7–42.

Naranjo Orovio, Consuelo. "Los rostros del miedo. El rumor de Haití en Cuba (siglo XIX)." In *Caleidoscopios coloniales. Transferencias culturales en el Caribe del siglo XIX =*

Kaléidoscopes coloniaux. Transferts culturels dans les Caraïbes au XIXe siècle, edited by Ottmar Ette and Gesine Müller. Madrid, Frankfurt am Main: Iberoamericana, Vervuert, 2010, pp. 283–304.

O'Brien, Colleen C. *Race, Romance, and Rebellion: Literatures of the Americas in the Nineteenth Century.* Charlottesville: University of Virginia Press, 2013.

Ogden, Daryl. "Byron, Italy, and the Poetics of Liberal Imperialism." *Keats-Shelley Journal*, no. 49, 2000, pp. 114–37.

Osterhammel, Jürgen. *The Transformation of the World: A Global History of the Nineteenth Century*, translated by Patrick Camiller. Princeton: Princeton University Press, 2015. (*Die Verwandlung der Welt. Eine Geschichte des 19. Jahrhunderts*. Munich: Beck, 2010.)

Padura Fuentes, Leonardo. *José María Heredia. La patria y la vida.* Havana: Unión, 2003.

Pagden, Anthony. "Die Auslöschung der Differenz. Der Kolonialismus und die Ursprünge des Nationalismus bei Diderot und Herder." *Jenseits des Eurozentrismus. Postkoloniale Perspektiven in den Geschichts- und Kulturwissenschaften*, edited by Sebastian Conrad and Shalini Randeira. Frankfurt am Main, New York: Campus, 2002, pp. 116–147.

Pagni, Andrea. "Traducción y transculturación en el siglo XIX. *Atala* de Chateaubriand por Simón Rodríguez (1801) y el *Cancionero* de Heine por José A. Pérez Bonalde (1885)." *Iberoamericana*, vol. 24, nos. 2/3 (78/79), 2000, pp. 88–103.

Painter, Nell Irvin. *The History of White People.* New York: Norton, 2010.

Pâme, Stella. *Cyrille Bissette. Un Martyr de la Liberté.* Fort-de-France: Désormeaux, 1999.

Pedraz Marcos, Azucena. *Quimeras de África. La sociedad Española de Africanistas y Colonialistas.* Madrid: Polifemo, 2000.

Pedraza Jiménez, Felipe B., and Eugenio Alonso Martín. *Manual de literatura hispanoamericana.* Berriozar, Navarra: Cénlit Ed., 1991.

Piqueras Arenas, José Antonio. *La revolución democrática (1868–1874). Cuestión social, colonialismo y grupos de presión.* Madrid: Ministerio de Trabajo y Seguridad Social, 1992.

Pons, André. "Blanco White Abolicionista." *Cuadernos Hispanoamericanos*, no. 559, 1997, pp. 63–76.

Popkin, Jeremy D. *Facing Racial Revolution. Eyewitness Accounts of the Haitian Insurrection.* Chicago: The University of Chicago Press, 2007.

Poumier, María. "José María Heredia et la révolution française (Cuba 1803–Mexico 1839)." *Cahiers des Amériques Latines*, no. 10, 1990, pp. 262–274.

Pratt, Mary Louise. *Imperial Eyes. Travel Writing and Transculturation.* London: Routledge, 1992.

Reinstädler, Janett. "*La répétition interrompue*. Representando la descentralización del caribe durante la Revolución Francesa." *Caribbean(s) on the Move. Archipiélagos literarios del Caribe. A TransArea Symposium*, edited by Ottmar Ette. Frankfurt am Main: Peter Lang, 2008, pp. 23–38.

Reinstädler, Janett. "Die Theatralisierung der Karibik. Postkoloniale Inszenierungen auf den spanisch- und französischsprachigen Antillen im 19. Jahrhundert." Diss. Berlin: Humboldt-Universität, 2006.

Rétat, Pierre. "Citoyen-Sujet, Civisme." *Handbuch politisch-sozialer Grundbegriffe in Frankreich 1680–1820*, vol. 9. Munich: Oldenbourg, 1988, pp. 75–105.

Riedel, Wolfgang. "Anthropologie und die Literatur in der deutschen Spätaufklärung." *Internationales Archiv für Sozialgeschichte der deutschen Literatur*, special issue #6, 1994, pp. 93–157.

Rimpau, Laetitia. *Reisen zum Ursprung: das Mauritius-Projekt von Jean-Marie Gustave Le Clézio.* Tübingen: Niemeyer, 2002.

Rivs, Zelideth María, and Debbie Lee-DiStefano, editors. *Imagining Asia in the Americas.* New Brunswick, New Jersey: Rutgers University Press, 2016.

Roldán, Inés de. "La diplomacia Británica y la abolición del tráfico de esclavos cubanos. Una nueva aportación." *Quinto Centenario*, no. 2, 1981, pp. 219–225.

Ronzón, Elena. *Antropología y antropologías. Ideas para una historia crítica de la antropología española.* Oviedo: Pentalfa, 1991.

Rosa, Richard. *Los fantasmas de la razón. Una lectura material de Hostos.* San Juan (Puerto Rico), Santo Domingo (Dominican Republic): Isla Negra, 2003.

Rössner, Michael. "Das Bild der Indios in der brasilianischen und hispanoamerikanischen Romantik." *Dulce et decorum est philologiam colere. Festschrift für Dietrich Briesemeister zu seinem 65. Geburtstag*, edited by Sybille Große and Axel Schönberger. Berlin: Domus Ed. Europaea, 1999, vol. II, pp. 1709–1726.

Said, Edward W. *Culture and Imperialism.* New York: Vintage Books, 1994.

Schmeling, Manfred, and Monika Schmitz-Emans. Introduction to *Das Paradigma der Landschaft in Moderne und Postmoderne. (Post-)Modernist Terrains: Landescapes—Settings—Spaces*, edited by Manfred Schmeling and Monika Schmitz-Emans. Würzburg: Königshausen & Neumann, 2007, pp. 21–36.

Schmidt-Nowara, Christopher. *Empire and Antislavery. Spain, Cuba, and Puerto Rico, 1833–1874.* Pittsburgh, PA: University of Pittsburgh Press, 1999.

Schmieder, Ulrike. *Nach der Sklaverei. Martinique und Kuba im Vergleich.* Berlin, Münster: Lit, 2014.

Schulin, Ernst. *Die Französische Revolution.* Munich: Beck, 1989.

Servera, José. "Introduction." *Sab*, by Gertrudis Gómez de Avellaneda, edited by José Servera. Madrid: Cátedra, 1997, pp. 9–93.

Smith, Lynn, and Vernon J. Parenton. "Acculturation among the Louisiana French." *American Journal of Sociology*, vol. 44, no. 3, 1938, pp. 355–364.

Sommer, Doris. *Foundational Fictions. The National Romances of Latin America.* Berkeley: University of California Press, 1991.

Staum, Martin S. *Labeling People. French Scholars on Society, Race, and Empire, 1815–1848.* Montreal: McGill-Queens University Press, 2003.

Steiner, George. *Extraterritorial: Papers on Literature and the Language Revolution.* London: Faber and Faber, 1972.

Strubel, Antje Ravic. *Die Arbeiter des Meeres.* 2003. Available online: http://www.dradio.de/dlf/sendungen/buechermarkt/165895/. Accessed 21 June 2016.

Tessonneau, Alex-Louise. "Dupré et la littérature jaune en Haïti sous Henri Christophe." *Haïti 1804. Lumières et ténèbres. Impact et résonances d'une révolution*, edited by Leon-François Hoffmann, Frauke Gewecke, et al. Madrid: Iberoamericana, 2008, pp. 183–200.

Thiem, Annegret. *Rauminszenierungen. Literarischer Raum in der karibischen Prosaliteratur des 19. Jahrhunderts.* Berlin, Münster: Lit, 2010.

Thoma, Heinz. "Von der Geschichte des *esprit humain* zum *esprit français*. Anthropologie, kulturelle Ordnungsvorstellungen und Literaturgeschichtsschreibung in Frankreich 1790–1840." *Die Ordnung der Kulturen. Zur Konstruktion ethnischer, nationaler und zivilisatorischer Differenzen 1750–1850*, edited by Hansjörg Bay and Kai Merten. Würzburg: Königshausen & Neumann, 2006, pp. 99–120.

Tietz, Manfred, and Dietrich Briesemeister, editors. *Los jesuitas españoles expulsos. Su imagen y su contribución al saber sobre el mundo hispánico en la Europa del siglo XVIII*. Proceedings of the International Conference in Berlin, April 7–10, 1999. Frankfurt am Main: Vervuert, 2001.

Tomich, Dale W. *Slavery in the Circuit of Sugar. Martinique and the World-Economy, 1830 –1848*. Albany: State University of New York Press, 2016.

Torabully, Khal. "Quand les Indes rencontrent les imaginaires du monde." *Worldwide. Archipels de la mondialisation. Archipiélagos de la globalización*, edited by Ottmar Ette and Gesine Müller. Madrid, Frankfurt am Main: Iberoamericana, Vervuert, 2012, pp. 63–72.

Torres Cuevas, Eduardo: *Antonio Maceo: Las ideas que sostienen el arma*. La Habana: Editorial de Ciencias Sociales, 1995.

Torres-Saillant, Silvio. *An Intellectual History of the Caribbean*. New York: Palgrave Macmillan, 2006.

Toumson, Roger. *La transgression des couleurs. Littérature et langage des Antilles, XVIIIe, XIXe, XXe siècles*. Paris: Éd. Caribéennes, 1989.

Trouillot, Michel-Rolph. "Zur Bagatellisierung der haitianischen Revolution." *Jenseits des Eurozentrismus. Postkoloniale Perspektiven in den Geschichts- und Kulturwissenschaften*, edited by Sebastian Conrad. Frankfurt am Main: Campus, 2002, pp. 84–115.

Turcotte, Paul, and Claude Brabant. "Ile Maurice: Nuvo Sime." *Peuples Noirs/Peuples Africains*, no. 31, 1983, pp. 100–106.

Vigier, Philippe. "The Reconstruction of the French Abolitionist Movement under the July Monarchy." *The Abolitions of Slavery. From Léger Félicité Sonthonax to Victor Schœlcher, 1793, 1794, 1848*, edited by Marcel Dorigny. Paris: UNESCO, 2003, pp. 248–254.

Vila Vilar, Enriqueta, and Luisa Vila Vilar, editors. *Los abolicionistas españoles. Siglo XIX*. Madrid: Ediciones de Cultura Hispánica, 1996.

"Völker am Wasser." http://www.wunderhorn.de/content/buecher/literarische_reihen/voelk er_am_wasser/index_ger.html. Accessed June 23 2016.

Walker, David. *Walker's Appeal, in Four Articles; Together with a Preamble, to the Coloured Citizens of the World, but in Particular, and Very Expressly, to Those of the United States of America, Written in Boston, State of Massachusetts, September 28, 1829*. Boston, 1830; electronic edition available at *Documenting the American South (DocSouth)*. University of North Carolina at Chapel Hill. http://docsouth.unc.edu/nc/walker/walker. html. Accessed June 23 2016.

Walker, David. *David Walker's Appeal, In Four Articles: Together With A Preamble To The Coloured Citizens Of The World, But In Particular, And Very Expressly, To Those Of The United States Of America*, revised edition with an introduction by Sean Wilentz. New York: Hill and Wang, 1995; excerpts online available at http://www.pbs.org/wgbh/aia/ part4/4 h2931 t.html. Accessed June 23 2016.

Walsh, John Patrick. *Free and French in the Caribbean: Toussaint Louverture, Aimé Césaire, and Narratives of Loyal Opposition*. Bloomington, Indiana: Indiana University Press; Chesham: Combined Academic, 2013.

Warning, Rainer. "Romantische Tiefenperspektivik und moderner Perspektivismus. Chateaubriand/Flaubert/Proust." *Romantik. Aufbruch zur Moderne*, edited by Karl Maurer and Winfried Wehle. Munich: Fink, 1991, pp. 295–324.

Watson, Tim. *Caribbean Culture and British Fiction in the Atlantic World, 1780–1870*. Cambridge: Cambridge University Press, 2008.

Weigel, Sigrid. "Zum 'topographical turn.' Kartographie, Topographie und Raumkonzepte in den Kulturwissenschaften." *KulturPoetik*, vol. 2, no. 2, 2002, pp. 151–165.

Werner, Michael, and Bénédicte Zimmermann. "Vergleich, Transfer, Verflechtung. Der Ansatz der 'Histoire croisée' und die Herausforderung des Transnationalen." *Geschichte und Gesellschaft. Zeitschrift für historische Sozialwissenschaft*, no. 28, 2002, pp. 607–636.

Wogatzke, Gudrun. *Identitätsentwürfe. Selbst- und Fremdbilder in der spanisch- und französischsprachigen Prosa der Antillen im 19. Jahrhundert*. Frankfurt am Main: Vervuert, 2006.

Wogatzke-Luckow, Gudrun. "Victor Hugo: *Bug-Jargal* (1826). Abgesang auf den 'bon sauvage' oder Inszenierung von Ambivalenzen?" *Pasajes. Homenaje a Christian Wentzlaff-Eggebert = Passages. Mélanges offerts à Christian Wentzlaff-Eggebert = Passagen. Festschrift für Christian Wentzlaff-Eggebert*, edited by Susanne Grunwald. Sevilla: Secretariado de Publicaciones de la Universidad de Sevilla, 2004, pp. 21–138.

Wolfzettel, Friedrich. *"Ce désir de vagabondage cosmopolite." Wege und Entwicklung des französischen Reiseberichts im 19. Jahrhundert*. Tübingen: Niemeyer, 1986.

Zacair, Philippe. "Haiti on His Mind. Antonio Maceo and Caribbeanness." *Caribbean Studies*, no. 33, 2005, pp. 47–78.

Zeuske, Michael. "Gran Caribe." http://www.ihila.uni-koeln.de/5593.html. Accessed 5 December 2010; site discontinued.

Zeuske, Michael. *Kleine Geschichte Kubas*. Munich: Beck, 2000.

Zeuske, Michael. *Schwarze Karibik. Sklaven, Sklavereikultur und Emanzipation*. Zurich: Rotpunktverlag, 2004.

Zeuske, Michael. *Sklavenhändler, Negreros und Atlantikkreolen*. Berlin, Boston: De Gruyter Oldenbourg, 2015.

Afterword

This work is a translation of my 2012 book, *Die koloniale Karibik. Transferprozesse in hispanophonen und frankophonen Literaturen*. I have fundamentally revised the German original and added the following sub-chapters:

III.9 "Digression: Sugar and Skin Color between Metropolis and Colonial Projection";

V.7 "Conviviality and Relationalism in the French Colonial Empire: A Transoceanic Comparison";

VII.3 "Khal Torabully";

VII.4 "J.-M.G. Le Clézio, Édouard Glissant, and Epeli Hau'Ofa: Avant-Gardes in Oceania."

I would like to thank Marion Schotsch and Leonie Meyer-Krentler for their crucial support in the genesis of this book. I would also like to thank Marie Deer for her outstanding translation and our productive as well as pleasant cooperation throughout the entire translation process. I should also note here that the German version of 2012 is based on my work as director of the German Research Association's Emmy Noether Junior Research Group on the "Transcolonial Caribbean" at the University of Potsdam. I would like to express my gratitude to the entire research group for the many enriching discussions (from 2008 to 2011), in particular, along with my two aforementioned colleagues, Johanna Abel. Ottmar Ette at the University of Potsdam provided decisive support to the project from the very beginning, facilitated the institutional formation of a research group there, and constantly supplied essential ideas and inspiration. I am very thankful for this. The discussions in his colloquia were also a major factor in the emergence of this book.

www.ingramcontent.com/pod-product-compliance
Lightning Source LLC
Chambersburg PA
CBHW032149010526
44111CB00035B/1257